INTENSITY

*An Essay in
Whiteheadian Ontology*

**The Vanderbilt Library
of American Philosophy**
offers interpretive perspectives on the historical roots of
American philosophy and on present innovative developments in American thought,
including studies of values, naturalism,
social philosophy, cultural criticism, and applied ethics.

General Editor
Herman J. Saatkamp, Jr.
Texas A&M University

Editorial Advisory Board
Kwame Anthony Appiah (Harvard)
John Lachs (Vanderbilt)
John J. McDermott (Texas A&M)
Joel Porte (Cornell)
Hilary Putnam (Harvard)
Ruth Anna Putnam (Wellesley)
Charlene Haddock Seigfried (Purdue)
Beth J. Singer (Brooklyn College)
John J. Stuhr (Pennsylvania State)

Other recently published titles in the series include

*Elements of Knowledge:
Pragmatism, Logic, and Inquiry*
Revised and Expanded Edition
Arthur Franklin Stewart

*The Loyal Physician:
Roycean Ethics and the Practice of Medicine*
Griffin Trotter

Genuine Individuals and Genuine Communities: A Roycean Public Philosophy
Jacquelyn Ann K. Kegley

Rorty and Pragmatism: The Philosopher Responds to His Critics
edited by Herman J. Saatkamp, Jr.

The Thought and Character of William James
new paperback edition
Ralph Barton Perry

The Relevance of Philosophy to Life
John Lachs

The Philosophy of Loyalty
new paperback edition
Josiah Royce

INTENSITY
An Essay in Whiteheadian Ontology

Judith A. Jones

Vanderbilt University Press
Nashville and London

© 1998 by Vanderbilt University Press
All rights reserved
First edition 1998
98 99 00 01   4 3 2 1

This publication is made from recycled paper
and meets the minimum requirements of
American National Standard for Information Sciences—
Permanence of Paper for Printed Library Materials. ∞

Rachel Hadas's "On Poetry," from *Slow Transparency,* © 1983 by Rachel Hadas, Wesleyan University Press, is quoted by permission of University Press of New England.

The last ten lines from William Butler Yeats's "All Soul's Night" is reprinted with the permission of Simon & Schuster from *The Collected Works of W. B. Yeats,* Vol. 1: *The Poems,* revised and edited by Richard J. Finneran, © 1928 by Macmillan Publishing Company, copyright renewed © 1956 by George Yeats, and by permission of A. P. Watt Ltd on behalf of Michael Yeats.

Reprinted by permission of Farrar, Straus & Giroux, Inc.:

Elizabeth Bishop's "Insomnia," from *The Complete Poems 1927–1979,* © 1979, 1983 by Alice Helen Methfessel;

Excerpts from Seamus Heaney's "Poem" from *Poems 1965–1975,* © 1980 by Seamus Heaney.

The last nine lines from W. H. Auden's "In Praise of Limestone" are reprinted with the permission of Random House, Inc., from *W. H. Auden: Collected Poems,* edited by Edward Mendelson, © 1951 by W. H. Auden.

Library of Congress Cataloging-in-Publication Data

Jones, Judith A., 1963-
   Intensity : an essay in Whiteheadian ontology / by Judith A. Jones. -- 1st ed.
     p. cm. -- (The Vanderbilt library of American philosophy)
   Includes bibliographical references and index.
   ISBN 0-8265-1300-X (alk. paper)
   1. Ontology. 2. Whitehead, Alfred North, 1861-1947. 3. Process philosophy. I. Title. II. Series.
BD311.J66 1997
111'.092--dc21
                                             97-21240
                                                CIP

Manufactured in the United States of America

Contents

Acknowledgments vii
Introduction ix
Abbreviations xiv

Chapter ONE: Intensity of Satisfaction 3
    Some Reflections on Whitehead's Use of Categories 4
    Intensity of 'Feeling' 8
    Contrasts 12
    Subjective Form and Balanced Complexity 14
    Aesthetic Order 18
    Satisfaction 23
    Intensity of Feeling Revisited: More Structural Considerations 33
    Contrasts Revisited: The Categories of Existence 40

Chapter TWO: Intensity and the Categoreal Obligations 44
    The Phases of Concrescence 45
    The Categoreal Obligations 46
    Conclusion 82

Chapter THREE: The Ontology of Intensity 84
    The Concrescence/Concretum Distinction 85
    Quantitative Satisfaction 98
    Being, Actuality, and Derivative Actuality 104
    Creativity and the Ontology of Atomism 109
    Intensive and Extensive Quantity: Some Historical Considerations 112
    Extensive Solidarity and Intensive Atomism 122
    Conclusion: Individual Existence and Persistence of Character 126

Chapter FOUR: Intensity and Intellectual Experience 132
    Intensity in the Higher Forms of Experience 133
    Symbolic Reference: The Status of Presentational Immediacy 149
    Some Historical Considerations 157
    Coordinate Analysis: Extensity and Intensity 159

Chapter FIVE: An Essay on the Morality of Attention 171
    Metaphysical Background 172
    Transcendent Decision and Control of Process 175
    The Metaphysics of Muddle 178
    'Individuality' in Moral Experience 181

CONTENTS

The Aesthetic Discernment of Individual Beings 185
A Defense of Whitehead's Concept of Value 188
"On God and Good": Ideals, Religion, and the Discipline of Attention 191
Conclusion: Sketch of an Ethics of Intensity 197

Epilogue on Atomistic Metaphysics 207
Notes 215
Bibliography 229
Index 235

Acknowledgments

In this book I will be defending a certain interpretation of Whitehead's relational atomism, asserting something about both the strong individuality and important internal connectedness of events that can be found in a process ontology. It is essential, then, that I acknowledge those connections and relationships which have contributed to the becoming of the present text.

Several forms of institutional support have been invaluable to the completion of this manuscript through various stages of its existence. Substantial late revisions were made possible by a Summer Faculty Research Fellowship generously granted by Fordham University. The first formulation of this work was supported by a Woodruff Fellowship and Lewis White Beck Research Fellowship from Emory University, where I earned my doctorate. I thank both institutions for their support and confidence. Finally, I am grateful for the opportunity to have this work appear in Vanderbilt University Press's Library of American Philosophy. Special thanks go to series editor Herman J. Saatkamp Jr. for his encouragement and for his ongoing leadership in a number of areas important to scholars in the American tradition. I also thank the editorial, production, and marketing departments at Vanderbilt University Press for making things go so smoothly on the practical side of this project.

The individuals whose influences are manifest in the present study (though I accept total responsibility for all the claims made herein) are truly too numerous to list, though I would like to extend a warm "thank you" to a handful of people without whom these speculations would probably never have occurred. The first is Elizabeth Kraus, with whom I was fortunate enough to study for several years at Fordham when philosophy first appeared in my mental landscape as an undergraduate. To Thomas R. Flynn of Emory University I am deeply indebted for years of patience, guidance, and friendship. I am also grateful for the atmosphere of broad and intensive philosophical inquiry that so many of us have found at Emory. Without the company of fellow process speculators David Kite and Edward Munn it would have been harder to remain focused and, at times, to keep life in perspective! Many of us during our years at Emory were also lucky enough to have George Lucas on hand for a time, with whom our inquiries took long strides. My colleagues at Fordham University have been an inspiration in every sense of the word. Their pluralism and keen philosophical instincts are inexhaustible resources, and their good will is a daily blessing. I especially thank the graduate students whose energy and insight have made my seminars in process thought so rewarding and sustaining in the preparation of this research. I am grateful to Anne Pomeroy for many hours of editorial assistance and good conversation.

ACKNOWLEDGMENTS

So many people in the Process Community have been important to me in bringing this study to completion, that enumerations are bound to be rudely incomplete. I must, however, thank Jorge Nobo, Lewis Ford, and George Kline for their comments, arguments, and encouragements. Thanks are also owed to Donald Sherburne, William Garland, and Joseph Grange for conversations that have been formative in the development of the present work. I am grateful to the Society for the Study of Process Philosophies for the opportunity to present some of my work at an annual meeting. Another debt reflects the shifting spaces of philosophical exchange in these last hours of the twentieth century—the Process Forum internet listserve is a community of inquirers in the best sense of the word, providing daily opportunities to exchange ideas and try out new concepts.

Finally, without the personal support of friends and family philosophy would be impossible and, in the end, perhaps pointless. I am deeply grateful for the love and support of my parents and extended family. For J. E. Runyon's sharp eye and rich sense of life I am always thankful.

Judith A. Jones
Fordham University, 1996

Introduction

The sort of thing I want to prove is that
a twittering of pigeons out of sight
is enough to adorn a sunset. That the sea
unscratched by swimmers is as cold and blue
as thirstiest thought could daub it. . . .

Forbid the old nostalgia
for what is recognizable,
intimacies of summerhouse and garden,
the contents of the labyrinth.
Tabula rasa or

embarassment of riches—
either way it's a solitary business,
not what the wayfarer pictured
when settling herself behind that corner table
she first unfolded the map,

lifted her eyes to an uncreased world.
—Rachel Hadas, *"On Poetry"*

In these lines the poet announces what to philosophical eyes is a recognizably "realist" interpretation of nature's self-investment with qualities. And not simply qualities—but a form of beauty, resident in nature independent of human perception: the sunset is "adorned" and the sea in its cold blueness possesses a satisfactoriness that is not a function of the slaking of thirst, either in the mouth or in the mind. Realistic philosophy, including Whitehead's, has always been the attempt to build something of a conceptual map, a representation of the contoured terrains of ocean, desert, forest, city, and cosmos we inhabit. And yet the usefulness of such maps is all too diminished by their inevitable need to be folded into some manageable shape. The need to impose manageability on our ideas of reality is likely to manage reality itself in a rather inopportune way—half the time the place we need is several folds away, or falls on one of the "creases" making that location, that reality, next to invisible.

This essay is an attempt to shift the consideration of Whitehead's ontology from some habitual and manageable notions of "individuality" to a less clear-cut, but perhaps more realistic, basis. By focusing on the concept of "intensity" as a description of the subjective experience of actual entities, we

ix

can come to an understanding of what kind of atomic actualities are posited in or implied by the relational ontology developed in Whitehead's mature system. Whitehead himself manifests considerable "nostalgia" for philosophical conceptions that in the end (in my view) are at odds with the insights guiding his own "solitary business" of constructing a realistic metaphysics adequate to science, religion, and everything between them in the "labyrinth" of nature and human experience. Not that he would have done better to begin from a "tabula rasa," as if various brands of objectivism and subjectivism had not already sculpted a landscape of philosophy that is itself, along with nature, an "embarrassment of riches." But certain conceptions, such as the contrasts of subjectivity and objectivity, final and efficient causality, present and past, and so on, crease Whitehead's landscape in a manner that distorts in advance the peculiar atomism of intensive acualities that the system maps out in its categories and in its own "wayfaring" exploration of the nature of existence.

In what follows I will argue for a certain version of Whiteheadian atomism that picks up on certain strains in Whitehead's system while downplaying others. Thus, the task is both exegetical and revisionist. The revision is a small alteration, but it makes all the difference. The exegetical dimensions of this interpretation concern the unpacking of Whitehead's use of the concept of "intensity" in various systematic applications. "Intensity" generally describes the quality and form of feeling involved in subjective experience, from the privacies of actuality involved in pigeons and sunsets to the conditions of perceptual apprehension in swimming and metaphysical map-making human beings. Because it is a notion that is formative for Whitehead's thinking about process at all naturalistic levels, it seems particularly useful as a lens through which to view just what is going on in this system of atomic, but internally connected, individuals.

But intensity is more than an exegetically useful concept, as I think it is the decisive component of Whitehead's particular brand of realism. In the essay on "Speculative Philosophy" beginning *Process and Reality*, Whitehead forwards his conception of metaphysical thinking as the attempt to frame a system of ideas that is an adequate and inclusive description of the dense texture of reality. Near the end of this essay he asserts:

> The conclusion of this discussion is, first, the assertion of the old doctrine that breadth of thought reacting with intensity of sensitive experience stands out as an ultimate claim of existence; secondly, the assertion that empirically the development of self-justifying thoughts has been achieved by the complex process of generalizing from particular topics, of imaginatively schematizing the generalizations, and finally by renewed comparison of the imagined scheme with the direct experience to which it should apply. (*PR* 16)

Realism is established to the extent that "self-justifying" thoughts find themselves applicable to the "direct experience" from which such concepts were ultimately derived. Now by itself this passage is somewhat curious, for "intensity of sensitive experience" seems to have a systematic referent that the essay itself does not unpack. But its meaning becomes clear upon close scrutiny of the intensive structures described throughout *Process and Reality*. It is the intensity of our sensitive (perceptual and intellectual) experience that convinces us simultaneously of its value-ladenness and its at least partial causation by events external to the percipient as such. Moreover, intense sensitive experience suggests that causation carries the valuative and evocative dimensions of actuality within its influencing force, and vice versa.

In intense experience the subject is aware of the emotion-laden impress of a world whose capacity for such impress does not belong exclusively to the subject him- or herself. The blue of the ocean and the quality of a sunset are not simply a function of the observer. The vivid colors of the first spring-like day, the searing emotional pains of a discovered betrayal, the ecstasy of religious insight, and the anxiety of moral terrors—these experiences in their evocativeness suggest the capacity for one thing to realize itself in and influence another. "Intensity" as the provocative, attention-capturing element in "sensitive" experience thus becomes a notion from which the causal structures operative in the world at large may be explored under the auspices of the "breadth of thought" characteristic of speculative metaphysics. The causally connective event of intensive human experience of an imposing world is the *empirical* underpinning of Whitehead's otherwise analogical use of human experience as a model for the description of reality in general. If qualities impose themselves in our experience in a quantitative manner which varies in degrees, perhaps this intersection of quality and quantity—form and magnitude of form—might be the fundamental component of the morphological and existential description of other natural events. The "ultimate claim of existence" is intensity of experience in its undermining of those skeptical gestures that deny the percipient subject speculative access to the world that is perceived. Existence announces a character of intensiveness that could undergird the formal and quantitative analyses of the natural sciences as well as the decidedly evaluative experiences involved in moral affairs.

It is my suspicion that certain problems in ontology introduced by Whitehead's atomism may be surmountable if close attention be paid to the kind of "ultimacy" enjoyed by "intensity" as the main description of the process of causal derivation and causal origination involved in the subjective experience of actual entities. I have in mind the curiosities that have been raised in Whiteheadian scholarship regarding the relation between a subjective concrescence and its satisfaction, or, to put it another way, the relation between subject and superject, or the subject and its objectifications in other ("future") subjects. From another perspective this is a question about the ontological status of "past" events. The ontological status of both past

xi

and future are a function of the understanding of present actuality. I wish to detach Whitehead's ontology of individuals from certain dimensions of his temporal description of them. There is a conception of temporalization that is essential to process metaphysics, but which does not subject past and future to absolutely derivative ontological status. This conception will involve the development of a notion of "ecstatic individuality," which asserts that an entity exists with the ontological status of *its* subjectivity to *some* degree in every subject in which it comes to have influence (and, to an extent, in every subject from which it originally derived). Thus, nature is to be seen as an affair of degrees of valuation (intensities) assuming a real and ontologically original (nonderivative) status in all other such degrees and perspectives of valuation (other intensive standpoints). Whitehead was mistaken to think that intensive, evaluative individuality had to be confined to a radically perishing conception of presentness. The way Whitehead (and consequently his interpreters) ontologizes the past, present, and future operates at a separate, more abstract analytical level than the actual process of temporalization. Temporalized intensive individuals are spread out across any and all temporal modes.

In order to develop this thesis, I first offer a general exposition of the notion of "intensity of satisfaction" in chapter one, noting immediately both the central place intensity assumes in the categoreal scheme and the vexing interpretive problems the very concept of "satisfaction" imposes on the reader. Chapter two then complements this initial discussion by unravelling the Categoreal Obligations in their dimension of being procurative of intense subjective experience. Various systematic notions will be introduced alongside the categories to "work the scheme" in order to understand its objectives and possible weaknesses.

In chapter three I offer my account of the "ontology of intensity," the unpacking of intensive individuality in order to resolve some knotty problems in conceiving of relational individuality. In that chapter I also begin to explore some of the stages in Whitehead's development of the notion, and how these developmental insights bear on our final construal of the atomism he adopted in the system of *Process and Reality*. Chapter four picks up the discussion of intensity at the level of "higher" forms of experience typical of human perception and intellectual feeling. This will occasion some further comment on the generation of the notion of intensity, as well as on the relation of the Theory of Extension to the atomistic intensive realism attempted in Whitehead's metaphysics. Here we will be able to see some of sources of Whitehead's own obscurity on the ontological issues his texts impose on their interpreters.

Chapter five departs from the systematic concerns of the other four chapters and inquires into the moral applicability of "intensity," given Whitehead's tendency to associate morally significant concepts such as responsibility with the conditions of agentive achievement of intense unity of feeling. I examine a model of moral agency derivable from Whitehead's intensive atomism, and bring this conception of agency into dialogue with the ethics of "attention" developed by philosopher-novelist Iris Murdoch.

In the epilogue some final reflections on doing metaphysics with an eye to the concept of "intensive individuality" will be offered, partially by way of anticipating critique of the interpretation. These reflections are meant to be suggestive leadings into further investigations of the problems facing any attempt at realistic metaphysics, particularly one that includes, as I think it should, some theory of individuation. I will highlight what I take to be Whitehead's unresolved attraction to both subjectivism and objectivism as a general perspective from which to work on a description of reality.

At the beginning of every chapter, as at the head of this introduction, there is an epigraph consisting of some poetry or literary art, and each chapter begins with a suggestion of the epigraph's relevance to the issues under analysis in the chapter in question. I have done this in order to evoke a state of mind in regard to the conceiving of certain ideas, much as Whitehead himself resorts to poetry when he knows he cannot stretch words far enough in discursive exposition to say what most needs saying. I hope that these poetic incorporations are not a distraction, as they are meant to bring out dimensions of Whitehead's thinking, which at some crucial points in the system are in fact unexposed, to the detriment of the system's coherence and loyalty to its own stated purposes. Poetic tastes may vary, but I have tried to select pieces from thinkers of a stripe quite similar to Whitehead's in one way or another.

I am not sure if any philosophy, and hence any interpretation of a philosophy, can be an uncreased map of its object, the "uncreased world." That the world suggests our need to crease it in thought is a given for the realist's sensibilities, but this is, in the end, what also keeps it at a distance, somewhere far across the "table" from where we sit and undertake our solitary ruminations. I have tried to set certain "nostalgic" and comfortably "recognizable" interpretive methodologies aside in order to clear the way for what might be in future work the development of a renewed vocabulary respecting the world to which we "lift our eyes."

Abbreviations

AI	*Adventures of Ideas*. New York: Free Press, 1967.
AE	*Aims of Education and Other Essays*. New York: Free Press, 1967.
CN	*The Concept of Nature*. Cambridge: Cambridge University Press, 1971.
PNK	*An Enquiry Concerning the Principles of Natural Knowledge*. New York: Dover, 1982.
ESP	*Essays in Science and Philosophy*. New York: Philosophical Library, 1947.
FR	*The Function of Reason*. Boston: Beacon Press, 1958.
IMM	"Immortality." In The Philosophy of Alfred North Whitehead, edited by Paul A. Schilpp. LaSalle: Open Court, 1951.
MG	"Mathematics and the Good." In The Philosophy of Alfred North Whitehead, edited by Paul A. Schilpp. LaSalle: Open Court, 1951.
MT	*Modes of Thought*. New York: Free Press, 1968.
PR	*Process and Reality*. Corrected Edition, edited by Donald W. Sherburne and David Ray Griffin. New York: Free Press, 1978.
RM	*Religion in the Making*. New York: Fordham University Press, 1996.
SMW	*Science and the Modern World*. New York: Free Press, 1967.
S	*Symbolism*. New York: Fordham University Press, 1985.
UA	*A Treatise on Universal Algebra, with Applications*. New York: Hafner, 1960.

INTENSITY

*An Essay in
Whiteheadian Ontology*

CHAPTER ONE

Intensity of Satisfaction

> The realities and passions, the rumors of the greater world without, steal in upon us, each by its own special little passageway, through the wall of custom about us; and never afterwards quite detach themselves from this or that accident, or trick, in the mode of their first entrance to us.
> —Walter Pater, "A Child in the House"

Whitehead's metaphysics could be described as an account of how the "greater world without" any entity "steals in" upon it, how one existent manifests itself in the very fabric of another. It is my thesis that the functioning of an existent in another existent must be ascribed to the internal account of the first existent, as much as it is to be ascribed to the present self-constitution of an entity in concrescence. The fully determinate feeling characterizing the "satisfaction" of any occasion includes elements whose sources lie in *other* entities that to some significant extent retain their character as determinate unities of feeling *in themselves* even as they are objectified in a present concrescence. The objective functioning of one thing in another, in other words, never completely loses the subjective, agentive quality of feeling that first brought it into being. The "accidents" or "tricks" of an actuality's insinuation in another remains a real and passional element in the satisfaction of that other entity.

Pater's quote seems to capture the problem left for the reader of Whitehead's somewhat unusual ontology. On the one hand, "the greater world without" any entity really is "without," in the sense that Whitehead wants to highlight the subjective self-constitution of every individual actuality or "atomic" entity. And yet, we are left with the task of unpacking how and to what extent an entity can really be said to contribute to the becoming of another such that this philosophy is, or can be revised to be, truly a *relational* (in the proper sense of "relational") atomism. In this chapter I begin to explore the general systematic framework within which the notion of the interpenetrating ontological subjectivity of entities can take shape. The present chapter introduces much of the basic metaphysical hardware Whitehead provides on the issue of "intensity of feeling," bringing to bear fundamental notions involved in the "Categoreal Scheme" of *Process and Reality*, and focusing particularly on the "satisfaction" of an entity to which intensity belongs. Chapter two will continue the general discussion of

3

intensity in the context of a more focused analysis of one type of category, the Categoreal Obligations, as it is in the context of these categories that "intensity" is introduced as a systematic notion. As I proceed with these analyses I will underscore what I take to be the issues raised by the categoreal scheme that point to the need to rethink the ontology to which the scheme is alleged to give rise.

One of the benefits of treating the daunting categories offered by Whitehead in *Process and Reality* in light of a single, centrally important concept such as "intensity" is that the scheme might thereby stand out as bearing a good deal more coherence and unity than it might at first blush appear to possess. Although I happen to think that "intensity" is the *best* such notion to use as a lens for examining the overall unity of the categories, we need not accord the concept such honorific status in order to appreciate its peculiar efficacy as a tool for the appreciation of such unity. In fact, it would be an interesting experiment to unpack the categories in light of alternative "lens" concepts, such as "subjectivity," "form," "harmony," "relation," and so on. This kind of analysis is particularly useful in unearthing Whitehead's often insufficiently elaborated purposes in crafting his presentation in the manner in which he does. Although contemporary deconstructive philosophy should warn us that authorial intentions are elusive at best in one's encounter with a text, such inquiries have a philosophical value of their own regardless of what they reveal to us about Whitehead's objectives. But since at present I am, in fact, interested in the philosophical objectives of Whitehead's relational atomism, I will, with all apologies to deconstruction, proceed as if textual and systematic coherence is worthy of discovery, even if only to establish the necessity of revising the system whose coherence is being tested.

Some Reflections on Whitehead's Use of Categories

As a preliminary to an analysis of what Whitehead's categories accomplish in regard to explicating the dimensions of an entity's achievement of "intensity of feeling," it might be useful to make some brief comments on the very employment of "categories" in this organic cosmology. Taking "categories" to refer to those modes of thought whereby the objects of our knowledge may be construed, Whitehead's lineage on this score is most easily traced to Aristotle and Kant. This kind of historical comparison gives us the opportunity to appreciate some unique turns of thought at the foundations of Whitehead's system, which is important to the comprehensive analyses undertaken in the present book. In the rough definition of categories just given, I have deliberately blurred the distinction between the metaphysical and epistemological uses of categories.

In terms of this distinction, we could for the sake of argument accept Aristotle's categories as metaphysical, delineating the basic modes in which we can and must describe reality or being, and Kant's categories as epistemological, delineating the modes in which the structures of our faculty of knowing give form to our experience.[1] Kant did not begrudge Aristotle the important task of searching for "fundamental concepts," for that is Kant's purpose as well. But in addition to the immediate problem of assuming that categories could be taken to refer relatively unproblematically to realities, there is for Kant a deeper problem in Aristotle's category-building effort, and that is the lack of a *principle* of discovery. Kant recommends his own complement of twelve categories on the basis of the following argument: "This division is developed systematically from a common principle, namely, the faculty of judgment (which is the same as the faculty of thought). It has not arisen rhapsodically, as the result of a haphazard search after pure concepts, the complete enumeration of which, as based on induction only, could never be guaranteed. Nor could we, if this were our procedure, discover why just these concepts, and no others, have their seat in the pure understanding."[2]

The historical disputes between Kant and Aristotle may be sidestepped in favor of a direct assimilation of Kant's comments into a discussion of Whitehead's use of categories. The conclusion of this discussion is that Whitehead's philosophical methodology is an interesting blend of both Aristotle and Kant, and as such forms a viable alternative to either. The inductive nature of Aristotelean category-enumeration does indeed present a difficulty for philosophy, as Kant points out. Kant's transcendental project is advanced, in fact, as a refutation of Hume's discreditation of induction as yielding metaphysically significant (certain) knowledge of events as they occur in nature. Whitehead shares Kant's interest in securing the legitimacy of scientific knowledge despite the curious epistemological problems posed by inductive inferences about natural events, but rejects the transcendentalist project of grounding inductive knowledge in categoreal conditions that form the basis for the possibility of experience of objects. Instead, he employs a more directly naturalistic Aristotelean method of exploring the conditions of the possibility of events in nature as disclosed in a thoroughgoing appreciation of the contents (not just the forms) of those events. Whitehead modifies Aristotle somewhat by undertaking this exploration of nature via the analysis of human knowledge of nature as an instance of the nature to be known. Thus knowledge is not, as it is for Kant, the basis for the characteristics of natural events, but is an instance of the conditions, whatever they are, governing the occurrence of those events.[3] Thus for Whitehead induction is to be grounded not transcendentally, but naturalistically, via the unpacking of the contents of experience treated as a natural occurrence. This involves the exploration of the experiential conditions that provoke inductive inferences via memory, physical causality, purposive thought, and our need to act in the world. Such a naturalistic metaphysical protection of induction may not amount to a "guarantee" on Kant's more certainty-oriented terms for knowing, but it does offer a plausible account of how probabilistic instances of knowing can occur.

Thus, while Whitehead formulates a system of categories that are fundamentally related to one another in some important way, he is not bound to employ a rule or principle for discovery, and in fact the exploratory and hypothetical character of metaphysics as he undertakes it would recommend against any principle that might blind us down the road to the need to elaborate categories as yet unformulated. The openness of categoreal formulation is a necessary guard against an error Whitehead associates with Aristotle, which is that we tend to conflate the conditions of reality with the forms of our speech about it. He objects that the "dominance of Aristotelean logic from the late classical period onwards has imposed on metaphysical thought the categories naturally derivative from its phraseology" (PR 30). The expectation that reality and its conditions will conform to the subject-predicate grammar of language must be broken, and this problem would set Whitehead at odds with Kant's categories as well in so far as they reflect an array of forms of judgment typical of subject-predicate forms of speech.

On a broader analysis, though, Whitehead applauds Kant's recognition that categories, whatever their derivation, express a kind of process and not merely a classification of objects. According to Whitehead, Kant "introduced into philosophy the conception of an act of experience as a constructive functioning" (PR 156). The synthetic acts of understanding in Kant are reformulated by Whitehead as synthetic acts of natural existences, but Kant retains the credit for framing a conception of experience as an incorporative, organizing process and not a simple reflection of a state of affairs external to a mind (or, on Whitehead's terms, a passive relation to an actual world wholly beyond or external to an entity in concrescence). Thus it would be fair to call Whitehead's categories somewhat Kantian in that they enumerate the various manners in which the processes that occur in nature participate in the conditions of process per se. We are, here, straining historical sensibilities in favor of *philosophical* similarities, but this is perfectly appropriate given Whitehead's own ignoring of historical narratives in favor of the discovery of unnoticed thought trajectories in the works of major philosophers of the western canon.[4]

In sum, Whitehead rejects the subjection of the real either to the structures of speech or the forms of logical judgment, while accepting the faith that speech is naturally about the real and that thought (or more generally experience) gives indications as to how we should conceptualize the reality of which experience is itself an instance. Whitehead's categoreal scheme avoids the realm of universals where we are ultimately left by the Aristotelean substance-accident model of predication, and from the realm of mere appearance to which we are circumscribed by the Kantian rules for the having of experience. Categories will, for Whitehead, explore the various kinds of things we need to hypothesize as being basic characteristics of nature such that our experiences (including linguistic practices and logical predication, but also religious sensibilities, scientific data, and art) have the content that they do. In a certain sense, Aristotelean and Kantian categoreal schemes commit what Whitehead called the fallacy of Misplaced Concreteness—the mistaking of a certain mode of abstraction about reality for the complete or definitive account of that reality or our knowledge of it. This fallacy, as Whitehead sees it, seems to be the result of a persistent flaw in thinking, which is our contentedness with a limited set of evidentiary elements in the construction of a rational scheme. Kant alighted upon judgment, Aristotle upon a fairly abstract list of the types of features things tend to have. Thus these schemes of categories lack the rich evidentiary basis of Whitehead's experimental, broadly experiential appeal in enumerating a categoreal system capable of legitimating our inferences about reality.

Upon first encountering Whitehead's own scheme of categories, one might be tempted to charge that, while trying to guard against a fallacy in conceiving the nature of categories, Whitehead violates a principle of parsimony in enumerating them. To begin, there are four kinds of categories: The Category of the Ultimate (Creativity), expressing the fundamentally processive and organismic nature of the universe; The Categories of Existence, expressing the eight types of proper entities comprising the actual universe; The Categories of Explanation, expressing the twenty-seven ways in which the processes involving the interaction of the proper entities can be understood; The Categoreal Obligations, expressing the nine requirements (or conditions) to be met in all process. The Category of Subjective Intensity, the point of introduction for the concept that is our main focus, is the Eighth Categoreal Obligation, governing the concrescence, or coming to be, of actual entities.

The multiplicity of categories enumerated by Whitehead may mark an expositional weakness, or it may mark an attempt to crystallize for the reader the basic notions that the entire system of *Process and Reality* is meant to elaborate. The total of forty-nine categories certainly gives the system undesirable rhetorical dimensions, and yet it serves as a reminder that a processive, interrelated cosmos is no simple thing to be grasped in an unduly thin set of notions. In this the scheme of categories reflects expositionally the broad experiential appeal which is the methodological starting point for Whitehead's particular brand of metaphysics. However one evaluates the unfortunate construction of the Categoreal Scheme, it does serve the purpose of emphasizing the need for a more embracing completeness in our abstractions about reality, since incomplete sets of notions are usually what lead us away from a respectful entertainment of that reality. In my final chapter I will explore some of the moral implications of the problem of incompleteness in our entertainment of the relevant features of the real.

The Categoreal Obligations are the last to be presented by Whitehead, presumably because without contextualization by the other categories they are largely mysterious and seemingly arbitrary. While the other three types of categories lay out the specific kinds of entities, their status in creative

7

process, and the kinds of relations they maintain in that process, the Categoreal Obligations express just *how* and more importantly *why* all this occurs. I would maintain, then, that the "Obligations" most explicitly exhibit "categoreal" status (that is, the status of principles in terms of which an adequate conception of the entities and states of affairs that comprise reality may be framed). Creative process happens with just these nine distinct aspects. It is, moreover, usually the Obligations to which Whitehead refers either individually or conjointly when he refers to the categoreal analysis of becoming (e.g., PR 246–55, 276–79). These categories allow for distinctions of metaphysical generality to emerge in and guide discussion of concrescence in a way that the interlocked and mutually illuminating Categories of Explanation (which address primarily our *analysis* of reality) do not. The Categories of Existence merely give us a listing of the basic types of entities requiring unity according to the obligations, and, moreover, their status as categories is made somewhat curious by a feature that will be dealt with later in this discussion. The Category of the Ultimate expresses a comprehensive feature of what it is one studies when one does metaphysics, but in order to have any useful content, it does so at a level of generality intrinsically requiring the other categories. It is not so much that the other three types of categories lack the metaphysical generality that is the very mark of categoreality for Whitehead,[5] but simply that the Obligations express those critical operations that lie "at the heart of" concrescence (PR 228) and therefore at the heart of a process metaphysics. The physiology of this "heart"—the complex workings of process as captured by the nine obligations—will be explored in the next chapter. Here I am simply concerned to establish a general sense of Whitehead's scheme, in order to situate the concepts that will be introduced in the initial analyses of intensity, which is the concern of the present chapter.

I will begin the exploration of intensity with a discussion of the notion of "feeling," and then will move on to fleshing out Whitehead's understanding of intensity of feeling by focusing on the concepts of "contrast" and "subjective form." The relation of the notion of "aesthetic order" to the achievement of intensity will then be probed so as to set up the discussion of intensity of "satisfaction," crucial to the overall ontological view I am trying to develop. Aesthetic order and contrasts will then be reintroduced in order to round out the basic contours of the concept of intensity, and to raise the questions that will move our analysis on to chapter two.

Intensity of 'Feeling'

Whitehead introduces the concept of intensity into his categoreal scheme in the following statement of a Categoreal Obligation:

> (viii) *The Category of Subjective Intensity.* The subjective aim, whereby there is origination of conceptual feeling, is at intensity

of feeling (α) in the immediate subject, and (β) in the *relevant* future.

This double aim—at the *immediate* present and the *relevant* future—is less divided than appears on the surface. For the determination of the *relevant* future, and the *anticipatory* feeling respecting provision for its grade of intensity, are elements affecting the immediate complex of feeling The greater part of morality hinges on determination of relevance in the future. The relevant future consists of those elements in the anticipated future which are felt with effective intensity by the present subject by reason of the real potentiality for them to be derived from itself. (PR 27)

Of greatest relevance to the present inquiry is the fact that Whitehead ties the ultimate teleological concerns of process—subjective aim—to the concept of intensity. Intensity will express the aimed at and enjoyed valuative feeling on the part of actual entities. Indeed, Whitehead at one point refers to this as the "Category of Subjective Aim" (PR 278). One last initial point to notice is the remark regarding morality, included in the very statement of an ontological category. I take this to denote the critical importance of moral experience to Whitehead's choice of metaphysical conceptions. Its inclusion in the Category of Intensity, moreover, necessitates a treatment of ethics in the complete analysis of intensity, which will be undertaken in the final chapter.

The centrality of the concept of final causes for Whitehead is indisputable, so the relative absence of a detailed systematic study of "intensity" as a concept in virtue of which to comprehend Whitehead's conception of purposive finality in occasions is a bit puzzling. Perhaps the overlap between intensity and the more general concept of "subjective aim" has made analysis and critique of the latter seem enough. The doctrine of subjective aim is the attempt to reintroduce into the discussion of all things as they exist a concept of an end to be achieved. The subjective aim of an entity is the "lure" by which the entity brings its "prehensions" of elements in its actual world into a *unity* of feeling. Subjective aim guides the "process of self-creation" (PR 25) to an internally complex determinate final form of feeling. "In its self-creation the entity is guided by its ideal of itself as individual satisfaction and as transcendent creator. The enjoyment of this ideal is the 'subjective aim,' by reason of which the actual entity is a determinate process" (PR 85). The entity's status as "transcendent creator" in this latter passage is a role accorded by the concern for the relevant future as noted in the Category of Subjective Intensity, while the entity as "individual satisfaction" is the rendering of the immediate concerns of the entity for its complex of feeling noted there as well. These aspects of the actual entity are inseparable, as made clear by their inclusion in a single Categoreal Obligation, but the fact remains that this inseparability is strained by certain renderings of Whitehead's account of the relation of an entity as subject to its objectifications (or superjections) in other things. This critical problem of interpretation is the initial driving force behind the present study. For now, I will note that the analysis of subjective aim to the exclusion of a broad analysis of intensity compromises the understanding of agency as it is present in actualities in concrescence. To understand the aim of an entity in abstraction from what it is accomplishing by way of feeling is to miss the sense in which the aim is *in* the entity that realizes value *by* feeling things in a certain manner.

One possible reason why intensity has been comparatively overlooked as a concept that might shed light on any number of important points in process philosophy is precisely *because* it has to do with the *immediacies of feeling* just alluded to. In the statement of the Category of Subjective Intensity Whitehead refers to the "intensity of feeling" involved in the concrescent process conceived either under the aspect of the present or of the derivative future. Although, in effect, the whole of the organic philosophy spelled out by Whitehead is an attempt to elucidate the modes and patterns of how entities "feel" other entities and groups of entities (i.e., it is a systematic elucidation of the principles involved in an ontological situation constituted by the transmission of feeling among things that exist), it is generally held or assumed that the "feeling" aspect of the process as subjectively undergone is a wholly private affair.[6] That is, although we might speak of the conditions of feeling, feelings themselves are the private affair of the entities under analysis; and although we might discuss the conditions of privacy, the experiential contents of privacy are, by definition, not open to analysis. And so we can employ the concept of intensity of feeling as a placeholder in the analysis of experience, but cannot on principle peer into the enjoyments constitutive of experience per se.

There may be a point to this somewhat skeptical gesture designed to highlight the privacy of individuality crucial to the reality of value as a function of individual feeling. Certainly Whitehead did not intend for his abstract analyses to deliver concrete actualities to us in nude form. In addition, the private intensity of experience is an important aspect of the relation of religion to the wider concerns of human culture. But this respect for metaphysical privacy, if it is indeed any part of the account of the absence of a systematic analysis of intensity, masks some crucial topics in an understanding of how Whitehead's scheme works. The vagaries prompting analysis of key Whiteheadian terms such as 'actual', 'concrete', 'existent', as well as the all-important concept of 'subjective aim', are further dispelled by including in such analyses a consideration of the intensive dimensions of occasions. The present study seeks to undertake this important supplementation.[7]

Basically, intensity expresses the *felt unity* of the "data" (prehensions of elements in the actual world) integrated by an entity in concrescence. It is the particular shape by which, for each entity taken individually, "the many become one, and are increased by one" (PR 21). Each actual entity, guided by its "ideal of itself," prehends those items presented to it by its actual world into a unity; it appropriates aspects of its actual world as elements determinative of the eventual character of the novel entity.

The actual world of any entity consists of those entities available to the concrescing entity for synthesis into the satisfaction of the aim of that entity. "Actual world" has no referent outside of the coming to be of some determinate actuality; that is, there are only the actual worlds of individual entities in process, and no "actual world" considered from a 'God's eye view' as having a perspective of its own. The fifth Category of Explanation asserts,

> That no two actual entities originate from an identical universe; though the difference between the two universes only consists in some actual entities, included in one and not in the other, and in the subordinate entities which each actual entity introduces into the world. The eternal objects [forms of definiteness, or possibility] are the same for all actual entities. The nexus [somewhat determinate togetherness] of actual entities in the universe correlate to a concrescence is termed 'the actual world' correlate to that concrescence. (PR 22–23)

Each concrescence intensely integrates elements of its actual world and the realm of eternal objects. Since the realm of eternal objects is available for all actualities, I will assume it to be implied with each reference to 'the actual world', for shorthand, even though the eternal objects are not, by definition, "actual." An "eternal object" is a pure potential for the becoming of actualities. Actual entities prehend each other via these eternal objects, which are forms of definiteness of character serving a function analogous to universals or Platonic Forms. It is in virtue of the eternal objects that discrete actualities manifest similar forms of definiteness, such as those we call color, shape, smell, attractiveness or repulsiveness, and so on. Each eternal object is some "pattern" accounting for a particular character of existence realizable by actualities via feeling.

The integration performed in each concrescence involves data being taken in two ways: (1) as discrete elements and (2) as elements with some relations to other elements by reason of participation in the same actual world (i.e., of a specific entity). Concrescence, then, involves the consideration of an actual world taken as a multiplicity (demonstrating individual potential contributions to concrescent process), *and* the consideration of the potential forms of unity under which alone this multiplicity can even *be* entertained. Data perform unique roles as 'bits of information', so to speak, but only if they occur under certain determinate conditions of unity (to be spelled out later). The consideration of data as discrete elements emerging out of and connected to the actual world of the entity is attempted in the sixth Category of Explanation:

> That each entity in the universe of a given concrescence *can*, so far as its own nature is concerned, be implicated in that concrescence in one or other of many modes [made possible by consideration of the world as sheer multiplicity]; but *in fact* it is implicated in only *one* mode: that the particular mode of implication is only rendered fully determinate by that concrescence, though it is conditioned by the correlate universe. This indetermination, rendered determinate in the real concrescence, is the meaning of 'potentiality.' It is a *conditioned* indetermination, and is therefore called a '*real* potentiality.' (PR 23)

This passage raises questions concerning eternal objects, which certainly are entities in the universe of any concrescence but by definition are 'pure' potentials rather than *actual* entities (PR 221). I deal with these questions in the analysis that follows, but here it is important to note that the passage does emphasize the mutual implication of *discrete* particular data, the correlate universe, and the subject in concrescence.

Intensity arises out of the aforementioned mutuality of the factors of concrescence. Prehensions must be brought under unity; there must be a 'how' of feelings integrated in the one concrescing subject in accordance with the "ideal" or "aim" which guides the self-creation and eventual satisfaction. What intensity expresses is the ordered patterning of the prehended elements of an entity's universe in accordance with, indeed realizing, this "ideal" (perhaps with some modification). The ideal is nothing more nor less than the maximum ordered valuation and inclusion of elements of the universe (though, to be sure, transformed by the process of concrescence itself). How this valuation and inclusion occurs is governed by the nine Categorial Obligations, as well as the four "grounds of order" and the four "conditions of satisfaction" outlined in chapters III and IV of part II in *Process and Reality*. Before entering into a discussion of these latter notions, which will eventually deepen our understanding of all nine of the Obligations as procurative of intensity, we must introduce the notion of "contrast" as the basis for the unifications of feeling leading to achievement of intensity.

Contrasts

A "contrast" is the positive relation of two or more discrete elements in the complex of feeling involved in concrescence, such that those elements are mutually compatible and enhancing rather than mutually inhibiting or indifferent. That is to say, prehensions involving a contrast of elements allow for more of the actual world to be positively and importantly involved in the concrescence of an entity. All prehensions are brought under some mode of contrast, either to the enhancement or diminishment of overall intensity of feeling. We should note at the outset that the concept of "contrast" allows Whitehead to avoid the metaphysical difficulty of describing an entity as feeling every item in its world separately, which is not only an unwieldy possibility but one that would fail to account for the possibility of eventual unification of all feelings in a single determinacy of feeling, called satisfaction. Thus feeling as occurring under "contrast" reminds us of the creative, synthetic character of process, in a way that feeling as the incorporation of a sheer multiplicity or manifold of possibility would not.

Some of Whitehead's comments on contrasts of eternal objects are helpful in introducing the general notion of contrasts as they function in his system, because an eternal object is one of if not *the* simplest element in the universe, capable of combination into "complex" eternal objects in virtue of some form of relatability among the forms of definiteness. This general notion of relatability is also reflected in the discussion of what a contrast does. The aspects of the actual world to be prehended are complex eternal objects expressing the achieved characters of the entities in that world, as well as the realm of eternal objects considered in itself as expressing relevant possibilities for the prehending entity. Whitehead refers to the relation of eternal objects to the actual world as "ingression." An eternal object ingresses into creative process in the sense that it is incorporated into the self-determination of an entity that evaluates that eternal object as important for the attainment of the full value of its ideal of itself. And so, when Whitehead reintroduces the Category of Subjective Intensity in the elucidation of the "higher phases of experience" late in *Process and Reality*, he reiterates the definition of the category presented earlier and offers the following explanation: "We first note (i) that intensity of feeling due to any realized ingression of an eternal object is heightened when that eternal object is one element in a realized contrast between eternal objects, and (ii) that two or more contrasts may be incompatible for joint ingression, *or* may jointly enter into a higher contrast" (*PR* 278).

A number of things can be concluded from this discussion, using an analogy with the aesthetics involved in a painting by way of illustration. First, intensity characterizes the feeling of any *individual* element in the complex of feeling constituting concrescence (such that it may be "heightened" via contrast). In a painting, each color contributes a basic intensive importance as just the shade or hue it is, such as periwinkle blue or daffodil yellow. Second, intensity is augmented by the mutual *compatibility* of such individual elements (realized ingression of eternal objects). The mutual juxtaposition of periwinkle blue and daffodil yellow in our painting intensifies the feelings of each, and of the two taken together. The feeling of the color complex is greater than the sum of its parts, and modifies the feeling of the parts. Third, there are some conditions under which it is impossible to achieve contrast and so impossible to enhance intensity in that respect, or there may at times be positive inhibitions of intensity in virtue of incompatible elements entertained for prehension in a single concrescence. Here we locate the source of what Whitehead calls the "enfeeblement of intensity," which, in its more significant occurrences, is called "evil" or "aesthetic destruction." The occupation of a certain region of the painting by periwinkle blue may make the choice of some accompanying colors by the artist aesthetically unlikely, or unfortunate, for the overall effect of the painting. Fourth, intensity may be somewhat geometrically enhanced by the combination of achieved contrasts under a higher form of contrast. Each addition of color and shape to a painting complexifies the forms of definiteness and their relations in the painting, such that the unity of the effect of the whole is not only more than additive of the individual effects (such as might be displayed on a color and shape pallette) but is something of a multiplication of the aesthetic effectiveness of the parts in their relations. These kinds of reflections on the greater aesthetic significance of wholes to their parts is an artistic commonplace.

The first conclusion drawn here concerns the notion of subjective form; the second and fourth concern the notion of aesthetic order; the third simultaneously concerns the idea of enfeeblement of intensity, suggests the consideration of "negative prehensions" (or the positive dismissal from relevance of some possibility), and enriches our sense of the entity as an attempt at "balanced complexity." My discussion now turns to a consideration of the first and third conclusions (issues concerning subjective form and balanced complexity, specifically) drawn briefly in the preceding, as these provide a frame of reference for understanding the concept of "aesthetic order" manifest in the second and fourth conclusions.

Subjective Form and Balanced Complexity

The subjective form of a feeling is the emotional tonality of that prehension as informed by the consideration of the aim at ideal intensity of satisfaction for the entity as a whole. That is, subjective form expresses the stamp of individuality in each prehension of determinate features of the actual world; it is the redetermination (in terms of immediate subjective aim) of features of the world that are determinate achievements of other actualities. Subjective Forms comprise the fourth Category of Existence, and are there described as "Private Matters of Fact" (PR 22) as opposed to the public matters of fact that are the aspects of the achievement of entities as graspable by other entities. Subjective form is the felt novelty of atomic actuality arising out of causal process:

> The breath of feeling which creates a new individual fact has an origination not wholly traceable to the mere data. It conforms to the data, in that it feels the data. But the *how* of feeling, though it is germane to the data, is not fully determined by the

data. The relevant feeling is not settled, as to its inclusions or exclusions of 'subjective form,' by the data about which the feeling is concerned. The concrescent process is the elimination of these indeterminations of subjective forms. The quality of feeling has to be definite in respect to the eternal objects with which feeling clothes itself in its self-definition. (PR 85–86)

A reference to the complete actuality is required to give the reason why such a prehension is what it is in respect to its subjective form. . . . In other words, final causation and atomism are interconnected philosophical principles. (PR 19)

It is important to note that in both of these passages the peculiarities of subjective form, such that a feeling is felt in a determinate *manner*, is referred to the entity taken as a *whole*. Subjective form seems to be the introduction of uniqueness of feeling to the extent required for the differentiation of one actuality from another, that is, for the creation of "a new individual fact." I point this out in order to counter a tendency to read Whitehead's discussion of novel feeling as being mostly about the value of such novelties of emotional tone in themselves; but it may be that the *novelty* of the feeling, as opposed to the simple *determinacy* of the feeling, has more to do with atomicity as such, the differentiation of one actuality from another, than about immediacies of emotionality. As the passages suggest, a *great deal* of the determinations of feeling do "steal in . . . each by its own special little passageway" from the actual world. Subjective form introduces the stamp of concrescent individuality, though not the total determinacy, on every feeling.

Subjective form has a significant role in the attainment of what Whitehead calls the "balanced complexity" of feeling expressed by the idea of intensity. That is to say, subjective forms contribute to the internal complexity of the entity as guided by its ideal of itself as attaining to a certain level of intensity. In light of this role, we note in the long passage quoted here that subjective forms derive their private character from the complex of relations in which they stand to other data being felt and to, ultimately, the subjective aim or final causality of the concrescence. Individual feelings do not in and of themselves yield the total emotional tonality they contribute to the total satisfaction; they are "indeterminate" until in-formed by the concrescing entity's consideration of itself as an eventual whole. This in-forming entails the modification of the feeling of the data by contrasting the elements of this feeling with the other eternal objects available to the entity in its self-constitution. Thus the last sentence of the passage, "The quality of feeling has to be definite in respect to the eternal objects with which feeling clothes itself in its self-definition" is understood to refer to the self-creation of the entity in toto as clothing the discrete elements of its inner complexity in terms of that complexity taken in its entirety. Feeling does not, technically,

15

"clothe itself" except in the sense that every feeling is an act of the entire subject as the locus of the agency of feeling. Individual elements are felt intensely as if alone (it is the subjective form of *this or that* prehension) but only because of complex relation and integration.

By way of turning to the idea of enfeeblement of intensity and to the concept of "negative prehension" and its roles in the procurement of intensity, let us recur to the notion of "balanced complexity" mentioned previously. Further along in the description of the Category of Subjective Intensity in the analysis of the higher phases of experience (cited earlier), Whitehead notes that "Here 'complexity' means the realization of contrasts, of contrasts of contrasts, and so on; and 'balance' means the absence of attenuations due to the elimination of contrasts which some elements in the pattern [of eternal objects available for feeling] would introduce and other elements inhibit." He continues: "Thus there is the urge towards the realization of the maximum number of eternal objects subject to the restraint that they must be under conditions of contrast. But this limitation to 'conditions of contrast' is the demand for 'balance.' For 'balance' here means that no realized eternal object shall eliminate potential contrasts between other realized eternal objects. Such eliminations attenuate the intensities of feeling derivable from the ingressions of the various elements of the pattern" (*PR* 278). If certain eternal objects actually incorporated into a concrescence were (*per impossibile*) not rendered somehow compatible with other incorporated eternal objects, there would be significant enfeeblement of intensity, as well as an impermissible lack of unity in the entity, brought on by the non-integration of its components. The "urge" or impetus to maximal incorporativeness is constrained by the equally important need for "balance" or mutual realizability of what is to be incorporated.

The confluence of this conception of an urge for inclusion and the concept of its constraint by the need for contrast can be used (if a short digression be indulged) as a way of understanding a very important aspect of Whitehead's thought, which will increase in significance as the present analyses proceed. Whitehead's description of an actuality haunted by infinite forms of potentiality does not leave each entity to the awesome task of fabricating ex nihilo all of the orderings and relations necessary to its incorporation of features of its world. The urge to include is simultaneously an implicit organization, for forms of definiteness competing for realization are in and of themselves comparable to one another.

In *Science and the Modern World,* Whitehead accomplished the internal organization of the realm of potentiality with the idea of an eternal object as possessing not only an "individual essence" (its unique character), but also a "relational essence" (its character in so far as it is to be compared to other forms of definiteness) (*SMW* 157–72). In *Religion in the Making,* this is supplemented by the conception of God as an original actuality whose self-creating valuation of the realm of potentiality establishes the intrinsic relationality of eternal objects without which the relevance of one such eternal object to another or to an actuality is impossible. Again, the idea is that sheer manifoldness of possibility is not a feature of our universe, just as no entity encounters a world of entities having the status of sheer manifoldness. A "many" in Whitehead is always to some extent an organized manyness (unless one has posited a manifold for some analytic purposes with no bearing on the intrinsic metaphysical status of the items so posited). Creativity, or the "urge" for inclusion, is always in a state of significant organizedness or comparability of its components. This point helps to take the edge of miraculousness off of Whitehead's account of the self-creation of actualities, a miraculousness that might rightly be taken as off-putting if not simply ridiculous to the newcomer to process thought.

Returning to the discussion at hand, we must introduce the concept of "negative prehension" and its role in the realization of balanced complexity in an occasion. Whitehead distinguishes the general concept of "prehension" into the two "species" of "positive" and "negative" prehensions. A positive prehension is the definite inclusion of the character of the datum prehended into the complex of feeling being established in the concrescence; the datum has lent its determinacy to the becoming-determinate of the entity whose datum it is. A negative prehension is the dismissal from relevance of a datum in the actual world of an entity, and this dismissal is itself in the interest of the overall unity being sought in the satisfaction. Negative prehension is not an ignorance of the datum, but the determinate and purposeful exclusion of some or most of the values resident in the datum from incorporation into the character aimed at. Negative prehension serves a role made necessary by Whitehead's incorporation of the totalistic or holistic sensibilities of idealism: "An actual entity has a perfectly definite bond with each item in the universe. This determinate bond is its prehension of that item. A negative prehension is the definite exclusion of that item from positive contribution to the subject's own real internal constitution" (PR 41). Although he does not give to negative prehensions the status of "feelings," as feelings are by definition positive incorporations of data, Whitehead does maintain that negative prehensions have subjective forms. There is a significance attached emotionally to the dismissal of the excluded datum, and this significance contributes to the overall value or intensity of feeling realized in the entity as a whole.

Negative prehensions facilitate the dismissal of irrelevant or incompatible details from the process of concrescence attempting to unify those feelings positively prehended. In this sense they contribute to intensity in two ways. First, their subjective form is a component of the final intensity achieved. Second, negative prehensions help avoid the incompatibilities of feeling that diminish intensity when they occur in the same entity. On the other hand, negative prehensions can cause genuine but unfortunate enfeeblement of intensity if they occur unnecessarily, as a way to avoid contrast that would

17

indeed be possible for the data in question. It is, in fact, one of the four "grounds of order" hypothesized by Whitehead that as much of the data of an occasion as possible *be* positively incorporated into that occasion, and not dismissed into negligibility by negative prehensions if it is at all possible for those data to be rendered compatible by contrast (PR 83). Thus negative prehensions have a precarious place in concrescence, performing a necessary office of dismissing the irrelevant (and thereby avoiding the monistic or ultimately undifferentiatable existents usually characteristic of idealistic schemes which assert a definite relation among all items in the universe), while at the same time being a source of risk insofar as they might be used so as to avoid realization of maximally intense contrast unifying diverse types of data.

In fact, to look ahead a bit, it is important to note that the complex task of contrasting widely divergent possibilities is most typical of and significant for those forms of experience described by Whitehead as "high-grade" or "higher forms," particularly human and cultural experience. These forms of experience exemplify the same general conditions of process as do all metaphysical entities, but involve a greater capacity for dealing with alternative possibilities than do, for example, the occasions in the history of a block of granite. Because dealing with diverse possibility is what defines such occasions, it is in such "higher forms" of occasions that the failure to realize maximal intensity—a failure wrought possibly through immoderate use of negative prehensions—is at its most costly. The possibilities of contrastive realization in the higher forms of experience will be explored in chapter four, though I raise the point here to suggest one of the important though touchy dimensions of negative prehension, as one of the modes creativity employs in the achievement of intensive forms of organized feeling.

Aesthetic Order

Earlier I drew a number of conclusions from Whitehead's way of stating the Category of Subjective Intensity, among which were the following: that intensity is augmented by the mutual compatibility of eternal objects (data) brought under contrast, and that intensity may be conceived as susceptible to something like a geometrical expansion on the basis of contrasts, contrasts of contrasts, and so on. Drawing on these ideas, I now turn to what I call the "structural considerations" governing the attainment of intensity according to the four "grounds of order" laid out in the "Order of Nature" chapter in part II of *Process and Reality,* and the four notions by which Whitehead claims satisfactions are to be "classified" in the chapter, "Organisms and Environment" (PR 111). These considerations may be elaborated into a more general portrait of the metaphysical work done by the concept of intensity. I will thus be able to clarify what the achievement of contrast entails, what the teleological nature of process implies, and how Whitehead centers his metaphysics on aesthetic considerations.

It is important to note at the outset that when Whitehead writes of the "order of nature" he is not appealing to an atemporal character of realization that imposes itself coercively on natural events. He refers, on the contrary, to the types of order that emerge from process such that we might get a glimpse of the conditions whereby there is any order at all in nature in the more usual sense of an overall shape or design. This conception of order does imply some notion of "design" (unpopular in metaphysics at least since Hume's famous arguments in the *Dialogues on Natural Religion*), but for Whitehead the design nature manifests is emergent from process, and is not its ground. The only ontologically "prior" form of order to which natural processes must respond is that imposed by the "primordial nature of God," which is postulated as the eternal envisagement of all possible forms of relatedness of eternal objects, as mentioned earlier. God is the "unlimited conceptual realization of the absolute wealth of potentiality," but Whitehead qualifies this form of divine basis for order by noting that "In this aspect, he is not *before* all creation, but *with* all creation" (*PR* 343). God's role is a function of the becoming of each natural existent individually, and is not an imposition of a totalistic form of order to which individual realities must submit. Whether this view meets all objections to the concept of "design" as of divine origination is immaterial to our understanding of Whitehead's irremediably emergentistic conception of "the order of nature."

The relation of God's ordering of the realm of potentiality to the forms of order emergent in the actual world is, as Dorothy Emmet observed, the answer to Leibniz' metaphysical problems in this area. In a consideration of "cosmic creation" as the "arising of definite types of order," she points out:

> We must bear in mind . . . that sheer, blind creativity and unbounded potentiality between them could produce nothing. There would be no sufficient reason for *any* course of creation whatsoever. Therefore, like Leibniz, Whitehead holds that if we are to say that the realm of possibility is wider than the realm of actuality (as we must, if we are to avoid Spinoza's determinism), we must say that there must be a primordial limitation on pure creativity in virtue of which there is a sufficient reason for *some* (though, unlike Leibniz, Whitehead would not say for this specific) actual course of events. This is the sense in which God is said to be the principle of concretion.[8]

God's initial determination that there be grounds of order in the very nature of process, but not that there be any particular (in Whitehead's terminology, any 'determinate') types of order which must emerge, avoids Leibniz' stipulation that God established that there be the order which in fact exists, a position that robs his monads of any direct participation in the creation of good orderings of things. Here Whitehead's role for God meets two requirements of metaphysics in this scheme: that we can find reasons for—that is, offer some explanation of—what there is (this is Whitehead's rationalistic bias), and that these reasons, according to the Ontological Principle expressed in the eighteenth Category of Explanation, are to be found only in the nature of specific actual entities, in this instance God as "primordial created fact."[9] God is the actuality among other actualities in whose individual character (not *will*, importantly) is to be found the reason for the existence of order in all of nature, as God's primordial valuation of possibility establishes the comparability of the realm of potentiality, and hence its organized relatability to the course of actual events. Order cannot be avoided completely, because comparability and hence contrastive complexity is of the essence of all that participates in the creative "urge"; and yet no particular order is coerced in these participants, whose response to the creative urge determines *what* forms nature shall take.

Whitehead's concept of order is coextensive with his concept of causality. "Order" expresses the relation of causal interaction between entities and their actual worlds, always, of course, under the conditions of novel valuation expressed in the ideal of subjective aim. "For the organic doctrine the problem of order assumes primary importance. No actual entity can rise beyond what the actual world as a datum from its standpoint—*its* actual world—allows it to be. Each such entity arises from a primary phase of the concrescence of objectifications [what other entities in its actual world have already become] which are in some respects settled" (PR 83). It is for this reason—the settledness of certain forms of determinateness in any entity despite its own subjective aim—that there are in fact recognizably stable orders in the natural and human environment. What separates this from sheer determinism is the fact that "disorder" is also given in the concrescence of any entity. Disorder expresses the inevitable partiality of the conformation of present becoming with past attainment, a partiality that expresses both the freedom and the potential failure of attainment on the part of things in their becoming. There is no reason to conclude from Whitehead's description of his scheme as an account of the self-creation of things that this self-creation is a principle of *abundant* novelty; it simply indicates that settled factors in the causally determinative processes of temporal flux occur in individual subjects that incorporate those settled factors along with what alternative possibilities are relevant to those individual occasions. Again, this attenuates the wildly counterintuitive sense that each of Whitehead's occasions must create the world anew. The role of disorder, freedom, and possible variations in the shape of attainment will recur in the consideration of the moral implications of Whitehead's metaphysics in chapter five.

The four "grounds of order" posited by Whitehead are:

> (i) That 'order' in the actual world is differentiated from mere 'givenness' by introduction of adaptation for the attainment of an end.

(ii) That this end is concerned with the gradations of intensity in the satisfactions of actual entities (members of the nexus) in whose formal constitutions the nexus (i.e., antecedent members of the nexus) in question is objectified.
(iii) That the heightening of intensity arises from order such that the multiplicity of components in the nexus can enter explicit feeling as *contrasts*, and are not dismissed into negative prehensions as *incompatibilities*.
(iv) That 'intensity' in the *formal constitution* of a subject-superject involves 'appetition' in its *objective* functioning as superject (PR 83).

The "superject" of an entity is its character as a completed actuality, which will lend its aspects to subsequent acts of becoming on the part of other actualities. What this passage makes clear above all else is that when we speak of entities we are rarely if ever referring to free-floating self-determiners outside of some temporal organization denoted by the term 'nexus.' That is, actual entities are found in paths of causal transmission of characteristics such that discernable orders are present in nature. Indeed, we should remind ourselves that Whitehead moved into metaphysics in order to provide more compelling answers to his initial philosophical questions concerning our capacity to gain scientific knowledge of the natural world. The natural world to be known is a scene of "permanences" and "recurrences" knit across a flux of temporal "passage." Science and metaphysics seek to elaborate the conditions of the "transmission" of character from one passing event to another (PNK 98).

The important point to note here, however, is that despite the prevalence of *paths* of transmission, the point of the whole process is the increase of intensity in the satisfactions of the *entities* constituting a given path (by grounds i and ii). This does not relegate ordered processes to importance only in the individual satisfactions of merely self-interested entities. By conditions (iii) and (iv) it is the convergence of data from the nexus as a multiplicity so as to yield effective contrast, which provides for heightened intensity. The *subjective* intensity of the individual realities provides for, in these realities' very aims, reference to those realities' participation in the nexus—their "*objective* functioning as superject," or as "transcendent creator" is integral to the *subjects* embedded in the nexus. The overall conclusion to be drawn from a consideration of these grounds of order is that the analysis of causal interaction is primarily concerned with intensity and only secondarily with other formal considerations as to the entity as subject-superject. I would go so far as to say that had Whitehead developed a vocabulary whereby the work of final and efficient causality could have been described in terms related to "order" as intensive actualization, the ontological problems we are identifying in his thought would have been minimized or avoided. The formal considerations concerning subject-superjects are discussed by commentators such as Nobo and Kline, and will be addressed in chapters two and three. Bearing in mind the focus of the grounds of order on intensity, I can now undertake clarifying the waters that Whitehead muddied subsequent to his laying out these simple grounds.

Intensity functions as the intersection, so to speak, of order and disorder in virtue of the fact that the quest for order is guided by "adaptation to an end." What is meant by an end here is twofold. It is both the "ideal of itself" entertained by any entity, and the determinate satisfaction that will characterize the entity as completed fact, which satisfaction may or may not realize the ideal entertained at the outset of concrescence. Now, remembering that Whitehead ties the "end" to be sought to the intensity of actual entities, we note, "The intensity of satisfaction is promoted by the 'order' in the phases from which concrescence arises and through which it passes; it is enfeebled by the 'disorder'. The components in the concrescence are thus 'values' contributory to the 'satisfaction'" (PR 84–85). There is tension between the maximum value realizable by an entity and the value eventually realized, a tension expressed by saying that 'disorder' is the correlate of 'order'" (PR 83). Significant problems of interpretation arise at once: Which meaning of intensity is that with which Whitehead is primarily concerned— the intensity an entity can possibly achieve (the felt lure of subjective aim which in fact gets the whole process of concrescence started), or the intensity it does in fact achieve given its location in paths of ordered transmission whose elements inevitably will yield up incompatible elements for synthesis and thereby attenuate contrast? In other words, is intensity best understood under the aspect of its privacy as an ideal, or as a completed attainment participating in determinate forms of order based on the need to inherit repeated patterns of characteristics?

Although we might be tempted to point to the doctrine of the modification of subjective aim to deal with this issue,[10] the disjunction of aim and satisfaction is not so simply dismissed, for it is a particular way of posing a broader issue of interpretation. Whitehead discusses "satisfaction" as the "closing up" of an entity; a satisfaction expresses an entity's status as "concrete" outcome of process considered in abstraction from its process of concrescence (PR 84). Discussions of the ontological obscurities of Whitehead's conception of process are born here. In the causally interactive world of actual entities in paths of transmission of character, are actualities in their most ontologically telling sense to be conceived in terms of their processes of coming to be, or in terms of what they become as "satisfied"? So far in Whitehead scholarship, these problems of ontological status have been dealt with in the absence of a close scrutiny of the concept of intensity which is really at their core, and the present discussion is offered to supplement existing strategies for dealing with the seeming noncoincidence of the ontological status of concrescence and of satisfaction. Our first step will be to consider the status of the satisfactions Whitehead describes on the heels of his analysis of the grounds of order governing the transmission of character along a nexus procurative of intensity in its members.

Satisfaction

A satisfied actuality is one that has completed the full circuit of phases involved in concrescence such that it has achieved a status as an "individual" arising from determined data brought under the unity of the entity's private aim. "'Satisfaction' provides the individual element in the composition of the actual entity—that element which has led to the definition of substance as 'requiring nothing but itself in order to exist'. But the 'satisfaction' is the 'superject' rather than the 'substance' or 'subject'. It closes up the entity; and yet is the superject adding its character to the creativity whereby there is a becoming of entities superceding the one in question. The 'formal' reality of the actuality in question belongs to its process of concrescence and not to its 'satisfaction'" (PR 84). The problem here is clear, for Whitehead has tied the most ontologically significant aspect of the actuality—that designated as its "formal" reality, borrowing the term from Cartesian metaphysics—to its concrescence. The satisfaction that enjoys a kind of "objective" reality (modifying Descartes's definition, which applied to the knowledge of an existent) insofar as it denotes the entity's functioning in other things, lacks the subjectivity and agency of concrescent process crucial to primary existential status in a process-oriented metaphysical scheme. In fact, Whitehead repeatedly incants Plato's phrase, "it never really is" (PR 84, 85) in discussing the status of satisfactions, suggesting that the concept of "existence" does not really apply to satisfactions at all. The Platonic denial of existence to satisfactions is echoed in Whitehead's equally favorite phrase from Locke regarding the "perpetual perishing" of actualities as they lose their immediacy upon satisfaction (PR 29,81,210). Finally, we have the offhand comment Whitehead made in one of his Harvard lectures, as reported in notes made at these lectures by William Ernest Hocking: "You can't catch a moment by the scruff of the neck—it's gone, you know."[11]

If "satisfaction" represents the fully determinate feeling aimed at in concrescence, but concrescence as agentive process is the locus of ontologically significant existence to the exclusion of the satisfaction, then Whitehead's system leaves us with an uncanny tension between the goal of process—intensity of feeling—and the process itself. Poetic phraseology about "perishing," and "never really existing," and not being able to "catch" an entity as it passes, fail to provide enough interpretive clues to deal with the tension just identified. It is my opinion that part of the problem here is Whitehead's unfortunate decision to adopt terms and hence concepts from the metaphysical schemes he was intending to overturn with precisely the notions he then obfuscates by using these terms. This is a common weakness in Whitehead's own exposition, but it is particularly disastrous in this context, for it raises questions about just how to construe this organic atomism—are the atoms really the concrescences, or the concrete results of concrescence, the satisfactions? I would like to spend a few moments exploring Whitehead's invocation of Cartesian language, to suggest one component of a solution to these ontological difficulties whose full elaboration is the project of the remaining analyses. We will then return to an analysis of satisfactions per se.

The passage quoted earlier regarding "satisfaction" as that which has "led to the definition of a substance as 'requiring nothing but itself in order to exist'" is an echo of a discussion in *Religion in the Making* where Whitehead is at pains to repudiate substance metaphysics as an inadequate conception of the individuality of existents. In *Religion in the Making*, the problem identified in substance metaphysics is the conception of the "individuality" of the substances therein identified. Descartes's dualism of "minds" and "bodies" is the context of the discussion at issue, and Whitehead's criticism is not aimed at the thrust of the dualism per se, for "in some sense no one doubts but that there are bodies and minds," but at the added supposition that bodies and minds are each "individual substances" wherein individuality amounts to substantial ontological independence of one thing from another (RM 105–8). Whitehead's complaint with Descartes's definition of substance as that "which requires nothing but itself in order to exist" is that this definition presupposes a concept of "individuality" which Whitehead denies applies to any entity, including God. In Whitehead's system, as it had been worked out up to the time of *Religion in the Making* (which is the text written between *Science and the Modern World* and *Process and Reality*), "every entity is in its essence social and requires the society in order to exist. In fact, the society for each entity, actual or ideal, is the all inclusive universe, including its ideal forms" (RM 108).

Interestingly, the broad contexts of the *Religion in the Making* and *Process and Reality* repudiations of the Cartesian definition of substance is the same—in both discussions Whitehead is talking about the broader orders of nature in which entities occur, and the paths of transmission of character involved in the social dimension of the determination of actualities. The *Religion in the Making* discussion is again instructive in understanding the PR version, and worth quoting at length. Taking "matter" and "mind" as a focus of discussion, since Cartesian dualism set the context in that text, Whitehead claims:

> Now, according to the doctrine of this lecture, the most individual actual entity is a definite act of perceptivity. So matter and mind, which persist through a route of such occasions, must be relatively abstract; and they must gain their specific individualities from their respective routes. The character of a bit of matter must be something common to each occasion of its route; and analogously, the character of a mind must be

24

> something common to each occasion of its route. Each bit of matter, and each mind, is a subordinate community—in that sense analogous to the actual world.
>
> But each occasion, in its character of being a finished creature, is a value of some definite specific sort. Thus a mind must be a route whose various occasions exhibit some community of type of value. Similarly a bit of matter—or an electron—must be a route whose various occasions exhibit some community of type of value. (RM 108–9)

Minds and bits of matter are here denied the status of true metaphysical individuality, which is reserved for "definite acts of perceptivity." A similar denial is found in *Science and the Modern World,* where Descartes had been chastised for taking his experience of self-value as a conscious mind as a sign of his "substantial independence" from other discrete existing things and for the "independent individual substance" model of existence *per se* (SMW 194–95). The two denials taken together suggest that when we take our attention away from the kind of "individuality" we think attaches to the self as a mind and to material objects as macroscopic things in nature, and turn toward "individual acts of perceptivity," or actual entities as individual existents, we are in fact looking at a different *kind of individuality* than attaches to a self or a bit of matter. Organized societies are individualities because of a route of transmission of character, a persistent reiteration of a form of order. But an individual occasion lacks the broad spatiotemporal thickness whereby it might possess individuality as we are used to experiencing individuality at the experiential scale of objects that are, in fact, *ordered processes of character-transmission.*

So then the question is, what kind of individuality does an entity possess? The short answer would be to say that individuation is a function of the "act" of perceptivity, what in *Process and Reality* is called prehensive unification. This would leave us with the model laid out in *Process and Reality* whereby the 'formal' reality of an occasion belongs to the agentive concrescence. But even in *Religion in the Making,* this is rendered ambiguous by recurrence to the notion of "finishedness" as definitive of individuality. To quote again: "But each occasion, in its character of being *a finished creature,* is *a value* of some definite specific sort" (emphasis added). Thus we are left with the tension between individual existence as a function of active, agentive concrescence, versus individual existence as a function of the finishedness or satisfaction of the entity.

Let us return to the *PR* 84 passage, which began our discussion of "satisfaction." Just before the section quoted earlier, Whitehead writes:

> Thus the notion of 'order' is bound up with the notion of an actual entity as involving an attainment which is a specific

satisfaction. This satisfaction is the attainment of something individual to the entity in question. It cannot be construed as a component contributing to its own concrescence; it is the ultimate fact, individual to the entity. The notion of 'satisfaction' is the notion of the 'entity as concrete' abstracted from the 'process of concrescence'; it is the outcome separated from the process, thereby losing the actuality of the atomic entity, which is both process and outcome. (PR 84)

It is my contention that the meaning of this passage is that the satisfaction as "product" that imposes itself on other things is *not existentially separable* from the atomic actuality most often referred to by Whitehead as belonging exclusively to concrescence as a "process." In other words, Whitehead misrepresents his position by proceeding to identify concrescence as the "formal" reality of an occasion, and relegating satisfaction to the status of merely "objective" or derivative existential status wholly parasitic on the concrescent actuality or agency of the entities in whose concrescences objectification occurs.

Adopting the Cartesian distinction between "formal and objective reality" undermines Whitehead's repudiation of the Cartesian definition of the individuality of existents, and leads to an inability to define individuality coherently within the organic atomism being advanced. To look ahead quickly, Whitehead needs to be modified in his expression of the individuality of existence in such a manner as to explicate the sense in which, as quoted previously, "every entity is in its *essence* social" (RM 108, emphasis added). This may lead to some conceptualization within which the individuality belonging to satisfaction and the individuality belonging to concrescence may be held to coincide, as they must for Whitehead's processive atomism to make sense. Subsequent discussions will develop just such a conceptualization. Let us return, for the moment, to a fuller analysis of the very notion of "satisfaction," so as to appreciate what is demanded of the concept of intensity that links an entity's closure to the processes whereby that closure is reached.

The first systematic analysis of the uncanniness of Whitehead's claims about "satisfaction" came in William A. Christian's highly regarded study of Whitehead's metaphysics in 1959, and these inquiries offer a good working blueprint from which to begin to explore the ontological problems posed by the concept of satisfaction. Christian discerns five distinct ways in which the satisfaction of an entity is referred to by Whitehead, only four of which need explicitly concern us here. The first has been hinted at previously, namely that the "satisfaction of an actual occasion is both aimed at and achieved in the experience of that actual occasion." In other words, it is conceived as expressing the ideal aim of the entity while it is also conceived as what the entity actually is as a completed process. Christian argues for an identity of aim and achievement gathered under the unitary term 'satisfaction,' citing the passage quoted earlier wherein Whitehead claims that "In its self-creation the actual entity is guided by ideal of itself as individual satisfaction and as transcendent creator."[12] I think there are good reasons to want to bring the conceptions of creative process and transcendently creative product together in a single conception of the individuality of an entity, but given Whitehead's statements about the status of satisfactions, and given the issues involved in the modification of subjective aim, this would require more development as a solution than is offered in Christian's text. If we include the modifications in our conception of the "aim" considered as such, however, this solution is a good start, if buttressed by further argumentation.

A second construal of satisfaction, perhaps the most problematic undertaken by Whitehead, is the notion of the internal experience of satisfaction on the part of the entity. This is, as Christian describes it, the idea that "the satisfaction of an actual occasion is a feeling immediate to that occasion."[13] What we have just seen in terms of Whitehead's denial of subjectivity (hence feeling) to satisfactions suggests that this notion of "internal experience" is out of the question, but there is ample textual evidence that Whitehead often thought otherwise. For example, he speaks of the "complex, fully determinate feeling . . . . termed the satisfaction" (PR 26). At PR 155, he states that satisfactions are "immediately felt." At PR 45 it is the satisfaction that expresses the actual entity as the unitary, wholly determinate feeling (including all positive and negative prehensions) of its actual world. Categoreally, moreover, the subjective unity of feeling sought in an entity entails that there be some single feeling expressing this unity as fully determinate for the entity in question, and it is unclear what else this feeling could be except the satisfaction under the aspect of intensity. So, when Whitehead states emphatically that "No actual entity can be conscious of [read: 'can feel'] its own satisfaction; for such knowledge would be a component in the process and would thereby alter the satisfaction" (PR 85), we are in the presence of genuine ambiguity.

This ambiguity is further brought to light in a third reading of satisfaction noted by Christian, that a satisfaction is "not a process of change."[14] It is here that Christian builds his own position on the issue of the status of satisfactions considered ontologically. If, as all of *Process and Reality* suggests, processes of actualization are the fundamentally real things, if "apart from things that are actual, there is nothing—nothing either in fact or in efficacy," and if actuality is "an act of experience" (PR 40), then a satisfaction as "the outcome separated from the process, thereby losing the actuality," (PR 84) is of ambiguous ontological status. Christian's approach here is to claim that while, certainly, satisfactions do not undergo the adventures of becoming that mark actualities in process, it is not the case that satisfactions are not involved in process, because it is "the outcome of the internal process of becoming, and it leads to the transition into the future. Thus the satisfaction as an immediate feeling stands between the two kinds of process and is internally related to both."[15]

The internal relation of satisfactions to both the present concrescence and the transcendent creativity of an entity is an intriguing notion, with some role in the position I will eventually lay out as my own interpretation regarding how to conceive of the individuality of occasions. But Christian goes a step further to what I would deem an excess of emphasis upon the satisfaction as the stamp of completed, felt unity on the part of the entity. He advances the position that "the satisfaction represents a pause in the midst of the flux. The pause is not empty; it is occupied by a single, complete feeling," a "halt" in the otherwise relentless passage from actuality to actuality in causal flow.[16] Now, Christian is careful to note that this is not some kind of "instant of enjoyment" distinct from the concrescent process, for outside the duration of a concrescent process there *is no time*. In Whitehead's epochal theory of time, time comes into being with the actualization processes of discrete atomic entities. "Indeed the satisfaction contains, one might say, the whole of the *temporal* duration of the occasion. For the genetic process that produces the final satisfaction is not itself in physical time. . . . It is by producing their satisfactions that actual occasions produce the temporally extended world."[17] The "pause," then, is simply the unitary *feeling* of the entire temporal duration or epoch of the entity as completely determinate in regard to its prehensions of its universe.[18]

This is not exactly the position ascribed to Christian by Ford. Even after noting Christian's adherence to the epochal concept of time, Ford attributes the idea of a real momentary "pause" in process to Christian's reading. Ford deems this necessary in Christian's position because of the latter's "unnecessarily severe interpretation of the perishing of subjective immediacy" with the completion of concrescence. The subject must enjoy itself in some final form before it loses its important ontological status as subject. Ford objects to Christian's purported "halt" by asking why, if the satisfaction can exist "for a moment," it cannot continue to exist? The satisfaction does indeed continue to exist via its objectifications in subsequent subjects.[19] On Jorge Nobo's reading, "becoming" is productive of the "being" of an entity (in the form of its satisfaction with transcendently creative efficient causality), and this does capture the real persistence of an objectified entity even after its immediacy has perished.[20] But this solution leaves it unclear just how the existence represented in the concrescence and that represented in the satisfaction, or superject, correlate in terms of how one identifies "individual" actualities. It would be unfortunate indeed if an atomism of any sort was premised on two fundamental *kinds* of individuation, one for subjects and one for objects. My reading, to be developed in the balance of this chapter and in the two subsequent chapters, will synthesize Christian's position on the internal relationship between concrescence and satisfaction, and Ford's and Nobo's correct assertions regarding the continued existence of the satisfaction in subsequent actualities, though I will at times part significantly from the overall interpretations of all three in order to frame what I think may be a more workable model of individuality that preserves what I take to be the spirit of Whitehead's adoption of atomism in his metaphysics.

Although the relation between the subjective and the objective sides of satisfactions is clearly problematic, the "objective" functioning of satisfactions in the transcendent universe is basically accessible. Christian's fourth thesis as to satisfactions easily acknowledges their functioning as *objects in subsequent actualities*: the "satisfaction of an actual occasion exists objectively for all occasions that supercede that occasion."[21] This objective functioning expresses what Whitehead calls the "objective immortality" achieved by all entities to one degree or another. But it may be that Whitehead was misled by the availability of his own doctrine of objective immortality so as to overemphasize perishing, in so far as it characterizes satisfaction as the *cessation* of immediacy, subjective existence, agency, and so on. To assert the "objective" functioning of the superject or satisfaction in the becoming of other entities need not require that subjectivity in all senses wholly perish, nor does it necessitate a view of an entity as a "closed-up" individuality. To say that outside of the decisions of actualities there is nothing—"the rest is silence" (PR 43)—need not lead us to strip past actualities of the same kind of existence which attaches to present concrescences. And if we can find a way to continue the subjectivity of existents into their objectifications, problems as to the ontological status of the past diminish in impact.

The upshot of Christian's problem is how to resolve the immediacy of feeling in the satisfaction of the entity as subject, which seems to perish, with the objective immortality in the superjected satisfaction in a single conception of what it means to exist. How can a satisfaction be both subject and object in a way that is not self-contradictory?[22] His resolution is to recognize two senses in which the existence of the satisfaction may be considered, two senses expressed alternately in the pairs of terms, "private and public," "intrinsic and extrinsic reality," and "subject and superject." The latter pair has the merit of substantially reflecting Whitehead's persistent use of terminology. It should, therefore, be taken seriously if it offers any way of resolving the present difficulties. We might also note that the other two pairs offer information as to *what it means to be* a subject-superject or to conceive of one.

The private-public contrast, in order to be considered in a manner that does not introduce a complete rupture between the two terms, requires that we bear in mind a crucial concept in the organic cosmology: that everything that comes to be is thus a potential for the becoming of other things. Thus, when we are considering an entity in its own internality as the realization of its unique subjective aim bringing about immediacy of feeling, we are referring to "the attainment of the private ideal, . . . a unity of aesthetic appreciation immediately felt as private" (PR 212). But when we consider it as a public fact, we are considering the modes in which that satisfaction may

29

enter into creative process beyond the entity in question: "In other words, the 'satisfaction' of an entity can only be discussed in terms of the usefulness of that entity" (*PR* 85). To refer this discussion to the Categories of Existence, which Christian does not, we note that privacy and publicity are the marks of two varieties of existence. Subjective Forms, the emotional tonalities of unified prehensions enjoyed by the subject in itself, are described as "Private Matters of Fact," as we have already noted. Nexūs, as also noted, are described as "Public Matters of Fact" (*PR* 22). The suggestion that existence is to be conceived differently for the private and the public aspects of an entity is somewhat legitimated, apparently, by these categoreal definitions. I will return to this notion later.

Whitehead uses the concepts of "intrinsic and extrinsic reality" only once, referring respectively to "the event as in its own prehension, and the event as in the prehension of other events" (*SMW* 103). This formulation has the appeal of simplicity, but it does little to elaborate on the connection between private and public existence. The terms do add the air of more strictly metaphysical description, though the fact that they do not recur systematically in the metaphysics of *Process and Reality* suggests that Whitehead may not have found them to convey his sense adequately. If we are attempting to elucidate the sense of an obscure scheme, it may be ill-advised to add terminology to an already obfuscating vocabulary. Jorge Nobo does make use of the intrinsic-extrinsic reality distinction in speaking about the existence of an entity, but in such a manner as to accent the duality of the entity without (if a coherent 'atomism' of intense becoming is our conceptual goal) satisfactorily resolving the problem of individuality created by this duality.[23]

The subject-superject expression of the dual guise of the actual entity is somewhat effective in driving home the need to conceive of satisfactions in two manners, but in the end does not solve our problem either, unfortunately. On the one hand, Whitehead does explicitly acknowledge the need to examine the entity in these two distinct ways. Christian cites a passage in *Process and Reality* which states that "An actual entity is to be conceived both as subject presiding over its own immediacy of becoming, and a superject which is the atomic creature exercising its function of objective immortality" (*PR* 45). Indeed, this is in effect a restatement of the eighth Category of Explanation, which claims "that two descriptions are required for an actual entity: (a) one which is analytical of its potentiality for 'objectification' in the becoming of other actual entities, and (b) another which is analytical of the process which constitutes its own becoming" (*PR* 23). On the other hand, Whitehead is here talking about 'conceiving' and 'describing' the entity, while it is unclear just how these analytical modes reflect the existential dimensions of actualities. In fact, this ambiguity between analysis and existential description infects much of Whitehead's scheme, despite (among other things) his deliberate construction of the Theory of Extension (and the doctrine of Presentational Immediacy underwritten by Extension) to overcome it. From the way in which the category is stated, one existential conclusion that could be drawn is that existence is primarily to be ascribed to satisfactions (mentioned first in the call for two descriptions), and secondarily to the "becoming" that produced the individuated entities which impose themselves objectively on other things. But this would contradict the thrust in Whitehead's system towards privileging the agentive ontological status of concrescence.

Christian does, by way of summary, make an observation that is quite helpful in coming to some kind of closure on the uncanny existential status of satisfactions. He notes that "the occasion aims at intensity of experience in other entities as well as itself. But it cannot contribute to the experience of other entities without ceasing to exist in its own subjective immediacy. Hence attainment of its satisfaction requires the perishing of immediacy and passage into objective existence. The subjective immediacy of an occasion *calls for* its objective immortality" and correspondingly, "the objective existence of an actual occasion *points to* its previous existence as an immediate experience."[24] Christian notes that the two modes of existence "require each other" but does not elaborate on just what it means to say that an entity in one mode of existence "calls for" another mode, and that this other mode "points to" the first. The language of 'pointing' and 'calling' does, despite its obscurity, capture the active "vector character" (as Whitehead calls it) of prehensions being *felt as coming from* distinct entities in the world, and as going out toward the world transcendent of the present feeler. Christian's language helps tag the vector character of the subjective-then-objective functioning of the entity. Taking up the issue of vector-feeling here will be helpful.

Recalling the grounds of order cited earlier, we note that the final causality, or end, of actuality "is concerned with gradations of intensity in the satisfactions of actual entities," and that "'intensity' in the *formal constitution* of a subject-superject involves 'appetition' in its *objective* functioning as superject" (PR 83). The existence of an actual entity clearly is being linked to its intensity, equally applicable to the subjective and objective dimensions of the satisfaction. The intensity embodied in the satisfaction is the link between the formal (private) existence of the actuality as agentive finality and its objective (public) existence as efficient cause in the formal constitutions of other entities. This is not merely a question of how we analyze or consider an actuality, but a question of what an actuality *is* in the creative process of becoming. Although Christian's somewhat metaphorical formulations may lack sufficient explanatory force, the "vector character" of feelings suggested by his language is crucial. Christian cites the following passage, with the omission of the first three sentences quoted here, which I have added to expand the analysis of satisfaction:

> The operations of an organism are directed towards the organism as a 'superject,' and are not directed from the organism as a

> 'subject.' The operations are directed *from* antecedent organisms and *to* the immediate organism. They are 'vectors,' in that they convey the many things into the constitution of the single superject. The creative process is rhythmic: it swings from the publicity of many things to the individual privacy; and it swings back from the private individual to the publicity of the objectified individual. The former swing is dominated by the final cause, which is the ideal; and the latter swing is dominated by the efficient cause, which is actual. (PR 151)

To be perfectly consistent, Whitehead should have added an observation to the effect that the final causation entails provision for the swing to efficient causation on the part of an entity eventually functioning as transcendent creator, a point that is implicit in the first three sentences. Moreover, this vectoral provision is critical to the very finality of the subject itself, as conveyed in the grounds of order and the Category of Subjective Intensity, where intensity in the relevant future is stipulated as a present concrescent concern.

Interestingly, the passage just quoted is once again concerned to distinguish the philosophy of organism from more traditional, particularly Cartesian, substance ontologies, and thus like the passages quoted earlier concerning individuality, and so on, should be unpacked in its significance as a statement of Whitehead's fundamental metaphysical objectives. I think this quote very strongly suggests that the individuality Whitehead is talking about as characterizing actualities must be tied to the satisfaction as the emergent product of concrescence, in some manner that does not relegate the all-important agentive subjectivity of concrescence to a derivative status like that accorded to satisfactions in certain other passages from *Process and Reality*. Descartes's claim that "I am, I exist, is necessarily true each time that I pronounce it, or that I mentally conceive it" is challenged for its implications regarding the process-product distinction: "Descartes in his own philosophy conceives the thinker as creating the occasional thought. The philosophy of organism inverts the order, and conceives the thought as a constituent operation in the creation of the occasional thinker. The thinker is the final end whereby there is the thought. In this inversion we have the final contrast between a philosophy of substance and a philosophy of organism" (PR 150–51). Connecting these comments to the earlier passage, which in Whitehead's text follows immediately the comments on Descartes just quoted, I think we have good reason to say that the all-important final causality of subjective aim concerns the satisfaction as transcendent efficient cause in much more than a derivative or secondary sense to the immediate concerns of enjoyment of feeling in a given concrescence. Tying finality to the satisfaction may in fact require the reconsideration of immediate enjoyment as the real locus of atomistic existence, for the atomic actuality of the organism is in these passages the superject *more than the subject*.

To some extent Whitehead's problem here, as in the passages about formal and objective reality, may be that he is adopting metaphysical distinctions from an ontology he is trying to subvert. The distinction between efficient and final causality that leads to excessive differentiation of the ontological status of concrescence and satisfaction-superject may in fact distort the ontological reconstruction of process that the philosophy of *organism* (over and against the philosophy of *substance*) is trying to accomplish. If we jettison the language of the two forms of causation for the moment, we can ask if there is a need for an ontological distinction between the present intensive concerns of the organism and its intensive superjection in transcendent process. And, to the extent that any distinction is required, is it a distinction of existential or ontological type? My answer to the first question is "Perhaps," with the immediate clarification by a "No" response to the second question. The intrinsic and extrinsic reality of an actuality are the same reality. What is needed is a reconstruction of Whitehead's claims to make this feasible, and this is what the rest of the present discourse undertakes.

To prepare ourselves for further advancement of the thesis that ontological distinctions between concrescence and satisfaction can be collapsed via a more organismic conception of organic atomism than is explicitly rendered in Whitehead's text, we should deepen our understanding of the intensive structures constitutive of satisfaction itself. This will involve taking a look at the factors in concrescent process that allow for or are the basis of what is called the eventual intensity of feeling expressed by the satisfaction. This, along with a second look at the concept of "contrasts" so crucial to intensity, will round out this first chapter's venture into the thickets of process metaphysics and its ontological difficulties.

Intensity of Feeling Revisited: More Structural Considerations

It was in a move to the structural consideration of intensity that we noted (1) that there is a tension between intensity as an ideal to be aimed at and the intensity actually achieved by an entity, (2) that this in part leads to questions about the existential status of satisfactions, and (3) that the constitution of the total subject-superject manifests what should be seen as a *unitary* concern for intensity. The source of the difficulty in the mutual entertainment of these three notions stems, I think, from (1), because it points to the two difficult to reconcile trends in Whitehead's handling of the subjective-objective, concrescence-satisfaction issue. I will argue for the dismissal of this difficulty on the basis of an unflinching conception of consideration (3).

Intensity, as noted, is *what is aimed at*, it is the goal of the process involved in the entity's becoming. Considered in this manner, intensity expresses the application of freedom and agency in the entity's self-creating unification of its feelings of its world, and thus intensity is the depth of immediate feeling resident in or, actually, constitutive of the subject. This is intensity considered as a fact of inalienable privacy, making Whitehead's a metaphysics of individual value-realization. On the other hand, intensity expresses what the entity *objectively is* for other entities in its status as a satisfaction or superject, and as we have seen this is taken account of *in* the subjective aim of immediate purpose in such manner as to modify the privacy of the entity in light of its possible function as a public fact. By situating a further elucidation of intensity in our interrupted discussion of "order" we may find a way to avoid thinking of intensity as systematically ambiguous in its referring to both the immediate experiential complex *and* to the objectification of any given entity.

The intensity embodied in the satisfaction of any entity arises from the degree to which the conditions of "triviality," "vagueness," "narrowness," and "width" are manifest in that entity's appropriation of factors in its environment. Although for brevity's sake I refer to these as the "structural" considerations involved in intensity, it must be remembered that they refer as well to the *evaluation* of data in a concrescence. Value and structural pattern wholly coincide, though I will use the language of structure to get at what could loosely be called the quantitative dimensions of intensive patterning or valuational structuring of feelings by entities. In fact, the coincidence of structure and value is in part one of the issues at stake in coming to terms with the ontological status of concrescences and satisfactions. One thought to keep in mind as our analysis proceeds is that one of the reconstructions of metaphysics that Whitehead's cosmology is attempting is the elimination of the fact-value dichotomy entrenched in thought by the scientific revolution of Descartes and his era. This is another dimension of the reason why it may in the end be wise to eliminate the distinction between efficient and final causality as hopelessly obscuring Whitehead's repudiation of the fact-value distinction.

Whitehead refers to the four considerations we are about to discuss as those notions by which a "classification" of satisfactions may be made. This at once alerts us to the *emergent* significance of the kinds of valuations performed within concrescence such that elements in the datum are contrasted in various ways. Aristotelean logic, in *Science and the Modern World*, is rejected for its emphasis on classification, since what was meant by the classification of natural objects into genera and species was the notion that every substance possessed a nature that defined it from within, in much the same manner as Descartes is criticized by Whitehead as holding that thought defines thinking from within the substance doing the thinking (cf. *SMW* 195). Thus Whitehead's sense of classification must be taken to refer to the products of process, the emergent intensities of satisfaction, rather than to any conception of subjectivity as a kind of nature that sustains the emergence of determinate characteristics.

"Triviality and vagueness," Whitehead writes, "are characteristics in the satisfaction which have their origins respectively in opposed characteristics in the datum" (PR 111). This tells us nothing yet as to what those characteristics are, but it does hint at something I take to be an essential ingredient in Whiteheadian metaphysics, which is that formative conditions of process are often, and at crucial times, described in terms of the functioning of contrasted considerations, "contrast" here meant in the strict sense of unity in difference. The pairing of terms here and elsewhere is no mere rhetorical flourish, nor is it a concession to ordinary dualism. It is a duality of conception that may, in the end, mark a kind of conceptual unity unique to process thought, as I hope the present study will suggest.

Triviality refers to an excess of differentiation in the data of the entity, such that this data fails to be brought under effective contrast for coordinated prehension. It "arises from lack of coordination in the factors of the datum, so that no feeling arising from one factor is reinforced by any feeling arising from another factor" (PR 111). Now, Whitehead does refer to these nonmutually reinforcing elements of the datum as something of a contrast, but they are not effectively contrasted so as to produce an important unity of feeling: "In other words, the specific constitution of the actual entity in question is not such as to elicit depth of feeling from contrasts thus presented. Incompatibility has predominated over contrast" and intensity is thwarted. Factors in the environment are relegated to the status of unimportant difference by means of negative prehensions arising either in response to the genuine mutual exclusiveness of the elements or in response to the lack of relevance of the differences therein embodied for the subjective aim of the entity. To recur to our example of a painting, triviality would be the result if the juxtaposition of periwinkle blue and daffodil yellow as different colors did not really add to the overall effect. The colors represent, in this instance, meaningless variety. Triviality, along with the other three notions we are discussing, is a structural issue—it expresses a necessary component feature in the constitution of any entity as it proceeds in its self-creation. Some multifariousness of data matters, some does not. Triviality is thus one structural manner in which the complete identification of entities with one another in a troubling monistic sense is avoided—it is a form of differentiating dismissal of what could be complete inclusion by emphatic relevance. Of course in the higher phases of experience, where coordination of diversities of data are the order of the day, tolerance of triviality in self-creation may border on vice.

Vagueness, on the other hand, refers to an excess of non-differentiation among the elements of the datum. "In the datum the objectifications of various actual entities are replicas with faint coordinations of perspective contrast. Under these conditions the contrasts between the various objectifications are faint, and there is deficiency in the supplementary feeling discriminating the objects from each other" (PR 111). Factors in the environment are dismissed as a fog of undiscriminated multiplicity provoking no significant response in the entity's self-constitution. Here we must distinguish between the simple physical feelings that initiate the process of concrescence as arising in the actual world, and the supplementary feelings that are the stamp of *novel* individual agency (but not agency per se). These supplementary, or "conceptual," feelings unite and clothe the feelings of the earlier "phase" according to the adaption to an end embodied in subjective aim. Thus, in the painting, vagueness is the condition wherein some elements in the scene fail to effect the aesthetic experience of genuinely meaningful variety. The shades of colors are meaninglessly (as opposed to purposefully) similar, the shapes are, with no end in mind, relatively indistinguishable. Vagueness need not be conceived as totally purposeless, for minute absences of purposive differentiation may be crucial to an overall aesthetic effect sought for what are very determinate purposes. Pointillism and French impressionistic painting make a virtue of such vagaries attending the low-grade distinguishability of one element of an overall scene from another.

It is with the notions of "narrowness" and "width" that what Whitehead calls "depth" (a fifth notion which, we will see, interestingly unifies the four structural considerations) of intense satisfaction in regard to trivial or vague environmental prehensions may be understood. "Intensity is the reward of narrowness" (PR 112). Narrowness imposes simplification of perspective, but with full appreciation of the differentiations (contrasts) realized out of the environmental field. That is, a great "width" of significantly diverse elements in the datum is brought into as "narrow" as possible a unity to as to be a harmony of efficiently contrasted component feelings. Elements in the datum have been harmonized so that they are mutually compatible insofar as that compatibility is possible for and essential to the aim of the entity in question, and these elements have entered into complex contrast so as to be felt as one. In the painting, some overall condition of unification (narrowness) stands as the principle of aesthetic unity, or elegance, in the work as a complex (wide) whole. Perhaps it is a representational scene, in which case details represented are put together so as to convey the concept of the theme being represented—a vase of flowers, a worker in the field, a man on a horse, and so on. Too much width or complex detail and the thematic unity may be lost; too much narrowness and the painting may approximate the line-drawings of a first-grader.

Triviality, vagueness, narrowness, and width conjointly function in the determination of oneness out of the manyness of the datum such that depth of satisfaction, or intensity, is reached. These are the terms in which the many are valued individually and mutually up or down in the realization of the aim at intense feeling *in and as* the one actual entity. These notions achieve a description of what it means for the entity not only to *have* but to *be* a perspective on the entire universe out of which it arises. They describe the background and foreground of the perspective which that entity *is*, such that it participates in the type of order out of which it arises and to which it seeks to contribute for its own sake as well as for the sake of the order. An actual entity that is part of the order constituting, for example, an enduring block of granite establishes a perspective making possible at one and the same time the maintenance of that order and that entity's transcendent role in that maintenance. An entity's role is to arrange background and foreground elements in such a manner that the order can be maintained, should the wider environment tolerate or demand it and should the possibilities for the entity in question urge in that direction. It is worth quoting Whitehead at length on this point:

> By reason of vagueness, many count as one, and are subject to indefinite possibilities of division into such multifold unities. When there is such vague prehension, the differences between the actual entities so prehended are faint chaotic factors in the environment, and have thereby been relegated to irrelevance. Thus vagueness is an essential condition for the narrowness which is one condition for depth of relevance. It enables a background to contribute its relevant quota, and it enables a social group in the foreground to gain concentrated relevance for its community of character [participation in order]. The right chaos [supplied also by the relegation to triviality of masses of elements in the datum], and the right vagueness, are jointly required for any effective harmony. They produce the massive simplicity which has been expressed by the term 'narrowness.' Thus chaos is not to be identified with evil; for harmony requires the due coordination of chaos, vagueness, narrowness, and width [significant variety]. (PR 112)

Triviality and vagueness provide a background of downgraded importance and decidedly insignificant elements that are the sources of disorder (chaos) against which narrow appreciation of wide contrasts of significant detail (forms of order exemplified in individual entities) arise. That is, a hierarchy of contrasts, emerging in the gradual unification of the entity's multiple feelings of its world, is made possible by the data and realized to some extent by the entity. There is a narrow contrast that elicits a depth of feeling supported by the wide range of lower level contrasts that the narrowness has managed to symbolize, so to speak, in the one unified intense satisfaction. But it is more than a symbol—it is the reality of the many feelings *actually in the one feeling* in virtue of a patterning of value which expresses that entity's finality individually clothing its feelings of its world.

It is important to note the mutuality of the structural conditions of intensity. Narrowness in large measure *is* the massive simplification afforded *by* triviality and vagueness and *by* meaningful width of detail. Narrowness is the contrast of elements in subordinate degrees of contrast (expressed by triviality, vagueness, and the details of width), such that what is essential to the entity stands out in its own intense feeling, and what is inessential lends its subjective form (to the narrowly felt contrast) as the dim but necessary feeling of the actual world as extending off in all directions from the entity. "Intensity" expresses the entity as an individual perspective on the many. In virtue of intensity the many are scaled or contrasted (patterned) into valuations of relevance and irrelevance according to the ideal of itself entertained by the actuality. The mutual implications of these terms do not undermine their significant pairing, however. Triviality and vagueness are contrast terms for the prehension of a background; Narrowness and width are contrast terms expressing the prehension of a foreground of simplification amid variety.

Whitehead might simply have referred to these conditions of depth of satisfaction as the stipulation that entities aspire to a harmonic situation of "elegance." Although his discussion of what I am calling the structural conditions of intensity does have an air of the appreciation of mathematical simplicity usually denoted by the term "elegance," it is better conceived as arising from a general appreciation for the aesthetic character of feelings brought under conditions of existential unity in the agentive phases of self-creation in concrescence. As Elizabeth Kraus notes, "An intense satisfaction will therefore manifest width in its earlier stages and progressively simplify that width in the later stages. It resembles a painting with a carefully detailed foreground set against yet growing out of a vaguely discriminated background. The right kind of narrowness is essential if the painting is not to become a cartoon; the right kind of width and vagueness if it is not to degenerate into chaotic busy-ness."[25] These right kinds of structural valuation refer to the significant contrasts possible for and aimed at in the ideal of the entity, an ideal with the crucial existential concern that the entity achieve a satisfaction appropriate to the various orders, or social structures, in which it is actually, to use Kraus's term, "nested."[26] There is little objective immortality for an actuality that fails to incorporate the right patterns so as to secure its significance in the interpenetrating natural orders in which that entity participates. For example, the occasions constitutive of the circulation of blood in my body fail their ideal of transcendent effectiveness (represented by an ideal intensity of satisfaction) to the peril of both the occasions individually and, what is the same thing, the wider social environments comprised by such occasions, here blood ph, circulation, oxygen delivery, nutrition of tissues, and so on.

Robert Neville stresses existential concerns that point to the need to opt away from the simple aesthetic concept of "elegance" and toward the more ontologically significant "contrast," but his reasons for doing so differ in an interesting and significant manner from my own in this context. Neville notes that "elegance" is "intended as a characterization of the value in anything, not just in cosmological entities. It is the simplification of the value in mathematical systems as well as in persons or buildings. The elegance appropriate to cosmological entities is called 'contrast' because 'contrast' connotes a greater independence between the harmonized constituents than connoted by 'elegance'. The reason for the greater independence is that all cosmological harmonies located in the experience of actual entities are harmonies of other, objectified actual entities. Those harmonized actual entities in their moments of subjective process are isolated from each other."[27] Neville's position here stems from the important recognition that the existential discreteness of entities has to be acknowledged in our description of how they come to incorporate features of one another. This may be taken as a given for any kind of pluralistic or atomistic view of process. But the question arises as to what kind of discreteness we are looking to protect. We cannot read into a pluralistic cosmos a standard conception of "individuality" that is itself the primary notion to be developed in just such a description of pluralism or, in Whitehead's case, atomism. What is to be protected is, at least, the sense in which those things that are incorporated as having "come from" or "stolen in from" the world "never afterwards quite detach themselves from this or that accident, or trick, in the mode of their first entrance into us," to recur to the quotation from Pater with which we began. The "mode of first entrance" is determined by what the entities from out of the world did to assure their objective immortality or transcendent effect. What needs protecting is a kind of "realism" about the past and about the world as such external to the entity, such that each entity is not in an "idealistic" sense responsible for the existence of everything else, nor is it truly "isolated" from other things.

The choice between the more existentially neutral term 'elegance' and the more ontologically significant 'contrast' shows itself to be an interesting decision for the purposes underway here, which is the entertainment of the ontological status of satisfactions vis-à-vis what goes on in concrescences. I would maintain, in something of an inversion of Neville's conclusion but in the interest of preserving his intention, that 'contrast' preserves at one and the same time the difference as well as the genuinely rich organic unity between the elements so harmonized. Neville's concern is to defend an axiological metaphysics (that is, a metaphysics of value-existence) against the charge of idealism that might arise if the unity of existents is stressed over their cosmological separateness. He is also distressed at the particular kind of separateness Whitehead's atoms enjoy. My position is that Whiteheadian axiology, in the form of atomism, may be defended axiologically without over stressing the ontological *separateness* of existents. Concepts of 'separateness' or 'distinctness' between existents within a process scheme are parasitic on or derivative from the more general conception of 'individuality' that must be defined by any such scheme.[28]

We have arrived, thus, at the point where a deeper appreciation for the nature of "contrasts" is very much in order so that a complete understanding of intensity and satisfaction might be possible. "Contrast" will be seen to contribute somewhat to the ambiguous ontological status of intensity as a systematic notion attaching both to concrescence and satisfaction, but will also be seen to be a centrally important dimension of any possible intensity, and will, moreover, frame the substance of an important gloss on the question of just what it means for something to "exist" in the organic philosophy of "orders of nature" developed by Whitehead.

Contrasts Revisited: The Categories of Existence

Contrasts stand as the eighth Category of Existence, and are described as "Modes of Synthesis of Entities in one Prehension, or Patterned Entities." Whitehead also notes that this category "includes an indefinite progression of categories, as we proceed from 'contrasts' to 'contrasts of contrasts', and on indefinitely to higher grades of contrasts" (PR 22). This latter qualification can be read as an acknowledgment that contrasts exist at different levels of complexity, and that these levels denote a certain difference in kind of existence. Indeed, this is consistent with the claim that satisfactions may be "classified" according to their intensities. That is to say, all classification is made on the basis of emergent similarities in achieved intensities such that the possibility likewise emerges that "occasions are gathered into various types," but that "from the metaphysical standpoint these types are not to be sharply discriminated" (though "as a matter of empirical observation, the occasions do seem to fall into fairly distinct classes") (PR 110). There are rough kinds of things—like minds and bodies—but these are results of complex orderings rather than their being the conditions of the orders. They can be results of order because of the paths of inheritance manifest by similar intensities achieved by entities and reproduced in other entities along the path, intensities made possible by grades of contrast in the datum, as supplemented by aim, and so on. These intensities do not express metaphysical generalities but imposing actualities. Likewise, contrasts and contrasts of contrasts express the indefinitely emergent ways in which potentialities—that is, the actual world of any entity taken as a multiplicity in conjunction with the realm of eternal objects—are brought under conditions of unity in the actual occasions without which there is nothing.

It is in this progression of types of existence as contrast that Whitehead ultimately grounds emergent evolution:

> But a multiple contrast is not a mere aggregation of dual contrasts. It is one contrast, over and above its component contrasts. This doctrine that a multiple contrast cannot be conceived as a mere disjunction of dual contrasts is the basis of the doctrine of emergent evolution. It is the doctrine of real unities being more than a mere collective disjunction of component elements. This doctrine has the same ground as the objection

> to the class-theory of particular substances. The doctrine is a commonplace of art. (PR 229)

Note that class theories are faulty because of their manner of handling "*particular* substances." Classification of individuals is, like the earlier question of the distinction between individuals, dependent upon the right understanding of the very *individuality* of the things to be collected in any manner. It is easy to think of the world as carved out into neatly classifiable sets of entities if a simple notion of individuality as rough correspondence to numerical oneness is in place. Without this particular definition of individuals, classification is a complex process of coming to terms with emergent forms of unique contrastive unification. Just what the alternative to numerical oneness might be must await our subsequent analyses. But it would be appropriate to note here that grounding emergent evolution in "contrast" is part of Whitehead's general denial of scientific reductionism—complex things simply *do not reduce to mere components*.

It is suggested thus far by Whitehead's analysis that "existence" taken as a categorical notion implies no particular forms of synthesis but all possible forms of synthesis. That is, "being" is emergent and takes on any number of determinate guises, and this multiplicity of guises suggests a certain leeway in our according ontological status to various types of entities in the world. Of course Whitehead does state that among the categories of existence "actual entities and eternal objects stand out with a certain extreme finality," and that "the other types of existence have a certain intermediate character" (PR 22). This is not to be taken to mean, however, that actual entities and eternal objects are what *really* exists, or, in an extreme reading of the ontological principle, that only actual entities exist because they are the "reasons" we ultimately seek when we look for the explanations for what occurs in the world. Actual entities and eternal objects "stand out" and the other forms may, indeed, be "intermediate" in the sense that they explain the relations of actualities and forms, but this does not suggest so much a hierarchy of what exists in the truest sense, but instead should be read to underscore the real interdependence of the categories of existence. Critical disputes about the ontological implications of actuality as concrescence, and satisfaction as completed process, stem in part from an overly strong reading of Whitehead's claims about the extreme finality, whatever it may be, of actualities qua subjective processes of coming to be. A treatment of the other types of existence as derivative, less critical, or secondary results to some extent in ontological quandaries about subjectivity versus objectivity that this system was designed precisely to overcome. It is important to understand that the other forms are "intermediate" in the sense that they are *the ways in which, or conditions whereby*, actualities and forms come to stand out in an analysis of reality.

The categories listed besides Actual Entities and Eternal Objects—Prehensions, Nexūs, Subjective Forms, Propositions, Multiplicities and

Contrasts—express the dimensions and modes of existence involved in any actuality's realization of forms of definiteness. This, in turn, is governed by the Categoreal Obligations, which are rendered in detail by the Categories of Explanation, and all of these collectively unpack the conjunction of process and product attempted in the Category of the Ultimate (creativity as how the "many become one and are increased by one"). Actualities and forms may have a finality about them, but the other categories express still more basic things about the more final types of existence.

I go out of my way to remove the mystique of ontological status from actual entities and eternal objects, in part because of the weak sense of "category" that should be taken to be operating in this particular set of categories. In the first place, "contrasts" denote the curious possibility of an "indefinite number" of categories of existence. Secondly, the categories of existence not only have a relation of mutual implication (the "intermediate" character of the nonfinal categories vis-à-vis the more final ones), but they also enjoy a relation of mutual penetration and explanation. "Every categoreal type of existence in the world presupposes the other types in terms of which it is explained" (PR 349). If types of existence explain one another, then the ascription of existential status to anything—including concrescences and satisfactions—is to be undertaken gingerly. There must be some complex considerations made for the formal conditions of determinacy provided for in the categories taken as a whole. This complexity is underscored by the fact that a contrast not only expresses a relation between two (or more) items but harbors reference to the particularities of those items—a contrast is *just this* contrast of *just these* particularities, the "special passageways" (recurring again to Pater) that the greater world beyond uses to steal in upon something (cf. PR 228). For the purposes of the issues at stake in the present discussion, this suggests a distinct overlap in our consideration of the realization in a present entity of forms of definiteness embodied in the satisfactions of prior actualities, and our consideration of the concrescent process of realization by which satisfactions are appropriated from the world. Again, the point is the penetration of one category of existence by another in the attempt to explain the ontological status of individually existing things.

The interpenetration of the Categories of Existence arises most resolutely from the following considerations. Actual entities feel the data presented under forms of contrast. These contrasts are then contrasted anew to provide for the mutual coordination of the subordinate contrasts (feelings) in the one complex of feeling that eventually issues in the satisfaction. Now, the contrasts are the basis for the ascription of intensity to the experience of an entity, and the entity eventually is its determinate intensity provided by these contrasts, some of which it has taken over from its actual world, some of which it has provided for itself via conceptual origination of feeling. In this sense, all of the categories of existence, as specifying elements in the constitution of actual entities, describe the modes in which an entity becomes a high-grade contrast signified by "intensity." This means that the indefinite progression of categories of contrast proceeds across the other categories presented, as well as extending the list of categories indefinitely. In fact, Whitehead notes that in a sense a "proposition" is a species of contrast (PR 24), and it might likewise be said that the other categories too are species of contrast. The only problematic category would be Eternal Objects, for these are Pure Potentials, by definition unrealized forms. Because a contrast is a felt comparison, Eternal Objects would be excluded. If, however, we called eternal objects potential contrasts as their mutual comparability established by the primordial envisagement by God provides, then this anomaly may be minimized.[29]

The position I am advocating is that we choose a new point of terminological emphasis in conceiving existence in Whitehead's cosmological metaphysics. If intensity of feeling is what all of the categories help bring about, why not read the categories in their existential implications as being about the operations of contrastive feeling procurative of intensity? This would provide a single terminus for our ontological discussions, rather than the cumbersome problem of adjudicating between the subjective actuality phase of things and the objective immortality phase of things. As tempting as this might be, however, we cannot rush headlong into the re-ordination of the categories of existence until we have really faced the cumbersome problem of subjective and objective existence just mentioned. These speculations about the status of the Categories of Existence help to round out this rather dialectical first run-through of the ontological problems raised by atomism, as it brings us back around to considering the status of categories as such in Whitehead's scheme, and this is where we began. Having gotten a look at some of the key terms involved in the study of the role the concept of "intensity" plays in Whitehead's system, we can now begin to build a case for using "intensity" as the central ontological point of reference in this scheme. Although I do intend the raising of "intensity" to central significance in the system to be a hypothetical experiment that might be performed as well with other notions, at the same time I think this particular notion has some important lessons to teach us about process metaphysics, so I will plunge ahead, treating "intensity" with a certain "extreme finality" so as to explore the full scope of its interpretive force.

CHAPTER TWO

Intensity and the Categoreal Obligations

> *... if*
> *Sins can be forgiven, if bodies rise from the dead,*
> *These modifications of matter into*
> *Innocent athletes and gesticulating fountains,*
> *Made solely for pleasure, make a further point:*
> *The blessed will not care what angle they are regarded from,*
> *Having nothing to hide. Dear, I know nothing of*
> *Either, but when I try to imagine a faultless love*
> *Or the life to come, what I hear is the murmur*
> *Of underground streams, what I see is a limestone landscape.*
> —W. H. Auden, *"In Praise of Limestone"*

In these lines Auden brackets the possibility of supernatural remedies for the incompletions and indiscretions of temporal life, and chooses to focus on the kinds of processes that concrete, temporal life has set in place for the overcoming of limitations met in this or that limited experience (the "sins" we commit, the "death" that awaits the body). The "limestone landscape" is the shape nature has taken in the long process of being carved, from the intrinsically soft stone of existence itself (the "matter" that can be "modified" by reorganization in new forms), by the old and subterranean force of water coursing its way through, or as, time. Limestone nicely represents the malleability of nature's forms, the capacity of this or that turn of events to shape creative existence as it will, into the sheer enjoyment of "innocent athletes" or "gesticulating fountains," the pleasures of private experience that yield the forms that will be regarded from the "angles" or perspectives of other things. I think Auden's "praise" for temporal processes in all of their aesthetic splendor, and his description of their participation in time and immortality nicely captures the point Whitehead is trying to convey in his somewhat more turgid presentation of subjective process and its products. Like Auden, Whitehead is articulating a joyful naturalism, a celebration of the processes that create the enjoyments that are their own source of immortality, that perfection of form which may be snatched at from within the relentless movements and reshapings constituting temporal passage.

In this chapter I explore the self-constitution of entities in accordance with the Categoreal Obligations that express the conditions under which subjectivity (and with it objective existence) takes shape. Focusing on "intensity," I will unpack the nature of the subject and its experience, and explore how this might contribute to a solution to the ontogological vagaries surrounding the adventures of these subjects (as superjects) in the concrescences of other things. The extent to which existents achieve "blessed" integrity undamaged by this or that incorporation in the "angled" becoming of other subjects will be hinted at to move us, like a "murmur," to the more definitive arguments about ontology in chapter three. In order to appreciate the various categories for what they involve vis-à-vis the achievement of subjectivity, it is first necessary to quickly sketch the "phases" of concrescence through which actualities move in the achievement of complete unity of feeling as "satisfaction."[1]

The Phases of Concrescence

A concrescence involves first a phase of "conformal feeling," which denotes primarily the reproduction in the novel entity of feelings belonging to other entities in the concrescent subject's world. Whitehead calls this the stage of "physical feelings," wherein there is genuine "transmission" of feelings from actuality to actuality. The sense of reproduction meant here is the new subject's feeling for itself, a feeling that markedly belongs to the being of another entity. This is the essence of causal influence in its barest form: "The deterministic efficient causation is the inflow of the actual world in its own proper character of its own feelings, with their own intensive strength, felt and re-enacted by the novel concrescent subject. But this re-enaction has a mere character of conformation to pattern" (PR 245). For our purposes, it is important to note that these feelings, bearing in themselves reference to the actualities whose objectifications they are (PR 245), are incorporated into the new entity in the guise of *their intensities*. Something in the satisfaction of a prior actuality goes to the satisfaction of the new actuality.[2]

Upon the initiation of the concrescent process by the causal objectifications or superjects streaming in (we recall that feelings are "vectoral" [PR 19]) from the actual world, there begins a phase of "conceptual feelings," whereby the novelty of each new actuality begins to take shape. This stage is characterized by the ingression of eternal objects, as noted earlier, "clothing" the feelings of data with "subjective forms." This stage begins the evaluative aspect of subjectivity. Feelings take on relative importance to the achievement of subjective aim and are clothed accordingly, in such a manner as to mark their original contribution to the eventual satisfaction, and to make possible their integration with other feelings arising from the original data or from these conceptual feelings. Feelings arise from feelings in accordance with subjective aim, which brings us to the third phase, that of "comparative feelings." In this phase of even more elaborate valuation of elements to be integrated in satisfaction, we have the introduction of higher forms of contrastive unity in which those elements assume a place. By this stage of comparison, complexity arising from meaningful contrast is deepened, and with it intensity (cf. *PR* 266). There is origination of conceptual feelings integrating massive varieties of data such that the satisfaction may be as emotionally complete or intense as conditions demand or allow. This is the multiplicative expansion of contrastive complexity mentioned in chapter one.

We are now in a position to consider the Categoreal Obligations, and how they bear on the procurement of intensity by each actuality as it proceeds through its phases of concrescence. Our run through the obligations will render more substantive our grasp of the structural conditions of intense becoming—triviality, vagueness, narrowness, and width. More importantly, problems in regard to how to conceive of (a) inheritance (causal influence from the past), (b) the present existence of an entity, (c) the satisfied entity, and (d) the status of the future, will come to light, suggesting the centrality of "intensity" as a concept leading to the resolution of these problems. One thing to point out is that I am here omitting a specific treatment of the Category of Subjective Intensity, because it has been introduced in chapter one and will be discussed in relation to all of the other obligations to be analyzed at present.

There is, it should be noted, a rough correlation between the order in which Whitehead discusses the obligations and the order of the phases of concrescence. The earlier Categoreal Obligations loosely mirror the early parts of concrescence, and the later Categoreal Obligations loosely mirror the later phases. This is not to be overemphasized, however, for all of the categories apply to the act of becoming *in toto,* though each assumes characteristic importance in certain aspects of concrescent process. So, for example, it is true that the Category of Subjective Intensity is particularly important in later phases of conceptual feeling integrating all of the data felt in concrescence, but the category is operative even in regard to what occurs in the "early" stages of physical feeling, for without aim (which is introduced by this obligation), there is no decision as to the subjective form of any feeling. Whitehead never explains the extent to which the obligations map onto the phases of concrescence, but the discussion of the various Categoreal Obligations and their operation in the stages of concrescence as dealt with in late sections of *Process and Reality* suggest the mapping is real though loose.

The Categoreal Obligations
THE CATEGORY OF SUBJECTIVE UNITY

The first Categoreal Obligation, perhaps the most counterintuitive and problematic, is that of "Subjective Unity." In virtue of this category, "the many feelings which belong to an incomplete phase in the process of an actual entity, though unintegrated by reason of the incompleteness of the phase, are compatible for integration by reason of the unity of their subject" (PR 26). If we had to point to one categoreal source for paradoxes about Being in Whitehead's atomism, we would need look no further than this obligation. What this category means is that, despite the fact that full determinacy, and thus the full 'subject' in question, awaits the completion of the entire concrescence, the feelings involved in the phases along the way can become part of the eventual completed determinacy in virtue of belonging to the subject being created. In order for there to be integration of feelings in incomplete phases, these feelings must point to the unity of their implied subject. Whose feelings are they? The subject undergoing the self-creative process. The answer to the question, *When* in concrescence, as self-determination, is the subject? is "All along." "Thus the superject is already present as a condition, determining how each feeling conducts its own process" (PR 223).

Although at first blush this Categoreal Obligation sounds quite implausible, it gains in plausibility if we remember a few things we have just seen. Recall that feelings are directed to an emergent subject, the superject to be precise, and they have a vector character as having come out from the world toward this new superject (cf. PR 151). The unity of the subject is to some extent supplied by the directionality of the feelings therein involved. Whitehead stipulates no need for, and in fact rules out the possibility of, a conception of the "subject" of feeling as in any way underlying the process of concrescence. An ever-present subject underlying concrescence would reintroduce into his atomism the same conception of individual substantiveness as substantial independence from which he is at pains to distance himself.

Another way to render this category somewhat more plausible is to highlight the fact that it calls our attention to the concept of "integration" as the central activity or characterization of concrescence. That which is unintegr*ated* is integr*able* by virtue of this condition. Subjective unity is first and foremost the expression of the eventual total integration of the many feelings involved in concrescence. To put that another way, "unity" is interchangeable with "integration" or at least "integrability."

At this point a very general observation can be made to render this notion more intelligible. The Whiteheadian process cosmos is in an overall sense conceived as a scene of possible unification of diverse elements—this is the essence of creativity. The universe as experienced testifies to gross and universal relevance of one thing to another. Unity would in general be defined as the capacity for things to be brought together which are somehow significantly diverse. As I have already pointed out, Whitehead recognized the need to render the sphere of potentiality a realm of diversity already compatible for integration in *any* concrescence (via God's primordial envisagement), or else all realization would be irrelevant to what went before. So, in terms of the specifics of this category, "subjective unity" would only need to be the integrability of diverse elements presenting themselves for incorporation in concrescence *with vectoral directedness towards a certain superject*. This last stipulation prevents "integrability" or "compatibility" from being, by itself, the ground of the unity of the subject, for if we attend back to Whitehead's statement of the category, this would invert his meaning: that the unity of the subject is the *condition for* the compatibility of that which is in fact unintegrated. In fact, there are reasons stemming from the nature of pure potentiality for the compatibility for integration of the feelings so concerned, but their compatibility *for this subject* depends also on vectoral flow.

The interesting suggestion that "each feeling conducts its own process" suggests that the kind of agency attributable to an entity need not be a seamlessly unitary thing, a notion that will be important as I move along. The agency of all feelings collectively may, if speculation be permitted, be as diversely textured as the eventual complex satisfaction that "determines" each process of singular feeling. Coupled with the weak definition of "unity" supplied by this category and demanded by the general metaphysics, the textured agency so readily described as "*an* actuality" may generate a very curious conception of "individuality" indeed.

If subjectivity be conceived as integration, it must be remarked that the conditions of integration, namely contrasts affording compatibility, are of paramount importance. Integration is the production of contrasts; the *contrasts are themselves the integration*. The subordinate contrasts afford the total integration that *is* the emergent subject. Total integration is none other than intense satisfaction. Part of the argument of the next chapter will be that the verbal similarity between "integration" as the concrescent activity and "integral intensity" (one of Whitehead's terms for individuality of satisfaction) is paralleled by conceptual equivalence as well. Here I must note that subjective unity and subjective aim, which is the provision *for* intensity, are to some extent coextensive notions: "For the subject is at work in the feeling, in order that it may be the subject with that feeling. The feeling is an episode in self-production, and is referent to its aim. This aim is a certain definite unity with its companion feelings" (PR 224).

The comment here that a feeling performs its function so that the entity "may be the subject with that feeling" is interesting. I have already speculated on the vectoral production of superjects by even the unintegrated phases of concrescence. There is a sense in which universal creativity is saying that a certain kind of subject is needed at a certain point in process, and the attention we have paid to the notion of "orders of nature" has been designed to underwrite such an idea. Now, this does not erase the free self-creation attending subjective becoming, but it does, again, render more plausible the kinds of unification performed by each humble entity as a perspective on the entire process of nature. The vectoral thrust of feelings pointing to a superject that will participate in many "nested" orders are the "settled" and "deterministic" elements of process unavoidable for all but the most free occasions in, for example, conscious experience. Another way to look at this comment is from an "analytical" perspective. Whitehead's conception of explanation is two-edged. There is "genetic" and "coordinate" analysis of actual entities, and these two modes correspond roughly, though not completely, to the two kinds of analysis mentioned earlier, that directed toward how an entity came to be, and that directed toward how it functions in the creative process beyond itself. Most coordinate analyses, the "division" of the "extensive continuum" of nature according to some analytical recognition of a significant factor of divisibility, may be expected to alight upon aspects of the continuum, which refer to ways in which satisfactions have imposed themselves on process beyond individual concrescence. The point is this: in any metaphysical or scientific explanation, we come upon actualities. We analyze feelings into phases just because we have noticed the superject adding its determinacy to the orders in which it has been recognized to have occurred.

Part of the issue of subjective unity, in other words, could be prompted by the metaphysical operation itself—having to hypothesize on the genetic conditions of concrescence of something we know to have the unity of character of the satisfaction that called our attention to it. Given the speculativeness of Whitehead's system, it is not implausible that the metaphysical impulse itself is reflected in the conditions that are posited to be the reasons why what is to be explained has the features we have already recognized it to have. Intensity is important here, because intensities are the reasons for the sustenance of the orders that occur in nature and most readily command recognition by beings with sense-organs such as ours. The conditions of order, whereby fully determinate subjects of adequate intensity emerge where they are needed and constitute the world of which we are aware when we look out the window at the breezy colors of an autumn afternoon, or when we accelerate particles in a physics laboratory, impose themselves on the observer as well as on the entities so ordered. Given the questions in empirical science from which Whitehead began his metaphysics, this is not far-fetched. One might object that this reduces metaphysics to a sort of sophisticated phenomenology that attempts to describe how reality must be, given how we experience it. Paul Weiss advances the possibility of just such a conception (without the concern about reductionism) in *Beyond All Appearances*.[3] It is unlikely that Whitehead would be troubled by this notion; he never denied the ultimately experiential origins and endpoints for metaphysical explanation. In this sense it is unfortunate that he never fully entered into conversation with much of post-Kantian critical philosophy and with the continental thought to which it gave rise.

THE CATEGORY OF OBJECTIVE IDENTITY

The "Category of Objective Identity" states that "[t]here can be no duplication of any element in the objective datum of the 'satisfaction' of an actual entity, so far as concerns the function of that element in the 'satisfaction'" (PR 26). What this means is that the many feelings a concrescent subject has of another entity in its world must eventually be united into one complex feeling of that entity, integrated with the complex feelings of other entities. In virtue of this category, a past actuality from which pattern is inherited is recognized as "obstinately itself," requiring valuation up or down (according to subjective aim) of the elements it contributes to the concrescence (*PR* 225). The multiple roles the entity might play must be gathered via contrast into a single role (*PR* 266). The contribution of complexity to intensity is in part what is at stake here. Some elements of the objectified entity will be compatible for realization with other elements of the same entity or elements of other entities according to what the valuational feelings of the concrescent subject perceive as most relevant. From this arise the considerations of triviality, vagueness, narrowness, and width, whereby what is most important (and *some* things *must* be more important than other things) may be raised into focal enjoyment (brought into complex compatibility by contrasts), and what is unimportant may be dismissed by negative prehensions into a background of supporting but irrelevant detail (definite incompatibility for the purposes at hand).

To use an example from experience, my halogen lamp is an object in my present activity, and is important to my purposes now in some respects but not in others. All of the respects in which it is important must be rendered compatible with other objects also prehended, and must be rendered into a unitary impact of the lamp on me, however complexly integrated into contrasts the various dimensions of the lamp's significance may be, or its relevances will not be appreciated at all. If the light of the lamp were contrasted with compatible elements of, say, the white desk, and the heat of the lamp contrasted with compatible elements of, say, my skin temperature, but the light and the heat were not compatible with each other or with the subconscious ways in which the lamp affects me causally (electromagnetic currents, and so on), my apprehension of the lamp would be as if it were in fact multiple objects instead of the one. Although in conscious experience such dislocations are common and permissible for the creativity they make possible, in physical experience the lamp's multiplicity would betoken a rupture in my sense of unity with a predictable environment, and may result in extreme and debilitating anxiety. These kinds of experientially dissociative states are not uncommon to various psychoses and chemically induced states. To generalize from this, we might say that the locatedness of an entity in its "nested orders" to some extent depends on this category.

Intensity is relevant to Objective Identity not only in terms of the interests of an entity in the compatibility and unity of its feelings, but also in terms of how intensity bears on particularity of existence.[4] Just as a subject in concrescence is aiming at its own present intensity of feeling *and* intensity of feeling in *its* future, the entities *objectified in* that subject did likewise. Just how obstinately the objectified entity gets to impose itself in the integrations constituting a subsequent concrescence depends upon how successful the objectified entity was in achieving balanced complexity in *its* satisfaction.

Once again I am turning attention to the fact that what goes on for an entity considered individually depends in very large measure on what has been going on and what will go on around that entity, though Whitehead very often did not assume this important perspective. The integrity of an objectified entity insofar as it functions in the satisfaction of a subject entity will be determined on the basis of whether or not the elements it lends the subject answer to the aim of that subject. This aim is, in turn, determined by the type of balanced complexity achievable by that entity in its environment(s), which is in most cases some kind of social order, however loose. Order implies that there is a statistical preponderance of entities being incorporated with integrity into the satisfactions of their successors; otherwise causal objectification, and causality in general, would be a meaningless chaos of maddening impositions.

We have a three-fold conception of the "functioning" of an objectified entity: (1) its superjected intensity apprehensible in terms of its satisfaction and provided for in its subjective aim; (2) the intensity it lends to the subjective unity or integration of concrescing entities (its degree of objective integrity or identity); and (3) the consequent role it will play in the intensity of feeling aimed at in the future (transcendent creative process) of the subjects in which it is being objectified. Intensity of satisfaction determines, in other words, the three modes of reality described in *Modes of Thought* as the entity being for itself, for the others, and for the whole (MT 110). These ideas will be integrated into the subsequent analyses.

The foregoing considerations make it possible to return to the concept of concrescence as having various "phases" despite its lack of actual division into time-frames. Can there be real succession of phases if time itself is only constituted by the passing of completed concrescences as epochal wholes? One approach would be to claim that the analysis of concrescence into phases is simply a function of the analytical standpoint, and need not imply any *actual* succession in an entity. If we maintain such a position, however, the activity of "integration" that we have seen to be the hallmark of entitative subjectivity is problematized, because integration into greater complexity requires actual passage of some sort from states of lesser complexity of contrast to states of highly complex contrast. Sherburne signals such a problem in his *Key to Process and Reality*, and casts suspicion on Whitehead's claim that "the analysis of an actual entity is only intellectual" (PR 227).[5]

Although Whitehead does not resolve all of the tensions created by his assertion of concrescence phases within an epochal theory of time, the passage in which the comment just quoted occurs may allow us to cast the issue in a new light. The passage in question is, importantly for our immediate concerns, a discussion of Objective Identity. It is worth looking at in its entirety:

> The incomplete phases with their many feelings of one object are only to be interpreted in terms of the final satisfaction with

> its one feeling of that one object. Thus objective identity requires integration of the many feelings of one object into the one feeling of that object. The analysis of an actual entity is only intellectual, or, *to speak with a wider scope, only objective*. Each actual entity is a cell with atomic unity. But in analysis it can only be understood as a process; it *can only be felt as a process*, that is to say, as in passage. The actual entity is divisible; but is in fact undivided. The *divisibility can thus only refer to its objectifications in which it transcends itself. But such transcendence is self-revelation*. (PR 227, emphasis added)

Not one of Whitehead's finer moments of clear philosophical prose, no doubt, but this observation is extremely important to a conception of the nature and task of philosophical analysis as it attempts to discern the individual characters of existents. Whitehead's vagueness may be instructive, as I think he is talking about two issues, in such a manner as to suggest that more than one consideration is necessary for the understanding of single or "individual" things. I think it fair to speculate that Whitehead is struggling with the unexplained relationship between genetic and coordinate analysis, hinted at earlier, and, importantly, the point may be that statements that refer to genetic analysis (such as those relating to the phases of concrescence) are to some extent parasitic on coordinate analysis, the division of the continuum (made possible by the inheritance of character from satisfaction to satisfaction) according to some principle of macroscopic recognition of relationships that appear to be occurring in the continuum. The objectifications of an entity in another entity must be, according to the category in question here, single but complex feelings. But in a concrescing entity these single feelings are but one factor among many feelings to be integrated into the one satisfaction. Two things follow: Although any entity unto itself is a "cell with atomic unity," its objectifications beyond itself precipitate, along with like objectifications on the part of other entities, a divisibility in the concrescing entity in which it is objectified. It (the objectified entity) also precipitates a revelation of its own internal complexity by the multiple feelings of it (which must be unified) on the part of the concrescent subject.

That is to say, genetic analysis, like coordinate analysis, is never the affair of looking at but one actual entity. An actual entity is noticed and analyzed, and its individuality of existence is stipulated, in virtue of its complex repetition (to whatever extent it occurs) in entities in its transcendent future. This sheds light on why intensity in the relevant future is posited as an interest of the actuality as an immediate subject. This is not merely the hope of immortality (though it *is* that to a degree) but an ontological recognition that the intensive character of an immediate entity is revealed in (because it resides in) its transcendent effects. An entity reveals itself for coordinate analysis in its complex functioning in the satisfactions of other entities, and suggests the possibility of its own genetic division into correspondingly complex "phases" of feeling (which involve the objectifications of still prior actualities) by this transcendent function in other things. Genetic analysis, and stipulation of the "individual" to be so analyzed, looks forward and backward in process before it can see what "can only be felt as a process, as in passage." Genetic analysis starts with ordered causal processes—it starts with a consideration of the "objective" dimension of things. This does not vitiate or epiphenomenalize the minutiae of Whitehead's genetic description of concrescence. It renders more intelligible the divergent trends in his approach to this problem by showing how objective analytizability and "subjectivity" might be coextensive. Indeed, as Lewis Ford informs us in the odyssey of *The Emergence of Whitehead's Metaphysics*, the "systematic correlation" of genetic and coordinate analysis was one of the philosopher's preoccupations in the final revisions of *Process and Reality*.[6]

To be absolutely clear here: the weak claim to be made on the basis of these observations is that the genesis of an occasion cannot be *understood* without reference to the coordinate analyses in which such occasions might be noticed. This would address only the analysis of the entity, and would make no further point about the existence of atomic actualities. However, I want to make the stronger claim that Whitehead's questions about the systematic correlation of genetic and coordinate analysis could have led him to claim more determinately the view I am building into his system: that what is *revealed* in coordinate analysis *is the entity* so revealed. The reason the metaphysical impulse finds itself, in this system, enmeshed in the overlapping analyses offered regarding subjectivity and objectivity is that the subjective and objective dimensions of the actuality qua individual are of a piece. This reading will be further developed as I go along, but in light of this interpretation as it is taking shape now, I can make some important observations about Whitehead's decision to make contiguous in his Categoreal Explanations the category dealing with the two modes of description required for actualities, and the category in which he states the "principle of process," which should be taken as some kind of fundamental statement of what his philosophy is about. The categories read thus:

> (viii) That two descriptions *are required* for *an* actual entity: (a) one which is analytical of its potentiality for 'objectification' in the becoming of other actual entities [roughly, coordinate analysis], and (b) another which is analytical of the process which constitutes its own becoming [genetic analysis].
> The term 'objectification' refers to the particular mode in which the potentiality of one actual entity is realized in another actual entity.
> (ix) That *how* an actual entity *becomes* constitutes *what* that actual entity *is*, so that the two descriptions of an actual entity *are not independent*. Its 'being' is constituted by its 'becoming.' This is 'the principle of process.' (PR 23, final emphasis added)

It is my position that the mutual requirement and nonindependence of the two modes of analysis indicates the nonindependence of the subjective and objective dimensions of an actuality; this is in the strong sense of suggesting that to even distinguish such dimensions obscures the point at hand. If incorporation in subsequent satisfactions is the only mode of self-revelation available for an entity, I think this may suggest that to be *that individual entity* means to *be objectified* just there, as much as it means to have been an original concrescence at some earlier metaphysical date. To deal with these issues fully will require closer scrutiny of the intensities that constitute the satisfactions of actualities, as this will yield further clues regarding the question of the ontological conception of individuals, as well as about the ontology of the past, both of which are very much at stake in a view that stipulates that self is only revealed beyond self.[7] As we proceed, we can recall Auden's words: "The blessed will not care what angle they are regarded from, Having nothing to hide." Although Whitehead's ontology is often taken to problematize past actualities in virtue of their incorporation in new, subjectively self-constituting actualities, and thus to render obscure just what sense anything can be said to remain itself through time, it may just be that presence in another thing is part of what a single reality is, that nothing is hidden by the angle of inclusion, that, on the contrary, inclusion is a dimension of blessed selfhood.

THE CATEGORY OF OBJECTIVE DIVERSITY

The connection between the ontological status and the self-revelation of things is emphasized further by considerations pertaining to the next Categoreal Obligation, "Objective Diversity." This Categoreal Obligation submits that "there can be no 'coalescence' of diverse elements in the objective datum of an actual entity, so far as concerns the functions of those elements in that satisfaction," and that "'[c]oalescence' here means the notion of diverse elements exercising an absolute identity of function, devoid of the contrasts inherent in their diversities" (*PR* 26). Whitehead is at pains in this category to preserve some aspect of the existential status of "diverse elements" themselves. That is to say, the possibility of 'contrasting' these elements via the supplementary comparative feelings in concrescence *presupposes* the real diversity of the objects thus contrasted. The sense of presupposition here is primarily ontological, because occasions are not logicians: the concrescence incorporates comparatively only on the basis of the real difference or real diversity of the existents (i.e. objectifications) thus involved. This is how we should read the following passage with ambiguous pronoun reference: "The Category of Objective Diversity expresses the inexorable condition—that a complex unity must provide for each of its components a real diversity of status, with a reality that bears the same sense as its own reality and is peculiar to itself. In other words, a real unity cannot provide sham diversities of status for its diverse components" (*PR* 227). The point is that for the experience of contrasts to be meaningful to the existence of the present entity, they must experience the component elements of the contrast (objectified entities) as realities of the same ontological stature as themselves. This is not just a new perspective on the meaning of past actualities—this is the real and actual inclusion of actualities as actualities in the full agentive sense in other actualities.

It is my opinion, if a moment of complaint be tolerated, that this Categoreal Obligation has been underestimated in its significance in much of the critical literature regarding Whitehead's concepts of causality, satisfaction, existence, actuality, and so on. It is generally acknowledged that this category states the necessity of maintaining diversity among the elements in the satisfaction of a concrescing entity (for the sake of its intensity, and so on), but the existential force of this Categoreal Obligation—its implications for the existential relations between past, present, and future actualities—is underappreciated.[8] The diversity commonly alluded to is simply the contrastive complexity in the satisfaction of the subject, but not necessarily the real ontological diversity of existents giving rise to this subjective complexity. The effects of this underestimation on the ontological exegesis of Whitehead's atomism will be explored in the next chapter.

It will be useful to trace two crucial aspects of this categoreal condition. At one extreme it affords, along with the other two categories already addressed, a metaphysically general grasp of the solidarity of the universe. At the other extreme it deepens our appreciation of the fundamental notion of a "contrast" as a basic component in individual becoming. What I hope will become apparent is the inseparability of the idea of "contrast" (which lies at the heart of concrescence conceived as integration) from the idea of the real solidarity of existents in the actual universe.

In this course of discussing contrasts in their relation to the conditions laid out in the Category of Objective Diversity, Whitehead makes two important claims, both of which bear on the idea of "particularity" or "individuality" as it stands in the organic philosophy. The first concerns the status of components of a diversity held in the unity of a contrast. The "real synthesis of two component elements in the objective datum of a feeling must be infected with the individual particularities of each of the relata. Thus the synthesis in its completeness expresses the joint particularities of that pair of relata, and can relate no others" (*PR* 228). A contrast effecting this synthesis is a "complex entity with . . . individual definiteness, arising out of determinateness of eternal objects" (*PR* 228). We note first of all that the concept of the "objective datum" (that is, the set of elements of the actual world to be intensely incorporated into the concrescent subject) is being closely tied to the concept of "satisfaction" (we remember that Objective Diversity concerns the functioning of elements in the satisfaction of the entity in process); this suggests, again, the close allegiance of genetic and coordinate analysis.

More importantly, we note that a contrast preserves some notion of the existential difference among the elements of the contrast, in the very process of the existential incorporation of these elements into the real satisfied unity of a present subject. This ontological or existential diversity among the elements in concrescence, maintained by the notion of particularity qua particularity demanded in contrasts, is Whitehead's point of divergence from Bradley, and idealism generally. Bradley's notion of relations condemn the relata to the status of "mere appearance" because, in Whitehead's view, a relation "fails to contrast." Thus relations without contrast are "the indiscretions of the absolute, apings of reality without self-consistency" (PR 229). Whereas Bradleyan relations "ape" reality, Whiteheadian contrasts constitute reality as the actual re-creation (hence "self-consistency") of one existent in another.

The second important claim Whitehead makes regarding individuality of existence while explicating the Category of Objective Diversity concerns the distinction between the particularity of the elements in a contrast and the particularity of actual entities themselves. It is, of course, part of my intention to claim in a manner not inconsistent with Whitehead that these two senses of particularity, though distinct in a certain way, are not separate in the actual contours of creative process. That this is valid is readily apparent in the following long passage concerning the real status of the past as preserved in a contrast. Whitehead is in the process of describing the general nature of particularity as it applies to entities:

> One actual entity has a status among other actual entities, not expressible wholly in terms of contrasts between eternal objects. For example, the complex nexus of ancient imperial Rome to European history is not wholly expressible in universals. It is not merely the contrast of a sort of city, imperial, Roman, ancient, with a sort of history of a sort of continent, sea-indented, river-diversified, with alpine divisions, begirt by larger continental masses and oceanic wastes, civilized, barbarized, christianized, commercialized, industrialized. The nexus in question does involve such a complex contrast of universals. But it involves more. For it is the nexus of *that* Rome with *that* Europe. We cannot be conscious of this nexus purely by the aid of conceptual feelings. This nexus is implicit, below consciousness, in our physical feelings. In part we are conscious of such physical feelings, and of that particularity of the nexus between particular actual entities. (PR 229)

Whitehead is expressing a realism about history here, underscoring the extent of his commitment to the real presence (in a concrescing entity) of entities with a recognized and resistant particularity of their own.[9] To say that "one actual entity has a status among other actual entities" is to suggest as much. A "datable" (*PR* 230) actuality (whether it is Rome, the breeze of ten minutes ago that has me cold now, or the slight of a friend from which my week has not recovered) re-emerges in the actualities in which it is objectified as *just the particular actuality it is*, and not as a *mere* pattern of eternal objects expressing characteristics that a present entity decides to exemplify.[10]

Whitehead reiterates this kind of realism in another discussion subsequent to the one just cited. As with the experience of history, so too with "perception," there is a temptation to limit the prehensive unity involved to the (conceptual) grasp or feeling of universals out of which can be constructed some kind of image of the "thing" we want to know. So that neither history nor what I perceive in my study while I write be a phantom—the "revels" of a cognitive Prospero, or the "indiscretions of the absolute"— Whitehead maintains that "our perceptual feelings feel particular existents." This feeling retains the "particular diversity" of which is felt (Roman guards, chariots, my lamp, my desk, my tepid coffee) "in its [the feeling's] uniting force" (*PR* 230), which is, likewise, particular. In a phrase that will lead us from this discussion of particularity to the other consideration noted at the outset of this section as to the implications of the Category of Objective Diversity (that is, its bearing on the solidarity of the universe), Whitehead emphasizes the real presence of actualities in each other by the strong claim that "actual entities are really together in all subsequent unifications [integrations] of the universe, by reason of the objective immortality of their real mutual prehensions of each other." (*PR* 230).

Although the doctrine of objective immortality is most often taken in relation to a single actuality's potential for objectification in later actualities, this last quotation suggests a more inclusive and mutual conception of objectification, one which, if nothing else, renders the concept of "creativity" less obscure. Indeed, it manifests a perspective from which it can be said that the actual world for an entity enjoys *as a world*, in the prehension of that entity by a subsequent actuality, "an objective immortality in the future beyond itself" (*PR* 230). Every particular realized contrast, and every particular entity effecting such contrasts, and every particular nexus of particular actualities, becomes a "standing condition in every subsequent actual world from which creative advance must originate" (*PR* 230).

INTERMEDIATE SUMMARY: THE ONTOLOGY OF REPETITION

The existential solidarity of the universe, via the perpetual reincorporation (objective immortality) of stubborn particularities by other particularities or individuals has now been asserted. This thesis, beautifully defended by Jorge Nobo in *Whitehead's Metaphysics of Extension and Solidarity*, will be developed further in succeeding analyses. I have worked it into the discussion of Objective Diversity because it puts us in a good position to understand Whitehead's own summary of the three categories discussed so far. It will be helpful to keep in mind that before the text of *Process and Reality* was corrected by Sherburne and Griffin, the following passage occurred immediately subsequent to the passage cited previously as evidence of the close interdependence of genetic and coordinate division.[11]

> Thus the process of integration, which lies at the very heart of concrescence, is the urge imposed on the concrescent unity of that universe by the three Categories of Subjective Unity, of Objective Identity, and of Objective Diversity. The oneness of the universe, and the oneness of each element of the universe, *repeat themselves to the crack of doom* in the creative advance from creature to creature, each creature including in itself the whole of history and exemplifying the self-identity of things and their mutual diversities. (PR 228, emphasis added)

If Whitehead were claiming anything less that the real existence of one thing qua *its individuality* in another thing by this summary, the phrase emphasized in the quote would be meaningless. So, too, would the paradox that defines the Category of the Ultimate, "the many become one, and are increased by one" (PR 21), be rendered merely pretty. Doom is the nothingness of that which lies outside intensively individuated process.

It is my aim to take this paradox in all its ontological seriousness and claim that Whitehead really means to assert that the presence of one thing in another is provided for by real repetition, a repetition that marks both the advance of time into the future and the real persistence—with retention of original ontological status—of individual elements of the past. This temporal ecstasis in the process of becoming grounds my claim that the conceptualization of any entity requires the acknowledgment of that entity's place in orders wider than itself, and that the intensities embedded in these orders are significant aspects of the atomic, individual existence of the entity in question. Though the chapter began with the words of Auden celebrating the blessed creations of a temporal earth process, some lines from Wallace Stevens seem to capture the present contention quite nicely:

> Let this be clear that we are men of sun
> And men of day and never of pointed night,
> Men that repeat antiquest sounds of air
> In an accord of repetitions. Yet,
> If we repeat, it is because the wind
> Encircling us, speaks always with our speech.
> —"Evening Without Angels"

THE CATEGORY OF CONCEPTUAL VALUATION

With the Category of Conceptual Valuation we begin a consideration of the conditions that bear most strongly on the achievement of intensity in a subjective process of coming to be. Whereas the Categoreal Obligations discussed thus far are crucial in terms of how we are to conceive of satisfied entities in their relation to process in general, that is, how achieved intensities come to bear upon the becoming of other intensities, this category and those that follow express more explicitly the intense ordering of feelings in every singular process of becoming. We can thus begin to grasp just what it means for every entity to repeat in itself the universe of entities from which it emerges.

Conceptual Valuation entails that "[f]rom each physical feeling there is the derivation of a purely conceptual feeling whose datum is the eternal object determinant of the definiteness of the actual entity, or of the nexus, physically felt" (PR 26). Whatever is physically felt in the actual world of the concrescing subject may be valued up or down (PR 247) in virtue of the conceptual feelings it (the datum) prompts in the subject. With conceptual feeling is born the novelty of each entity as self-creative. Indeed, it marks the origination of what Whitehead calls the "mental pole" (as opposed to the "physical pole") characteristic of every entity, the aspect of Whitehead's scheme that has controversially earned him the label, "panpsychist." The mental pole of any entity involves the entertainment of eternal objects and contrasts of eternal objects such that the task of integration may proceed in accordance with the subjective aim.

Conceptual Valuation is the process of each actual entity, in effect, asking itself whether or not what is unavoidably felt as in its world is going to contribute to the depth of satisfaction of the subject doing the valuing. Indeed, Whitehead notes that the "valuation" aspect of this category involves questions of subjective form: writing of the relation of the mental pole to the physical pole of the entity, he notes that "the subjective form of a conceptual feeling is valuation" (PR 248). Although the conceptual feeling arising from the physical feeling is relatively straightforward, the subjective form of this feeling introduces a note of interpretation, "the subject as a determinant of its own concrescence" in light of its "ideal of itself" (ibid.). Conceptual Valuation is the locus of the basic autonomy (conceptual embellishment and integration) of entities of all types. It is the "subjective readjustment of the subjective forms" prehended in the objective data such that in the very basic integration of physical feelings by means of conceptual feelings derived from them there is a note of novel emotional tone (ibid.).

Although the intensification of feeling by valuation up or down for purposes of the complex integration necessary to realize the subjective aim involves other categoreal processes, there is an extremely important point regarding valuation where the concept of "intensity" is particularly relevant. This notion, Whitehead's concept of "physical purposes," will help us think together the idea of integrating order in an entity and the reproduction of one entity by another. It is in part by the Category of Conceptual Valuation that "physical purposes" find their place in the general metaphysical description of reality.

PHYSICAL PURPOSES: A GENERAL INTRODUCTION

Physical purposes are the type of comparative feeling whereby the entity in concrescence begins to decide the extent of its conformation to the prior actualities it feels, and the extent to which the entity will consider its interests in imposing lasting patterns of definiteness on the future. "The constancy of physical purposes explains the persistence of the order of nature, and in particular of 'enduring objects'" (PR 276). That is to say, physical purposes account for an important level of genuine causal transmission of character (intensive pattern) along a route of occasions.

Physical purposes are "physical" in that they stem from the initial physical feeling of entities and nexūs in the actual world of the subject; they are "purposes" in that the contrast of the conceptual feeling and the physical feeling from which it is derived is felt in the context of subjective aim. In this way, the physical pole of the entity is felt as purposive, as urging a certain dimension of intensive satisfaction rendered possible by the subjective aim of the whole entity. Another way to put this is to say that efficient causality operates within final causation such that there will be an autonomous repetition of pattern in the subject and potentially in transcendent subjects, manifesting a stable ordering of character—lamps that persist while I blink, coffee that remains coffee as it sits neglected at my side, fingers that remain anatomically organized so as to continue typing once a word has been begun. This is another instance where one wishes Whitehead had performed a thoroughgoing critique of the classical conception of the "four causes," particularly the efficient and final causality that time and again rub elbows in this strange atomism. If we bracket the alleged distinction between the two "kinds" of cause here operating, physical purposes can be conceived to manifest a very significant influx of design from the world, to be repeated *as* the autonomous functioning of the subject.

The subjective form of the feeling of the contrast between the conceptual feeling and the physical feeling from which it is derived can take two general forms. Whitehead calls these "adversion" or "aversion"—the "desire" so to speak, to either maintain or modify the order proposing itself for realization in the final satisfaction of the subject. Of course, if the influx of "efficient" causation be melded into the general conception of "self-causation" in a subject, adversion and aversion seem less "panpsychist" than the word "desire" we have just used might imply. The less mentalistic-sounding "decision" might be more appropriate to convey the sense of maintenance or nonmaintenance of intensities proffered by the actual world.

It might be helpful to quote Whitehead substantially on physical purposes to understand how this valuational activity of subjectivity is manifestly concerned with the entity's placement in orders beyond itself:

> In such a physical purpose, the datum is the generic contrast between the nexus, felt in the physical feeling, and the eternal

object valued in the conceptual feeling. This eternal object is also exemplified as the pattern of the nexus. Thus the conceptual valuation now closes in upon the feeling of the nexus as it stands in the generic contrast, exemplifying the valued eternal object. This valuation accorded to the physical feeling endows the transcendent creativity with the character of adversion, or of aversion. The character of adversion secures the reproduction of the physical feeling, as one element in the objectification of the subject beyond itself. Such reproduction may be thwarted by incompatible objectification derived from other feelings. But a physical feeling, whose valuation produces adversion, is thereby an element with some force of persistence into the future beyond its own subject. . . .

When there is aversion, instead of adversion, the transcendent creativity assumes the character that it inhibits, or attenuates, the objectification of that subject in the guise of that feeling. (PR 276)

The immediate valuations in becoming here involve concern for the "objectification of the subject beyond itself," echoing the notion introduced earlier, that feelings are directed *at a superject and not from a subject*. Whatever else concrescence is, it is a creative operation designed to procure transcendently effective intensities. Much of the natural universe as we know it depends on just this kind of procurement at the base of enduring characters such as trees, books, atmospheres, and so on.

Jorge Nobo, in his landmark book, *Whitehead's Metaphysics of Extension and Solidarity*, has brought to process scholarship an unrivaled systematic presentation of certain central, but overlooked, dimensions of Whitehead's metaphysical project. It would be very helpful for my purposes if the reader would indulge a rather lengthy digression to engage certain dimensions of Nobo's interpretation, for in many important senses his reading and my own are complementary, but in one significant sense they are not.[12] In his text, Nobo embarks on a discussion of physical purposes in order to buttress his thesis that what we find in Whitehead are really two kinds of processes, "transition" (whereby we analyze the metaphysics of passage from one entity to another in the wider sweep of creativity) and "concrescence" (whereby the more properly subjective conditions of realization are manifest).[13] Physical purposes would witness to the former as a separate process (Nobo calls the two processes "radically different") from concrescence, because they concern merely the objective flow of data from actuality to actuality. It should be evident by now that on the reading being developed here, what might be called the "merely objective" cannot be so called, and should be seen to be a revelation of subjectivity as much as a flow of objective character.

Though I maintain that the programmatic use to which it is put to be unwarranted (or at least, as we shall see, an exaggeration of Whitehead's claims), Nobo's explanation of physical purposes is excellent. If we read the word "transition" in the following not as a "radically" separate process, but as a different perspective on the one process of actualization, Nobo's exposition is quite useful to my own purposes here. Physical purposes,

> are those elements in the constitution of an actual occasion that *decide* how the transcendent creativity of transition is to objectify that occasion into an objective datum for later occasions. Each occasion, then, decides how it is to be objectified in later occasions. Inasmuch as such a decision refers to what is essentially beyond the occasion making it, Whitehead terms it a 'transcendent decision' [PR 164]. . . . Hence, the effectiveness of an actual occasion's physical purposes depends on the transcendent creativity which takes the completed occasion into account, and which serves as the *vehicle* for that occasion's transcendent decisions.[14]

Although this quotation locates the entity quite nicely in the orders constituting its "relevant future," Nobo may be pushing Whitehead's description of physical purposes too far by, effectively, placing efficient causality in the separate process of creative "transition" as opposed to the concrescent "decision" characteristic of final causality. Thus my interpretation takes issue with Nobo's claim that the "joint functioning of the physical purposes and of the transcendent creativity provides a link between final causation and efficient causation."[15] If we can develop a view of ontological individuality that can collapse the strong existential distinction between efficient and final causality, despite Whitehead's own use of these terms, then no "link" would be needed to close any apparent gaps between the subjective agency of concrescence and the objective imposition of character on subsequent subjects.

Whitehead's concluding statements about the notion of physical purposes (which Nobo also cites in support of his interpretation) can be read so as to assert that entities themselves supply all the "linkage" necessary to bond the "two" aspects of causality. The passage in question is as follows, and I begin quoting three sentences before Nobo, and include one more sentence at the end, so as to contextualize my alternative reading:

> The mental operations [of which Conceptual Valuation is a crucial dimension] have a double office. They achieve, in the immediate subject, the subjective aim of that subject as to the satisfaction to be obtained from its own initial data. In this way the decision derived from the actual world, which is the efficient cause, is completed by the decision embodied in the sub-

jective aim, which is the final cause. Secondly, the physical purposes of a subject by their valuations determine the relative efficiency of the various feelings to enter into the objectifications of that subject in the creative advance beyond itself. In this function, the mental operations determine their subject in its character of an efficient cause. <u>Thus the mental pole is the link whereby the creativity is endowed with the double character of final causation, and efficient causation</u>. The mental pole is constituted by the decisions in virtue of which matters of fact enter into the character of the creativity. (PR 277)

First, if the operations in regard to physical purposes as appropriations of the past are located solely in the concrescing entity in so far as these purposes will contribute to the satisfaction of the subject, it is doubtful whether the "double office" of these mental processes should render half of this office over to the creativity of "transition" for the disposition of the entity in *its* future. To separate the completed decision undertaken with a view to subjective aim from the borrowed decisions (from the actual world as "efficient cause") would seem to bisect the activity of contrasting that is the essential fabric of agentive subjectivity. All of the elements of a contrast need to somehow belong to the contraster, including things describable as efficient causes of the contrasting subject. Otherwise, the merely conceptual contrast begins to look more like a Bradleyan relation rather than an existential inclusion of diverse elements. To be sure, Whitehead does sometimes write as if a subject is incompletely present in the early stages of process where objectification of other actualities is paramount (cf. *PR* 212). But the incomplete presence of the subject is not the absence of *that subject* (as stipulated by the Category of Subjective Unity), and whatever causality is present in the early stages of becoming needs somehow to be a function of the subject coming to be.

Second, there appears to be no need for a "mediating" function of creativity, at least in so far as Whitehead describes the situation in this passage. Nobo cites Whitehead's description of transition as a kind of "vehicle" for transcendent decision, and this is another way to describe a mediating creative process, but this disrupts what I want to protect in Whitehead's calling his organic philosophy a form of "atomism." Can we, in fact, describe both the "subjective" and "objective" dimensions of actuality as a function of individuality itself? We can if we develop our conception of individuality along the lines implied in Whitehead's overall pattern of thought (though this pattern is non-explicit due, in part, to his tapping into the conceptual vocabularies of the traditional metaphysics he was rebelling against). In a sense, I would like to do a coordinate analysis of a certain persistent train of thought to see what it may imply genetically (that is, about the internal character) of that thought. An interesting alternative to transition as a mediating creative function can be built on a strict reading of sentences like, "the mental operations determine their subject in its character of an efficient cause," and our remaining analyses will "coordinately divide" Whitehead's system to reveal the "murmur" of this kind of notion as an "underground stream" in the system.

Third, Whitehead locates the "character" of the creativity in so far as it contains "matters of fact" (the objective functioning of entities) *in the subjective constitution of the mental pole of discrete entities*. It would be more reasonable to assert the distinction between concrescence and transition if subjectivity were not here linked in an immediate sense with the character, not merely the functioning, of the creativity alleged by Whitehead himself to be the *other* process.

Part of the interpretive difficulty Whitehead generates on these matters is due to the fact that he is clearly incorporating the operations of subjective aim into the valuation of contrast involved in physical purposes, although he doesn't "officially" introduce the Category of Subjective Intensity (where subjective aim is focused) into his discussion until he addresses the "second species" of physical purposes produced by Conceptual Reversion. This postponed introduction suggests that novelty (via subjective aim) is a supercessionally "later" phase than the objectification of pattern whereby there is repetition. But the necessity for subjective aim to be functioning already in the process of repetitive feeling involved in physical purposes suggests otherwise. Although Nobo has no problem admitting that final causality is present in physical purposes, he does maintain that there is a separation of final and efficient causality in terms of the supposedly distinct and supercessive processes they imply.[16]

Nobo's contention that the two species of process are "radically different" in Whitehead's cosmology is certainly substantiated by Whitehead's repeated use of forms of speech referring to the activities of the "transcendent creativity" as if it were in fact something different from what individual agency does creatively. Accommodating efficient causality in the process of transition seems legitimate given such statements as those we have seen in this discussion of Conceptual Valuation. In valuation, we recall, the "valuation accorded to the physical feeling endows the transcendent creativity with the character of adversion, or of aversion" (PR 276). This does sound as if creativity has some status apart from the subjective integrations performed by actualities aspiring to self-perpetuation. But this is at odds with what appears to be the wider intent of Whitehead's atomism, for it is, after all, the actualities themselves as superjects, which are the "transcendent creators," as we have seen.

All references to the transcendent creativity should be read as references to the creative function of actualities qua superject, which superjection is, (a) provided for in the subjective aim at intensity in the relevant future, and (b) the primary locus of the revelation of individual ontological character (noted earlier). What Nobo tries to accomplish with transition, I would want to accomplish with a notion of universal self-transcendence on the part of individual entities, that is, a concept of individuality inclusive of the transcendent creative function that alone reveals subjective character of the subject-superject. Efficient causation is accomplished by the collective efforts of every individual insinuating itself *as itself* (and not an "aping" of itself) in other things. I think this kind of idea was what Whitehead had in mind in calling his decidedly relational ontology an *atomism* despite the celebration of things' organic interpenetrations. Whitehead describes the physical purposes experienced as adversions or aversion as subjective forms that have "acquired a special appetition" (PR 184). Because appetition always belongs to, and is indeed the constitutive feature of, a subject in its quest for intensity of satisfaction (in the present and future), any suggestion of a species of process decentered from the subject begins to sound troubling.

More than his employment of certain figures of speech, however, Whitehead's very deliberate and, in Nobo's words, "unusually" clear and explicit, discussion of the two processes seems to undermine the unitary conception of causality I am trying to advance, and would at first blush seem to substantiate Nobo's hypothesis that "transition is the process of efficient causation whereby a new occasion is begotten and partly determined by its correlative universe of attained actualities, whereas concrescence is the process of teleological self-determination whereby the already begotten occasion autonomously completes itself."[17] In the chapter on "Process" in Part II of *Process and Reality*, Whitehead writes of "two kinds of fluency" in the world, alighted upon with varying emphases by different philosophers in the history of metaphysics. The one kind of fluency refers more explicitly to the active creations of novel acts of becoming, while the other notes the relentless passage or perishing of things. The first is what he calls concrescence, the second transition. "Concrescence moves towards its final cause, which is its subjective aim; transition is the vehicle of the efficient cause, which is the immortal past" (PR 210).

Nobo finds the emphasis on transition as a determinate process unto itself to be an important dimension of understanding the extensive solidarity of actual occasions to be actually productive of novel occasions. On this I substantially agree, that Whitehead wants to incorporate a view of the world as causally productive of the subjects whose final stamp of emphasis is presented in terms of the generative processes of feeling involved in "concrescence." Whitehead sees the world as conspiring to produce an entity as positioned in a standpoint in the continuum which, in the subject's initial phases, does not yet possess full determinacy of character that the subject will itself impose. Such a view is critical to understanding this process philosophy to describe not a miraculous reinvention of the universe by every entity, but a connectionistic, highly organized temporal flow of balanced character and novel "modifications of matter."[18] Yet, I think Whitehead need not have gone so far as to suggest a radical separateness of processes, provident of some kind of "mediation," and accomplishing the work of the various kinds of causality metaphysics is alleged to have to deal with.

My hesitation in following Nobo (and the strain in Whitehead's thought he builds on) stems from our angles of emphasis in interpreting the differences among the feelings involved in the various phases of concrescence. Nobo emphasizes that the initial phase of what Whitehead calls "mere reception" of feeling coming from diverse existents in the world of the entity, bereft of real final causality, is the scene of "transition" as the process whereby the world is objectified for the nascent occasion. This is the time of pure efficient causality, with intensive concerns of the telic demands of process coming to play only with the supercessionally later addition of aesthetically supplemental feeling by conceptual valuations, and so on. According to Nobo, the prehensions in the various stages require different understandings. The first are merely objectifications, the imposed natures of previous things in the (not-quite-present-yet) new subject. With supplementation, they acquire immediacies of feeling typical of what is commonly understood as concrescent experience.[19] I am, however, determined to highlight the fact that Whitehead does not in any existentially important sense distinguish the "realities" felt in the one phase as opposed to the other. In other words, the external existence felt in the prehension of mere objectification, mere reception, remains in the prehensions of those existences as clothed by the intensive considerations of subjectivity.

> In this second stage the feelings assume an emotional character by reason of this influx of conceptual feelings. But the reason why the origins are not lost in the private emotion is that there is no element in the universe capable of pure privacy. If we could obtain a complete analysis of meaning, the notion of pure privacy would be seen to be self-contradictory. Emotional feeling is still subject to the third metaphysical principle, that to be 'something' is 'to have the potentiality for acquiring real unity with other entities.' Hence, 'to be a real component of an actual entity' is in some way 'to realize this potentiality.' Thus 'emotion' is 'emotional feeling'; and 'what is felt' is the presupposed vector situation. (PR 212)

Refocusing our discussion on the Category of Conceptual Valuation at issue here, we can say that although valuation adds intensive significance by introducing private emotion, it does so in a manner inclusive of the publicity of the data objectified.

If the external sources of what is felt remain during the telic phases, I am hesitant to call the "efficient cause" phase a wholly separate process. It is one thing for Whitehead to deny that pure privacy is possible, or that it is the fundamental notion in process metaphysics, which it is not (though many commentators do not take this into much account). It is one thing to assert that "the notion of 'passing on' is more fundamental than that of a private individual fact" (PR 213), a concept that very much squares with the account I am offering, of "satisfactions" being the first consideration in coming to apprehend the individual ontological status of what are alternatively called "subjects." But it is another thing altogether to divide causal operations in two, especially in an ontology that trades so significantly on the agency of subjects as the central (indeed in some passages, the sole) locus of "existence." Thus, my difference of interpretation from Nobo hinges on whether or not the protection of different kinds of causality is essential to metaphysics, or more particularly, to this atomistic process metaphysics. I do not think it is. Surely Nobo is absolutely correct to identify the real causal power of one thing in another thing. I simply do not think we have to call it a different kind of power than the power being manifest in the new thing's self-creation. My analysis of the "ontology of intensity" in chapter three is designed among other things to defend this claim.

THE CATEGORY OF CONCEPTUAL REVERSION

Whereas the Category of Conceptual Valuation accounts for the characterization of subjective form according to the conceptual reproduction and enriching of physical data, the Category of Conceptual Reversion accounts for the production of conceptual feelings somehow different from the physical data. By this obligation, "There is secondary origination of conceptual feelings with data that are partially identical with, and partially diverse from, the eternal objects forming the data in the first phase of the mental pole. The diversity is a relevant diversity determined by the subjective aim" (PR 26). In the restatement of this category later in the "Theory of Feelings," Whitehead recasts the last line as a continuation of the first: "mental pole; the determination of indentity and diversity depending on the subjective aim at attaining depth of intensity by reason of contrast" (PR 249). It is the deepening of intensity that is at stake in the introduction of novel feeling via reversion. The importance of "intensity" in understanding all of the Categoreal Obligations is clear given its use in defining or elaborating the various obligations, as we see here.

We have already seen what it means for something to be a "relevant" diversity in the analysis of the Category of Objective Diversity. Things are relevantly diverse if they are really and purposely experienced as different from but contrastible with one another, and the felt difference advances the aim at intensity of satisfaction. The conditions of contrast made possible by the mere fact of relevant diversity in the objective data are operative here as well, the difference being that Conceptual Reversion is an introduction of *new* feelings on the part of the concrescent subject. Diversity in the objective data provides intensive dimensions of the new occasion, but with reversion intensity is *deepened* by the production of novel diverse feelings. Let us examine how this crucial deepening occurs.

A certain degree of intensity is made possible by the contrasts effected in the feeling of the various elements of the physical data, but reversion takes things a step further along the way to the completed determinacy required in the satisfaction being aimed at. Reversion is "the process by which the subsequent enrichment of subjective forms, both in qualitative pattern, and in intensity through contrast, is made possible by the positive conceptual prehension of relevant alternatives. There is a conceptual contrast of physical incompatibles" (PR 249). Data physically felt are enhanced in significance by conceptual comparison with potential forms of arrangement designated as various complex eternal objects prehendible by the subject but not in fact part of the physical transmission of feeling from objects. For example, right now my feet are cold and my head, being closer to the halogen lamp I have referred to, is much warmer. Physically, these two aspects of my experience do not announce, themselves, their comprehendibility under some broader single intensity; but in my total experience of the moment I find some way to effect such a unity, perhaps by conjecturing (maybe half-consciously) that the cold of the feet excites wakefulness in the body to which the warm head and brain is connected—the system, overall, works more efficiently for the contrasting of the intrinsically non-contrasted coldness and warmness in remote regions of the body.

In this example, it is the mere entertainment of a relevant possibility for integration, itself in contrast with the physically realized facts, that is of greatest significance in the deepening of intensity. Reversion does not mean replacement: it means the feeling of novel patterns in a definite contrast to those patterns that are in fact being physically reiterated and conceptually reproduced from the past actual world. Reversion adds (contrastive and multiplicative) depth by locating the range of prehensions involved in broader patterns of significant contrast, productive of the intensity being sought in the occasion as a whole, including its interest in transcendent creative action in other things. Thus Whitehead describes this as the category whereby we can understand the aspect of our experience that yields a sense of the simultaneous identity with and diversity from the past that attends any present.

It is necessary that experience significantly conform to data physically felt from the past, but at the same time it is necessary for there to be novel experience stemming from diversity from the past. This double necessity is at the heart of Whitehead's atomism. In his discussion of the Theory of Feelings Whitehead refers us, for a description of what the conceptual prehension of relevant alternatives (via reversion) amounts to, to his previous text, *Religion in the Making*. The birth of any new "aesthetic experience" is an instance or moment of what he means by the "creative process," and requires two things. (For "ground" and "consequent" in the following, read "physical feelings" and "conceptual feelings.") "1. The novel consequent must be graded in relevance so as to preserve some indentity of character with the ground" and "2. The novel consequent must be graded in relevance so as to preserve some contrast with the ground in respect to that same identity of character" (RM 115). To be a new instance of experience, that is, to be an actual occasion or entity, requires the production of conceptual feelings deepening experience in virtue of the continuities affirmed with the past and the discontinuities produced in virtue of the entertainment of relevant alternatives.

In other words, the determinate individuality of an entity depends on the activities of reversion producing content-rich feeling of ownership of *its* experience by the entity. There are limitations imposed by the actual world on the possible character of individuality a subject can attain, and yet to be *any* subject at all (to become a superject demanded by nature in that location) involves the feeling of some degree of relevant novelty from the feelings streaming in from the world. "Novelty" need not mean wildly diverse quality; all it needs to be qua novel is new perspective arrangement of the qualities proffered by the world, an arrangement that is felt in its intensive significance as possessing relative degrees of triviality, vagueness, narrowness and width. Felt structural novelty is qualitatively diverse enough to warrant a new actuality (with interest in its own value-experience) in a given position. As Whitehead writes in *Religion in the Making*, "[t]he limitations are the opportunities. The essence of depth of actuality—that is of vivid experience—is definiteness. Now to be definite always means that all the elements of a complex whole contribute to some one effect, to the exclusion of others. The creative process is a process of exclusion to the same extent as it is a process of inclusion" (RM 113). "Exclusion" here can be read as dismissal to the vague or trivial background in the interest of some foreground perspective on the "limitations" or "opportunities" provided by the world.

Contrasts are effected by reversion in order that "the ultimate creative purpose that each unification shall achieve some maximum depth of intensity of feeling, subject to the conditions of its concrescence [subjective aim]" (PR 249) can be realized. It would be beneficial to pause at this point and remark that Whitehead's use of the phrase "depth of experience" must be understood as more than a description of intense private enjoyment. "Depth" of actuality is not a metaphor. Misconstrual of the meaning of this and other similar descriptions has led to the view that Whitehead's metaphysics is what might be called a kind of universal aestheticism. Nature seems to be reduced to the whims of rich private feeling on the part of actualities that puff back out of existence just as soon as they have shown up on the scene. This is a more extreme and externally critical version of the problem that may be more neutrally stated as Whitehead's problematizing of the ontology of the past. But this to me seems to miss what is being proposed in the idea of depth of actuality, or depth of satisfaction, or depth of experience, or depth of intensity. These notions are not descriptive of the merely private (there is *no such thing as mere privacy* anyway, as we have already seen) intensive enjoyment of experience by a subject, but indicate the full ontological connectedness and real continuity with—or as—what has gone before, and, significantly, what will come later. Intensive privacy is in part the presence of the public in the subject, and involves the anticipation of the subject's presence as itself, and not, again, an "aping" of itself, in the intensive privacy of future beings.

Depth, in other words, is at once referent to the individual satisfaction and the creative process provocative of that satisfaction via the "urge" toward "balanced complexity" manifest in subjective aim. The drive toward satisfaction and "creativity" are not two things but two ways of describing the same thing. Depth is how the world achieves "growth of reality" (*RM* 152) via atomic experience. In a discussion that anticipates the *Process and Reality* description of Conceptual Reversion as the production of novel conceptual feelings of potentialities, *Religion in the Making* gives us some perspective on the question of "depth of actuality":

> The grading of ideal forms arises from the grading of the actual facts. It is the union of the forms with the facts in such measure as to elicit a renewed feeling-value, of the type possible as a novel outcome from antecedent facts.
>
> Depth of value is only possible if the antecedent facts conspire in unison. (*RM* 151–52).

"Renewed feeling value" is the perpetuation of the past in the present activity of the subject. It is in part the renewal—or real repetition—of the actual past in the actual present that requires a new subject and accounts for the experienced continuity of one event with those that precede and follow it. A new subject is not required by some remorseless necessity, though as noted earlier Whitehead permits a note of determinism in his sense of "efficient" causal presence of one thing in another. A new subject is required because reality *is* creativity, which Whitehead denotes in the oft-quoted sentence: "The creativity of the world is the throbbing emotion of the past hurling itself into a new transcendent fact" (*AI* 177).

It would be valuable to quote a passage from *Adentures of Ideas* that helps to clarify what I am claiming about "depth of actuality" as a kind of existential depth in addition to, or described as, emotional depth. Writing of the experience of continuity from one immediate moment of experience to another, Whitehead notes that past actualities "enter into experience devoid of any perceptible medium intervening between [them] and the present immediate fact." A past fact "is gone, and yet it is here." He then goes on to explain,

> Yet the present occasion while claiming self-identity, while sharing the very nature of the bygone occasion in all its living

activities, nevertheless is engaged in modifying it, in adjusting it to *other* influences, in completing it with *other* values, in deflecting it to *other* purposes. The present moment is constituted by the influx of *the other* into that self-identity which is the continued life of the immediate past within the immediacy of the present. (AI 181)

Conceptual reversion (along with valuation) achieves "depth" and relevant novelty because of the real presence of other actualities in the subject, and, it should be remarked, the subject's real presence in the satisfactions of entities transcendent of but provided for in concrescent subjectivity.

ECSTATIC EXISTENCE

This would be an excellent point at which to introduce a concept I think is helpful in understanding Whitehead's full conception of atomic actuality. Conceptual Reversion's role in procuring feelings partially identical and partially diverse from the physical influx of the world led us to a discussion of novel becoming in the language of "ground" and "consequent" from *Religion in the Making*. At that point, I equated "ground" with physical feeling and "consequent" with conceptual feeling for purposes of explicating the category at hand, but clearly "ground" and "consequent" refer to the existential "throbbing" of creative process from one actuality to another; it is the elaboration of the "passing on" of things that is of fundamental significance to Whitehead's organic cosmology and that ultimately reversion and the other Categoreal Obligations procurative of intensity of satisfaction make possible. Though Whitehead describes the "ground" and "consequent" (in *Process and Reality* the physical pole and mental pole of an actuality) as aspects of a single act of becoming, we have seen that these single acts are curiously intruded upon by other individuals and will intrude themselves upon other such acts.

I have elected to term this capacity for intrusion that appears to be the very mark of what Whitehead means by actuality the "ecstatic existence" of an individual subject. Past and future aspects of the intensive actuality procured by concrescence are to be conceived as existentially of a piece with the subject of concrescence considered as an atomic fact. An actuality is intensively deep in the rich ontological sense of being ecstatically located in (a) whatever contributes to it so as to be provocative of it as an occasion, and (b) whatever includes it as an element in its (the future actuality's) satisfaction. In Auden's words from "In Praise of Limestone,"

> These modifications of matter into
> Innocent athletes and gesticulating fountains,
>   Made solely for pleasure, make a further point:
> The blessed will not care what angle they are regarded from,
>   Having nothing to hide.

Readers of existentialism will hear in "ecstatic existence" the echos of Sartre's "phenomenological ontology," particularly in its emphasis on temporality. The temporality of every "*pour-soi*" or "for-itself" is always outside of itself. Sartre's ontology, like Whitehead's, is premised on the unavailability, to each act of experience, of a God's-eye view of Being as a whole. An act of experience never succeeds in being a substantial existence in the sense of a permanent endurance. Sartre captures the essence of what I am affirming in Whitehead's philosophy of passage and individuality. Writing of the "psychic" experience of duration (our seeming persistence through time which, if we identify the for-itself, or our agency, with it, becomes the basis of inauthenticity), Sartre claims, "*cette durée psychique qui ne saurait être par soi doit perpétuellement être etée. Perpétuallement oscillante entre la multiplicité de juxtaposition et la cohésion absolue du pour-soi ek-statique, cette temporalité est composée de <<maintenant>> qui ont été, qui demeurent à la place qui leur est assignée, mais qui s'influencent à distance dans leur totalité; c'est ce qui la rend assez semblable á la durée magique du bergsonisme.*"[20] I have provided the French here because I want to make a simple point based on the language, but this passage translates very simply: "this psychic duration which cannot be by itself must perpetually *be made to be*. Perpetually oscillating between the multiplicity of juxtaposition and the absolute cohesion of the ek-static for-itself, this temporality is composed of 'nows' that have been, which remain at the place assigned to them, but which influence each other at a distance in their totality; it is this which renders it comparable to the magic duration in Bergson's philosophy."

What I am forwarding as the ecstatic existence of actualities is captured in the notion of "multiplicity of juxtaposition and the absolute cohesion of the ek-static for itself." Like the for-itself that is always and everywhere outside of itself in its temporalized existence, the individual atomic actuality is a temporally reiterated subject-object whose locations cohere as "one" despite their physical "distance" from one another as absorbed in other things. The way in which the reflexive verb is presented in the French suggest a tighter, internal immediacy than what we may be tempted to read into the English statement of a *pour-soi* or an entity's cohesion or internal unity of activity: "*s'influencent*" sounds much less like an actual multiplicity than does the phrase "influence each other."[21]

Just how we are to understand the ecstatic unity of individuality enjoyed by atomic actualities in Whitehead's system will be explored in the next chapter. I have introduced the notion here so as to cease beating around the bush about the ontological claims that can be made on the basis of a full understanding of the "intensity" of experience constitutive of actuality. Reversion's introduction of relevantly novel feelings in contrast with physically reiterated feelings of (other) actualities is more than a provision for a fortunate continuity with the past or a wished-for immortality—"if sins can be forgiven, if bodies rise from the dead, / . . . Dear, I know nothing of /

Either"—it is a concept on which to build an understanding of the "vibratory" conception of atomic reality advanced in this organic cosmology. The "ground" asserts that which must be reiterated or reproduced so as to maintain an order or social organization in which the entity in question is "nested" to use Kraus' term. The consequent asserts that which is novel such that this is a new temporal quantum of that order, expressed most definitively as the persistence of a certain intensive pattern. Contrast under conditions of important identity of character (which, in intensity, is not simply pattern but the very existence of the thing in question, as I will argue later) is the principle of physical existence: "In the physical world, this principle of contrast under an identity expresses the physical law that vibration enters into the ultimate nature of atomic organisms. Vibration is the recurrence of contrast within identity of type. The whole possibility of measurement in the physical world depends on this principle. To measure is to count vibrations" (*RM* 115–16).

A similar discussion is undertaken in *An Enquiry Concerning the Principles of Natural Knowledge* as a recognition of "rhythm" as a fundamental feature of the natural world: "Now a rhythm is recognizable and is so far an object. But it is more than an object; for it is an object formed of other objects interwoven on the background of essential change. A rhythm involves a pattern and to that extent is always self-identical. But no rhythm can be a mere pattern; for the rhythmic quality depends equally upon the differences involved in each exhibition of the pattern. The essence of rhythm is the fusion of sameness and novelty, so that the whole never loses the essential unity of the pattern; while the parts exhibit the contrast arising from the novelty of their detail" (*PNK* 198). Reversion is a significant aspect of the presence of order provocative of subordinate intensities in a natural world that is physically and metaphysically atomic, providing three key necessities: weight of repetition, intensity of contrast, and balance among the factors in the contrast. "In this way the association of endurance with rhythm and physical vibration is to be explained. They arise out of the conditions for intensity and stability" (*PR* 279).

Reversion sheds further light on the atomic nature of temporal actualities if we consider it in light of the role of God's primordial nature. In explaining how it is that a potentiality can come to function as relevantly diverse from prehensions that are physically felt, Whitehead notes that the Category of Reversion by itself provides no answer. How can an entity decide that one potentiality is more or less remote or interesting than another? (cf. *PR* 250). This refers us ultimately to the primordial nature of God in reference to actuality. Unrealized potentialities are graded in relevance to a concrescent entity's limitations in virtue of the mutual adjustedness of all potentialities in the divine nature. Ultimately, this relevance is embodied in the subjective aim that is derived from God. But it is reversion that provides some of the feelings in which the entity's subjective aim as derived from God is operative in procuring intensity, and these feelings involve the futural being of the actuality.

Part of the intensity sought in present becoming, as noted already, is measured by the entity's "anticipatory feelings of the transcendent future in its relation to immediate fact. This is the feeling of the objective immortality *inherent in the nature of actuality*. Such anticipatory feelings involve realization of the relevance of eternal objects as decided in the primordial nature of God" (PR 278, emphasis added). According to the divine decision (itself one of the "limitations" imposed by actuality) thus felt, potentials will be experienced as more or less proximate or remote. It is the role of reversion to establish the identity and contrast implicit in this feeling of potential futural existence according to possibilities ordained by the divine envisagement. Again, the intensity marking the existence of an actuality both provides for and is enhanced by the experience of its temporal location both in present and future. Sartre describes this external locatedness of the temporality of the *pour-soi* as a "virtual unity," indicative of the impossibility of the *pour-soi*'s actual existence across time in a durational sense. But because Whitehead has available a rich conception of "efficient" causality (I will be marking this term whenever I use it to indicate its merely intellectual difference from "final" causality in my interpretation) that actually links one occasion internally with another, the unity of an intensive individual across temporal modes is not "virtual" but "actual" in the "vibratory"—that is, discontinuous but persisting—sense of actuality Whitehead is trying to develop.

THE CATEGORY OF TRANSMUTATION

Problems in how to conceive of "existence" in Whitehead's overall ontological project are made deeper by the Category of Transmutation, whereby a nexus comes to function as if it were a single entity with its own "categoreal type of existence" (PR 251). It is in virtue of this category that an enduring object, which is a complex nexus or society of nexus, might be said to be characterized by a certain quality. Some feature is shared among the actual occasions constituting the life-history of an enduring object such that a quality may be predicated of the object with relative accuracy, despite the fact that all characters of any kind can only be said to belong to actual occasions. The Category of Transmutation states:

> When (in accordance with category [iv] {Conceptual Valuation}, or with categories [iv] and [v] {Conceptual Reversion}) one and the same conceptual feeling is derived impartially by a prehending subject from its analogous simple physical feelings of various actual entities in its actual world, then, in a subsequent phase of integration of these simple physical feelings together with the derivate conceptual feeling, the prehending subject may transmute the *datum* of this con-

ceptual feeling into a characteristic of some *nexus* containing those prehended actual entities among its members, or of some part of that nexus. In this way the nexus (or its part), thus characterized, is the objective datum of a feeling entertained by this prehending subject. (PR 27, curly brackets enclose my own interpolations)

Although earlier categories have provided for the separate (though contrasted) functioning of diverse prehended occasions in the becoming of a new occasion, this category accounts for the fact that an entity may feel its environment to be a genuine community in virtue of certain persistent characters or qualities. As was the case for the operations of the other Categoreal Obligations, intensity is once again at stake in transmutation's making an environment "feelable" as a unity of character.

It might appear at first that transmutation would tend to diminish intensity, as it seems to favor a narrowness that is eliminative of certain kinds of diversity provident of width. But the narrowness of feeling achieved is its own kind of intensification, bought at the expense of eliminating the subordinate intensities of physical detail. Transmutation "transformatively" gathers the several conceptual feelings arising from the several physical feelings of diverse entities, into one powerful, complex physical feeling. The role of this Categoreal Obligation is to lift into effective prominence some reiterated pattern occurring throughout a portion of the environment, such that its attribution to a nexus or part of a nexus is an added impetus to its incorporation, valuation upward, and therefore intense realization. Transmutation's role could be described as a feeling of the structuredness of the environment by the relations of various actualities sharing intensive qualia. Via transmutation, "the world is physically felt as a unity, and is felt as divisible into parts that are unities, namely, nexūs" (PR 250). It is important that it be possible to feel the world as such a unity, or as composed of unities, for this is a significant portion of the way "order" inside an entity reflects and contributes to "order" in nature beyond the entity: "Transmutation is the way in which the actual world is felt as a community, and is so felt in virtue of its prevalent order. For it arises by reason of the analogies between the various members of the prehended nexus, and eliminates their differences" (PR 251).

Now this last passage betokens a note of elimination that seems to be actually dismissive of content rather than simply an organizational and intensifying function. Indeed, Whitehead likens transmutation to a kind of abstraction, noting its similarity to propositions, conscious perceptions, and judgments (PR 254). And, in a statement that for all intents and purposes undermines transmutation as a metaphysically general Categoreal Obligation, Whitehead claims that given the eliminations of physical content performed by transmutation of conceptual feelings into single physical feelings, it is "evident that adversion and aversion, and also the Category of Transmutation, only have importance in the case of high-grade organisms. They constitute the first step towards intellectual mentality, though in themselves they do not amount to consciousness" (PR 254). It is contended that adversion and aversion (the subjective forms of those feelings called physical purposes) depend upon physical feelings that are themselves consequent upon the conceptual reversions performed by supplemental feeling. Here we wind up at an interpretive impasse, for Whitehead stipulates elsewhere that "all actual entities include physical purposes" (PR 276), and the existence of order in nature (in societies like rocks, lamps, trees and daffodils that do not appear to be bordering on consciousness) depends on these physical purposes, which must, qua feelings, have their subjective forms.

It is certainly the case that transmutation has its best applications in the context of intellectual activity (which is discussed in its intensive significance in chapter four). Taking account of Whitehead's own ambiguities about this category, I come down in favor of its categoreal generality or relevance for occasions of all types to one degree or another. It is important for the general notion of existence implied by the philosophy of organism that every entity take account of the orderedness of occasions external to it. Not merely the patterned intensities are felt, but the relations of the satisfied intensities as carving up the actual world into spatiotemporal arrangements of form. Although it is absolutely essential in the intellectual experience of organisms capable of "sensation" that some provision be made for an occasion's "symbolization" of an organized "external" world (Whitehead's theory of presentational immediacy does just that), a similar concern is present to a lesser degree in occasions generally. Indeed, in a passage that undermines his claim that transmutation belongs only to high-grade occasions, Whitehead acknowledges that, "[i]n general, and apart from high-grade organisms, [the] spatio-temporal association of the sense-datum is integrated into a vague sense of externality. The component valuations have in such cases failed to differentiate themselves into grades of intensity" (PR 314). Failure to differentiate here should not be taken as a total failure of intensive becoming, for as we have seen, relegation to vague background status is important for the lifting into prominence of certain other details, and for the feeling of "depth" (in the existential, as well as the emotional, sense) of actuality.

We could view Whitehead's lack of clarity on the issue of transmutation as a symptom of his general failure to completely come to terms with the correlation of coordinate and genetic analysis, and I do in fact view it this way. Nobo's systematic elucidation of the metaphysical status of extension (which is the focus of coordinate analysis) successfully demonstrates that the ontological solidarity of all occasions, and experienced by all occasions, cannot be ignored in its elucidation of the modes of objectification and superjection crucial to the creative process of genesis as such. We will meet with these issues again in later chapters. For the present, it must be noted that it is impossible that the feeling of any physical presence in the becoming of an actuality could have the status of being a "contrast" unless the subject actuality does indeed feel the real externality of that which is present in it. Whitehead's "realism" about the past, discussed earlier, hinges entirely on the entity's recognition that what is in it (the entity) is not *only* in it. In those instances where Whitehead finds it necessary to emphasize elimination and absence of one thing from another, it is likely that he is neglecting his own assertions about the vibratory character of the real. And, it is not surprising that these instances of erroneous emphasis, as happens in regard to transmutation, occur largely in those contexts wherein Whitehead incorporates the classical distinction between final and efficient causality into his system (unnecessarily, in my view).

Let us bring the discussion of transmutation to a close by returning to the point with which we began, which was Whitehead's comment that via this Categoreal Obligation a nexus comes to function as if it were a single entity with its own "categoreal type of existence." A transmutation is a contrast arrived at through the impartial feeling of an analogous pattern embodied in various members of the physical datum. The contrast is between the one complex conceptual feeling of the recognized pattern, and the consequent physical feeling of the nexus so symbolized.

The categoreal status of the existence of the nexus arises because it is a particular kind of unity of a particular kind of diversity. The curiosity here is that "nexūs" get categoreal status by what concrescent subjects do in order to feel them. This bears quite interestingly on our consideration of the ontological significance of the privacy versus publicity issue. We recall that as listed in the Categories of Existence, a nexus is defined as a "public matter of fact" (*PR* 22). Thus, this type of categoreal existence is really a function of the others—nexūs can only function as public matters of fact in the contrasts resident in actualities. It is extremely interesting that the "public" mode of existence be a function of contrastive activity. It is for this reason, among others, that I find it a good idea to jettison the dual language of efficient and final causation so as to capture the overlappingness of the public existence of one thing and the private existence of something else, in order to capture the sense in that the public existence bears in itself a reference to (indeed, as I shall argue, a form of) the private subjectivity from which it proceeds as superject. Whitehead should, perhaps, have found some manner besides transmutation in which to account for the presence of the organized dimension of nature in the existents that comprise nature. It is perhaps due to his system's derivation from the contours of human experience that this particular obscurity arises.[22]

THE CATEGORY OF SUBJECTIVE HARMONY

The logic of the Category of Subjective Harmony follows very closely from the logic of the first Categoreal Obligation, Subjective Unity. Subjective

Unity asserted that all the feelings to be integrated in a concrescence must be compatible by reason of the unity of their emergent subject, and we saw that this refers to the unity afforded by the emerging intense satisfaction sought in concrescence. The Category of Subjective Harmony might be said to put the flesh on the bones of the implied subjects of concrescence operative in the first obligation. In fact, since what must ultimately be harmonized are all of the feelings an entity has (with their subjective forms of emotional valuation), Whitehead's quotation from Ezekiel in illustration of the notion of subjective form is relevant here: "So I prophesied as he commanded me, and the breath came into them, and they lived, and stood up upon their feet, an exceeding great army" (*PR* 85, Ezekiel xxxvii:10). Subjective forms "clothe the dry bones with the flesh of a real being, emotional, purposive, appreciative." The Category of Subjective Harmony stipulates that all such "fleshing out" or "breathing" life into things must effect an aesthetic mode of togetherness; the fully developed conceptually embellished entity of both physical and mental origin must be a harmony of enjoyment, structure, and purpose.

The harmony achieved in an entity is a question of the final form of valuation of the elements presented for feeling in the one intense satisfaction. The category states: "The valuations of conceptual feelings are mutually determined by the adaptation of those feelings to be contrasted elements congruent with the subjective aim" (*PR* 27). Again we note the inclusion of subjective aim, which is at intensity, in the definition of another Categoreal Obligation. Whereas the Category of Subjective Unity demanded the absence of incompatibilities that would attenuate intensity by preventing contrast, the Category of Subjective Harmony demands actual contrasts marking the specific adaptedness of all feelings to the 'end' that is the one unified intensity of satisfaction. Thus, Whitehead describes the "joint function" of the categories of Subjective Unity and Subjective Harmony in expressing the "pre-established harmony in the process of concrescence of any one subject" (*PR* 27). Subjective Unity stipulates something about the data, while Subjective Harmony governs the unity of the subjective forms of the data as felt. What Whitehead means by "pre-established" harmony is that the prehensions in the incomplete phases of a concrescence conspire in unison even though the subject to whom they belong emerges from, rather than underlies, that unison.

Because the production of conceptual feeling providing for the unique integration of data that is the entity is the functional content of "harmonization," we must note that this Categoreal Obligation overlaps significantly with the Category of Conceptual Reversion. Indeed, Whitehead expands his concept of the joint functioning of the categories and asserts that the triad of Subjective Unity, Subjective Harmony, and Conceptual Reversion account for "the ultimate particularity of feelings" in a concrescence. "For the superject which is their outcome is also the subject which is operative in their production. They are the creation of their own creature. The point to be noticed is that the actual entity, in a state of process during which it is not fully definite, determines its own ultimate definiteness" (PR 255).

The Category of Subjective Harmony secures the superject's status in the future by demanding that present becoming yield an intensive structure inclusive, broad, and deep enough so as to minimize the chance that the future as derivable from the entity will be such as to thwart that satisfaction's self-imposition in creative process. The more harmonized the entity's total feeling of its world, including the "nested" set of social orders that it "vaguely senses," the less likely that some unaccounted for environmental factor can disrupt its objectifications in transcendent subjects. In this, Subjective Harmony is a crucial factor in the explanation of what Whitehead sees as the fundamental orientation of nature toward the maintenance and increase of order, rather than toward disorder or decay of achieved complexity.

In a discussion in *Religion in the Making*, Whitehead equates "evil" with aesthetic destructiveness, the accidental failure or deliberate intention to obscure the intensity possible via one course of realization by entertainment of an alternative intensive structure that excludes it. The obstructive intensities might have been brought under more refined contrast, but were not (RM 95–97). He notes that "the evil lies in the loss to the social environment," suggesting yet another dimension in which this philosophy privileges public functioning despite the dependency of public functioning on private attainment. A rich social environment will support more harmonizing actualities, and more harmonizing actualities will support a rich social environment, and so on. Evil, in its simple forms unaided by human deviancy, tends towards self-annihilation, for it undermines the objective conditions of the maintenance of orders of its type. This helps unpack the correlation of society and individuality stipulated in the four "grounds of order" discussed earlier. What is important to note is that Whitehead believes that there is a basic impetus in nature toward the maintenance of rich environments and deep actualities: "The fact of the instability of evil is the moral order in the universe" (RM 97, 95).

Interestingly, in discussing the "mutual sensitivity of prehensions" effected via the Category of Subjective Harmony, Whitehead provides a rule for the discovery of the genetic components of an actuality that involves the combined considerations of the two categories of explanation cited earlier in support of the notion that Whitehead was groping after a way to unite coordinate and genetic analysis. We are referred to the eighth and ninth categories, which refer to the two modes of analysis required to grasp the being and the becoming of an actuality. In the course of this discussion, we are instructed to begin with the satisfaction, which is the entity as one, and work our way back to individual prehensions: "take any component in the objective datum of the satisfaction; in the complex pattern of the subjective form of the satisfaction there will be a component with direct relevance to this element in the datum. Then in the satisfaction, there is a prehension of this component of the objective datum with that component of the total subjective form as its subjective form" (PR 235).

Subjective forms are presented here as an organized totality from within which such discriminations can be made (with careful analysis) as to identify the component elements individually. Thus, the modes of harmonization in an entity, its scaling of the relative values accorded each element of the datum, and such elimination of direct valuation as is needed to effect relevant overall structure, are to be conceived as constituting an internal process of quasi-totalization. The product is an entity that functions as an intensive lens through which the self-revelations of other objectified entities in the datum of the subject may be discovered with some degree of integrity. Thus Subjective Harmony, although suggesting a focus on the intense internal experience of an actuality so as to define its own enjoyment of itself, has a critical role to play in what is actually the objective solidarity of occasions in a continuum of mutual revelation of character. That which appears to be "made solely for pleasure," to recur to Auden, has "nothing to hide."

THE CATEGORY OF FREEDOM AND DETERMINATION

If we were following the expositional order of Whitehead's presentation of the Categoreal Obligations, this would be the point where the Category of Subjective Intensity would be addressed, but as I have already introduced Category of Subjective Intensity in chapter one, and have noted its function across the other Categoreal Obligations, I will now pass on to a treatment of the last Categoreal Obligation in Whitehead's table, that of freedom and determination.

All of Whitehead's metaphysical efforts are devoted to the exploration of "really real" things as *causa sui*. It is through self-creation that what are traditionally called final and efficient forms of causality come to have sway (cf. PR 85ff). Somehow the degree to which something is free is consequent upon the degree to which it is determined. The category is stated thus: "The concrescence of each individual actual entity is internally determined and is externally free," and in his explanation Whitehead states that this means essentially that,

> in each concrescence whatever is determinable is determined, but that there is always a remainder for the decision of the subject-superject of that concrescence. This subject-superject is the universe in that synthesis, and beyond it there is nonentity. This final decision is the reaction of the unity of the whole to its own internal determination. This reaction is the final modification of emotion, appreciation, and purpose. But the decision of the whole arises out of the determination of the parts, so as to be strictly relevant to it. (PR 27–28)

If one were to wish to disabuse one of Whitehead's detractors of the misconception that this atomism is the wildly implausible account of how "limestone" occasions and other inanimate stabilities are really, deep down, free self-constitutors, this category would be a good place to start. Efficient causality is the order of the day, it seems, determining what residual decisions are left for the occasion, and then provoking just those decisions required for creative process just here in the continuum.

We need not be uncomfortable with what appears to be the mildly deterministic slant of this axiology. For an individual to be a self-value requires that it be a deeply relevant form of intensive valuation; this has to mean that what agentive activity there is to speak of seeks mostly to secure its place in the environment of its ecstatic existence. Acquiescence in determinism is, however, another mode of accepting a binary conception of two major kinds of cause (efficient and final) and opting for one of them at the expense of the other. This is just the kind of philosophical blunder Whitehead constructed the philosophy of organism so as to avoid. This is also why it is unfortunate that he maintained the two-cause conception, as it obfuscates the novelty of his conception of Creativity. Be that as it may, the skeptic can be assured that natural objects in which one would not expect to find the kinds of choices made by sentient beings are in fact not making those choices. Nature's order demands strict relevance, even if the exaggerated abstraction of determinism (abstract because it divorces the causes from one another) is absent. Relevant decision is adequately permissive of the kind of self-value champions of a more enlarged concept of final causality might demand, because it secures the depth of value of an occasion whose intensive structure embodies and feels the bonds of character that pervade its immediate world. Without this kind of strict relevance to that which is traditionally marked as "efficient" cause, individual decision would mean the non-entity of chaos via irrelevance—the collapse of actuality rather than its deep experience. Existentialism's neglect of a philosophy of "Nature" has left it open to this complaint.

What is distasteful about even a mild determinism might be avoided if we remember that the course of creative process is, in the end, only referable to the pulsing creativity of individual actualities. Whitehead notes that together the Ontological Principle (that the reasons for things are to be found only in the experience of actual entities) and the Category of Freedom and Determination jointly explain the "peculiarity" of the course of history. "The evolution of history can be rationalized by the consideration of the determination of successors by antecedents. But, on the other hand, the evolution of history is incapable of rationalization because it exhibits a selected flux of participating forms. No reason, internal to history, can be assigned why that flux of forms, rather than another, should have been illustrated.... There is no reason why there could be no alternative flux exhibiting that principle of internal determination. The actual flux presents itself with the character of being merely 'given.' It does not disclose any peculiar character of 'perfection.' On the contrary, the imperfection of the world is the theme of every religion that offers a way of escape, and of every sceptic who deplores the prevailing superstition" (PR 46–47). It is internally determined that there be a course of history's flux, and yet it has been the individual decisions of actualities constituting the flux that have given the flux *that* shape. Actualities are, in Sartrean terms, "condemned to be free," to be the sole responsible agents, in the solidarity of their individual existences, for what transpires in the world. The orders demanding reiteration in actualities are intensities produced by actualities, limited to and by actualities, and are the marks of the creativity that cannot exist apart from actualities. As I think is the case for the old dyads of subject-object, final and efficient cause, and so on, Whitehead would have done well to avoid the dichotomous conception of freedom and determination. The concept of ecstatic existence, the real presence of subjects as subjects in other subjects, helps to ease the curiosities surrounding the ultimate description of the individual atoms of experience whose possible freedom or determination is under scrutiny here. Given the intractability of issues of free will and deterministic causality in the history of philosophy, we are entitled to suspect that we are laboring under a misstatement of the question.

Conclusion

The first two chapters of the present discourse have served to lay the groundwork for a full statement of the "ontology of intensity" that frames the backdrop for the concept of ecstatic existence I am offering as a corrective re-interpretation of some crucial themes in Whitehead's atomism. In the first chapter various questions were raised about the categoreal status of "contrasts" so as to suggest the fundamental importance of "intensity" in conceiving what it means to exist in this scheme. Interpretive difficulties regarding "satisfactions" were introduced so as to suggest a point of entrée for the revisionist reading of existence the balance of our discussions will elaborate. In the present chapter I have used an elaboration of the Categoreal Obligations under the aspect of their procurement of intensity so as to begin to advance the conception of ecstatic existence, a conception that might resolve the ontological tensions raised by the dualities of subjective and objective dimensions of actuality, final and efficient causality, present and future functioning of satisfactions, and so on. Because of the omnipresence of concerns for intensity, it is reasonable to assert that any Categoreal Obligation selected for analysis must be understood to overlap significantly with the operations of the other obligations.

There can be no intensity arising from subjective harmony without the process of valuation whereby certain elements in the datum assume the status of a foreground narrowness and others assume the status of a background vagueness. Likewise, there can be no such valuation without the harmony established by the aesthetic unity being sought under subjective (aim at) intensity that cues the entity as to its valuative needs or importances. There can be no transmutation unless objective diversity provides for genuinely diverse elements to be transmuted into the feeling of a nexus. Reversion complicates and deepens the process of transmutation by introducing complexities of novel feeling that may result either in intensification in future concrescences or in the mutual obstruction of possibilities reverted and transmuted in the community of entities. The ultimate goal of all of the forms of adjustment obliged by these categories is the balanced complexity of intense feeling in the satisfaction of the novel creature.

My concentration thus far has been on unpacking certain fundamental categoreal assertions, as this helps to locate any necessary reinterpretation of the scheme at the heart of the system rather than around the "fringes." This is aimed, of course, not at dismantling the cosmology Whitehead presents, but at making more plausible some of what I take to be its finer assertions, especially the insight that "value" is referable to individual existents as the locus of a vibratory creative process. Our discussion will now turn to a less category-bound and more free-ranging discussion of the nature of "existence," with direct engagement of some provocative critical renderings of Whitehead's ontological commitments. We will undertake a philosophical enactment of the discovery hinted at by the narrator who speaks in the lines that opened this chapter: "when I try to imagine a faultless love / Or the life to come"—when we try to imagine an individual self-same existent, in its adventures beyond itself—what is found is something subterranean and hard to make out, discernible only by its ever-changing results: "what I hear is the murmur / Of underground streams, what I see is a limestone landscape." What can we imagine about the existences whose intensive satisfactions make up the landscape of the known universe?

CHAPTER THREE

The Ontology of Intensity

He who binds to himself a joy
Does the winged life destroy;
But he who kisses the joy as it flies
Lives in eternity's sun rise.
   —William Blake, *"Eternity"*

The view of "ecstatic existence" or "ecstatic individuality" that will be further developed in this chapter takes a clue from these lines of William Blake. It is my contention that the over attention paid to the private subjectivity of an entity as the main, or even sole locus of its proper individuality and agency amounts to a kind of ontological "binding" of actuality. An actuality is a "joy" in Blake's sense because it is an enjoyment, the agentive experience of joy that is the essence of life. But to circumscribe that joy within the prison of immediacy, as Whitehead himself unfortunately sometimes does, "destroys" the sense of "life" that must attend our sense of existent individuals in this scheme, a metaphysics in which "vibration" is the telltale sign of physical existence. I think there is something nonvibratory and non-life-like about the description of subjectivity as something somehow causally and ontologically different from objectivity. Whitehead's more careful remarks on the fundamentally "passing" character of creative process—the progression from satisfaction to satisfaction that hints at the microscopic processes from which the satisfactions emerge—manages a mode of conception in which we might "kiss the joy as it flies," thereby respecting the ontological integrity implicit in its inherent tendency toward "flight" or "passing on."

In this chapter I attempt a conception of actualities as passing joys. The sense of "passing" meant here is not the relentlessness of perishing that marks a boundary between existents, but the persistent vibratory achievement of intensive feeling that marks the interpenetration of individuals in a non-idealistic and nonmonistic sense. This interpenetration of existents is what it means to "live in eternity's sunrise," to witness the objective immortality of atomistic beings whose life is a relatively perpetual new day, a repetition "to the crack of doom."

I think this conception is an effective way of thinking about Whitehead's difficult-to-conceive Category of the Ultimate, or creativity. Charles Hartshorne calls Whitehead's expression of the ultimate character of creative process in the statement, "the many become one, and are increased by one," his "novel intuition" in philosophy. It is in the development of this novel intuition that the greatness of Whitehead as a thinker stands forth.[1] And yet it is also in the development of this principle of organic process that the seeming incoherence, obtuseness, and equivocation in Whitehead's philosophy occur. We have already seen some problems on this level in the analyses that raise the question of how the existence (in the ontologically most significant sense of being an individual, or an "atomic" experience) of things is to be conceived in this scheme, and also in terms of William A. Christian's attempts at untangling Whitehead's apparently contradictory claims about the "satisfaction" of an actual entity. In this chapter, I unpack my vision of Whitehead's creative atomism with special attention to the role of intensity, in the course of addressing what I take to be a few of the significant critical questions raised in regard to his ontology. There will be recourse to the question of how the notion of intensity came to be formulated in Whitehead's scheme, as this may be helpful to understanding the final expression of that scheme, particularly as the account of how "the many become one, and are increased by one" (PR 21).

The Concrescence/Concretum Distinction

By now it should be clear that much of the significance of the notion of intensity in Whitehead's metaphysics is that it stands at the crossroad, or indeed *is* somehow the crossroad between subjectivity and objectivity. We have seen that the achievement of a fully determinate intensity of feeling is the purpose and nature of subjectivity, and have noted that this intensity is the offering of any entity as objective matter for prehension by subsequent concrescences. The intensive pattern achieved in an entity's subjective process will either be objectified in other entities or modified as relevantly diverse from the original intensity. And yet when we stop to ask how we should think about the objectifiable satisfaction (the superject) of the entity in light of its relation to the agency of concrescence (subjectivity) that it (the superject) supposedly lacks, we meet great difficulties. The perplexity of the subject-superject notion of the entity is not to be underestimated, and despite the evidences adduced so far for seeing these perplexities as necessary to Whitehead's process-based system, for seeing the crossroad not as a vanishing point but as a significant existential scene with its own characterization, one might at this point be inclined to tag the matter as a morass of equivocation.

In fact this inclination has been engaged thoroughly, though not skeptically, by George Kline in his seminal paper, "Form, Concrescence, and Concretum." Kline's analysis is a helpful tool in laying out some of the issues that I want the concept of "ecstatic existence" to address. While noting Whitehead's consistency in using the neologisms critical to his novel approach to metaphysics ('concrescent', 'ingression', 'physical prehension', and so on), Kline goes on to claim that Whitehead "is much less consistent in his use of such traditional, and traditionally vague or equivocal, terms as 'actual', 'concrete', 'constitute', 'decision', and 'function/ing', all of which are of central importance for his thought."[2] We might conclude, with Kline, that this penchant for inconsistency is due to Whitehead's "cryptosubstantialism," his importation of metaphysical conceptions characteristic of substance ontologies. Whitehead's equivocation would then simply be yet another instance of a traditional carelessness about terminology, his vagueness yet another instance of a traditional failure to achieve clarity and distinctness about all-important concepts regarding existence, his cryptosubstantialism a bit of evidence for the incoherence of an event-based metaphysical atomism.

It is philosophically tempting to see such a radically novel thinker as Whitehead falling into these traps about traditional questions of Being. It would be proof that the classical conceptions are in fact insurmountable and the philosophy of organism is a failed attempt to move beyond them. Kline may, in fact, be correct in attributing Whitehead's terminological obfuscations to something like a "cryptosubstantialism," for as I have pointed out earlier, it is probably Whitehead's failure to completely revise the classical concepts in ontology that gives rise to his own ontology's manifestation of just the kinds of dualities it was designed, in my view at least, to overcome. I prefer to see the situation not as a cryptosubstantialism in thinking as much as an overcoming of substantialism that makes the unfortunate choice to clothe itself in the language of "substance" discourse. It is my view, however, that even in the course of these manifestly unclear expressions of just what he means by his own organic atomism, Whitehead does convey a possible mode of conception—actuality as intensive satisfaction—which avoids substantialism and its dichotomy of subject and object, final and efficient cause, and so on.

Kline presents a very careful and painstaking analysis of Whitehead's use of terms, and I do not propose in what follows to contest his elegant sorting of vocabulary. Kline is perfectly correct in stating that Whitehead uses terms in a manner that is frequently "misleading" and systematically confusing.[3] Terminological vagueness, however, does not suffice as proof of Whitehead's final failure in expressing his novel intuition. In addition to Whitehead's own lack of clear expression, part of the problem regarding key terms may also be in the presuppositions we bring to interpreting this philosophy. Although there may indeed be "nothing new under the sun," I would be curious to know if someone whose features, garb, and mannerisms were curiously different from my own, and yet who used many of the words familiar to me in quite a different manner from the way they were used in my language, were not in the end referring to things differently from how I do, and hence meaning very different things. This, I think, is the curiosity we must have about Whitehead's terminology, not so much that it really is a wholly new metaphysical language, but that what it says resists our hearing the words in the usual ways.

Reconstructing our conception of the embracing concepts through which to think the Whiteheadian insight in terms of intensity and contrast suggests that the neat sorting possible in Kline's analysis may itself represent a kind of "cryptosubstantialism" that crops up in interpretive work on Whitehead's nonsubstantialist scheme. To be clear, it is Kline's ultimate objective to preserve the integrity of the temporal *atomism* put forth in this system. Thus, although his analysis gives us important matter for thought, I will disagree with Kline when he comes to the fundamental question of just what the "atoms" are in this system. I think, in fact, Kline's meticulous study of Whitehead's verbal ambiguities gives us an excellent starting point from which to entertain the need for the revised conception of individuality I am forwarding in the present study.

The central purpose of Kline's analysis is to argue for the "sharp ontological—as opposed to merely functional—distinction between concrescence and concretum," between entities in the process of coming to be, and entities that have already become.[4] According to Kline, 'concrescences' are 'actual' in the most fundamental sense possible in Whitehead's atomic scheme. They alone possess the subjectivity, immediacy, or agency characteristic of the "final realities" (PR 22) elucidated by that scheme. A 'concretum' is a closed or completed entity available for objectification in subsequent processes of becoming. A concretum may have efficacy in subsequent entities, but it lacks the subjective agency properly attributable to the fully actual, concrete—that is, subjective—process of concrescence.[5] Let us examine how it is that Kline arrives at this sharp ontological distinction set forth as preservative of Whiteheadian atomism.

As already noted, Kline's method follows the discovery of inconsistent use of crucial terms and finds two basic types or contexts of usage for such critical concepts as the 'actuality', the 'constitution', and the 'concreteness' of entities. The two types of usage correspond roughly to the distinction, already set forth, between those things that have agency and are truly active and those things that lack agency and thus have only passive yet efficacious roles in process. Kline uses subscripts to indicate his sorting of the meanings of the terms in question, designating as $actual_1$ those references to things as actively in the process of actualization and therefore self-significant, and as $actual_2$ those references to things as no-longer-active, already actualized, and efficacious (other-significant) but not possessed of agency.[6] Thus, in reading the sentence, "Each actual occasion defines its own actual world from which it originates" (PR 210), we are to read the first reference to actuality as $actual_1$ and the second as $actual_2$. The actual world, as the available-for-concrescence-past-actualities, is not, properly speaking, $actual_1$; it is by definition the locus of actualities that have completed their processes of coming to be, and therefore is properly construed as a realm of potentiality. Kline cites

87

Process and Reality 65, where Whitehead discusses the real potentiality of the past, and category of explanation (vi), which asserts that the determination of the final role of a 'real potentiality' depends upon the decision of actual occasions in concrescence (*PR* 23). This distinction between the two senses of 'actuality' running through Whitehead's texts and the preference for 'actual$_1$' as the more strict meaning hinges on Whitehead's claim, borne out by much of the system, that "agency belongs exclusively to actual occasions" (*PR* 31).

We may pause here and note with interest the sentence just quoted and set forth what may be a problem in maintaining the sharp ontological distinction between those things that are active, coming-to-be, and those that are passive, having already come-to-be. The agency to which Whitehead is referring is agency of "comparison," the ability to make a meaningful evaluation of the relevance of various potentialities in becoming. We know from our analyses thus far that this comparison is the formation of contrasts, and the valuation of potentials occurs in the mode of forming effective, minimally eliminative contrasts in the interest of achieving maximal intensity. If, as has been suggested at various points in the first two chapters, the contrasts achieved substantially repeat contrasts and intensities achieved in past occasions (which, I must add, looked forward to such inclusion in a relevant future), can we really make a sharp *ontological* distinction between the feelings witnessing to the agency in concrescing actualities and the merely past agency (which is, allegedly, not truly agency) of completed actualities? In other words, if their intensities and contrasts are truly, to whatever extent, reiterated, or even significantly modified (which would include a recognition of the true character of that achievement from which departure is being made), can past actualities$_2$ really be stripped of actuality$_1$? The question, as we will see more clearly as we move on, concerns our conception of *where* or *how* an entity is to be conceived as existing. For now it is enough to remark that agency is linked to the activity of comparison, which leaves us on the doorstep of the concept of contrasts and thereby intensity.

The idea of the 'constitution' of entities receives similar analysis. Whitehead uses the word in a variety of ways, most significantly for my purposes as both verb and noun, the syntactical ambiguity Kline refers to as the "'-ing/-ed' ambiguity of many '-tion/-sion' words."[7] Constitution$_1$ refers to the "*process* of constitut*ing* or creat*ing*" and constitution$_2$ refers to the "*state* or *condition* of having-been-constitut*ed* or creat*ed*."[8] Thus Whitehead's concern that his philosophy explain the generic conditions governing the processes involved in the "real internal constitution" (borrowing Locke's phrase) of entities means two things, according to Kline: the activity of self realization when used in regard to concrescences (*PR* 29, 41, 53), and the "static structure or make-up" when applied to concreta (*PR* 24, 29, 219).

I am not convinced, however, that such a distinction between active self-realization and static achievement is intended in the texts referred to by

Kline. To take the section cited in favor of both usages, *Process and Reality* 29, it seems, indeed, that Whitehead is stretching language so as to avoid the type of ontological duality asserted by Kline and typical of any interpretation that emphasizes the agency of concrescence at the ontological expense of public existence. It is important to look at the entire passage in question, rather than the selected sentences in which the suspect vocabulary occurs:

> It is fundamental to the metaphysical doctrine of the philosophy of organism, that the notion of an actual entity as the unchanging subject of change is *completely abandoned*. An actual entity is at once the subject experiencing and the superject of its experiences. It is subject-superject, and neither half of this description can for a moment be lost sight of. The term 'subject' will be mostly employed when the actual entity is considered in respect to its own real internal constitution. But 'subject' is always to be construed as an abbreviation of 'subject-superject.' (PR 29, emphasis added)

What it is tempting to treat as an ontological distinction is here treated by Whitehead as a subordinate, abbreviating distinction in vocabulary to treat of the one ontological reality which is expressible only as the hyphenated subject-superject. The abbreviated reference to simply 'a subject' is for the purposes of considering some aspect of the entity, but because this is an abstraction from its complete being, we cannot assume that that aspect is more fundamental.

According to this passage, it is never appropriate to treat the metaphysical situation of an entity as if it were truly distinguishable as having two different ontological levels. The only thing in Whitehead's scheme that is bereft of inherent activity is an eternal object. The "complete abandonment" of modes of speech that treat actuality, anywhere it is met, as static, precludes the type of strong distinction reached by Kline (and implicit in much scholarship in this field) as a conclusion in his consideration of equivocal vocabulary. By looking at the "constitution" of an actuality in terms of its status as an intensity of contrast, we would note that, qua actual, there is no distinction between the agentive decisions and the contrasts effected in those decisions; the decision *is* the contrast. This is how we should read Category of Explanation ix (discussed earlier, and which is troubling to Kline and others), which states "that *how* [the free decision manifest in subjective form] an actual entity *becomes* constitutes *what* the actual entity *is*; so that the two decriptions of an actual entity are not independent. Its 'being' is constituted by its 'becoming.' This is the 'principle of process'" (*PR* 23). It is my opinion that Whitehead means what he says in these statements about the ultimate character of creative process, and that the seeming paradox of the many

89

becoming one and being increased by one should be conceived as referring to one ontologically significant thing, not two ("being" as somehow different from "becoming").

It is on the two senses of 'concrete' that Kline focuses his most sustained attention. Indeed, because of its "serious ambiguity" Kline abandons the term 'concrete' altogether, including his own subscript distinction between concrete$_1$ as active and concrete$_2$ as passive. He substitutes instead a triadic distinction between concrescent (active self-constitution$_1$), nonconcrescent (the status of forms, or eternal objects, which do not become at all), and postconcrescent (having achieved an internal constitution$_2$ and no longer active).[9] Let us turn to Whitehead's statements about concreteness and unpack their existential import.

Whitehead's texts are replete with references to "past actualities" as if he were indeed talking about something in a post-concrescent stage. The passages in which we noted troublesome issues as to the status of a satisfaction sound very much as if Whitehead adopts such a viewpoint. But the question arises, prompted by Kline's curious appellation of a concretum as 'post-concrescent': From what perspective is an entity's status as post-concrescent to be judged? If time truly is "incurably atomic," from what perspective can any judgment as to the 'post'-anything status of an entity be made? There is no large-scale temporal perspective from which to make such a determination.

Now, a metaphysician, including Whitehead, is sure to need to make reference to the past; these are the kinds of references to past actualities collected by Kline as descriptions of 'concreta.'[10] But there is no perspective, other than the present becoming of an actuality, from which something may be said to be, ontologically, past. But this pastness is not invoked by Whitehead as a separate ontological level, for pastness is only the operation of achieved intensities of feeling in the present becoming (achievement of intensity of feeling) of an entity. If Whitehead had conceived of the past as existing at a separate ontological level from the present he might be expected to have made such an observation, because this issue bears so strongly on his atomism. Unfortunately Whitehead often leaves the drawing of obvious implications to the inductive capacities of the reader, so we cannot take refuge in the mere absence of an ontological designation of pastness as different from the ontological designation of presentness. Also, one would expect some comment as to 'pastness' to appear in the categories of existence, but nothing of the kind occurs. We find there only a reference to nexūs as "public matters of fact," as noted earlier. If there is no perspective on the past (or future for that matter) except from the perspective of a present entity, then no ontological status can be granted in our metaphysics to the pastness of an actuality in itself. But to be honest, again, the mere absence of the "past" from the categories is no telling point either, for as we have seen the categories are not possessed of a great deal of rigid structure so as to be exclusive of much of anything.

This point about the Categories of Existence does, however, steer us in the right direction. What if "public" matters of fact are included in the list, and elaborately described throughout the Whiteheadian corpus, to suggest that publicity—the capacity to exist outside of one's center of organization—is not to be thought of primarily in temporal terms but in more straightforwardly creative terms? In other words, is it the pastness of the past that is important in the present becoming of existents, or is it the "sense of externality" these existents are felt with? Perhaps it is possible to conceive existentially temporal passingness without a strong sense of temporal quanta that effectively bound off agents from each others' agencies. This is what the concept of "ecstatic individuality" is designed to suggest.

It might be interesting to naively speculate (that is, without presupposition born of long familiarity) on what the philosophy of organism really requires in a philosophy of time. There is no doubt that Whitehead was concerned to make sense of the obvious flux involved in what is real, and his statement in *Science and the Modern World* that "temporalization is realization" makes this point quite nicely. However, claiming that "time is atomic (i.e., 'epochal')" does not necessarily translate into a conception of radical pastness and radical futurity as somehow *ontologically* distinct from present actuality. Whitehead continues: "It is to be noted that this doctrine of the epochal character of time does not depend on the modern doctrine of relativity, and holds equally—and indeed, more simply—if this doctrine be abandoned. It does depend on the analysis of the intrinsic character of an event, considered as the most concrete finite entity" (*SMW* 126). What this suggests is that the view of temporal atomicity being forwarded in the system is not dependent upon this or that general theory of time, and is instead subordinate to the ontological examination of actualities in their intensive agencies. As with some of the reconceptualizations we have seen so far, this, too, would help minimize one of the aspects of "process" philosophy that is manifestly unattractive to proponents of other metaphysical schemes: its apparent subordination of ontological stabilities to temporal passage for temporal passage's sake. I am attempting to reverse this subordination by emphasizing those instances in which Whitehead himself points to the reversal.[11]

Kline's imperative to draw an ontological distinction between past and present actualities stems from his entertainment of the question as to whether, despite what he sees as a complex but regular equivocation between actual$_1$ and actual$_2$ (and their analogues in other active/passive terms), concreta are "in *any* sense agents."[12] I think, though, that Kline begs the question here for he seems already to suppose a "no" response to the question that is supposed to be up for consideration. Kline sees as "cautious and accurate" Whitehead's statements that would answer the question in the negative—the reference to a past entity as a "dead datum" for objectification (*PR* 164), for instance.[13] He then characterizes as "less cautious" those claims that seem to ascribe agency to past entities as 'provoking' something in, or 'intervening' in concrescence (*AI* 176, *PR* 220). Outright "incautious" are any statements that directly characterize the past as engaged in some activity: the "creativity of the world is the throbbing emotion of the past hurling itself into a new transcendent fact" (*AI* 177), the 'throbbing of emotional energy' characterizing the transition from past to present (*PR* 116), and the "energizing of the past occasion as it claims its self-identical existence as a living issue in the present" (*AI* 182). Kline insists that Whitehead's doctrine requires that all activity be a function of present actualities alone, that concreta are incapable of anything like provocation, energizing, and so on, that any energy that might be ascribed to them is derived from that of a present actuality$_1$. Again, it is my intention here not so much to challenge Kline's reading individually, as to use it as a manifestation of a common and widely defended interpretation which I take to be significantly assailable if we come at the system from another angle, that provided by a close analysis of "intensity."

It is significant, though not signaled by Kline, that many of the 'incautious' statements cited do occur in the context of a discussion of the satisfaction of an entity. Others occur in discussions of the creative universe in which an atomic actuality finds itself. By unpacking these wider contexts in light of the suggestions raised thus far in our apprehension of the concept of intensity, we will be able to circumvent the ontological distinction that strips concreta of agency simply because of their "pastness."

If the language of 'provocation' be an incautious way of describing the impact of the past on the present, then Whitehead has incautiously formulated his entire discussion of subject-object relations in *Adventures of Ideas*, for there he develops the doctrine of the immanence of the past in the present as an unpacking of the following statement: "The subject-object relation can be conceived as Recipient and Provoker, where the fact provoked is an affective tone about the status of the provoker in the provoked experience. Also the total provoked occasion is a totality involving many such examples of provocation" (*AI* 176).

Objects (past actualities) are described consistently as provocative of essential characteristics of the subjective character of an experient occasion; indeed this is asserted to be the *definition* of being an object. It is also claimed that our conception of an object often runs the risk of being defective if that conception suggests "that an occasion of experiencing arises out of a passive situation which is a mere welter of many data" (*AI* 179). Objects are essentially components in the generation of a final, emotionally complete subjective unity of experience on the part of an entity (*AI* 177). Moreover, we must carefully understand the sentence that states that "the fact provoked *is* an affective tone *about the status of the provoker in the provoked experience*" (emphasis added). The subject *is* the emotionally clothed incorporation of the provoker; it does not 'have' reactions to objects, but other actualities have the status of objects in virtue of the affective (intensive) incorporation of them in the subject. If there is no such thing as a "passive situation which is merely a welter of many data" it is worth asking if the "past" has been well-characterized in those descriptions which employ such epithets as "dead data," the "dry bones" prophesied to by Ezekial.

Now, on what basis may the nonpassivity of the past be claimed given what we know of the general metaphysical conditions governing the coming-to-be of an actuality? We recall Whitehead's making categoreal the provision by an entity, in the present, for the intensity of that entity in the future. This is the actual entity's provision for its intervention in subjects that transcend it. Indeed, the reference to actualities described as 'intervening' in this sense, rejected by Kline, is very much supportive of my position if considered in context. The "objective intervention of other entities" is the "creative character which conditions" a concrescence in process (*PR* 220). It is true that Whitehead does describe this as "real potentiality," suggesting an ontological distinction between the actual/active and potential/efficacious as made by Kline, but the suggestion is misleading. Let us consider the context in which the notion of 'intervention' is discussed:

> The peculiarity of an actual entity is that it can be *considered* both 'objectively' and 'formally.' The 'objective' aspect is morphological as far as that actual entity is concerned; by this it is meant that the process involved is transcendent relatively to it, so that the *esse* of its satisfaction is *sentiri*. The 'formal' aspect is functional so far as that actual entity is concerned: by this it is meant that the process involved is immanent in it. . . . [The] formal consideration of one actual entity requires reference to the objective intervention of other actual entities." (*PR* 220, emphasis added)

If it is a "peculiarity of an actual entity" that it be thus construable simultaneously as objective and formal, "pragmatic" (having consequences in entities subsequent to itself) and processive (feeling the consequences of prior actualities into its own immediacy of becoming) (*PR* 220), we are warranted to ask whether the distinction between formal reality as agency and objective reality as merely morphological and derivative being (*esse* as *sentiri*) is in fact more a function of the "consideration" of actualities than of the ontological status of the entities. If the formal consideration of one actuality "requires" reference to objective intervention by other entities, isn't the distinction suggested by analysis absent in fact? Restating the last line as "the formal constitution of one actual entity requires the objective intervention of other actual entities" highlights the strained sense of the formal and objective reality distinction being used here. If we take the distinction seriously, just how are we to *think* the *presence* of the merely objective in the manifestly subjective? The answer is, I maintain, that we cannot, but that we need to be able to seems to be the very point of Whitehead's relational, creative atomism of subjects whose characters infuse themselves in the continuum of being that beckons the attentive analyses of the metaphysician.

The implications of Kline's formulation of systematic semantic consistency, and the fairly common and understandable reading of Whitehead they represent, amount to an ontological misrepresentation. The 'being' of an entity as objective may be at certain times and places in its being 'perceived,' but Whitehead *is* forwarding it as (part of) *its* existence, in the only manner in which existence is conceivable in a scheme that asserts the primacy of internal relations, whereby the individuality of things "does not mean substantial independence" (SMW 70). Indeed, in discussing Berkeley's doctrine of perception as a model for the philosophy of organism, Whitehead concludes that for Berkeley's notion of perception as constituting the entire being of natural entities we "can substitute the concept, that the realization is the gathering of things into the unity of a prehension; and that what is thereby realized is the prehension, and not the things. This unity of a prehension defines itself as a *here* and a *now*, and the things so gathered into the grasped unity have essential reference to other places and other times" (SMW 69).

If the reference to other places and times (other actualities past and future) is essential, can we limit the location of the proper existence of an entity (and therefore its agency, activity, etc.) to the aspects of itself considered merely as subject, or must we not confer existential status to the provocative effectiveness of the entity in entities which transcend it? The "here" and "now" aspect of prehension refers to the position of the subject, but this positioned subject refers, in its subjectivity, to other times and places. The passage at issue proceeds: "The things which are grasped into a realized unity, here and now, are not the castle, the cloud, and the planet *simply* in themselves [this would be Berkeley's troubling idealism]; but *they are the castle, the cloud, and the planet* from the standpoint, in space and time, of the prehensive unification. In other words it is the perspective *of* the castle over there from the standpoint of the unification here. It is, therefore, *aspects of the castle, the cloud, and the planet* which are grasped into unity here" (SMW 69–70, emphasis added). Whitehead likens this description to Spinoza's "interlocked plurality of modes" of the one substance which for Whitehead is "creativity" (not as substance, however, but as act).[14] I have emphasized certain terms in this description in order to highlight the sense in which "objectified" actualities are yet themselves, in the ontologically significant sense of individuality of existence: "individualization does not mean substantial independence." What is not "independent" (i.e., separate, boundaried, etc.) is the central character of existents as agencies of contrast. Provocation belongs to objects because, in other words, they are not merely objects, but perspectives *of* (not *on*) the subjects from which they originate.

To repeat a passage cited earlier, Whitehead's description of prehensive incorporation can be seen to invite the reading I am advancing over the view that limits agency only to concrescence: "the present occasion while claiming self-identity, while *sharing the very nature of the bygone occasion in all its living activities*, nevertheless is engaged in modifying it, in adjusting it to *other* influences, in completing it with *other* values, in deflecting it to *other* purposes. The present moment is constituted by the influx of *the other* into that self-identity which is the continued life of the immediate past within the immediacy of the present" (*AI* 181, first emphasis mine). Kline objects to this claim to the self-identity of an entity as existing in its own immediacy and in the immediacy of subsequent entities that will modify it because, according to him, it violates the principle that locates agency only in the process of concrescence.

It was noted at the outset of this discussion that Kline asserts the necessity of making a sharp ontological distinction between concrescence and concretum in order to preserve Whitehead's *atomism*. He contends that given the tension in Whitehead's texts between formulations suggesting the purely passive status of concreta versus the active status of concrescences, the issue can probably not be settled exegetically; the textual conflicts, he claims, are "a manifestation of an underlying tension between Whitehead's ontological atomism and his lingering cryto-substantialism."[15]

I have tried to suggest, through questions posed in terms of some systematic considerations, that the ambiguity Kline correctly identifies in some of the texts in question stems not from a cryptosubstantialism in Whitehead but from misstatements (and hence misunderstandings) of his atomism. My suggestion is not merely exegetical; I borrow Kline's method and advance, as he does, a proposal referent to the philosophical needs of the system. Although I share with other readers of Whitehead the frustration with ambiguous terminology, I think some sense may be made of Whitehead's atomism, which does not require the sharp ontological distinction that seems to lurk behind the verbal ambiguities. Such a distinction seems to me to participate in a major error identified by Whitehead in philosophies of substance: it asserts a kind of independence—the independence of agency—which isolates each individual as such in its own ontological "space," if you will. We recall it was precisely this isolation, *not* the fact of persistence, of substances that Whitehead deplored. It is the interpretive strategy that ontologically privileges the concept of merely private agency that emerges, if we understand Whitehead correctly, as cryptosubstantialist, though of course he himself at times seems guilty of just this lingering attachment to radical individuality.

Hitherto in this chapter I have spoken in systematically general terms, addressing and extrapolating from Whitehead's doctrines regarding actual entities, subjects and objects, and so on, without much particular reference to the concepts of intensity and contrast. There are two reasons for this temporary hiatus from the conceptual vocabulary of the present thesis. First, it is important to the viability of my thesis that its contentions be to some degree expressible in the terminology usually employed by Whitehead (as well as, and especially, by his commentators), or at least that the issues I focus on be expressible in those terms. This approach helps us to understand Whitehead to have really meant what he claimed at critical junctures about seminal ideas in his system. Second, there is the converse intention to demonstrate that a different perspective from that which is usually taken is necessary to understand this terminology. In other words, the problematic character of Whitehead's novel intuition when conceived in the absence of a developed vocabulary of 'intensity' had to be established. Similar difficulties of conception, due to Whitehead's nonrejection of the distinctions of classical ontology, will be introduced later. It is hoped that some of the difficulties at least, as well as a hint of a way to avoid them, have been made clear in the preceding section.

I now turn to a discussion of the resolving force of the concept of intensity in Whitehead's ontology. I begin with a slight shift in primary terminological focus, one that speaks to the general issue of what should be our primary conceptual vocabulary in the construal of the meaning of existence in Whitehead's scheme. Our move will be to a consideration of "creativity" as aesthetic realization. In *Science and the Modern World,* organic atomism is developed as an alternative to a physics of "simple location" and to an epistemology of subjectivism amounting to "solipsism." In the development of this view, there is a simultaneous concern to explain both "enduring things" and the processes at work in reality such that there is evolution, change, even dissolution. Whitehead concludes: "One all-pervasive fact, *inherent in the very character of what is real* is the transition of things, the passage one to another. This passage is *not a mere linear procession* of discrete entities. However *we fix* a determinate entity, there is always a narrower determination of something which is *presupposed* in our first choice. Also there is always a *wider determination into which our first choice fades* by transition beyond itself" (*SMW* 93; emphasis mine).

We are to conceive this transition of things as occurring via 'events' that are emergent unities actualizing value. But we are warned not to fixate on the discreteness implied by the concept of an event: "The name *'event'* given to such a unity, draws attention to the inherent transitoriness, combined with the actual unity. But this abstract word cannot be sufficient to characterize what the fact of the reality of an event is in itself. A moment's thought shows us that no one idea can in itself be sufficient. For every idea which finds its significance in each event must represent something which contributes to what realization is in itself" (*SMW* 93). If we cannot terminologically or conceptually locate the reality of things in a single representation of an individual unity, we cannot try to force the metaphysics to imply this singular location either. In other words, if we are warned of the self-transcendence of an entity beyond the confines of our conception of it as an individual, then we must admit that the metaphysical atomism being conveyed is prohibitive of our attempts to locate the being of things in overly monadic singular entities. We must consider individual entities only in the guise of their placement in the extensive continuum of entities. The "doctrine of the continuity of nature . . . balances and limits the doctrine of the absolute individuality of each occasion of experience" (*AI* 183).

The continuity of nature is predicated on the fact of reiteration of aesthetic achievement. Both the individualty of events and the massive unity of enduring objects emerge from the ultimate fact of creative realization of value via reiteration and adjustment. It is worth quoting Whitehead at length on this point:

> The endurance of things has its significance in the self-retention of that which imposes itself as a definite attainment for its own sake. That which endures is limited, obstructive, intolerant, infecting its environment with its own aspects. But is is not self-sufficient. The aspects of all things enter into its very nature. It is only itself as drawing together into its own limitation the larger whole in which it finds itself. Conversely it is only itself by lending its aspects to this same environment in which it finds itself. The problem of evolution is the development of enduring harmonies of enduring shapes of value, which merge into higher attainments of things beyond themselves. Aesthetic attainment is interwoven in the texture of realisation. (*SMW* 94)

If something is only itself in virtue of its location in future entities and its continuity and interwovenness with previous entities, then it can metaphysically only be conceived as thus 'ecstatic' in its being. The atomicity Whitehead wishes to preserve is the atomicity of aesthetic attainment, which we have seen is expressed in the concept of intensity of feeling via contrast. An individual existent is nothing other than the felt unity of aesthetic achievement. This aesthetic achievement is 'self-retentive,' 'infectious,' requiring for its very essence the presence, internal to it, of former aesthetic achievement. The concluding sentence of the passage just quoted, "Aesthetic attainment is *interwoven in* the texture of realization," must not be read, 'Aesthetic attainment is *woven into* the texture of realization,' as if realization were ontologically anything other than the aesthetic realization. The texture of realization is an interpenetrating atomism of aesthetic intensities. Only by clearly understanding the operations involved in aesthetic realization of value can we hope to understand atomism as proffered by Whitehead.

We must tenaciously stick with the vocabulary of aesthetic attainment, of realization as creative achievement of intensity, and avoid the tendency to view creativity, attainment, intensity, and so on, as *predicates of* the things that really exist (actual entities, construed as if they were something else besides the intensity of contrast achieved in a concrescence). Whitehead is fond of invoking Plato's phrase, "It never really is," in the attempt to describe the actual entity as a temporal atom (e.g., PR 82, 84, 85). The reason an entity can never be said to truly 'be' in the ordinary sense, despite the fact that it is an obstinately individual atom, is because of its curious double status as self-creator and transcendent creator, as subject-superject. Time is "perpetual perishing" because we cannot ascribe any spatiotemporal 'being' to an entity as if that were anything else than its internal relations to spatiotemporal atoms prior and subsequent to that entity, as if it were anything else than the intensity of feeling that borrows from and infects other intensities. Thus the superject, which is the satisfaction, is at once the "pragmatic" consequence of the entity and its internal conditions of aesthetic unity.

In elaborating on the Category of Subjective Intensity in regard to some operations typical of complex organisms (addressed in chapter four), Whitehead repeats in *Process and Reality* the conditions for aesthetic realization stated in *Religion in the Making,* already quoted, as to the process of realization involving reference to a ground and consequent. He repeats the claim that "an actual fact is a fact of aesthetic experience" and that "all aesthetic experience is feeling arising out of the realization of contrast under identity" (PR 280). Keeping to this identification of actuality and aesthetic attainment, we can analyze to good end some complex statements as to the status of satisfaction as the superjective nature of the entity. From a renewed analysis of satisfaction in light of its representation of aesthetic attainment (intensity), we can draw some conclusions regarding the ascription of existence, actuality, and being in Whitehead's atomism.

Quantitative Satisfaction

Whitehead identifies the satisfaction of an entity with its final quantitative intensity of feeling (PR 116), as we have already seen. The phrase "quantitative satisfaction" is used to convey the final intensity achieved in the unification of forms of feeling (ibid.). In this light, the individual being of an entity, which is in question in the present analysis, is represented as a determinate emotional quantity, the degree of presence and importance of the feelings unified as a subject. It is in this sense that the pair of terms, 'integrate' and 'integral', can be considered more than etymologically connected, as suggested earlier. Each occasion is an integral integration—its integral character is constituted by the integration effected, and the integration effected is influenced by the necessity that it be an integral becoming. In other words, the emergence of an entity as an individual being, or, to put it another way, the metaphysical identification of an individual entity, is in virtue of its specific satisfaction embodying a "tone of feeling" (PR 85). It is interesting to note that the identification of an individual is dependent upon its satisfaction, because this satisfaction is supposedly merely the consideration of the entity in terms of its consequences in other entities, or its pragmatic usefulness (ibid.). If the atomic individuality of a creative entity is indeterminate except in light of a consideration of its effectiveness as transcendent creator, any attempt to conceive of the agency and activity of an actuality without the prominence of the idea of its final and objectified quantum intensity is falsifying of its individuality. Can we make the sharp ontological distinction made by Kline if actuality$_1$ qua individuality requires the *simultaneous* recognition of actuality$_2$?

To address this question, let us read the following passage (noted earlier) in terms of the construal of a satisfaction as an quantum of emotional intensity:

> The notion of 'satisfaction' is the notion of the 'entity as concrete' abstracted from the 'process of concrescence'; it is the outcome separated from the process, thereby losing the actuality of the atomic entity, which is both process and outcome. 'Satisfaction' provides the individual element in the composition of an actual entity—that element which has led to the definition of substance as 'requiring nothing but itself in order to exist.' But the 'satisfaction' is the 'superject' rather than the 'substance' or the 'subject.' It closes up the entity; and yet is the superject adding its character to the creativity whereby there is a becoming of entities superseding the one in question. (PR 84)

We would expect, given many of Whitehead's own explanations of the process of concrescence, and the general tenor of the conceptualization characteristic of his commentators, that Whitehead would identify the factor of individuality of an entity with its subjectivity and not its "objectification" or what is here called its superject. If subjectivity is ontologically prior somehow, such that the actuality$_1$-actuality$_2$ distinction seems feasible, there would be no point in identifying the satisfaction as that in virtue of which an actuality has such significant ontological status as to be the reason for the mistaken concept of substance as "requiring nothing but itself in order to exist." Satisfaction conceived as a quantitative achievement of emotional intensity helps us unravel these difficulties.

Our first step must be to remove any substantializing of our conception of the "satisfaction" as some "thing." Satisfaction amounts to closure, the perishing of immediacy, the completion of creative unification (PR 85). It is an aspect of a process, and not of a thing. It is the manifestation of the process as having achieved a determinate quantity of emotional intensity that is fit for two roles: the prehensive unification of feelings imposing themselves as past actualities, and the transmission of feelings of determinate forms to a future partially determinate on the basis of the concrescence in question.

Private enjoyment is the emergent feature of these basically functional requirements. The entity meets the quantitative needs of creative realization at a determinate point. Its quantum organization of emotional tone (its intensity) is what is needed (though not fully determined) by the order in which it finds itself. Certain quantum arrangements of emotional valuation are necessary for the maintenance of any given environmental order, and necessary for that entity's own unique role in the spatiotemporal continuum.

The quantitative intensity of satisfaction of an entity will be revealed as reiterated in or provocative of subsequent intensities conforming to some extent to it. How it can and eventually does infect its environment by providing quantitative achievements of effective contrasts of relevant data is determinative of the subjective unity of the entity in the present. In other words, the pragmatic usefulness of the entity is as descriptive of its individual existence as the decisions of feeling whereby it came to embody useful forms of intensive order. "Pragmatic usefulness" does not amount to an adventure of a static product, but is revelatory of the full actuality that is both subject and superject. Satisfaction marks the "termination" of concrescence, but not necessarily the production of something called a "concretum," which exists at some other ontological level. The objectifications (in the form of reiterations or modifications) of the quantum intensity achieved by an actuality are part of its individual character, for it is the quantum intensity that is in question all along in its concrescence. The question before any entity is: how can a maximum of productive contrast be effected such that the emotional unity of feeling takes account of the full sweep of relevance of past and future? A certain quantity of emotional richness of feeling is required to be just that spatiotemporal locus of an ever-transcending creative process. That quantitative intensity achieved, as the individualization of creativity, exists so long as it is effectively embodied in subsequent actualities, and this existence will always be marked by the datability of the concrescence. This datability, however, does not mean "substantial independence" because spatiotemporal quanta are relative to and internally connected to each other in the scheme of extensive relatedness.

We cannot underestimate the role of quantum emotional intensity in determining the ultimate character, and therefore ontologically most significant sense of individuality, of an entity. The temptation to view an actual entity as agentive and as an individual existent only as considered in its concresence (as if disjoinable from its 'concrete' life) is possibly due to a misconstrual of what a "character" of an occasion of experience is. We are used to thinking of a character along the lines of a predicate belonging to a subject, this predication being localized in a subject that is usually construed to exist within fairly defined limits. But in Whitehead's atomism, the limits of individuality are established precisely by the *emergence* of character(s) as intensive patterns of emotional achievement. Moreover, that individuality of character is *present in* later entities, and is constructed on the basis of the *presence in it* of other entities' achieved intensive character. Much consideration of

Whitehead's system seems influenced by an abiding habit of seeking subjects to which important 'predicates' such as existence, agency, immediacy, and character may be attached. But the truly processive character of this atomism as expressed Whitehead's rejoinder, "It never really is," precludes such a search. My claim here is a systematic elaboration of the consequences of Whitehead's overall rejection of subject-predicate language and logic, and substance-accident metaphysics.

QUALITATIVE AND QUANTITATIVE PATTERN

The link between intensity and character (indeed, their identification) can be made clearer in light of a difficult passage in which Whitehead describes the two "factors" in the subjective form in which any feeling occurs. Subjective form is, as we have noted, that aspect of feeling whereby the unique character of an individual entity emerges. The two "factors" involved in subjective form are "its qualitative pattern and its pattern of intensive quantity" (PR 233). Now, we might be inclined to read this as a challenge to the view being forwarded here—that the character or qualitative achievement of an actuality is not the same as its intensive achievement. But this reading would imply that a "factor" is a "part" or "separate aspect" as if such parts or aspects were substantially separate from each other. Whitehead denies this: "But these two factors of pattern cannot wholly be considered in abstraction from each other. For the relative intensities of the qualitative elements in the qualitative pattern are among the relational factors which constitute that qualitative pattern." In other words, intensity characterizes the very qualitative pattern (of eternal objects brought under contrast) in virtue of the fact that the elements in the pattern are essentially relational; it is "*its* pattern of intensive quantity" and this is not something 'extra.' Meaningful arrangement thus always implies intensity. Whitehead continues: "Also conversely, there are qualitative relations among the qualitative elements and they constitute an abstract qualitative pattern for the qualitative relations." The intensities represented in the arranged (balanced) elements of the qualitative pattern constitute, as balanced in complexity, an "abstract" intensive pattern for the whole that enters into the very constitution of its elements as arranged. "The pattern of intensities," the passage goes on to say,

> is not only the variety of qualitative elements with such and such intensities; but it is also the variety of qualitative elements, as in such-and-such an abstract qualitative pattern, with such-and-such intensities. Thus the two patterns are not really separable. It is true that there is an abstract qualitative pattern, and an abstract intensive pattern; but in the fused pattern the abstract qualitative pattern lends itself to the intensities, and the abstract intensive pattern lends itself to the qualities. (PR 233)

It is only the "fused pattern" that "exists" in the sense of being something actual. The two abstract patterns are what abstract analysis may discern for the sake of explaining how the fused pattern can be said to be what it is, an intense qualitatively determinate feeling, an achieved "character." They are not the recourse to more primitive "parts" out of which actuality is constructed, but are simply considerations necessary in the description of the incurably atomic balanced complexity of feeling that any individual thing is. As parts these patterns (of eternal objects) exist only as factors in actuality; they have no status outside the determinations of actual entities in concrescence. An interesting example of what Whitehead is talking about here may be found in recent attempts to develop facial recognition software for security applications. Recognition of a face is not best accomplished by a computationally thick matching process, whereby face parts, or features, are compared to a standing inventory of possible ways in which such parts may be manifest. The software works much more effectively if designed to discern layers of *patterning among* various features. Features are most reliably found to belong to the individual whose features they are if the features are surveyed via a patterned network of patterned relations of various key points on the facial surface.

Returning to the description of the individuality or character of individuals as "ecstatic," we can gain insight as to the facility of conception made possible through the language of intensity by drawing the implications of Whitehead's continued discussion of subjective form, which follows his comments as to the fusion of quality and intensity.

> [The] subjective form cannot be absolutely disjoined [read: 'is not ontologically disjoined'] from the pattern of the objective datum. Some elements of the subjective form can be thus disjoined; and they form the subjective form as in abstraction from the patterns of the objective datum [considered in abstraction for the sake of noting the occurrence of change in creative orders]. But the full subjective form cannot be abstracted from the pattern of the objective datum. The intellectual disjunction is not a real separation. Also the subjective form, amid its own original elements, always involves reproduction of the pattern of the objective datum. (PR 233)

The *pattern* of the objective datum, or better, the pattern that the objective datum *is*, is internal to, constitutive of, the subjective form (patterned, balanced complexity) of feeling in a concrescent entity. In other words, the subjective form *is* to a great extent the pattern of the objective datum, as repeated or reiterated in this spatiotemporal quantum. The intensity characterizing the subjective form of feeling in a concrescent subject ontologically overlaps with (though is not exhausted by) the intensity of its objective datum. The disjunction is "intellectual," not "real."

CRYPTOSUBSTANTIALISM AND THE SUBJECT-SUPERJECT

To return to our purposes of conceiving Whitehead's atomism as a description of entities that are equally subject-superject, concrescence and satisfaction, we can advance a defense of this atomism against the charge of cryptosubstantialism. I contend that the effort to attach ontological status to anything in the Whiteheadian system—objective datum, satisfaction, subjective form, feeling, character, actuality, and so on—as if anything else were being discussed except the achievement of aesthetic intensity, will inevitably produce a picture of Whiteheadian atomism as cryptosubstantialist, when in fact such an effort is itself the cryptosubstantialism infecting the subject matter with its presuppositions about the nature of individuality. Whitehead is not wholly innocent of this tendency, to be sure. But it is the difficulty of expressing, in the language available, the novelty of insight achieved in the organic philosophy that leads him to engage in such explanatory indiscretions. The spirit of the system, wherein Creativity is the Category of the Ultimate, demands a reconstruction of its explanations in light of its core insights and principles. The principles all refer to the attainment of balanced complexity of feeling, expressible as intensity. If the entities whose individuality we are concerned to accord ontological status to are nothing but their intensity of feeling, and this intensity is not substantially separate from the intensities reiterated from the "past," then we must find a way to speak of ontological status that does not sunder concrescence and concretum, actuality$_1$ and actuality$_2$.

Just as the intensity of an occasion, or to be consistent with what was just claimed, the intensity that *is* an occasion of experience, includes the intensities of past occasions, we can make analogous claims as to the status of the satisfaction considered as the usefulness of the entity in a concrescence beyond itself. Its intensity will be repeated, reiterated as the objective datum that is a large factor in the intensity of that subsequent occasion. That repetition will include, indeed is, a reference to the former concrescence as an individuality, because the intensity incorporated is a contrast and not merely a relation. This expands our understanding of the doctrine of reiteration that was merely hinted at in chapters one and two, as one of the essential aspects of an entity's appropriation of the past, and quest for intensity of feeling in its future. The "completion" of an entity in its satisfaction says as much about the subject's status in things that transcend the subject entity, insofar as they are the appropriators of the intensity of that satisfaction, as it does about the concrescence itself; otherwise the claims that the entity *is* subject-superject are mere hyperbole. The satisfaction of any entity thus must be construed on the analogy of that entity's inclusion of other satisfactions in its self-constitution. To paraphrase a claim made earlier, the being of an entity extends forward and backward in the present becoming that constitutes that being—it is "ecstatic."

It is my position that an overattention to the claim for uniqueness made on behalf of every entity has obscured just what is to be achieved via that uniqueness and subjectivity, such that a misconstrual of what ontology could possibly mean in this atomic, organic philosophy is common in the critical literature. The question of the unique nature of ontology in a Whiteheadian vein affords us entry into a discussion of the work of Ivor Leclerc, who is credited with having tidied up Whitehead's messy claims about being, but whose perspective requires revision given the conclusions at which we have just arrived.

Being, Actuality, and Derivative Actuality

Ivor Leclerc is unsatisfied with Whitehead's atomism in light of its failure to accord acceptable ontological status to the kinds of substances encountered macrocosmically—the enduring objects purported by Whitehead to be somehow composed of more primitive ephochal entities or events. In this context, Whitehead is to be seen as an exemplification of certain pernicious trends in the scientific mentality that *Science and the Modern World* sought to repudiate: that which saw physical bodies, macrocosmic substances, as composites of more basically real atoms. The metaphysics of this mentality "is that the ultimate physical existent or substance in the strict sense of the term is to be identified with the final constituents, and that consequently no compound entity can be a substance."[16]

On this view, the existence of a large-scale substance such as is ordinarily encountered in the natural world—a lamp, a tree, a human—is derivative from the existence of the more fundamental atomic constituents. This, in Leclerc's view, strips them of the ontological status that it appears should attend them as unitary substances. Conceived as "mere aggregates," which they must be on any view that ascribes existence strictly to atomic components, they are deficiently substantive and their unity is insufficiently accounted for. The problem is, "that we have the conception of a group which has a particular character as that group, with a group structure and behavior which is something over and above and not reducible to the individual characters of the constituents. For there is nothing in the concept of material atoms whereby a togetherness of atoms in a group in a particular pattern or structure should result in a particular character of the group."[17] Leclerc finds contemporary science, Leibniz's metaphysical theory of mutually adjusted monads, and Whitehead's metaphysics of atomic process equally unable to accommodate the obvious unity of composite substances. His critique of Whitehead, if examined in terms of the concept of intensity as fundamental to Whiteheadian ontology, is unfounded and the unity he quite rightly wishes to protect for the sake of both metaphysics and common sense is very much available within atomism if conceived along the lines being developed here.

In Whitehead's view, a composite substance of the kind Leclerc wishes to include with more than a derivative status in an ontology is to be construed, generally, as a society of occasions. A society, as we have seen previously, is an ordered genetic relationship among actual entities such that there is significant retention of characteristic forms of definiteness. It is more than a "class" of entities in virtue of the factor of genetic derivation of some members from others (PR 89). The prehension of fellow members of a society by concrescent members of a society accounts for the retention of the dominant characteristics of that society.

Leclerc's objection is raised in regard to the very nature of prehension. The characteristic of prehension, that it is a realization in a subject entity of some feature(s) of entities elsewhere in space-time, precludes the possibility of a macrocosmic substance being any more than an aggregate, for the perspective on the whole society is always a question of the subjective, individual experience of a singular actuality. On Leclerc's reading, which is an instance of what I have used Kline's analysis to identify regarding the conception of "actuality" prevalent in Whitehead studies, inheritance from one actuality to another does not prevent the unity of the society from being relegated to the status of an aggregate with merely derivative being, and a derivative being without the unity critical to the aggregate as an enduring object. "In Whitehead's theory the act of feeling of the felt actual entity is strictly over when it becomes the object of the feeling of the prehending actual entity. Thus that the feelings are conformal does not suffice to render the constituent actual entities any less existentially separate than are Leibniz's monads. . . . [T]he conformity of the feelings . . . does not effect the point about the existential separateness of the constituents."[18]

Leclerc's objection is not decisive against Whitehead's view for three reasons: First, Whitehead's view of societies is more robust than Leclerc acknowledges; second, Leclerc does not take into account the full thrust of the meaning and function of what I am calling intensive re-enaction; and, third, underlying the first two reasons, the objection involves a misconstrual of the individuality of actualities, though one that is certainly understandable given Whitehead's texts. Let me begin my analysis of these three points by looking at how they are manifest in the very passages cited by Leclerc as descriptive of the process of feeling or prehension. The passages appealed to state fundamental facts about the nature of conformal feeling in concrescence: "A 'physical feeling' is . . . the feeling of another actuality" (PR 225); "a simple physical feeling is one feeling which feels another feeling" (PR 236), which (Leclerc notes) Whitehead explains via the idea that "the subjective form of a physical feeling is re-enaction of the subjective form of the feeling felt" (PR 237). Leclerc concludes from these statements that the nature of prehension amounts only to being "an item within the prehending actual entity," and means by this the ontological denuding of what is prehended and the society constructed in virtue of such prehensions.[19]

Much dispute has occurred over the second of these passages cited from Whitehead, the claim asserting that a feeling in a concrescence feels another feeling. Kline, Leclerc, Christian, and others agree that "feeling" is an act in the becoming of an actuality, and that strictly speaking it can exist only in a present occasion.[20] Therefore, a feeling cannot be said to feel another "feeling," because the felt actuality is no longer in act. What is felt is an objectification, a satisfaction, a "dead" datum (PR 164).[21] An ontological gap is posited between (to use Kline's mode of expression) an actuality$_1$ that feels, and an actuality$_2$ or concretum that can only *be felt* but which by definition *does not feel*. The only "feeling" and therefore active existence belongs to the present feeler, on this view. Indeed, it is Leclerc's general position that not only do macrocosmic substances have derivative existence, but so do past actualities as prehended in what are the only true agents of becoming, present actual entities.[22] As far as the question of ontological status is concerned, this puts him in agreement with Kline and therefore open to the objections stated against that view in the previous section.

In my view, one can consistently claim that a feeling feels another feeling, because all any feeling *is*, is an achieved intensity of contrast, and because a component of any present feeling is its determinate re-enaction (and, of course modification) of determinate intensities markedly external. Indeed, this is Whitehead's explanation of the third claim cited by Leclerc about "the subjective form of the feeling felt." Let us look at the entire passage from which that quote is taken:

> Apart from inhibitions or additions, weakenings or intensifications, due to the history of its production, the subjective form of a physical feeling is re-enaction of the subjective form of the feeling felt. Thus the cause passes on its feeling to be reproduced by the new subject as its own, and yet as inseparable from the cause. There is a flow of feeling. But the re-enaction is not perfect. The categoreal demands of the concrescence require adjustments of the pattern of emotional intensities. The cause is objectively in the constitution of the effect, in virtue of being the feeler of the feeling reproduced in the effect with partial equivalence of subjective form [emotional intensity]. Also the cause's feeling has its own objective datum, and its own initial datum. Thus this antecedent initial datum has now entered into the datum of the effect's feeling at second-hand through the mediation of the cause. (PR 237, emphasis added)

Regardless of degree of re-enaction, the intensity of any satisfied actuality is present in subsequent prehending actualities; it is either total conformation, which is largely the case in inanimate natural objects, or partial conformation, the realization of "aspects" of the castle, the lamp, and so on, with significant regard, via the structure of negative prehensions, for what has been deviated from. An intensity, whether perfectly or imperfectly re-enacted, is prehended as belonging to a subject that is in the causal "past" of the prehending actuality. "The reason why the cause is objectively in the effect is that the cause's feeling [intensity] cannot, as a feeling, be abstracted from its subject which is the cause" (ibid.). The importance of this passage for a resolution of Leclerc's difficulty is evident in the next sentence: "This passage of the cause into the effect is the cumulative character of time. The irreversibility of time depends on this character."[23]

The unity of a society required by Leclerc to account for macrocosmic substances depends upon the cumulative character of time. Leclerc underestimates the importance of this concept because, I contend, of the underappreciation of the significance of intensive re-enaction to Whitehead's ontology. Also, the very nature of a society is thereby compromised, as stated earlier. Let us return to our examination of "societies" such that the cumulative character of time as re-enaction of subjective form (intensity of feeling) can be better understood.

I noted in chapter one that it is the significance of societies that they are procurative of intensity in their component entities, and that the procuration of this intensity is necessary for the maintenance of the order and intensity required for that society; the processes involved feed into each other. Whitehead admits that the entire notion of "order," which I see as so significant to the doctrine of intensity of feeling (based on the narrowness, width, triviality, and vagueness achieved in the valuation of data, and requiring the four "grounds of order" discussed earlier) in actual entities is more usually used in regard to the arrangements of actual entities in what are properly viewed as societies. This "derivative" (not different) sense of "order" is a question of the achievement and maintenance (through transmission of feeling, inheritance) of intensities.

A "set of entities is a society (i) in virtue of a 'defining characteristic' [determinate intensity] shared by its members, and (ii) in virtue of the presence of the defining characteristic being due to the environment provided by the society itself" (PR 89). Leclerc's misplacement of emphasis stems from an underestimation of the importance and implication of the second part of this definition of society. The individual entities of a society would not have the intensities they do without the massiveness of emphasis provided by the collective of entities in genetic relationship. In other words, the society provides the environment that is procurative of the desired intensity. The inheritance of feeling has a cumulative result that defies Leclerc's characterization of the society as a mere aggregate. The society's contribution is cumulative in two senses, each of which has to do with the achievement of intensity of feeling. The first sense is that the possibility of prehension of the components of the actual world that form the society in question is by reason of their compatibility for contrast; an identical intensity will not obstruct and thereby attenuate itself. Thus there is real inclusion of multiple elements (actualities) that proffer the same intensity. The integral intensity achieved is massive in regard to both the real diversity of entities therein represented and in the absence of much necessity for negative prehensions. The second sense in which the society's contribution is cumulative is that, by the Category of Transmutation, a shared characteristic will be attributed to a nexus as a real unity, by the concrescing entity. This will also produce a massiveness of feeling that is more than an acknowledgment of a multiplicity, as Leclerc's thesis as to the "aggregative" nature of a society implies. As asserted earlier, entities do enjoy a feeling of a social order as a structured geometry of intensities reflected throughout the constituent members.

To understand fully how a society is not a mere aggregate, consider the circumstances under which social order is maintained. Each actual entity really includes, via repetition and structuring according to the conditions of intensity, its entire past actual world, in this instance under forms of dominant intensities repeatedly transmitted. It also provides, in its present, for the real possibility of its re-enaction in future actualities. In any given present moment in which we might consider a macrocosmic object (keeping in mind of course that no such absolute moment of consideration exists), the actualities that are "contemporaneous" at that moment all inherit the intensities achieved in their pasts and provide for the intensities to be achieved in their futures. The actual worlds objectified exhibit important similarity of intensities in respect to the defining characteristic being maintained, and in virtue of the fact that the actual worlds of entities comprising the social order of an enduring object contain by and large the same entities with only minor variation. Given the cumulative character of time as established via the presence of causes in their effects, the macrocosmic object is guaranteed ontological unity. Thus actualities in their feeling of their actual worlds, particularly in social orders, are engaged in a process that is "the cumulation of the universe and not a stage play about it" (PR 237).[24]

It is also to be remarked that the attempt to ascribe ontological status primarily to enduring objects is a philosophical perspective that Whitehead's philosophy of organism rejects as a starting point. It runs just as much risk of the "Fallacy of Misplaced Concreteness" as does the ascription of true reality to the abstract entities of science or philosophy. Of course Leclerc is rightly concerned with just what status they *do* have, given Whitehead's ontology. The response to this question is that they have enough status (via the massive re-enaction of the intensities required to be that object, that is, that form of massively inherited order) to be an enduring unity, but not so much that change becomes accidental to its being.

Leclerc's underappreciation of the operations of societies in Whitehead's scheme is tied to his (and others') more general view of the ontological status of individuals. To be sure, Whitehead's position is that actual entities in their processes of concrescence are the fundamentally real things or *res verae* in the universe (PR 18, 166); that "apart from the experiences of subjects there is nothing, nothing, nothing, bare nothingness" (PR 167). But it is simply not the case that an actual entity exists in ontological isolation or even radical separation from its predecessors or successors, for its is nothing other than the reiteration and modification of the aesthetic order pulsing creatively as the universe considered as a solidarity of the *res verae* (ibid.). It is in this sense that we are to understand Whitehead's claims as to how actual entities are impersonations (PR 237) or qualifications (PR 88) of the creativity that is the ultimate fact about the universe (PR 21).

The view adhered to in the established interpretation of Whitehead, to represent which I have explored in depth the positions of Kline and Leclerc, seems to me a direct repudiation of Whitehead's statement as to the nature of his scheme as a reversion to a pre-Kantian mode of thought (PR xi) whereby radical subjectivism is avoided. In my view, the typical reading of the subjective immediacy of actual entities as being the sole locus of ultimate ontological status turns Whitehead's scheme into one in which an actual, objective world must be derived in some subsidiary way from the experience of subjects. But this was not Whitehead's vision of his "reformed subjectivism" (PR 157).

> The philosophy of organism is the inversion of Kant's philosophy. *The Critique of Pure Reason* describes the process by which subjective data pass into the appearance of an objective world. The philosophy of organism seeks to describe how objective data pass into subjective satisfaction, and how order in the objective data provides intensity in the subjective satisfaction. For Kant, the world emerges from the subject; for the philosophy of organism, the subject emerges from the world—a 'superject' rather than a 'subject.' (PR 88)

Whitehead's atomic realism is, despite its atomicity, "communitarian" in the sense that any individual being is an individual only as engaged in a "community of common activity [achievement of aesthetic intensity] involving mutual implication [reiteration, derivation, objectification]" (PR 79).

Creativity and the Ontology of Atomism

The view expounded in this chapter, relying as heavily as it does on the notion of objectification, could be said to lean inordinately far in the direction of emphasizing those aspects of Whitehead's scheme that deal with "transition" as opposed to those aspects particularly important in "concrescence." This objection would imply that there is some weight to the thesis that transition and concrescence refer to two different processes, or two discrete phases of a single process. On the contrary, I take these two aspects of Whitehead's discussion simply to be the tracing of what it is necessary to ascribe to the one process of actualization alternately considered as transition and concrescence. It is hoped that the presentation thus far has established good grounds for maintaining that the kinds of causality allegedly represented in the "two" kinds of process need not be distinguished as radically as Whitehead himself does at times. The rejection of a two-process interpretation of Whitehead's scheme is premised on the understanding of ontology whereby there is no existence ascribable to anything except in terms of the achievement of aesthetic complexity of emotional detail, or intensity of subjective form. Those factors in the scheme that seem to point to two kinds of causality must be interpreted in light of how they explicate the one existentially unitary task of actualization, to realize intensities. Tensions amid elements of the scheme arise as tensions of explication, and not ontology, on this view.

The emphasis placed here on the actualization of intensity, the creative achievement of balanced complexity of temporally cumulative detail, might be said to be in line with William Garland's thesis as to the "ultimacy of creativity" in Whitehead's scheme.[25] Garland aims his analysis at a repudiation of Christian's thesis that "creativity" is not one of Whitehead's final metaphysical categories, that it is ultimately to be spoken of primarily in terms of "statements about the concrescences of actual entities," because actual entities are the final realities explicated in the Categories of Explanation, Categories of Existence, and Categoreal Obligations.[26] Garland claims, on the contrary, that "creativity" is, among other things, the ultimate principle behind both transition and concrescence.[27] Garland's view, however, on the level at which it describes what is going on metaphysically in the universe, shares in some of the notions that I have argued thus far require revision. It presupposes a substantive distinction between transition and concrescence, such that creativity is the urge toward self-creation in the latter, and the receptacle of what becomes in the former.[28]

An ontological gap is introduced between things considered as objective and things considered as subjective. The contention is forwarded that "transition processes must occur if we are to have any new processes of concrescence, for the past must be transcended in order for new actual entities to arise."[29] Transition is treated as a preparatory process to the eventual becoming of new actualities. Garland cites *Process and Reality* 85, a text usually cited in favor of viewing transition as a process somehow different from concrescence proper. "The process of concrescence terminates with the attainment of a fully *determinate* 'satisfaction'; and the creativity thereby passes over into the 'given' primary phase for the concrescence of other actual entities." Garland stops quoting here, but Whitehead continues, as we have already seen in discussing this passage earlier, "This transcendence is thereby established when there is attainment of *determinate* 'satisfaction' completing the antecedent entity. Completion is the perishing of immediacy: 'It never really is.'" Whitehead's text then continues into a discussion of the satisfaction of an actual entity as its pragmatic usefulness in transcending entities, beginning with the notion that no entity can be conscious of its own satisfaction.

In light of the view being advanced here, certain aspects of this description of transition stand to the fore. Notice, first, that "transcendence [in virtue of which there is transition (PR 85)] is . . . *established when* there is attainment . . . completing the antecedent entity" (emphasis added). The occurrence of transcendence of one entity by another is simultaneous with the completion of the entity superceded. The transcendence is considered in this passage from the perspective of the transcending actuality, such that the objectified entity is described as "antecedent." The satisfaction is very much a question of the appropriation of the completed entity by its successors. Thus the discussion of the "usefulness" of the entity and the impossibility of the entity's own consciousness of its satisfaction that follows this passage. If this is the case, then there is no perspective from which transition may be conceived as a separate process from concrescence, because transition is, on this view of the satisfaction, simply the view of the past from the perspective of a concrescent entity.

But because this process of appropriation is also describable from the perspective of the past entity, it appears at times from Whitehead's discussions as if transition were a "transitional process" (readers will please excuse the redundancy) between concrescences. Thus Garland writes that "In transition creativity receives the actual entities which have already achieved satisfaction and gives them to new actual entities as initial data which again demand unification" (229). This statement is a view of transition considered from the perspective of a present entity that is to lend itself to the transcendent creativity of the universe of actualities beyond itself. From the perspective of this entity it might indeed be posed as necessary that something "receive" the satisfaction that they might be "given" to future entities not yet existent. But it is a view based in part on an idea repudiated by Whitehead, that the initial situation of any actuality is a "welter of unsynthesized data" (229) that must be brought under unity solely through the agency of the new subject coming to be. Although it is true that unification is the aegis of subjective becoming, it is not true that the initial datum possesses no unity *until* such togetherness is effected by the novel agency of the new entity. It retains the unity of the satisfied entities contributing to it, and the unity effected by and in the subsequent concrescence *just is* the factual "togethering" that is purportedly performed by the "creativity" on Garland's (and Nobo's) view.

Whitehead describes his "reformed subjectivism" as a departure from Kant's view of the "datum" of experience as a mere unorganized flux of sensations that achieve unity solely on the basis of the construction of the subject (PR 72, 113, 248). In Whitehead's atomism, an individual emerges as a unique experient subject appropriating an actual world possessed of compelling order. It is the subjective experience of intensities achieved elsewhere, with a recognition of present intensity as genetically derived from, though not *fully* determined by, those intensities realized elsewhere. Nothing must be "given" for in being a potential the actualities of the past—those aesthetic patterns that are "elsewhere"—are in fact already objectified in the transcendent world—the "here" of concrescence. To repeat the claim argued earlier, the occurrence of transcendence of one entity by another is simultaneous with the completion of the entity superceded. This is the essence of "vibratory" existence, to which I have given the label "ecstatic" so as to be expressive of the ontological unity of all of the "vibrations" referable to the intensity of "an" actuality.

Intensive and Extensive Quantity: Some Historical Considerations

It is necessary at this point to pause in the programmatic argument being developed, in order to understand certain historical influences that did or may have contributed to Whitehead's development of the concept of intensity as expressive of something fundamental about reality. These historical insights do contribute to the understanding of Whitehead's scheme being developed via the arguments forwarded thus far.

A DISPUTE WITH KANT

We now reintroduce Kant as a foil for explicating Whitehead's conception of his own atomism. In *Science And The Modern World*, Whitehead cites two texts from Kant's *Critique of Pure Reason* concerning quantities, and puts their contrast to service in the explication of the epochal theory of time he (Whitehead) is trying to develop. The first text is from "The Axioms of Intuition" and concerns "extensive quantity." What Kant calls an extensive quantity is "that in which the representation of the whole is rendered possible by the representation of its parts, *and therefore necessarily preceded by it*" (emphasis Whitehead's). Thus just as the conception of any whole line requires the drawing of its successive segments in imagination, "the same applies to every, even the smallest, portion of time. I can only think in it the successive progress from one moment to another, thus producing in the end, by all the portions of time, and their addition, a definite quantity of time."[30] What is asserted is the divisibility of extensive quanta, in the sense that the whole is constructed of its parts, and therefore in some sense derivative from them, qua temporal.

The second passage, from "The Anticipations of Perception," asserts the opposite about intensive magnitudes.[31] Whitehead quotes, "This peculiar property of quantities that no part of them is the smallest possible part (no part indivisible) is called continuity. Time and space are quanta continua, because there is no part of them that is not enclosed between limits (points and moments), *no part that is not itself again a space or a time. Space consists of spaces only, time of times. Points and moments are only limits*, mere places of limitation, and as places *presupposing always* those intuitions that they are meant to limit or determine. Mere places or parts that might be given before space or time, could never be compounded into space or time."[32] This statement concerns the indivisibility of intensive magnitudes, those that "can be apprehended only as a unity."[33] No part-whole juxtaposition is possible for intensive quanta; in this case, the whole renders the parts possible.

Whitehead holds that, if we are concerned with Zeno's paradox as to the impossibility of time and movement given the infinite divisibility of portions of spaces and times, these two extracts are inconsistent (if taken concurrently to represent the character of space-time). A "vicious infinite regress is involved" if every portion of time requires first that some portion of itself be traversed. Whitehead opts for the view of the second passage, which accords with the relativity of atomic space-time positions he is developing in the chapter in question.

> I accept the later, and reject the earlier, passage. Realisation is the becoming of time in the field of extension. Extension is the complex of events, *qua* their potentialities. In realisation the potentiality becomes actuality. But the potential pattern requires a duration; and the duration must be exhibited as an epochal whole, by the realisation of the pattern. . . . Temporalisation is realisation. Temporalisation is not another continuous process. It is an atomic succession. (SMW 126)

If taken as a commentary on Kant, this juxtaposition of passages and the conclusion drawn from them, that they are fundamentally inconsistent with each other, constitutes, according to George Lucas, a misrepresentation of Kant made to Whitehead's own end (the justification of an epochal theory of time). On Lucas's view, the passages are not mutually inconsistent, for, despite what Whitehead might take the passages to imply, "Kant is at pains to show here that there is a marked difference between the way pure space and time are conceived *a priori* in intuition, and the way that spatial and temporal *objects* are necessarily perceived in actual experience."[34]

Although it is true that the status of the two passages differs in Kant's analysis in just the manner remarked by Lucas, Whitehead is not merely being careless in the midst of constructing his own alternative. Lucas sees this instance of Whitehead's appropriation of Kant as symptomatic of a wider tendency on Whitehead's part to be vague, unsystematic, and inaccurate in his understanding of Kant.[35] In the case of the fundamental characterization of space-time at stake in this dispute, however, Whitehead's reading of Kant goes right to the heart of the distinction between the two systems.

The distinction between the offices of the Axioms of Intuition and the Anticipations of Perception does not eliminate the mistake Whitehead is at pains to underline and repudiate. Although the Axioms concern the pure conditions for the possibility of objects and the Anticipations concern the conditions for the empirical apprehension of objects, the two principles nonetheless render categoreal both characterizations of time. Whitehead's objection is to the very categoreal status of *any* construal of time as extensive, particularly if this status concerns the preconditions of any experience. Whitehead applauds Kant in many places on the basis of his insight into the nature of experience as a synthetic construction. But in this instance, one of the conditions of such construction involves a primordial mischaracterization of the nature of space-time. Space and time in themselves do not contain extensive quantities (as really divisible portions) in Whitehead's atomism, except in virtue of the actual relations of temporally epochal events of realization, and even then what is present are extensive *relations* that may be measured by quantities, but not extensive quantities as the ground of the relations. Extensive *quantity* is not a condition that an experience must obey, but is a condition that emerges from and in the experience of actualities. There are no minimal or even infinitesimal or, in general, *any* extensive units at the base of space or time. I will return to the notion of extensive "relations" later.

In *Process and Reality* Whitehead reiterates his criticism of Kant on this point, in a way that helps clarify what is going on in the *Science and the Modern World* text. In a discussion of the nature of physical measurement, he repudiates the notion of an infinitesimal integral of distance out of which units of distance to be used in measurement are constructed. I here quote the passage at length, for it serves at once as an illustration of his problem with Kant, and as a clue as to the genesis of the notion of intensity in Whitehead's scheme, to which we will presently turn. As to the basis of measurement,

> There is no systematic theory possible, since the so-called 'infintesimal' distance depends on the actual entities throughout the environment. The only way of expressing such so-called distance is to make use of the presupposed geometrical measurements [of the Einsteinian method of finding constants expressive of relations among positions of actualities]. The mistake arises because, unconsciously, the minds of physicists are infected by a presupposition which comes down from Aristotle through Kant. Aristotle placed 'quantity' among his categories, and did not distinguish between extensive quantity and intensive quantity. Kant made the distinction, but considered both of them as categoreal notions. It follows from Cayley's and von Staudt's work that extensive quantity is a construct. . . . Further, the fact is neglected that there are no infinitesimals, and that a comparison of finite segments is thus required. For this reason, it would be better—so far as explanation is con-

cerned—to abandon the term 'distance' for this integral, and to call it by some such name as 'impetus,' suggestive of its physical import. (PR 332–33)

Kant's general mistake is the categoreal characterization of space-time quanta as extensive in any sense except that derivative of the intensive quantities realized by actualities (cf. PR 97). Any conceptualization of the quantitative aspects of spatiotemporal relatedness or character of experience is derivative from the intensive pattern of aesthetic achievement, the complex but continuous, or integral, quantity achieved in actualization.

THE MATHEMATICAL ORIGINS OF THE CONCEPT OF INTENSITY

Whitehead's rejection of a physical infinitesimal on which might be based a geometric primitive for the purposes of measuring or explaining the physical universe is a clue in addressing the question of how intensity came to have the status it does in his system. Also, it marks a point of contact between the theory of extension and the theory of concrescence, and analogously, the connection of genetic and coordinate division. The latter point shall be addressed in the following chapter. Here we pause to investigate the concept of intensity as it came to be the cornerstone of Whitehead's categoreal scheme.

The reference to the work of Cayley and von Staudt in the earlier quotation bespeaks the mathematical origins of Whitehead's metaphysical concept of quantity as primarily intensive.[36] The first appearance of "intensity" in Whitehead's work is in the very early *Universal Algebra* (1898), wherein Whitehead attempts to establish the unity of the many mathematical systems that were in process of proliferating, via a mathematical theory of the general abstract relations of non-physical, mathematical spaces. Granville Henry explains that "A generalized concept of space is an abstraction from many areas of mathematics, and hence has an applicability to those areas of mathematics that in themselves have no apparant relationship to the 'spaciness of space.'"[37] But Whitehead's efforts in this work bespeak his difficulty in leaving off completely the intuitive content of geometry in the attempt to frame an abstract grounding for any mathematical scheme whatsoever (e.g., UA 12). Henry notes that Whitehead typically manifests the conviction that "there is always some ontological content corresponding to mathematical reality."[38] Henry's analysis of the general task of *A Treatise on Universal Algebra* is helpful, but certain details of the treatise itself are of peculiar interest here. To my knowledge, no one has investigated the presence of "intensity" in *A Treatise on Universal Algebra* as it might be brought to bear on the development of Whitehead's metaphysical thought. The concept of intensity is introduced in the volume as a fundamental principle in the abstract rendering of the modes of togetherness of elements of positional manifolds. Whitehead describes his treatise as engaging the ongoing struggle to imaginatively construct workable conceptions of "originals" (*UA* 12), and intensity is offered as one of the most necessary notions in such a construction. Our questions as to the status of Whitehead's primary entities may be to some small extent illuminated by the notion of intensity as set forth in *A Treatise on Universal Algebra*.

Whitehead writes: "The properties of a positional manifold will be easily identified with the descriptive properties of Space of any number of dimensions, to the exclusion of all metrical properties" (*UA* 119). Whitehead is working with the most abstract notion of the general properties of spatiality and spatial relations (because these are positional manifolds), and proceeds to assert that "Each thing . . . involves a quantity special to it, to be called its intensity. The special characteristic of intensity is that in general a thing is absent when the intensity is zero, and is never absent unless the intensity is zero" (*UA* 119–20). The presence or absence of an element in a manifold (note the ontological overtones) is linked to its quantitative intensity. The existential presence of something is being established on the grounds of a notion of "degree," such that any quality possessed by a thing will vary according to that particular thing's degree of manifestation of that quality (*UA* 121). But as the quantitative measure attaching to the qualitative character of a thing, intensity is yet considered a "secondary property" of things, quality being here seen as more fundamental (*UA* 121).[39]

We have seen that by the time of the mature articulation of the system in *Process and Reality,* quality is no longer seen as more fundamental than quantity; the two aspects have parity as referring to the same existential conditions in an entity. But the continuity between the very early *Treatise on Universal Algebra* and the mature *Process and Reality* is the establishment of a notion of "degree" as expressive of something critical to the (internal) constitution of any thing that presents itself in some locus in a manifold of things. An analogy between the idea of "intensity of feeling" and this basic concept of degree of presence is not farfetched.

The precise terminology of "intensity" disappears from Whitehead's writings between *Universal Algebra* and the passages in *Science and the Modern World* to which I referred in noting Whitehead's departure from Kant on the concept of quantity in general. But the thought, we might say, behind the notion of "degree" implicit in the idea of intensity (as the concept of the degree coordinate to the presence of some object) is developed tenaciously in these intervening writings. For the concept of degree is essentially comparative. In his early philosophical writings, Whitehead is at pains to develop a theory of nature and knowledge of nature based not on the ontology and mathematics of scientific materialism, but on the comparison of spatiotemporal events in their aspects of spatiality, temporality (together, their extensity or duration), quality, and so on. Although the doctrine of intensity as the ontological expression of the essentially comparative character of metaphysical entities is undeveloped, the modes of thought out of which such a concept could be regenerated from a more purely metaphysical and less purely mathematical perspective were fully engaged. In addition, the intervening works concentrate heavily on the development of the concept of "value," also fundamentally comparative in its nature (noncomparative value, as noted, is not value but irrelevant chaos). It is my conjecture that in the early metaphysical works the theory of extension converged with the theory of value as to produce in the mature system the theory of intensive subjectivity belonging to internally related atomic actualities, difficult to pluck out of process, but necessary to hypothesize.

One of the critical achievements in the early works is the development of the notion of extensive abstraction, whereby, among other things, the geometrically central concept of a "point" could be defined on the basis of comparison of events, or as a limit in a group of abstractive sets. This conception of a mathematical point could be generalized to a conception of points of space and time. The "abstractive elements" that would qualify as such "points" of space or time "must in some sense exhibit a convergence to an absolute minimum of intrinsic character" (*CN* 85, 103). From this definition of points and the other basic geometrical entities such as straight lines and volumes that could likewise be conceived on this model of ideal limits of abstractive sets, an entire theory of natural explanation and measurement could be generated.

Whitehead's eventual theory of extension as expressed in *Process and Reality* shares this agenda. The goal is to express in purely formal terms the character of extensive relationship without the introduction of fundamental extensive quanta.[40] Thus the extensive relationships actually achieved by concrete entities could be established, and measurement (science) grounded, without recourse to a metaphysics of extensive quantities either open to Zeno's objections or reductive of the contents of the natural world.

PROJECTIVE GEOMETRY AND THE CONCEPTION OF INDIVIDUALITY

The critical principle arrived at in Whitehead's early work is a repudiation of the absolute individuality of events in nature: "An isolated event is not an event, because every event is a factor in a larger whole and is significant of that whole" (*CN* 142). The connection between this insight, the critique of Kant's conception of quantity as applied to space and time, the reference to Cayley and von Staudt, and the rejection of infinitesimal quantities depends upon the repudiation of any substantialist or Euclidean or Newtonian conceptualization of unitary elements in nature. There is no such thing as a completely individual event in the sense of an existent possessed of determinate and conceivable boundaries. There is no sense in which space and time as such are subject to extensive quantity, which seems to be the implicit assumption made in the conception of a completely individual event, except on the basis of the *intensive* reality of actual events. With a discussion of the significance of Cayley and von Staudt, and the rejection of mathematical or physical infinitesimals we may bring this historical discussion into greater focus. We can then rejoin the discussion with Kant by theorizing on a critical aspect of the period between Whitehead's early theories and the construction of the scheme of *Process and Reality*.

The mathematics of projective geometry were established by Arthur Cayley, with supplementation by Karl von Staudt, in the mid to late-nineteenth century. Like Whitehead in *Universal Algebra,* projective geometers sought to establish a science of geometry of such generality that any other geometry could be derived as a special case of the general scheme. (Methodologically, this has much in common with Whitehead's conception of metaphysics.) Thus, the "extensive" quanta with which we are ordinarily familiar in the arena of measurement, and with which our ontological conception of the "being" of spatiotemporal entities is infected, are simply constructs established on the basis of more general geometrical relations having to do, given the findings of projective geometry, with the comparison of positions of elements in a spatiotemporal manifold. The theory of projection held that certain geometric properties of spatially related elements remained constant in any "projection" of that arrangement of elements.

To simplify greatly, a "projection" is the striking of a perspective. The entire notion is derived from the discovery of the consistent properties of perspectival relations in Renaissance art. To achieve a representation of spatial depth, and therefore veridical spatial representation of actual scenes, artists imagined lines of light emanating from every point in the scene and converging, for simplicity, on one eye. The canvas was imagined to be as a glass screen interposed between eye and scene at any given angle. On the theory of projection, certain critical aspects of the spatial relations of the original scene would be preserved on the glass or canvas despite the particular perspective taken. Theorems were developed such that the representation of constant spatial properties on a canvas (which has not the convenience of the imaginary glass plate) would be possible, and the mathematics of projective geometry came to investigate the general scheme of such relations of projection.[41] A good example to think of here would be the face-recognition problem mentioned earlier. We recognize faces not because of measurable quantities corresponding to the features of the face conceived as a Euclidean plane, but because certain relations amongst the features of the face are retained no matter what angle we view the face from, no matter how that angle "distorts" what appear to be the "extensive" distances among face-parts, no matter what expression the owner of the face is wearing so that the face "distorts" or "deforms" itself. The realistically preservative angles permitted by "the face" considered as "one separate thing" (which of course it is not) are infinite. The face is, and is recognized, in all of *its* perspectives (to allude to the passage from *Science and the Modern World* cited earlier).

Extrapolating from projective geometry, then, the ultimate ground of all spatial and temporal relations could be conceived as comparisons among elements in a field. The smallest possible unit of space-time (the "originals" that we might be inclined to discuss in physics or metaphysics) would depend on that unit's relation to all other space-times. To bring this discussion directly back to the concept of intensity as it is employed in Whitehead's scheme of the relatedness of actual occasions, we can note and shed light on a curious comment made by Whitehead in the midst of his discussion of the structural conditions of intensity (triviality, vagueness, narrowness, and width). The need for effective contrast (or ontological comparison) of elements in the actual world of a concrescent entity, which demands narrowness (simplification) and width (variety), is expressed as an ultimate condition for the intensity of experience sought in subjective aim. Whitehead writes, "The subjective aim [at intense experience] is seeking width with its contrasts, within the unity of a general design. An intense experience is an aesthetic fact, and its categoreal conditions are to be generalized from aesthetic laws in particular arts" (PR 279). Without awareness of Whitehead's familiarity with and excitement over projective geometry, this comment about laws generalized from the arts may be read simply as an acknowledgment of the fundamentally aesthetic character experience, and of our explanation of it. But the reference to laws in the arts suggests more. It suggests some law of aesthetic relationship, such as is discovered in projective geometry, and as is generally advanced in Whitehead's own theory of extensive abstraction. The categoreal conditions alluded to, Whitehead goes on to explain, are the notions of conformity to a ground, and novelty of a consequent that emerges in significant contrast (unity in diversity) to that ground (an exact reiteration of the theory forwarded in RM and cited earlier; PR 279–80).

Thus, the notion of an individual act of intense experience emerges as an essentially comparative event, generalized from the discovery of an idea of spatiotemporal relationship that preserves meaningful constancies despite alterations in perspective. The possibility that there are some basic properties of relationship that are constant for *any* spatiotemporal relationships, despite the peculiarities of the entities in question (in other words, the question of whether or not there are any fundamental patterns at the base of all particular intensities of feeling), will be explored in the next chapter when we speculate as to the ultimate relationship between genetic and coordinate division.

THE REPUDIATION OF INFINITESIMALS

Our final consideration of the mathematically formative elements for Whitehead's eventual doctrine of intensity is his repudiation of infinitesimals. The very notion of an infinitesimal quantity is predicated on the notion of division of quanta as extensive wholes and parts. What is sought is simply infinitely small, though it is conceived to be extended in some way. The problems raised by infinitesimal time units in the construction of a mathematical theory of motion were monumental and eventually resulted in the reconstruction of the ultimate principles of the calculus involved.

A smallest increment of change was construed in the earlier view as an infinitely small quantity, greater than zero but less than any determinate numerical quantity. "Both time and motion," Kraus explains, "were thus construed as the summation or serial addition of these now existential units. They were, in a sense, the mathematical equivalent of the simply located particle of the physicist, and posed similar philosophical dilemmas" centered around the conception of how such units are to be conceived as "connected."[42] If externally connected, as was ordinarily thought to be the case, Zeno's problem remains at the heart of mathematics, physics, and metaphysics. Whitehead's reconstruction amounts to a reconception of talk about such infinitesimal quantities as talk about comparisons of classes or sets of finite entities (PR 328). That the "originals" to be discovered were essentially comparative entities, not "bits" or portions or parts or extensive quantities, is the essential point. Berkeley labeled as "infidel mathematicians" any theoretician who refused to acknowledge the fundamentally comparative foundation [for him "perception"] of any such unit, and satirically suggested that infinitesimals might best be construed as the "ghosts of departed quantities."[43]

Whitehead as a realist sought a revision of our ultimate mode of thinking about the "things" connected in experience, and more importantly, about the modes of such connection. Like Berkeley, Whitehead demands that "unity" in its fundamental conception be referred to unification—a process rather than an amount of some kind. The acceptance of intensive quantity against the "infection" of thought by notions of extensive quantities is the conclusion of this debate. Whitehead's antipathy to the infecting Aristotelean classificatory logic, noted at the very beginning of chapter one, can ultimately be traced to his association with it of the tendency to treat individual things (things that can be classified) as if they were extensive "ones" instead of intensive "ones." The consequences of Whitehead's repudiation of this form of thinking in his own atomistic theory are, as has been suggested, monumental.

SAMUEL ALEXANDER AND WHITEHEAD'S DISPUTE WITH KANT

In addition to his own mathematical investigations into the theory of quantitative relations and extensive properties, Whitehead had the benefit of the insights of Samuel Alexander in the construction of a metaphysical explanation of nature, and these insights, we may speculate, form the crux of the argument between Whitehead and Kant as to fundamental assumptions about the nature of experience. In the preface to *Science and the Modern World* (viii), Whitehead remarks that he is "especially indebted to Alexander's great work," *Space, Time, and Deity*, as a formative element in the thought behind the philosophy of organism. The point of interest to the present thesis is the development, in Alexander's work, of a critique and reconstruction of Kant's distinction between intensive and extensive quantity. Alexander accepts the distinction, and expresses it thus: "Extensive quantity is an affair of addition; intensive quantity is an affair of concentration, or in numerical language, of division."[44] The concentration involved in intensity is the inclusion of many spaces in a unit of time, or many times in a unit of space. The details of the theory are not important to our purposes here, but the conclusion is that space-time quanta are essentially comparative and internally complex.

Kant's insight, according to Alexander, was in his recognition that an object of experience must have intensive magnitude, or degree.[45] But Kant's weakness was in not being able to account for how this is so. Alexander's and Whitehead's analyses support a long-standing conviction on my part that the concept of "degree" as applied to empirical objects amounts to an incoherence in the first *Critique*. Kant recognized, according to Alexander, that there must be something in experience itself to account for the *filling* of time, since time could not be experienced itself. The notion of "degree" in the quality of experience was thus postulated by Kant as an "anticipation" on the part of the mind of any possible experience. Like Whitehead, Alexander concludes to the ascription of intensive quantity to natural events, and not to a property of the mind in the act of constructing the idea of a natural world, for Kant can give no account for this requirement of experience except "the empirical fact that a given intensity of sensation can decrease to zero in time."[46]

In thus reducing the very conception of intensive, continuous quanta to empirical conditions, that is, the additive property of quanta, intensity is founded on a concept of extensive quantity that is empirical and metrical in origin, and therefore subject to the same objections as the infinitesimal "fluxions" in Newton's physics. Also, and more critically, a fundamental condition for experience is articulated and defined in terms of empirical intuitions, which flies in the face of Kant's attempts to found experience transcendentally, and mathematics' and physics' attempts to ground measurement and science on relations of events that did not depend on the intuitive apparatus of the observer as empirically engaged. The significant point here is that Whitehead probably found in Alexander's account support for his own developing insight, that intensive quantity is a property of spatiotemporal events as comparatively constituted and mutually inclusive, and that any confusion of such intensive quanta with our expectations of extended quanta (derived from abstractive sense experience) precludes our properly understanding the intensive nature of "unity" or "oneness" as such.

With *Science and the Modern World*, the idea that a vision of natural orders, indeed metaphysical orders, could be predicated on the concept of comparison of durational atomic events took hold and molded Whitehead's mature system. Comparison became incorporation in the form of prehension. Events came to "be" comparatively, as incorporations of the full sweep of actuality and the incorporations embodied therein, and so on. This is Alexander's "intensive quantity" translated into a more sophisticated atomism, wherein the "realization" effected by one experiential event is inclusive of the aesthetic realization effected in other events. Temporalization, in this view, is "the realisation of a complete organism. This organism is an event holding in its essence its spatio-temporal relationships (both within itself, and beyond itself) throughout the spatio-temporal continuum" (*SMW* 127).

Extensive Solidarity and Intensive Atomism

We have seen that certain aspects of the peculiarity of Whitehead's temporal atomism often lead to misconceptions about ontology in the critical literature devoted to an illumination of this sometimes inscrutable philosopher-mathematician. In speculatively tracing the origins of the concept of intensity as it was to be employed in the mature system, we have seen that the properties of intensity as the aesthetic experience of existential comparison and incorporation of alien aesthetic experience has its origins in the same inquiries as does the extremely dense theory of extension. Two things follow: First, if it is the case that Whitehead's theory of extension is the attempt to frame a nonmetric ground for all geometric components of spatiotemporal relationship, such that knowledge of the natural world may be free of *arbitrary* intuitive content, then we must eliminate from our metaphysical interpretation of the scheme anything that might reintroduce the "infection" of categoreally real extensive magnitude. It is my contention that the notion of a "concretum" as something ontologically different from a "concrescence" represents just such a reinfection.

Likewise, when in an attempt to account for macroscopic substances of sufficient unity to be enduring objects, Whitehead's theory of societies is accused of being merely "aggregative," the horns should be sounded that a concept of metaphysical quantification (as is represented in the idea that ordered entities could in any sense be called an "aggregate") inconsistent with Whitehead's thought is being introduced. We cannot create the metaphysical equivalents of entities repudiated by Whitehead at the mathematical and physical level and expect them to adequately interpret the metaphysics derived from this repudiation. An "atom" is not a most small portion of space-time, if we mean by portion something that is essentially individual in the sense of being existentially separate from other such portions of space-time, for the notion of smallness of portion is a construct, whether we are employing it geometrically, physically, or metaphysically.

Second, the unitary source for the theories of intensity and extension is of great interest. It implies the necessity of conceiving the entire notion of subjective experience as developed in the organic scheme in light of the doctrine of extensive relation. In other words, extensive connection is not a corollary to the scheme in the event that we might wish at some time to measure scientifically the universe described in the rest of the work metaphysically. It is, on the contrary, of the essence of the possibility and nature of subjective experience.

NOBO AND THE EXTENSIVE SOLIDARITY OF ACTUALITIES

This view was arrived at, without a specific or detailed analysis of the concept of intensity, by Jorge Nobo, in the work to which we have already called attention, *Whitehead's Metaphysics of Extension and Solidarity* (1986). The repetition of his results under new experimental conditions in the present work is evidence, if we adopt a scientific criterion for the moment, of its tenability as an interpretation of Whitehead's scheme. The present work concentrates on the intensive subjectivity of agents, while Nobo concentrates on the extensive relations provident of such individuals. The two interpretations supplement one another. Despite my disagreement with Nobo's thesis as to the status of the two causal processes in Whitehead's philosophy, I am in complete agreement with his fundamental conclusion as to the extensive solidarity of subjective experient occasions. Not only *is* there extensive solidarity among subjects, this solidarity is *necessary* to the very achievement of subjective experience.

Although every event enjoys a unique "position" in the spatiotemporal continuum (such that the epochal atomism does not coalesce into a monism undifferentiated in any way except phenomenally, as in Leibniz), it is also literally "located" in every other position in the continuum in virtue of the relativity of the regions constituting the individual standpoints (positions considered as perspectives). Nobo acknowledges this general principle in the chapter, "Objectification, Position, and Self-Identity," and cites Whitehead (I will add the beginning of the first sentence to what Nobo actually quotes, for clarity of context):

> Every actual entity in its relationship to other actual entities is in [a] sense somewhere in the continuum, and arises out of the data provided by this standpoint. But in another sense it is everywhere throughout the continuum; for its constitution includes the objectifications of the actual world and thereby includes the continuum; also the potential objectifications of itself contribute to the real potentialities whose solidarity the continuum expresses. Thus the continuum is present in each actual entity, and each actual entity pervades the continuum. (PR 67)

Whitehead concludes by restating this succinctly: "Extension, apart from its spatialization and temporalization, is that general scheme of relationships providing the capacity that many objects can be welded into the real unity of one experience. Thus, an act of experience has an objective scheme of extensive order by reason of the double fact that its own perspective standpoint has extensive content, and that the other actual entities are objectified with the retention of their extensive relationships" (PR 67).

Extensive relationship is the "most general" scheme of relatedness making possible the determinate forms of objectification that occur between actualities. It is not ontologically prior in the sense of being something more primordial to which actuality must conform, but is "prior" in the sense of being the original determination of ordered actualities as they do atomize the continuum. Extensive connection is general not because it is before all creative entities, but because it is a feature of all of them, taken individually and collectively, and it "expresses the solidarity of all possible standpoints throughout the whole process of the world" (PR 66; also 80, 128). Nobo's great work is to have unpacked the significance of this existential solidarity of actualities that is possible in virtue of their real extensive mutuality. We have seen that upon this extensive mutuality is predicated the intensive mutuality of subjective experience, via repetition and relevant diversity from objectified entities.

"REPETITION" AND EXISTENCE

My position involves what Lucas has identified in Nobo as a rejection of the *conflation of material and efficient* causation implicit in the "usual" interpretation of Whitehead's notions of "being" and "becoming." The past actual$_2$ world assumes secondary ontological status, and is divested of the capacity for determinism on the basis of its relegation to a state of potentiality for the wholly autonomous self-construction of present entities in the "usual" view, but as already remarked the past has much more than an inert, merely material status. Again, we need to take Whitehead literally in statements about the fundamental nature of the scheme.[47] The real presence of one actuality in another, so often asserted at the core of this curious atomism, implies no possible split in ontological status between the past and the present (or the future, for that matter).

Although my reading departs from Nobo's in rejecting the sharp distinction between final and efficient causation, both interpretations rely heavily on the doctrine of "repetition" of one entity in another (as developed in chapters one and two above). Lucas notes that "[t]he notion of 'repeatable particulars' within a system that stresses the uniqueness of each particular does seem paradoxical," and that "this concept is not especially attractive from the standpoint of ontological economy," but also points out that it does seem to render intelligible Whitehead's claims as to the main agenda of his philosophy being "the analysis and clarification of this notion of 'being in another entity,' which he defines as objectification" (PR 50).[48]

The possible objections to the ultimacy of "repetition" in this scheme, Lucas contends, concern the possibilities of monism or the presence of a *reductio* in Whitehead's argument. Monism would result if repetition involved no uniqueness on the part of the concrescent subject. This is impossible given (a) the fact that there is no repetition without the guidance of the subjective aim of the subject, and (b) the real diversity of extensive standpoints constituting the unique position of each as well as their connection. The possibility of a *reductio* speaks directly to the problems of ontological status that I have been addressing. If "the reproduction is not exact (as it must not be), then what relation obtains between an original entity and its myriad reproductions—indeed, in what sense are the latter reproductions?"[49] The answer as asserted by Nobo and reiterated by Lucas is the notion of "creativity" as implying two separate species of process. One process, transition, effects the conjunctive unity of the many actualities such that the universe may be said to be expanding in a cumulative and non-eliminative manner. The other process, concrescence, signifies the unique subjective experience of individual entities. On this view, there is actuality both for the past and the present, and on the same ontological level, but in virtue of a processive situation that is two-edged. Objectification is made possible by transition, and subjective immediacy is accomodated by concrescence. Thus repetition is a factor of transition, to be distinguished from the concrescences that produce uniqueness.

But this will not do, for the reasons already stated. The atomization of the creative universe by actualities is one process of intensive patterning, wherein there are no grounds for an ontologically sharp distinction between objectification and concrescence. Lucas's question, "in what sense are [reproductions] reproductions?" requires the specific answer given here, that they are replications of intensive harmonies of prior subjects, marked by the individuality of those subjects, and contrasted with other elements of other subjects in the actual world. Lucas objects to Nobo's position on the basis that, "In the absence of any structure or criterion for order and selection [of what is to be objectified via repetition, and what is to be eliminated and how], it is impossible to see how mere repetition can be creative or can result in a synthesized 'datum'."[50] This objection, and Nobo's position against which it is aimed, can only be made from a perspective that ignores the fact that the criteria in question are precisely those conditions of "order" procurative of intensity via relevant contrast outlined in great detail in *Process and Reality*. Also, the centrality of the concept of a "contrast" is omitted. A "contrast," from which the intensity of any concresence emerges, is unique, selective, and eliminative, without ontologically effecting a radical pluralization of unique individual entities, and without failing to repeat patterns despite selection among actualities, and without ignoring the existence of eliminated entities (via the positive contribution to intensity by the subjective forms of negative prehensions).

Indeed, Whitehead himself entertains the question of how actual entities, depending so strongly on repetition of intensities realized elsewhere, can be 'rescued' "from being undifferentiated repetitions, each of the other, with mere numerical diversity." To answer this question he posits "the 'principle of intensive relevance'" whereby each actuality manifests a unique, graded perspective on the entire realm of potentiality. Every actuality grades its universe in relations of greater and lesser relevance, or importance to that subject entity (*PR* 148). The protean nature of the universe (including the realm of eternal objects, and the divine nature) considered as potentiality for creative becoming grounds the differentiation of feeling-character for each actuality despite its enormous repetition of earlier intensities. The subjective forms of even repeated elements of feeling are modified by this totalistic grading of (alternative) possibilities. The character of every existent item in the universe—actualities, eternal objects, nexus, and so on—to be in an essential disposition of *comparability* to every other item underwrites the agentive rearrangement of forms of feeling in every novel standpoint.

It seems to me that this was the major metaphysical project of *Religion in the Making* and *Science and the Modern World* taken together. In *Religion in the Making* the essentially comparative nature of value, and the divine nature in which it is founded, was elaborated; in *Science and the Modern World* the theory of eternal objects as possessed of detailed orders of comparison among one another was advanced (a project with originated in *Religion in the Making* as well with the acknowledgment of ideal forms) along with the relations view of atomic becoming. The principle of intensive relevance stipulates that to be an "atom" or an individual means to be a given and unique center from which the realm of possibility, in all of its remote forms, is graded in relevance. Because no two entities share precisely the same standpoint for this grading, no two entities clothe even their most insistent and provocative repetitions in *precisely* the same manner. Thus, there is massive accumulation of spatiotemporal actualities, significant retention of subjective pattern, and individuality marked by unique achievement of subjectively formed feelings.

Conclusion: Individual Existence and Persistence of Character

I would like to make some final comments on how we are to understand that the ontological *character*, and not merely the status, of actualities as they are objectified via the process of repetition (that may involve definite elimination of certain aspects of achieved intensities), is everlasting. Given the partiality of the inclusion of any subject in the existence of another subject, and given the description of a satisfaction as an incurably individual intensity, how can it be said that the *same individual* is still present in its objectifications? It may be that in any given instance, this is an empirical question, and that there is no metaphysically general condition that guarantees perpetual maintainance of the totality of achieved form. Whitehead introduced the concept of "God" as an answer to this problem of everlastingness in *Process and Reality,* such that the immediacy of full subjectivity of each entity persists in the consequent nature of the divinity, wherein there is no discordance of achieved intensity. In God there is ultimate harmonization, and therefore everlasting retention of intensity for every actuality (*PR*

88). Every intensity is thus preserved for its own sake, and for the sake of its possible prehension by future actualities.

This function of the divinity is not without problems, which is why I have attempted to develop a view without direct recourse to the status of God, except as that element of the universe in virtue of which each entity entertains an ideal of itself in its subjective aim.[51] Subjective aim might be derivable from the general nature of the universe itself, without recourse to a primordial actual entity, though how this is to be done without stretching the ontological principle to the point of unintelligibility is unclear to me. The grounds of order and the unique possibilities of intense order proper to a particular atomic standpoint do not in principle point to the necessity for any *singular* entity, however. Indeed, the doctrine of "God" introduces "a note of interpretation" (not metaphysical necessity) as to certain fundamental attitudes of thought in the midst of which a metaphysic assumes its relevance (PR 338, 341).

The "interpretive" aspect of the doctrine of the divine standpoint will be addressed in the following chapters, where thought in general and the question of "higher forms of experience" in particular will be addressed, in order to begin the entertainment of the moral dimensions of Whitehead's scheme. But the question remains, to what extent is a partially conformed-to individual still the same individual? No doubt the seeming implausibility of agentive self-sameness throughout objectifications is what underpins the ready entertainment of the view embodied in Kline and Leclerc's analyses; its prevalence in the literature is no doubt due to the intuition that in rejecting "substance" Whitehead was rejecting all forms of enduring self-sameness. But given the problems that arise from the absence of any plausible way to entertain some kind of self-sameness (to account for real internal relations without curious ontological dualities), and given the fact that in those passages where Whitehead most explicitly repudiates "substance," he goes after its definition of "individuality" rather than "self-sameness per se," it appears our problem is not endurance of *any* kind but of *which* kind. A strictly enclosed individual remaining self-same is indeed a philosophical conception that precludes an understanding of change. But perhaps in revising the concept of "individuality" we need to revise the concept of "sameness" as well.

The usual conception of "sameness" as everlasting retention of achieved character, that is, the exact identity of individual existence incapable of modification by temporal flow, may itself involve what Whitehead has described as the infection of our habits of thought by the notion of a categoreal status being granted to extensive quanta. In other words, in looking for a persistent quantum of existential character, are we not employing a concept of a spatiotemporal constant that is derivative and not formative in this metaphysics? Are we perhaps thinking of "same thing" as "one thing" with a concept of "oneness" that is extensive in origin and not intensive? The *one-*

ness of anything that exists in this universe of creative, aesthetic realization is nothing else but its *multiple realization* in the universe of events, and thus its oneness, or self-sameness, is not established simply by the boundaries of its own becoming considered in abstraction from the transcendent universe. This would indeed be a processive conception of "one" that does not confine the "one" within the distinctly non-processive boundaries of its concrescence. The entity as subject-superject, concrescence and satisfaction, may thus retain its coherence without forcing Whitehead to adopt dualities of description (subject-object, final-efficient causation, etc.) that undermine the novelty of his scheme. Also, we have new insight into the ultimate fact that, "[t]he many become one, and are increased by one."[52]

One important challenge that the reading being developed here must face is the strange fact that it seems to undermine the "specialness" of concrescence. If an individual is that subject wherever its contrasts are embodied (and I will spell out what I think this means later), then what is the point of Whitehead's highlighting the manifestly subjective conditions of aesthetic achievement within distinct concrescences? I think the way in which my reading can address this question is fairly revealing as to how to think about atomicity. The challenge at hand may be restated thus: In the ecstatic conception of the atomic actuality of subjects, why should we think of this individual as a *subject at all*? Even if we take his claims about the nonexistence of *absolute* privacy seriously, we still are faced with the decidedly subjectivistic (albeit a "reformed subjectivism") cast to Whitehead's theory of events. By unpacking one of Whitehead's statements of his "reformed subjectivism" in light of the ecstatic conception, we may elaborate the way in which existential ecstasis can accommodate the strong theory of subjectivity advanced by Whitehead.

> It is the basis of any realistic philosophy, that in perception there is a disclosure of objectified data, which are known as having a community with the immediate experience for which they are data. This 'community' is a community of common activity involving mutual implication. This premise is asserted as a primary fact, implicitly assumed in every detail of our organization of life. It is implicitly asserted by Locke in his statement ([*Essay Concerning Human Understanding*] II XXIII, 7 heading), "*Power, a great part of our complex ideas of substances.*" The philosophy of organism extends the Cartesian subjectivism by affirming the 'ontological principle' and by construing it as the definition of 'actuality.' This amounts to the assumption that each actual entity is a locus for the universe. (PR 79–80)

In this passage, as in the case of Whitehead's many other references to the conception of "substance" as being rightly understood as "power" (see especially *PR* 56–58 for the extended discussion of Locke), the point at hand is the power of one thing to influence another—what Whitehead unfortunately adopts the phraseology of "efficient causation" to designate. Power, in other words, is first of all attributed to satisfactions, that which the entity contributes to processes beyond itself. The passage also makes clear that the operations of other satisfactions in a subject entity are powers, and together with the entity's own process of self-constitution, form a "community of common activity." It is interesting that the subjectivist principle likening concrescence to the perceptual activity highlighted by Descartes, Hume, Berkeley, Locke, and Kant is framed as a discussion of the "pragmatic" or "transcendent" effectiveness of actualities. Thus, it is my contention that the present activity of subjects and the transcendent activities (*qua* activities, not "dead" or static givens) of objects are of a piece. This is one reason for my resistance to Nobo's accentuation of two processes to cover two forms of causation. Power is power is power. The distinction of power into kinds seems to undermine the unitary sense of universal creative process being sought in this philosophy.

This passage would seem to deepen our problems as to the seeming removal of immediate subjectivity in concrescence as being anything special, but I think it puts us at the doorstep of an answer. Just what do we think we need to mean by the agentive subjectivity of an actuality? In different phraseology, this is the famous question of panpsychism in Whitehead, but this phraseology is unfair to the system, as Whitehead never openly espoused such a doctrine.[53] The power of effecting intensity of satisfaction is the power of entertaining relevant possibilities of contrast on the basis of the limitations (also contrasts) imposed by the world. Much of this power depends on the origination of conceptual feelings in an individual concrescence. The occurrence of such origination is the reason for the designation of creative process as belonging to individual subjects—novel contrasts originate somewhere. The question is, *how* do they originate in subjects? Reverting to our assertion that "past" actualities may be said to "provoke" character in subsequent actualities, subjective agency may be described as the combined effect of a threshold provocation of the world *immediately* occasioning the influx or, better, immediate relevance of entertainable possibility called "subjective aim." When a threshold is present, so is the principle of "intensive relevance" operative.

The agency of a concrescence, such that it effects contrast and clothes feeling with novel subjective forms, is both borrowed and new *at the same time*. This is the reason for describing creative process as a "pulse" or "throb"—it happens all *at once* (though it is supercessionally "thick" so as to be productive of the temporal quantum designated in the "at"). The immediate relevance of potentiality to the active self-insinuation of the provocative occasion is the meaning of the all-important "immediacy" attributed to concrescence as an "immediate" subjectivity. It differs from objectification only in being the locus of that immediate relevance, not in being an ontologically separate process from objectification. Describing agency as the dynamic activity involved in the feeling of contrasts helps us to appreciate the absence of any magical sounding force of origination in concrescence proper. In fact, it is to be noted that in the statements of the various Categoreal Obligations governing subjective concrescence, origination is described quite passively, rather than as active production: "there is origination" is the phrase used in many instances of reference to the activity involved in concrescence. This does not imply any peculiar power of invention that could not be said to be manifest in the entity's superjection. In both subject and superject, power is equivalent to being possessed of contrast of a certain intensive character.

Once intensive relevance is occasioned, the contrasts thereby effected remain active contrastive ingredients, in whole or in part, in all subsequent process. Moreover, the subject's real potentiality to be derived from the contrasts effected in its past, which contrasts shepherd in the eventual relevance that occasions a "new" atom, constitutes the life it lives out behind (in the past of) its present occasioning. Thus the ecstatic conception may accommodate concrescence within the rather expansive and diremptive conception of existence being developed here. This conception, moreover, helps to diminish the deus ex machina appearance of the doctrine of subjective aim as provided by the divine nature. Subjective aim loses its sense of being a kind of divine orchestration of process and may be seen as the ever-potential intensive relevance of a definite scheme of potentiality to a given instance of provocation. God, in the primordial nature, *just is* the relevance of the realm of potentiality to whatever contrastive unifications are being provoked—and this is no mean feat! "Thus God in the world is the perpetual vision of the road which leads to the deeper realities" (*RM* 158). The question as to why there should be relevance at all is the unanswerable proposition at the heart of a value metaphysics.[54] Its thorough answer is the reason for the recourse to a richer conception of God and religious experience in the broader frame of reference for Whitehead's thought. God "is the mirror which discloses to every creature its own greatness" (*RM* 155).

Both individuality of concrescent process and "sameness" of enduring character refer to intensive achievement. Intensive achievement is the formed agency of contrastive feeling. It is my suspicion that the denial that a subject is "the same" in its objectifications stems from a conception of agency as something that belongs to the unitary subject of concrescence, rather than being identical to the emerging subject of the concrescence. The agency of contrast *is* the subject, the subject *is* the agency of contrast. To be a subject is to be a provoked instance of the agency of contrast, and that is all it is. Thus, wherever the contrasts achieved by an individual are reiterated in another individual, the original individual *is* there in the agentive sense. The pattern involved in an intense contrast is more than a mere arrangement of eternal objects. It is the feeling of the dynamic presence of the (other) individuals felt into the unity of a subject's intensity. This is the only way to understand Whitehead's repeated assertion of the vibratory character of actuality. No vibratory character has only one cycle *qua that vibratory character*—to be a vibratory character is to be an intensive imposition on all subsequent process, and, on the other end, to have emerged from the enduring vibrations of other insistent agencies of contrast. I see no other way of understanding why provision for future intensity is included in the category respecting "subjective" concrescence.

The agency of an "individual" Whiteheadian subject, such that it could be called the "same" subject wherever it appears and however partially it appears, is a "winged life," unconfinable to the alleged boundaries of the standpoint of its total intensive unification. Each actuality is hence itself a "murmuring underground stream" lying in real potentiality in the contrasts being effected by its past; it emerges as a unitary entity with just those contrasts that have demanded its appearance, clothed with what new form the unique standpoint affords as provoked; it lends itself *as itself* to the contrastive "landscape" of all determinacies that succeed it. Individuality can only be "kissed as it flies"—it is ecstatically a unitary one. Too "extensive" (in the derivative, measuring sense) a conception of self-same oneness "destroys" this intensive and eternal "joy."

CHAPTER FOUR

Intensity and Intellectual Experience

> *Such thought—such thought have I that hold it tight*
> *Till meditation master all its parts,*
> *Nothing can stay my glance*
> *Until that glance run in the world's despite*
> *To where the damned have howled away their hearts,*
> *And where the blessed dance;*
> *Such thought, that in it bound*
> *I need no other thing,*
> *Wound in mind's wandering*
> *As mummies in the mummy-cloth are wound.*
> —W. B. Yeats, *"All Souls' Night"*

The general purpose of this chapter is to explore the relevance of the concept of intensity to those aspects of the experience of entities, which pertain specifically to human mentality. Thus our concerns will be at once metaphysical and epistemological. For Whitehead, one of the hallmarks of distinctively intellectual experience is its increased capacity to suppress inherited forms of determinacy in favor of the entertainment of novel intensive structures. In Yeat's poem the thinker "holds tight" to his interests until all aspects of the subject matter are brought together in a unity of imaginative construction. Such construction feels itself distinctively capable of dismissing the expectations of habitual thought in favor of the unmanifest, the previously rejected, the as yet unheard of: "Nothing can stay my glance / Until that glance run in the world's despite / To where the damned have howled away their hearts, / And where the blessed dance." Intellectual occasions are the seat of creative rebellion from the bonds of physical inheritance, and yet in order to be relevantly novel they have to recognize a certain origination in the run of the ordinary, the imposing, which constitutes the environment in which such intelligence is occurring. Thought's inventive self-containedness of originality ("I need no other thing") imposes itself as if it were an obstinate physicality, rich with fascinating detail and preservative force: "Wound in mind's wandering / As mummies in the mummy-cloth are wound." Yeats' infatuation with the imaginative and physically reconstructive powers of thought forms an interesting backdrop to our consideration of aesthetic unification, or intensity, in the higher phases of experience. It also hints at one of the poignancies of such thought—despite the richness of intellectual experience's contours, it is not always a good thing to be a tightly wound mummy.[1]

The goal of the present chapter is twofold. First, determination must be made as to the salient intensive features of the metaphysical situation involved in occasions of intellectual experience, or to speak more strictly, in occasions of experience typical of the types of entities that are capable of intellectual feelings. Second, the employment of our knowledge in regard to philosophic explanation requires elucidation. This will round out certain claims that have been made in earlier discussions regarding the insinuation of our modes of *conception* of actuality into our description of reality's own contours. The first goal will be met via a discussion of intensity in 'the higher forms of experience' characteristic of human intellection. Also, Whitehead's two-mode epistemology, or theory of perception, will be addressed in order to discover the relevance to it of the concept of intensity. It will be seen that meeting this first goal really involves the achievement of the second, as to the status of our philosophic conceptions. A synthesis of the first and second goals may be found in the analysis of the relevance of the Theory of Extension to Whitehead's ontology, because this theory developed as a ground for not only metaphysics, but for our knowledge of the world as enjoying the kind of extensive observable (spatiotemporal) relations with which we are familiar.

It will be important at various stages of this discussion to point out the relevance of the conclusions reached to the project of the final chapter, that of the applicability of the concept of intensity to morality conceived in a Whiteheadian mode. Thus these final two chapters will work together in building a model of what is needed in moral thinking, and in thinking about morals.

Intensity in the Higher Forms of Experience

In a very general sense, the achievement of intensity in the forms of experience that involve sufficient organization so as to be "conscious" or "intellectual" is a direct result of the capacity for greater complexity. The more complexity entertainable in the subjective aim of an actual occasion, the greater the possibility for intensity via contrast of variety of detail in the subjective form (as we saw in chapter one). Those types of occasions that are marked by a high degree of conceptual experience, such that the possibilities for valuation, reversion, and transmutation are great, are open to intensities unimaginable for predominantly physical occasions. No doubt Whitehead's description of the subjectivity of occasions possessed of intellectuality is influenced by Alexander's account of knowledge as a mode of enjoyment.[2] Higher forms of experience are enjoyments, feelings, of greater intensity than those of more purely material entities of the physical universe.[3] That intensity describes both physical and mental experience, and that intensity of mental experience is held to be "greater" somehow than that of physical experience, is a cue to the nonsubstantialism of Whitehead's characterization of experience in general, and here specifically the nonsubstantialism of his account of 'mind'. If the quantitative aspect of mental experience is "greater" somehow than that of physical experience (which seems to us to possess greater dimensionality and solidity), then we are well advised to take pains to not misconstrue Whitehead's ontological assertions. This is a point to which we will return in the conclusion of this chapter.

THE ENTERTAINMENT OF POSSIBILITY: PROPOSITIONS

The greater complexity, and therefore intensity, possible in the 'higher forms of experience' is a function of the entertainment of possibility. There is a greater degree of freedom on the part of the entities involved to entertain the relevance of possibilities somewhat remote to merely physical experience. These possibilities may be entertained in a number of ways according to what type of feeling is being enacted. Whitehead enumerates a number of general kinds of particularly mental experience that may or may not attain consciousness, but all of which tend to characterize the complex occasions involved in the highly organized societies constituting a human life. Note at the outset that mentality is not linked to a singular form of experience, nor is it linked to a singular mode of organized being that performs a variety of functions—there is no 'mind' as a singular entity that is at one time 'imaginative' and at another time 'intellectual' or at another time 'believing'. Each of these modes of mental experience indicates the experience of individual occasions that societally function as what is ordinarily denoted by 'mind'. To emphasize this point, that mentality is in no way the property of a substance of any kind, I quote Whitehead on an issue to which I shall return later. In a moment of pointed hyperbole Whitehead notes that the mind "is perhaps some thread of happenings wandering in 'empty' space amid the interstices of the brain. It toils not, neither does it spin" (PR 339).

Let us turn, then, to a brief discussion of the types of occasions described as the 'higher forms of experience'. The most pervasive elements of these occasions are the 'propositional feelings', which are involved in all of the more specialized mental occasions such as judgments, beliefs, and intellectual feelings. The consciousness that we usually universally associate with mental experience is merely a certain subjective form, not always present, of a propositional feeling (PR 256). A propositional feeling involves two basic elements—a proposition, and the other physical or conceptual feelings with which the proposition is to be integrated. Propositions have a categoreal status of their own, and are referred to as a type of 'entity'. As a Category of Existence, Propositions are defined thus: "Matters of Fact in Potential Determination, *or* Impure Potentials for the Specific Determination of Matters of Fact, *or* Theories" (*PR* 22). Propositions are not to be described simply as actual entities or eternal objects, though they cannot be described outside of reference to the functioning of eternal objects and actualities. The best way to conceive of them without violating the Ontological Principle and without suggesting a mode of potentiality separate from the eternal objects, is to claim that they are certain existential features of actual occasions manipulating the realm of potentiality in a manner of complexity consonant with the nature of the occasions in question. Thus, propositions are a type of 'entity' in virtue of the operations of the actual entities of which the universe, which is in process of realizing potentialities, is constructed. They are inside the actual entities with which we have already become familiar.

The entitative status of a proposition derives from the fact that it is a *pattern* of potential determinacy entertained in reference to a really determinate actual world ('matters of fact'). The relation of a proposition to matters of fact is that some of the actual entities constituting the matters of fact (actual world) of an occasion of experience are denoted as the 'logical subjects' to which the 'predicative pattern' of the proposition might apply (*PR* 256–58). The 'predicative pattern' is a constellation of eternal objects, or a complex eternal object, that is entertained as relevant to elements in the actual world of the occasion entertaining the proposition. The elements in the world are entertained as merely 'logical' subjects, subjects to which the proposition might apply. Thus there is at once the limitation imposed on the propositional feeling by the actual world out of which alone such logical subjects may be selected, and abstraction from the bonds of realized actuality, because the proposition has indeterminate reference to any set of the actualities in question. The specification of the 'any', and the ultimate decision as to the meaning of the proposition in regard to the logical subjects, as that meaning will influence the texture of realization, is the affair of the actual occasion in question.

Given the analyses of chapters one through three, I maintain that wherever questions of 'pattern' arise, there too arise issues as to 'intensity'. Because an act of realization is finally the achievement of a determinate pattern of organized potentiality, any situation involving the entertainment or realization of such patterns prima facie can be held to influence the intensity of subjective form in an occasion. Thus, a proposition will invoke certain intensive elements of feeling in regard to its very entertainment. But the role of a proposition in procuring intensity is far more specific. A proposition is precisely a 'lure for feeling' (*PR* 259), and the function of any lure for feeling is to enhance and maximize the intensity of experience of the entity that is the subject of those feelings. The issue attending any proposition is the *valuation* to be made as regards its relevance in the experience of the subject in which it occurs. "The subjective forms of propositional feelings are dominated by valuation, rather than by consciousness" (*PR* 263). Before we acknowledge the intensive functioning of a proposition, we must note that it occurs as a 'contrast' between a physical (or physical and conceptual) feeling of determinate elements in the actual world, and a pattern of possibility (novel potential order) that *could* to some extent be realized in relation to that actual world. The valuative aspect of this felt contrast, and thus the intensity experienced in the entertainment, is the functioning of the proposition as a lure. "A propositional feeling is a lure to creative emergence in the transcendent future. When it is functioning as a lure, the propositional feeling about the logical subjects of the proposition may in some subsequent phase promote decision involving intensification of some physical feeling of those subjects in the nexus. Thus, according to the various categoreal conditions, propositions intensify, attenuate, inhibit, or transmute, without necessarily entering into clear consciousness, or encountering judgment" (ibid.).

A number of observations may be made about this passage. First, we must add to Whitehead's own description the clarification that a proposition cannot help but effect the intensity of experience in the subject entertaining it. How that effect will manifest itself is a question of the resolutions achieved (decided, realized in synthesis with physical data) in the "subsequent phases" referred to in the passage. Second, another clarification: the attenuations, inhibitions, or transmutations possible in virtue of a proposition are not effects different from intensification, but really specific modes of intensive relevance. What is attenuated, inhibited, or transmuted are the feelings eventually definitive of the intensity involved in the experience, which can always be greater or less. Finally, the passage reiterates the double office of 'lures for feeling' in the procuration of intensity. We recall that subjective aim seeks intensity in the present and in the relevant future. A proposition is one vehicle for the realization of this double aim. The present intensity of an occasion of experience looks ahead to (existentially anticipates) the transcendent functioning of that entity in its own future. Given the fact that entities characterized by propositional feelings are related to highly complex social organizations, this transcendent function is highly relevant and unavoidable. Also, the status of the society as procurative of intensity is not to be detached from the status of propositions procurative of intensity.

The moral application of this double concern for enhancement of intensity in the present and future via the entertainment of propositions (potential novel forms of order) is fairly obvious, and will be explored in the next chapter. The application to be made, to look ahead, concerns the effective and influential entertainment of relevant possibilities as a significant means of a society's (the enduring human personality, the relationship between enduring personalities, etc.) procuration of relevant novelty. It is the office of such novelty to insure that the society may endure and its members flourish amid the inevitable fluctuations in the environment. It is the effective intensity involved in such novel feeling that determines the moral contours of such experience.

SPECIALIZED FORMS OF PROPOSITIONAL FEELINGS

The three types of more specialized mental experience I wish to explore are 'consciousness', 'beliefs', and 'judgments'. The ways in which intensity is involved in and produced by such occasions are in part the explanations as to how novel conceptual experience comes to be morally relevant in human life. The subjective forms of such experiences are those with which we are most immediately familiar in our intellectual self-exploration.

Consciousness

As noted earlier, consciousness is a feature of only *some* mental occasions. It is not an aspect of human experience that attends any and all of the experiences constitutive of what we ordinarily designate as the 'mind'. Two points must be noted. First, this is in great measure the explanation of just how fundamental Whitehead's departure is from the types of 'subjectivism' characterizing the philosophies of Locke, Hume, Kant and the idealists (explored in PR 144–67). Although there are metaphysical conditions of connection and physical causality among subjective experiences of *any* kind, which establishes Whitehead's scheme as a 'reformed subjectivism', there is a further reform made to the 'mind' experiences from which the post-Cartesian philosophers began. This reform concerns precisely the elimination of directed consciousness as the starting point for philosophic analysis and metaphysical description. Although metaphysics may (perhaps unfortunately) borrow metaphors from cognitive experience, the dualism or idealism that results from the primary or exclusive origination of metaphysics in cognition are unnecessary philosophical gestures. Whitehead's reconstruction of the epistemological problem will be addressed later in the discussion of his account of sense-perception.

Second, the intentional consciousness asserted as definitive of human *experience* in phenomenology is by application of Whitehead's analysis limited to certain mental experiences. But Whitehead's departure from phenomenology is only via this limitation, for two important continuities remain. The ontology behind Whitehead's general theory of events—described here as the "ecstatic individuality" manifest by all events—borrows the sense of the dislocatedness of experiential content suggested in the idea of an "intention." And, Whitehead's definition of consciousness in particular is that it is characteristic of occasions in which there is explicit recognition that a possibility entertained *is not* definitive of the actualities in regard to which it is entertained. The contrast involved here is what Whitehead calls the 'affirmation-negation contrast' (PR 24, 243, 256, 261, 267). In consciousness, or 'awareness',

> actuality, as a process and in fact, is integrated with the potentialities [propositions] which illustrate either what it is and might not be, or what it is not and might be. In other words,

> there is no consciousness without reference to definiteness, affirmation, and negation. Also, affirmation involves its contrast with negation, and negation involves its contrast with affirmation. Further, affirmation and negation are like meaningless apart from reference to the definiteness of particular actualities. Consciousness is how we feel [the subjective form of] the affirmation-negation contrast. (PR 243)

Negation is essential in the experience of consciousness. The similarity to phenomenology is evident, though perhaps the closest tie is not with the twentieth-century thinkers as much as with Hegel. Ernst Wolf-Gazo has noted that for both Hegel and Whitehead, negation tied to affirmation in the structure of conscious experience is "logical in function but ontological in import."[4] The difference of Whitehead from both Hegel and his successors is that consciousness is limited by a physical experience of which it is not the sole determiner of ontological status (thus the references to the necessary tie of entertained potentiality to the definiteness of actualities in the earlier quote).

The intensity significant in 'conscious' feelings emerges not only because the feeling in question is a contrast of complex data (physically prehended actualities and conceptually prehended unrealized potentialities significantly diverse from that physical data), but because the awareness of the diversity is shot through with determinations of 'importance'. In the affirmation-negation contrast, a proposition is entertained in regard to a nexus of actualities, considered as a set of logical subjects. "Consciousness is the way of feeling that particular real nexus, as in contrast with imaginative freedom about it. The consciousness may confer importance upon *what* the real thing is, or upon what the imagination is, or upon both" (PR 261). Intensity will vary in character as well as degree (which is itself a mode of character) according to where emphasis is placed, and how this emphasis will effect the entertainment of other data in the feelings that together constitute an occasion of experience. It is important to note that consciousness is not in itself bound to place importance on the influential physical data in the feeling. Consciousness is thus not necessarily an organ of attention to what merely is, but is equally the vehicle of attention to what might be or what significantly might not be. Indeed, it emerges as the very occasion of the indetermination of mentality by sheer physical data—"nothing can stay my glance." Alongside the affirmation of the contribution of physical data to the propositional feeling, there is the fact of its negation by the more or less intense imagination of alternatives, which entertainment could result in a form of realization modifying the physical environment. This imaginative departure from the obligations of actuality will be explored in chapter five.

Belief

Whitehead's definition of 'belief' as a mode of propositional feeling is somewhat circular, or at least ambiguous, though it does help us understand the operations of intensity in mental occasions. In fact, intensity is most explicitly discussed in regard to the constitution of the subjective forms of beliefs, out of all the mental forms of experience. He explains: "A feeling is termed a 'belief', or is said to include an element of 'belief', when its datum is a proposition, and its subjective form includes, as the defining element in its emotional pattern, a certain form, or eternal object, associated with some gradation of intensity. This eternal object is 'belief-character'. When this character enters into the emotional pattern, then, according to the intensity involved, the feeling, whatever else it be, is to some degree a belief" (*PR* 267). In one sense, the definition states that a feeling is a belief when it is a belief, or contains belief-character, which is unhelpful. But in another sense, Whitehead is not being circular because the character of anything is always explicable in terms of the particular prehensions of eternal objects that occur in its act of realization. In this case, the pattern of eternal objects in question is that which is provocative of a certain form of intensity. What is interesting here is the tying of a determinate trait of an experience (belief) to a determinate intensity, relatively constant in its derivation from a set of eternal objects, or a complex eternal object. This is evidence of the fact that intensity and character are very much of a piece in Whitehead's scheme, despite the instances wherein Whitehead may appear to imply that intensity is merely a description of the element of privacy in feeling. The character is the product of a structural pattern of eternal objects, which patterns, qua actualized, are always indicative of intensities, potential or actual. (This fact will be of interest in our discussion of the Theory of Extension, wherein the basic spatiotemporal relations that obtain in all actualities, and in virtue of which there is extensive connection, will be construed as intensities, upon the background of which all other intensities are woven.)

The important aspect of belief as a peculiar intensity, or as possessed in part of a peculiar intensity among others, is that it does not require proof as to the truth or falsehood of the proposition entertained. Thus it is belief and not a 'perceptual feeling' or a 'judgment', in both of which the veracity of the proposition entertained is or can be significant. Belief is intense and compelling in the absence of certainty, and its compellingness is internal to its occasion. The intensity of belief-character can attach itself, in principle, to any mental act. It would be worthwhile to note how this conception of belief as the enjoyment of a certain kind of compelling intensive experience might help to shed light on the Humean claim that certain fundamental notions whereby we organize our experience, most notably that of "causality," is a kind of "custom," productive of the "belief-that" certain experiential continuities can be expected to remain in place in our lived worlds. Hume's conviction that experience is productive of such beliefs fails to explain the mode of their production, short of a vague allusion (but certainly one that Hume had a degree of conviction about) to a kind of natural conditioning of our capacity to know, a conditioning seized upon in behaviorist psychology and now enjoying renewed vogue in certain forms of materialistic or naturalized epistemology. Whitehead's description of the intensive enjoyment of certain propositions that take on a compulsory aspect when entertained in light of certain environments forms the basis of an interesting analysis of the origins of 'belief' in this and other senses. Belief is not sheer imprinting, but is a form of enjoyed origination felt with such force as to be productive of reiteration such that what we call imprinting or conditioning occurs at all.

Judgment

The last type of intellectual feeling to be explored is the 'judgment' form of a propositional feeling. There are three species of judgment: the yes-form, the no-form, and the suspense-form (*PR* 270). In a 'yes' judgment, there are significant grounds of unity between the physical nexus objectified in the feeling and in the proposition entertained, while in a 'no' judgment there is significant "incompatible diversity." In a 'suspense' judgment, there is diversity from the physical data, but not incompatibility (ibid.). We can infer, because the differences amongst judgment forms depends upon issues of identity and diversity, compatibility and incompatibility, that each species of judgment is attended by typical intensive structures. We cannot say that all judgments of each of the types would have identical intensities, or even certain identical intensive elements in the form of a specific eternal object attaching itself to the occasion, because all depends on the peculiarities of the nexūs and propositions involved, and the forms of compatibility and incompatibility achievable, and under what aims. There does, however, seem to be room to assert a certain general invariance of style of intensity amongst members of each species. In other words, the general contrast effected in each, as 'yes', 'no', or 'suspense', confers a general intensive structure (or form) on the peculiar intensive elements involved. This will involve arrangements of eternal objects, but they may be presumed to vary according to what is thus styled.

This extrapolation of an account of judgment forms in terms of a 'style' of intensity is attempted so as to provide, within Whitehead's scheme, a way of distinguishing between a judgment and a belief. Belief may attend any judgment, and indeed Whitehead's own account fails at times to distinguish between the belief character and the form of the judgment (e.g., *PR* 272: "Thus an intuitive judgment may be a belief, or a disbelief, or a suspended judgment"). It may at times, however, be critical to be able to make such a distinction. The account given here, though an extrapolation, is consistent with Whitehead's claim, noted in chapter one, that entities are to be classified in terms of their intensities of satisfaction. There should be, then, some *(emergent) intensive regularity* among the members of any "classification," whether of lamps, stones, beliefs, or judgments.

General Relation of Intellectual Feelings and Intensity

The general approach in this section, of eliciting the relevance of intensity in each of the forms of intellectual feelings, even where this relevance is unexplored by Whitehead, is demanded by Whitehead's own claims as to the "main function of intellectual feelings." This function is not the procurement of truth or even necessarily of belief, but instead, of intensity.

> The main function of these feelings is to heighten the emotional intensity accompanying the valuations in the conceptual feelings involved, and in the mere physical purposes which are more primitive than any intellectual feelings. They perform this function by the sharp-cut way in which they limit abstract valuation to express possibilities relevant to definite logical subjects. In so far as these logical subjects, by reason of other prehensions, are topics of interest, the proposition becomes a lure for the conditioning of creative action. In other words, its [the proposition's] prehension effects a modification of the subjective aim. (PR 272–73)

The "sharp-cut-ness" of the limitation of possibility suggests the order to be effected in virtue of the experience of foreground and background elements in the potentials entertained by any actuality. We have seen that the narrowness of foreground and vagueness of background conspire to produce intensity in an occasion of experience. Subjective aim thus employs an organized complexity of feeling in the decision as to present realization and transcendent efficacy. The "interestingness" of the "logical subjects" (feelings of aspects of the actual world, which, as we have seen, is a mode of agentive intrusion upon the present subject) itself establishes the provocativeness of the proposition as lure *"for the conditioning of creative action."* Again, feelings, physical or propositional, are directed at the superject, not from the subject. The aim, which is the locus of all that can be called agentive self-creation, is the throbbing force of the creative impetus resonating throughout the actual world. With the kinds of depth of implication a proposition can bring about, this force is felt with peculiar "vivacity" (*pace* Hume).

PROPOSITIONS AND PHYSICAL EXPERIENCE

The most important focus on transcendent creative action comes in virtue of the proposition's ultimate relationship to the physical datum (the actualities represented as logical subjects) with which in some manner it is being contrasted; thus the reference to physical purposes in the preceding quote, and in the passage immediately following:

> Intellectual feelings, in their primary function, are concentration of attention involving increase of importance. This concentration of attention also introduces the criticism of physical purposes, which is the intellectual judgment of truth or falsehood. But intellectual feelings are not to be understood unless it be remembered that they already find at work 'physical purposes' more primitive than themselves. Consciousness follows, and does not precede, the entry of the conceptual prehensions of the relevant universals. (PR 273)

Intellectual feelings broaden, deepen, and thereby intensify, both for the present and for the future, the purposes felt in an occasion of experience. Moreover, intellectual feelings are predicated on the antecedent reality and present relevance of the physical feelings involved in the orders of entities below the level of intellectual functioning.

The link here established between physical purposes and the enhancement of purpose possible through the imaginative entertainment of novel potentials systematizes the connection of mind and body, mental and physical occurrence, as they pertain to humans, elaborated in general terms in *The Function of Reason* and *Modes of Thought*. In each of these works the obvious interplay of mental and physical life is appealed to on the basis of a variety of experiences of our situatedness in a body, including memory, purposive action, and evaluative response to events. Intellectual experience, for all its freedom (absence of total determination) from the bonds of physicality, is concerned with the same kinds of intensive placement in the nested social orders transcendent of self that mark purely physical experience. Such notions will be relevant to our discussion of moral life in the next chapter.

PSYCHOLOGICAL PHYSIOLOGY: WHITEHEAD'S THEORY OF MIND

The obvious solidarity of mental and physical experience, as it pertains to humans, requires further systematic elucidation in terms of the metaphysics of higher experience of concern to us in this chapter as well as in the one that follows. In particular, how is it that we are to speak of the unity of mental experience so important in our ultimate conception of 'mind' and of the 'mind-body' connection? What is the 'life' of an embodied intellectual experient being, in this scheme? Influenced by the fledgling psychological inquiries of his day, Whitehead offers his description of "psychological physiology" as the outlines of a theory of 'mind' adequate to our purposes.[5]

Psychological physiology is a set of principles forwarded to describe the operations of living organisms of complex mental experience. Whitehead does not assert these principles as metaphysically general, but as "fit for the facts" as disclosed in a cosmos populated by beings such as ourselves that have emerged from the creative process (*PR* 103). The principles are an extension of the general description of societies, with the addition of special provision for the introduction of the "novelty" of experience characteristic of "living societies." The traditional picture of 'mind' or 'soul' as an enduring substance, the abiding entity responsible for the entertainment and realization of sometimes outrageous novelty, is on Whitehead's terms contradictory. An account of originality and freedom is sought, and the answer is that "the soul need be no more original than a stone" (PR 104).

According to Whitehead, the characteristics of a living society center on the society's capacity to engage in novel experience (be it locomotion, nutrition, entertainment of ideals, or any other more primitive or more complex realization) that transcends inherited data. In other words, what is most significant about living societies is their freedom, even in the midst of massive organization of patterns of inheritance in "living" bodies. Whitehead goes so far as to say that the "social" aspect of a living society is entirely the affair of the animal body (anything that is "animated") and not of the aspect of the society in virtue of which that society is deemed 'living'. Life "cannot be a defining characteristic. It is the name for originality, and not for tradition" (PR 104). Thus life is the signal that the capacity for origination typical of entities in general has been increased by the bonds of social order that sustain, but do not define, that capacity for origination.

The major goal of any living society (though from now on our focus will be on the 'life' associated with human 'mind' or 'personality') is precisely, in accordance with the thesis here, the achievement of intensity of experience. "The characteristic of life is reaction [to organic influences] adapted to the capture of intensity, under a large variety of circumstances. But the reaction is dictated by the present and not by the past. It is the clutch at vivid immediacy" (PR 105). The dictation of intensity by the present rather than the past bespeaks the enlargement of freedom characteristic of occasions of living experience. (It is important to note here that intensity is tied to immediacy in a manner suggestive of the thesis that immediacy of experience *just is* intensity, the metaphysics of which claim have been argued in the preceding chapters.) Although any actual entity is novel and enjoys its unique, private act of becoming, there is, in the absence of life, a great weight of determination by objective data involved in such becoming. Indeed the capacity for origination in such entities we have described as simply the becoming-relevant of forms of potentiality on the basis of threshold physical provocation by the actual world. We have described this weight, which is ontologically significant, in terms of the reiteration of patterns of intensive feeling. But for a living occasion, in a living society, "There is intense experience without the shackle of reiteration from the past. This is the condition for spontaneity of conceptual reaction" (ibid).

Now, to be sure, there is no living occasion without its definite bonds to the complex interweaving of inorganic societies comprising the animal body. Spontaneous conceptual reaction must react to something, and its reactions will be conditioned by the type of organism involved. Also, though intensity does not occur via sheer reiteration, there is certainly a significant conceptual valuation of those intensities proffered by physical objectification, such that the propositional novelty is relevant. Without grounds of relevance, there is no intensity because there can be no meaningful contrast. Thus the living occasion receives some determination in virtue of the physical organization of energies from whence it emerges. But, *qua living*, there is no shackle of reiteration to oblige such an occasion.

The occasions constituting the 'nonsocial nexus' that is the 'mind' are those that are free in this sense, free from mutual determination, but not free from the obligations of their material referents. "The characteristic of a living society is that a complex structure of inorganic societies is woven together for the production of a non-social nexus characterized by the intense physical experiences of its members. But such an experience is derivate from the complex order of the material animal body, and not from the simple 'personal order' of past occasions with analogous experience" (*PR* 105). Strangely, this appears to assert that the mind is more determined by the body than by occasions analogous to itself. The nonsubstantiality of the mind, along with the mind's obvious connection to physical bodies in our experience, are both neatly handled by this strange thesis. It also undergirds Whitehead's assertion that we are only intermittently conscious, insofar as we could stretch the claims made here about life to suggest that the characteristic of a living occasion is that it *does not have to happen*. The strange departure of life from deceased animal bodies is thereby nascently, though perhaps not completely, explained.

In his exploration of Whitehead's account of psychological physiology as a germ of a theory of mind, Sherburne has characterized the type of inheritance involved as a kind of tangential influence. The living occasions wander in the "empty space" of the physically spatial bodily occasions (*PR* 105), deriving influence from their order but not the determination that would characterize the mental occasions if they formed a truly social nexus. Sherburne develops his thesis in the interest of defending Whitehead against the charge that the 'personally ordered society' usually "uncritically" associated with personal identity in humans is, if it is Whitehead's sole explanation, open to the same objections raised by Whitehead himself against the substance theory of the mind. A personally ordered society is almost as dominated by inherited character as a substance, and has as much difficulty accounting for the radical novelty of psychic life. The doctrine of a wandering, nonsocial nexus, capable of 'clutching the vivid immediacy' obtainable through significant novel appetition, while still connected to and influenced by complex organic systems, solves this problem.[6]

I do not disagree with Sherburne; it is important to establish the grounds whereby there is significant but relevant freedom for mental occasions. I also do not disagree with the assertion that this doctrine echoes "the notion of the conscious ego" associated with "the dimly conscious regions of the 'depth' dimension of the psyche, flittingly illuminated by the movements of the ego, so often referred to under the imagery of a searchlight probing now this, now that, region in the largely obscure psychic depths."[7] Similar notions will return in our discussion of "attention" in what follows and in the subsequent chapter. But I do think that an important aspect of Whitehead's theory of mind may be appended to Sherburne's analysis by paying attention to the operations of intensive experience.

Sherburne's position links the 'being' of the mind almost exclusively to its capacity to be persistently relevant to the bodily functions from which it tangentially inherits. Beyond preserving the important freedom of the mind, this conception may be expanded so as to appreciate the ontological significance of such a mind's freedom. In the late essay, "Immortality," Whitehead writes extensively of personal identity, addressing this issue as to the balance of endurance and change in the life of human personality. Whitehead reiterates in this essay the thesis set forward in *Process and Reality*, that the intense experiences in these mental occasions themselves stand out with a certain ultimacy of character in their own right. What is not emphasized in Sherburne's view, and what makes a difference in our ontological consideration of mental experience, is how thoroughly Whitehead has recast 'being' in terms of *value* instead of substance, matter, or any of their imposters as they might insinuate themselves into the philosophy of organism.

Any society of occasions may stabilize a 'personal identity' via the maintenance of a certain character of value (what we have been analyzing as intensity) despite variations in the subordinate details out of which that character arises (*IMM* 688–89). "This preservation of a type of value in a sequence of change is a form of emphasis. A unity of style amid a flux of detail adds to the importance of the various details and illustrates the intrinsic value of that style that elicits such emphasis from the details. The confusion of variety is transformed into the coordinated unity of a dominant character. The many become one, and by this miracle achieve a triumph of effectiveness—for good or for evil" (*IMM* 690). Gallagher cites this passage in his attempt to account for the "unity of aim" binding the free and novelty-seeking intense aesthetic experiences characterizing human life.[8] This, too, is a helpful observation, but like Sherburne's reading, it does not address an important element in the quest for value-experience as outlined by Whitehead.

Value is real at any and all levels of generality of perspective. There are grades of aesthetic achievement varying in a spread of infinite dimensions (*IMM* 692). The levels of greater generality in any line of development we might explore (such as the increase of generality as we trace the systems in the human being on a scale of complexity, especially as regards capacity for novel realization) indicate higher types of value (*IMM* 692). Higher, broader, less physically bound types of value are as real as those values that constitute the character of physical realities. Thus, the types of experience in mental occasions "free of the shackles" of physical reiteration are still as ontologically significant as those complexly organized experiences from which they emerge and that they eventually condition. Because they do not possess the kind of tight and obvious unity of character of predominantly physical experiences and the societies thus engendered, these mental occasions can be misconstrued as deficiently actual in so far as they are not tightly knit to the physical societies with which they are associated. Sherburne sets out to salvage Whitehead's view from the charges of excess identification that compromise the substance theory of mind or personality, but describes a scheme that does not preserve the ontological significance of the mental occasions as the organs of novelty advanced against the substance position. The tangential inheritance model is important, but only half the story. The other half is the ontological significance of the value experience (intensity) of the mental occasions themselves.

My critique of Sherburne on this point is borne out by Whitehead's interjected discussion of God's role in temporal realization, in the midst of the elaboration of the theory of living societies in *Process and Reality*. The issues of preservation and novelty that permeate our consideration of the living orders that constitute human mentality and personality are, in the metaphysically most general sense, only secondary to the ultimate concern for intensity. "In the foundations of his being, God is indifferent alike to preservation and to novelty. He cares not whether an immediate occasion be old or new, so far as concerns derivation from its ancestry. His aim for it is depth of satisfaction as an intermediate step towards the fulfillment of his own being. His tenderness is directed towards each actual occasion, as it arises" (*PR* 105).

The reference to the fulfillment of God's own being here is unfortunate, for it suggests a divine agency with a directive office somehow transcendent of the creative process in which there is aim at intensity of satisfaction. But Whitehead's God has no such office. God's "primordial appetitions" (*PR* 105), whereby there is this aim at intensity, are not transcendent of creative process but primordial in it. God is, as we saw before, that in virtue of which there are grounds of order (procurative of intensity) *in* the universe. The better formulation of God's role in regard to intensity is in the succeeding paragraph: "Thus God's purpose in the creative advance is the evocation of intensities. The evocation of societies is purely subsidiary to this absolute end" (ibid.). The "absolute end" is intensity in the creative advance. 'God' as a metaphysical posit is the explanation as to why it should be so, that creativity appears to evolve creatures of ever greater capacity for intense experience. This is in obedience to the ontological principle, that the reasons for anything are to be discovered solely in the experience of actual entities, in this case God. God is that actual entity that explains the general character of creativity as the quest for intense experience.

Thus, the enlargement of Sherburne's view attempted here is predicated on the thesis that intense value experience is the absolute end of creative process, and that 'ontology' such as we are to conceive it, for persons or stones, is a question of intensity, and not vice versa. In other words, our conception of the ultimate existential status of persons, and their capacity for novel experience in the midst of bodily influence, is measured by the ultimate ontological condition of intensity. The status of human existence as inclusive of highly intensive valuational experience should be constructed starting from those peculiar intensive experiences, and not guided by preconceptions of what kind of entity we are looking for from the outset. Surely, unity of personality is important, as is novelty of appetition, but it is important to construe both of these in light of the more fundamental ontological concern for intensive contrast procurative of depth of actuality. So, it is not merely the freedom of mental occasions from direct physical obligations, along with their indirect inheritance from these occasions, which is most significant in describing the organisms to whom the principles of psychological physiology are applied.

Freedom and inheritance are ontological concerns subordinate to the intensive requirements of creative process, and the character of intense experience in living minds is thus definitive of its own ontological character. We certainly require the unity born of inheritance, and the novelty born of freedom, but these needs are subordinate to the ultimate ontological need for intensity. In fact, to bear out the suggestions made toward the end of the last chapter, we might do well to jettison the language of "freedom versus inheritance" in favor of a descriptive terminology of intensive valuation happening in varying forms, styles, and emergent characters. "Freedom" is not a force in itself but is the shape of noninherited but relevantly novel intensive character realized by some events considered in relation to other events. Thus the general question of the "agency" of all events is dealt with via the claim that intellection, which is a traditional locus of the most definitively agentive kinds of activity, is itself not willfully agentive in the sense ordinarily meant by "will." Panpsychism in the pejorative sense is thereby undermined and the continuity of metaphysical conditions governing all actualities may be asserted without its counterintuitive presumption. We will explore the question of the "will" in chapter five.

The recourse to statements about the divine nature once again finds us at the limits of descriptive metaphysics. The appeal to God, as an account of a metaphysically general and quite ultimate condition of process, is in large measure an appeal to interpretation. The primordial functioning of God as the actuality in virtue of which the realm of possibility is relevant to each occasion individually does not have to be given the name "God" except in so far as we address ourselves to issues broader than the conditions governing the coming to be of events. Developing the interpretation guiding the present inquiry as to the status of intensity in this scheme, we could simply stipulate that a creative universe is *in toto* and *in itself* the demand for intensive unification, and implies a realm of potentiality standing in such relationship as to explain and make possible those intensities that do in fact occur and add themselves to the process procurative of further intensities. In other words, intensive relationship is as much a condition for the solidarity of the universe as are the extensive relations ordinarily appealed to as the basis for this solidarity. Indeed, it may be (as I hypothetically suggest later) that extensive relation is ultimately a question of intensive relation.

The final answer on this issue depends upon, perhaps, the interpretive intuitions that guide one's inquiry. But for our purposes, we might claim that the ultimate end of intensity is imposed in the characters of the existents that enjoy solidarity with each other, "to the crack of doom." This account does not escape circularity, for it claims that "entities seek intensity, because entities seek intensity." But the seeking appealed to in the second clause refers to the universe of entities as a community, conditioning the universe of entities conceived as individuals as in the first clause.

The circularity simply mirrors the paradox of how "the many become one, and are increased by one." The mutual implication of community and individual in the existential demand for intensities explains the demand without the appeal to some one entity who is the condition of this demand in a special sense. The conditions of oneness in any experience are imposed by the conditions of oneness that pervade the continuum. These conditions of oneness are in both instances the conditions of intensive pattern. In *Adventures of Ideas*, in which the concept of God is not systematically appealed to as the ground of intensity, there is yet the Unity of Adventure enjoyed by all occasions as individualizations of the adventure itself. This individual and unified adventure involves the realization of 'Beauty' (*AI* 295), which is the ideal of intensity in the mutual adaptation of the factors in an experience to one end (*AI* 252; cf. *MT* 94). It is in virtue of Beauty that "the Universe achieves its justification" (*AI* 295). There is no appeal beyond Beauty, or intensity. In a vibratory cosmos, intensities must come to be. Of course such an interpretation evades a more thorough answer to the ontological question as to why vibratoriness of intensive character should exist, at which point an appeal to religious experience may be unavoidable.

THE "END" OF THE WANDERING MIND

The provisional conclusion to our discussion so far is that our "primitive" in the construction of a vision of human experience is, as for metaphysics generally, the intensive character of the experiences inspiring our attempt to construct such a vision. I have in this section attempted to trace out when possible those aspects of the various typical mental experiences that refer to this intensive character. To bring this discussion to a conclusion, we would do well to ask, what the status is of the broad intensive experience possible for human beings as characterized by these wandering 'mind' occasions. In the unity of adventure, to speak metaphorically, is the wandering to some end? Despite their particular character, these experiences find themselves always in the solidarity of occasions, particularly those physical occasions out of which they arose. Indeed, this is the point of the wandering—the potential for transcendent influence possessed by occasions free to entertain possibilities more or less remote.

Whitehead concludes his own discussion of the higher forms of experience by reintroducing the Category of Subjective Intensity. This category helps to explain the origination and operation of lures for feeling that have in them provision for the future. Nowhere are such lures more relevant than in the experiences constituting human purpose as conceptually entertained. In virtue of the reversions, valuations, and transmutations possible in high-grade experience, possibilities initially entertained conceptually may be brought to realization physically. I entertain the possibility of listening to a Mozart piano concerto, though I am nowhere near a stereo and not presently engaged in any activity suggestive of music. I act so as to bring the listening to pass, which involves vast modification of the physical environment, of the room, my body, and, to conceive the environment inclusively, my mind. There has been a realization of intensities at all levels, as a result of an ideal entertained in abstraction from what was going on in the sphere of physical causality. In all acts initiated by thought, there is adjustment of the intensities involved in all the occasions affected (*PR* 278–79). This transcendent function of the lures for feeling realized in thought as ideals is the focal point of any discussion of morality (*MT* 26–28), as we shall see in the next chapter. What is most significant here is the enlargement, through the realization of value experience in acts of mind, of the metaphysical import of 'purposes' beyond the possibilities realizable by 'physical purposes.'[9] Thus the "end" of the mind is the deepening (in the systematic sense) of the "ends" that pervade nature. Such a conception goes a long way to diminish the attractiveness of a mind-body dualism by denying that either physicality or mentality can carry off its ends in ignorance or independence from the other.

Symbolic Reference: The Status of Presentational Immediacy

The kind of sense experience with which we are familiar in epistemology and theories of mind, and from which many metaphysics and ontologies are begun, is highly derivative in Whitehead's scheme. The experience, largely visual, of objects contemporary to us and possessed of determinate boundaries, clothed in color and texture and all the 'secondary qualities', and enjoying perspective spatial relations with each other, is "derivative" in the sense that this is not the most immediate nor the most primitive form of encounter involved in the human experience of the world. Like the pragmatists,

Whitehead rejects this version of immediate experience as the foundation for a concept of knowledge and of experience in general, and opts for a view of immediate encounter that is thoroughly causal and interactive.[10] Perception of the contemporaneous environment in human experience involves Whitehead's two-stage epistemology of symbolism, wherein 'presentational immediacy' and 'causal efficacy' conspire to enable the percipient to apprehend aspects of the contemporary world via a 'symbolic reference'.

Whitehead's two stage epistemology of perception grows out of the need to describe how it is that we do appear to apprehend a contemporaneous environment, when the conditions of prehension, whereby there is metaphysical connection with this world, by definition preclude experience of contemporary occasions. I see the world as "now," not as the immediate past or potential future with which alone I am causally connected. 'Causal efficacy' is the operation of the prehensive connections of the animal body to the actual world to be perceived, and involves precisely those conditions of order already addressed in regard to experience in general. 'Presentational immediacy' is Whitehead's account of the forms of experience usually meant by 'perception'—the display of a present environment under those aspects alluded to earlier.

Until we come to show how the two modes of perception unite in a symbolic reference, and how this symbolic experience involves concerns centering on intensity, I will confine my attention to 'presentational immediacy', because causal interaction has been dealt with extensively in the foregoing. It is important to explore the relevance of intensity to those forms of experience involved in presentational immediacy, because it is at this level that we usually perform operations of analysis in regard to moral situations. Also, misunderstandings of what is really (though not acknowledged to be) a function of 'presentational immediacy' are involved in some of the metaphysical errors against which Whitehead formulates his system (PR 168). These errors will be of direct relevance in the balance of this chapter. Such errors are also not unconnected to some of the problems in moral thinking that a concept of aesthetic intensity might help resolve.

'Presentational immediacy' is basically an experienced display, by and for the percipient subject, of the present environment. Whitehead refers to this display as a 'projection', on the part of a percipient, of 'sense-data' enjoyed in virtue of our particular capacity to be affected by stimuli. (We recall the conception of 'projective geometry' that was of influence in Whitehead's philosophical development, and that forms the backdrop to the description of Presentational immediacy). The endowment of the environment with sense-qualia is as much an affair of the bodily subject as of the objects thus sensed. Presentational immediacy is "the experience of the immediate world around us, a world decorated by sense-data dependent on the immediate states of relevant parts of our own bodies. Physiology establishes this latter fact conclusively" (S 14). The notion of projection is thus grounded in the causally interactive connection of body and perceived environment, and the projection is as much a part of the environment as anything else: "There are no bare sensations which are first experienced and then 'projected' into our feet as their feelings, or onto the opposite wall as its color. The projection is an integral part of the situation, quite as original as the sense-data" (ibid.).

The notion of projection centers on the fact that the display presents an *extended* environment *contemporary* to the percipient. Roughly, it is a display, as present, of the extensive relations experienced in the causal connections of the bodily subject to the environment. The ways in which this projection is grounded for extensive accuracy depend mainly on the universality of certain aspects of spatial relationships. "This relatedness of spatial extension is a complete scheme, impartial between the observer and the perceived things. It is the scheme of the morphology of the complex organisms forming the community of the contemporary world. The way in which each actual physical organism enters into the make-up of its contemporaries has to conform to this scheme" (S 22). A symbolic reference is, therefore, the way in which causally connected organisms in temporalized relationship (one being in the relative future of the other) are apprehended as in genuine community in the present moment as a "cross-section of the universe" (PR 168). Thus, the projection symbolically refers to, or "means," the causal solidarity of the organisms involved.

Because presentational immediacy is a mode of experience peculiar to high-grade organisms, it emerges in virtue of the purposes engaged by those organisms. We have already seen some of the "purposiveness" of occasions of intellectual experience, and now may enlarge this understanding in more familiar experiential terms. Presentational immediacy emerges as a means of apprehension of the relevance and importance of aspects of our environment prehended in causal efficacy. By the "originative power" of the conceptual supplementation occurring in high-grade occasions, "what was vague, ill defined, and hardly relevant in causal efficacy, becomes distinct, well defined, and importantly relevant in presentational immediacy" (PR 172). There is a "vivid distinctness" of elements in our present perceived world, such that what I am causally related to is now related to in a mode of enhanced importance (PR 172–73). An annoying quality of illumination from a lamp is all the more annoying (in a raw sense of physical irritation) for being noticed visually as "right there."

What the conditions of 'order' (triviality, vagueness, narrowness, width) accomplish in any prehensive act, presentational immediacy accomplishes for high-grade acts of perception. Both involve the intensive relation (patterned valuation) of perceived factors in the environment relative to a subject. Symbolic reference procures intensive relation for high-grade subjects, though not necessarily those involving 'consciousness': "The two modes are unified by a blind symbolic reference by which supplemental feelings derived from the intensive, but vague, mode of efficacy are precipitated upon the distinct regions illustrated in the mode of immediacy. The integration of the two modes in supplemental feeling makes what would have been vague to be distinct, and what would have been shallow to be intense" (PR 180). What emerges is a refined intensity of experience, whereby the intensities realized causally, important to the formation of the organism, are enhanced as a presentational intensity according to the requirements and purposes of perception.

The critical question then becomes, what are the requirements and purposes of perception? In one sense, the intensity of this experience alone is its foremost justification. There is, however, another sense in which broader concerns do introduce a note of justification. "Symbolism can be justified, or unjustified. The test of justification must always be pragmatic. In so far as symbolism has led to a route of inheritance, along the percipient occasions forming the percipient 'person', which constitutes a fortunate evolution, the symbolism is justified; and, in so far as the symbolism has led to an unfortunate evolution, it is unjustified" (PR 181).

I will explore the moral import of 'fortunate evolution' as a pragmatic test later. Here I am concerned to spell out the relevance of the experience of symbolic reference to our discussion of intensity, and vice versa, though this relevance is not without direct connection to the moral dynamic that I take to be implicit in and everywhere in the background of Whitehead's scheme. Whitehead acknowledges that the way in which symbolic reference is "chiefly" to be conceived is in regard to the elucidation of causal efficacy by the "intervention of percepta" that occur in presentational immediacy. What is possible in virtue of symbolic reference is an enhancement of our apprehension of our "character" as embedded in a world intensively significant to us. It is worth quoting Whitehead at length on this point, as his language helps situate our discussion, and portrays some of what I take to be the foundational insights of this scheme, relevant metaphysically and morally:

> [Causal efficacy] produces percepta which are vague, not to be controlled, heavy with emotion: it produces the sense of derivation from an immediate past, and of passage to an immediate future; a sense of emotional feeling, belonging to oneself in the past, passing into oneself in the present, and passing from oneself in the present towards oneself in the future; a sense of influx of influence from other vaguer presences in the past, localized and yet evading local definition, such influence modifying, enhancing, inhibiting, diverting, the stream of feeling which we are receiving, unifying, enjoying, and transmitting. This is our general sense of existence, as one item among others, in an efficacious actual world. (PR 178)

The deliverances of causal efficacy are effective; but without the focus and discrimination possible in the forms of definite perception that occur in presentational immediacy, the effect is limited on the scale of macroscopic experience at which human organisms function. "The percepta in the mode of presentational immediacy have the converse characteristics. In comparison, they are distinct, definite, controllable, apt for immediate enjoyment, and with the minimum of reference to past, or to future. We are subject to our percepta in the mode of efficacy, we adjust our percepta in the mode of immediacy. But, in fact, our process of self-construction for the achievement of unified experience produces a new product, in which percepta in one mode, and percepta in the other mode, are synthesized into one subjective feeling" (PR 179). Conscious control of the activities of "self-creation" in human life begins in the perceptual definition achieved in symbolic reference. There is no guarantee of the rectitude of such control, or even of its "evolutionary fortunateness," but the potential for either good or evil in macroscopic behavior is born in these processes. Symbolic reference "lifts the meanings" of the causally efficacious elements of our world "into an intensity of definite effectiveness—as elements in knowledge, emotion, and purpose. . . . The object of symbolism is the enhancement of the importance of what is symbolized" (S 63).

The concern for intensity in the experience of symbolic reference thus involves the definition of the emotional content controlling and being controlled by us. The distinctness and intensity required at the level of intelligent experience are lacking in the pure mode of causal efficacy, though the raw materials for depth of intensity—the emotionally heavy impresses of the environment—are present. Whitehead asserts that it is the very purpose of mentality to, as we have already suggested, enhance the possibilities of realization that occur on the physical level, to the end of further conceptual potential, and so on. The introduction of novel patterns of eternal objects (potentialities) for intense realization of relevant alternatives, interestingly contrastible to the physical situation, is here, as always, the goal. Presentational immediacy is an extreme case of the eliciting of intensities that occurs at all levels of process. "It is the function of mentality to modify the physical participation of eternal objects: the case of presentational prehensions is only one conspicuous example. The whole doctrine of mentality—from the case of God downwards—is that it is a modifying agency" (PR 325).

I wish at this point to pause and comment on the centrality and broad significance of these issues. Not only is it the case that symbolic reference finds its place in the systematic concern for elaborating the conditions of intense subjective experience, but also, the experience of symbolic reference itself is seen to be formative of these systematic concerns. Whitehead's comment about perception in the mode of causal efficacy being our "general sense of existence" as embedded in an efficacious actual world is not mere hyperbole. He is expressing the insight upon which his system, and the doctrine of existence developed therein, are founded. "Philosophy is the attempt to make manifest the fundamental evidence as to the nature of things. Upon the presupposition of this evidence, all understanding rests" (*MT* 48). We must be aware of what Whitehead considers the fundamental evidence beginning an inquiry into the existence of things. Whitehead's mature system began in the protest of *Science and the Modern World* against the misconstrual of the primary evidence offering itself for our exercise of philosophic explanation. The warnings forwarded in that work against what Whitehead calls the "Fallacy of Misplaced Concreteness" are by now common knowledge. Appealing to various trends in the history of scientific and philosophic thought, but also and especially to the Romantic poets, the philosophy of organism joins the voices raised in "protest against the exclusion of value from the essence of matter of fact" (*SMW* 94). The survival of the poets' appeal, according to Whitehead, "is evidence that they express deep intuitions of mankind penetrating into what is universal in concrete fact," and the universal elements intuited are "aesthetic values" (*SMW* 87). Without a sense of the ultimacy of value in existence, our inquiries will be off on the wrong foot.

I am not so much concerned with the status of Romantic poetry in Whitehead's explorations of what is to count as evidence for philosophy, but with the conclusions of those explorations—that the ultimate evidentiary claims in philosophy concern immediate value experience, and that such experience involves the "self-evident" status of the realities dimly recognized in "the world around—the world of fact, the world of possibility, the world as valued, the world as purposed" (*MT* 49–50). The dimness of our recognition fades with more penetrating insight. In philosophy this insight is the unpacking of the two fundamental facts obvious in the nature of things, according to Whitehead—unity and diversity. In seeking deeper penetration, he suggests we "start from the notion of two aspects of the universe. It includes a factor of unity, involving in its essence the connexity of things, unity of purpose, and unity of enjoyment. The whole notion of importance is referent to this ultimate unity. There is also equally fundamental in the universe, a factor of multiplicity. There are many actualities, each with its own experience, enjoying individually, and yet requiring each other" (*MT* 51).

This description is frequently echoed in Whitehead's acknowledgment that philosophic (or scientific) explanation begins with the fact of an embodied percipient, with felt physical connection to the entire environment. These physical connections ground the very sensations appealed to in our reasoning. "In being aware of the bodily experience, we must thereby be aware of aspects of the whole spatio-temporal world as mirrored within the bodily life." In this bodily experience, we are self-evidently aware of the "distant environment" and the "transcendent world" in general (*SMW* 91–92) The long passages from *Process and Reality* cited previously echo these programmatic claims more systematically. Our perception reveals, and renders more definite, the felt interconnection of our subjectivity with the efficacious, emotionally heavy world around. Intensive perceptual discernment, woven on a basis of intensive emotional causality, is the fundamental evidence of our intuition, from which philosophy begins.

Thus, we can return to the passage quoted in the introduction concerning the insight guiding Whitehead's construction of his philosophic scheme. The "demand for an intellectual justification of brute experience" concludes with "the assertion of the old doctrine that breadth of thought reacting with intensity of sensitive experience stands out as an ultimate claim of existence" (*PR* 16). The intensity of sensitive experience with which our thought reacts occurs at the emotional and perceptual and intellectual levels simultaneously, as this discussion of symbolic reference, as well as the analysis of the higher forms of experience, points out. Likewise, our breadth of thought—our entertainment and realization of remote conceptual possibilities—ultimately concerns this intensive experience.

Any doctrine of existence must begin with existence as it reveals itself in this primarily intensive human experience. Whitehead is aware that we are here at the limits of the applicability of proof and argumentation. The appeal is to intuition, but to Whitehead, it is an intuition unburdened by the presuppositions about knowledge that undermined rationalism, empiricism, and idealism, generating a dualism of nature and mind, and rendering unintelligible the value experiences that permeate our lives. The retreat into ultimately solipsistic empiricism, substantialist rationalism, or subjectivistic idealism is on Whitehead's terms not a triumph of rationalism but instead marks its retreat, "the great refusal of rationality to assert its rights" (*SMW* 92). The occasion of knowing is an occasion of existence, revelatory of the general contours of this existence; we do not work *from* knowledge *to* being, whether our chosen path be empiricist, substantialist, or idealist, but discover being existing objectively in knowledge.

> We have to search whether nature does not in its very being show itself as self-explanatory. By this I mean, that the sheer statement, of what things are, may contain elements explanatory of why things are. Such elements may be expected to refer to depths beyond anything we can grasp with a clear apprehension. In a sense, all explanation must end in an ultimate arbitrariness. My demand is, that the ultimate arbitrariness of matter of fact from which our formulation starts should disclose the same general principles of reality, which we dimly discern as stretching away into regions beyond our explicit powers of discernment. (*SMW* 92–93)

Immediate experience discloses existence as the interconnection of one act of experience with the world that stretches away beyond that occasion in space and time.

Whitehead goes out of his way to distance himself from Santayana in a passage that nicely captures the sense in which the "being" discovered existing "objectively" in knowledge can be thought of as the kind of ecstatic subjectivity I have been arguing for. Santayana's relatively solipsistic account of cognitive "intuition" makes the strange-sounding claim that "nothing given exists," because existence belongs to things that are not present to intuition (things that can be apprehended only by "animal faith"). In a manner that relates Santayana's account of intuition simultaneously to sense experience and to actuality in general, Whitehead chides (the otherwise "genius") Santayana for his denial that the contents of intuition stand in any existential relationship with other things or intuitions. He then claims that the philosophy of organism is precisely the acceptance of the premise that the immediate contents of one experience—its "*act* of experience"—finds itself in ("becomes a datum for") the existential immediacy of another occasion—*its* "act of experience" (PR 142).

The point against Santayana is his distinction between present immediacy of intuition and other kinds of existences in a manner that asserts both their separateness and their difference, and Whitehead claims to be rejecting both as introducing a "veil" between an experient and its world. It is for such reasons that I feel it appropriate to close the analytical gap between what is called "final" and what is called "efficient" causality by Whitehead. Intuition is the entertainment of essences, for Santayana, just as immediacy is for Whitehead the entertainment of possibility, but Santayana's intuition of essences cannot transfer itself to or claim itself as existentially insinuated in another being, whereas Whitehead demands just this. This is an interesting point at which to offer a gloss on this passage as a statement on how to think of eternal objects' role in actuality. If the objection to Santayana be taken as a point of reference, eternal objects (essences) convey not just a form, but an actuality as formed, when they are considered as the vehicles of objectification of one actuality in another. To call them "forms of definiteness" inert in themselves does not circumscribe their function in objectification to inertness as well. When there is transfer of form between actualities, it is a transfer of agentive contrast, a mode of activity shared between subjects.

To return to our discussion, then, presentational immediacy is at once an instance of the ultimate aim at creative realization of intensity of feeling, and the first point of evidence that this ultimate aim is what is to be discovered upon investigation of the universe. In sensitive experience we feel our ecstatic presence to and in other things, and their genuinely ecstatic presence in us. It is this feeling on the part of the knower of intensive unity with other times and places from which metaphysics proceeds. In the final section of this chapter, I will return to this point of departure in Whitehead's thought, and discuss what may be taken as its systematic justification (so far as arbitrariness may be justified!). The conclusion here is that human experience is the foundation for Whitehead's systematic description not only in the sense that all subjects are conceived on the analogy of the purposive conceptual agency we enjoy, but on the deeper point of the intensity characteristic of this enjoyment, whereby purpose, conceptuality, and agency come to have meaning in our experience of embeddedness in an emotionally and valuatively impressive world.

Some Historical Considerations

The sources of Whitehead's intuition as to the ultimate evidentiary status of intensive experience are probably various. We have already seen that the basic distinction between intensive and extensive quantity as it manifest itself in the history of philosophy was of concern to Whitehead in his fundamental mathematical speculations about how we are to conceive the quantitative aspect of things, scientifically or metaphysically. We will return to this issue later.

As to the epistemology of intensity, there is particular appeal to be made once again to Samuel Alexander, and also to some insights of Henri Bergson. In *Space, Time, and Deity*, Alexander asks straightforwardly whether the intensity characteristic of space and time, which involves the compression of multiplicity in an individual unity, is also characteristic of sense experience and thinking. He concludes that for sensation, intensity is present in the quantitative spatiotemporal relations involved in the perception of objects, but is separate from the qualitative aspects of those perceptions. Thus intensity indicates the degree of presence of a quality apprehended, but the ordered patterns constitutive of quality and quantity differ ontologically.[11]

We have seen Whitehead's rejection of this distinction between the qualitative and quantitative patterns earlier, and may speculate that he goes out of his way to do so in dialogue with Alexander's thought. Alexander notes that Bergson forwards the position that "intensities really are qualities" and that thus a distinction between the two in sensation is erroneous, though he himself will not go so far.[12] Alexander does not indicate which of Bergson's works he is referring to, but in *Creative Evolution* we find the following passage, which seems to establish a link between the general issue of qualitative intensity, and the primary intuitions from which inquiry begins. Discussing our deductive abilities in regard to our knowledge of the perceived world, Bergson invokes the idea of a "latent geometry" integral to all acts of intelligence. We bring to any perception or deduction the obligation that quantitative intuitions will be formative of any other apprehension.

> Thus prior to the science of geometry, there is a natural geometry whose clearness and evidence surpass the clearness and

> evidence of other deductions. Now, these other deductions bear on qualities, and not on magnitudes purely. They are, then, likely to have been formed on the model of the first, and to borrow their force from the fact that, behind quality, we see magnitude vaguely showing through. We may notice, as a fact, that questions of situation and of magnitude are the first that present themselves to our activity, those that intelligence externalized in action resolves even before reflective intelligence has appeared.[13]

This kind of action is closely associated with 'instinct'.[14] Bergson's idea of the quantitative impress of our perceived environment in light of the requirements of action is echoed in Whitehead's repudiation of subjectivism in *Science and the Modern World,* passages from which have already been quoted as to the primitive fact of the body's feeling of the world. "Just as sense-perception seems to give knowledge of what lies beyond individuality, so action seems to issue in an instinct for self-transcendence" (*SMW* 90). It should be noted, too, that the passage from Bergson is in part explicative of how it is that intellect always "spatializes" and thereby distorts its subject matter, mainly by the mis-ascription of extensive quantities to things that in Whitehead's improved terminology are really intensive quantities.

The quantitative aspect of intensity, whereby pattern is the primitive feature of existents, receives elaboration in regard to perception by Alexander and Bergson, in a manner that may certainly have influenced Whitehead, inspiring him at the same time to devise a revisionist scheme in which unnecessary distinctions between quantitative and qualitative patterns could be maintained by a firmer metaphysical grasp of the nature of intensity per se (particularly its ontological rescuability from infection by the notion of measurable extensive quanta). Some other specific differences emerge between Whitehead's analysis and that of his sources. For example, Alexander denies that thinking itself involves intensity. To be sure, he asserts that there is an indirect intensity in thinking, in respect either to the effort of attention required in regard to some particular object, especially upon the promptings of bodily circumstance, or to the intensity of belief that may attach to any thought.[15] I will explore the connection of intensity and attention in thinking in the next chapter, where it will be critical to the development of the moral applications of Whitehead's scheme. We have already seen, however, that attention to definite detail in our environment is very much a product of the intensive discriminations made possible in symbolic reference, which involves the causal objectification of and the presentational emphasis on intensive contrasts and hence their proper presence in that which is called thought. The influence of Bergson on Whitehead's conception of mental experience, and the extent to which it presented some difficulties to be overcome, will be explored in the final section of this chapter.

In order to appreciate this influence and its implications in our understanding of the role of intensity in Whitehead's scheme, however, I must turn to my discussion of the Theory of Extension, for in this context the issue of the connection between the nature of our conception of reality and the fabric of reality itself is of the essence.

Coordinate Analysis: Extensity and Intensity

In chapter two it was argued that our apprehension of the *subjective* conditions of genesis (becoming) of an actuality somehow hinged on our consideration of that actuality's *objective* functioning in other entities. In other words, the analysis of the satisfaction and superjection of an actuality is precedent to an analysis of its coming-to-be. The problem at hand then was an initial attempt to construe the relationship between the subjective immediacy of actuality in process, which is supposedly of some sort of ontologically primary status, and the objective efficacy of an actuality, which is supposedly ontologically derivative, or set off from the subjective becoming. We have since engaged in numerous discussions that have attempted to eliminate the analytic perspective from which such a separation or ontological distinction might be, or need to be, made. It was noted in chapter two that Whitehead's awareness of the connection between genetic and coordinate division—the connection between analysis of concrescence and analysis of the concrete—appears to have increased as the writing of *Process and Reality* proceeded, if we are to take Lewis Ford's conjectures as accurate.[16] It would be helpful at this point to return to this discussion so as to clearly understand the relationship between the operations of thinking and the dynamic of being. The argument of this section is that the ontological problems I have been addressing are generated by a misapplication of notions that are really, though unconsciously, derived from a misunderstanding of coordinate analysis.

Let us begin with a consideration of Ford's explanations as to how the theory of coordinate division came to be introduced into the system. The section on coordinate division was, according to Ford, probably "the last to be included in *Process and Reality*." The supposed reason for its inclusion was to provide a "bridge" between the theory of concrescence and the theory of extension. Ford hypothesizes that Whitehead only gradually became aware that the analysis of concrescences and the analysis of concrete relations amongst concrete entities are commensurable.[17] I would expect that because the intimate connection between subjectivity and objectivity, concrescence and concreteness, subject and superject are constantly entertained, though not without perplexity, throughout the scheme, Whitehead would have been more careful to document the relationship of genetic and coordinate analysis. And yet it appears that Ford is correct in claiming that the theory of coordinate division or coordinate analysis remained insufficiently integrated into the system as laid out in regard to the genetic account.

It is my view that what the theory of coordinate division might have rendered clearer to Whitehead was that our *analysis* of an entity as concrete influences our *analysis* of an entity as concrescent, such that certain conceptions we might be tempted to have about the *being* of a concrete entity fail to capture *the sense* in which it *is one* with (or "constituted by") the *becoming* of a concrescent entity. The parity between the two levels of analysis and the two (apparent) levels of ontology needs to be very carefully understood so as not to generate confusions about the existence of actualities. Thus, the notion of coordinate division could serve to indicate how one not only can but must think together the two types of analysis offered in the scheme, one in regard to concrescence (the transmission of influences, as Whitehead refers to it in the section now in question), and the other in regard to extension (the scheme of relations providing the "conditions to which all transmission must conform" [PR 288]), in a manner that accounts for both the distinctness that seems to apply to the concrete over and against the concrescent, *and* the intimate ontological connection between them.

COORDINATE ANALYSIS AND THE THEORY OF EXTENSION

The theory of extension has two roles in Whitehead's scheme: first, to account for the solidarity of actualities in a continuum throughout which causal influence is possible, and second, to account for how scientific measurement that is not merely a function of the knowing mind itself is possible. The point of the theory is that the two roles are not disjoined, that the understanding gained in science is founded on and referent to the metaphysical situation as it exists. Thus the oft-quoted comment by Whitehead, "Science is *either* an important statement of systematic theory correlating observations of a common world, *or* it is the daydream of a solitary intelligence with a taste for the daydream of publication. But it is not philosophy to vacillate from one point of view to the other" (PR 329).

The theory of extension explains how the observations made by science, which depend on sense perception, pertain to a universe really connected in a scheme of extensive relatedness to which the measuring efforts of science may be applied. The connection between scientific observation and related actualities is grounded on the fact that presentational immediacy really can disclose actualities, in some fashion, and that extensive relations among actualities generate those relations observed by science that is always done in the mode of presentational immediacy (PR 333).

Now, a coordinate analysis concerns the analysis of the purely concrete aspects of actualities functioning objectively in other actualities. The 'satisfaction' of an actuality is objectified in subsequent actualities. The coordinate divisibility of the satisfaction into its constituent feelings arises from its objectification in these other actualities. In other words, a satisfied entity may be analyzed into its component prehensions in virtue of that entity's presence in other entities under some aspect. This kind of analysis abstracts from the full immediacy of subjectivity and considers the entity only as concrete. There is elimination of some of the fullness of actuality in the subjective form of the totality of feelings, but there is preservation of some elements of definiteness achieved (PR 283–93).

The division of entities in coordinate analysis has been taken to have ontological conclusions or has undergirded ontological distinctions between concrescence and concreteness in the minds of commentators, but in my view this involves a misapprehension of what coordinate division tells us about how to construe the individuality of entities. What is revealed in a coordinate analysis is not ontologically separate from the subjectivity of an actuality. Concreteness can emerge for observation because of the extensive divisibility of the region of the extensive continuum actualized by an entity. An actuality realizes an 'extended quantum' that is not in fact divided spatially or temporally ("such a view is exactly what is denied by the epochal theory of time"), but may be divided for purposes of analyzing the objectifications of the actual world (the individual prehensions) realized in that region (PR 283).

Because of the quantitative nature of the extensive region—"the problem dominating the entire concrescence is the actualization of the quantum *in solido*" (PR 283)—we may be led to believe that individualities may be construed in a kind of separation from each other on the analogy of *discrete quantities*. But the notion of coordinate division, whereby objectifications assume the nature of subquanta in virtue of being the divisions of a quantum region, does not allow any such notion. For the divisibility in question arises solely from the systematic relatedness of all regions. In other words, the quantitative aspects of any coordinate division are not individual—they emerge on the basis of extensive *relatedness*, not some fundamental notion of extensive *quantity* or merely numerical oneness.

It is here that we must recur to a possible debt to Bergson. In his discussion of the relation of soul and body, Bergson argues against the thesis that in metaphysics we are left with a sundering of the unextended-qualitative from the extended-quantitative elements in experience. Materialism is rejected as the derivation of the first from the second, and idealism is rejected as the derivation of the second from the first.[18] We have seen in general metaphysical terms that Whitehead's rejection of materialism and idealism is founded on the same insight as that forwarded by Bergson against the dualism of the extended and the unextended. Whiteheadian subjects are at once productive of qualitative character and quantitative extension, in virtue of the complete systematic connectedness of all such entities—the many really do become one, and really are increased by one.

Bergson and Whitehead both object that the dualism of quality and quantity stems from a misconstrual of what the individual things in reality are, and how to conceive of them in analysis. An equivalence is erroneously established, to put it simply, between the particular, discrete individuality of an object of thought, and the mode of existence of the thing referred to in the intellectual analysis. Intuition (direct experience) for Bergson is a complex unity of experience that intellect may subdivide into discrete quantitative components, but which in fact is not so divided.[19] Bergson attempts to effect the unification of the qualitative character of spatiotemporally extended realities and their extension, rather than continuing the mistake easily made in light of practical interests of inquiry, that the extensive quantities encountered in the course of such interests are misconstrued as fundamental in themselves.[20]

The important idea is the repudiation, in both Bergson and Whitehead, of the idea that existing objects have determinate, sharp existential boundaries conceivable on the analogy of the clear cut objects studied and measured in science. In Bergson's words, "All distinction of matter into independent bodies with absolutely determined outlines is an artificial division."[21] The problem in coordinate division, then, is to conceive of extensive properties of atomic quanta of qualitative character, without introducing such *artificial* divisions. The notion of extensive *relation* replacing as fundamental the notion of primitive extensive *quantities* achieves this goal. Relation establishes the simultaneously quantitative and qualitative nature of the texture of reality conceived as intensive integration adapted to an aim.

The multiplicity of atomic actualities, and the divisibility of any one of these multiple atoms, depends on their genuine unity. "The atomic unity of the world, expressed by a multiplicity of atoms, is now replaced by the solidarity of the extensive continuum. This solidarity embraces not only the coordinate divisions within each atomic actuality, but also exhibits the coordinate divisions of all atomic actualities from each other in one scheme of relationship" (*PR* 286). The participation of all actualities in the one scheme of extensive connection is that property in virtue of which each may be subdivided so as to indicate its appropriation of the others, and such that the others may be revealed in their complexity in virtue of their presence in the entity being divided. But the scheme of extensive connection is thoroughly relational. There is a difference between being an *extended* quantum, suggestive of numerical unity qua separation from other such unites, and being *extensively* related as a subjective actuality to all other such actualities. The quantitative aspects an extended region displays are derivative of the fact of relationship that is not itself divisible in extendedly quantitative terms. This is one of the main points of the geometry of the Theory of Extension. The pure notion of relationship founds the modes of connection (and therefore quantity) with which we are familiar in the extended world perceivable (symbolizable) in presentational immediacy and describable by science. Hence Whitehead's chastisement of Kant for making both modes of quantity categoreal, when only one (intensive quantity) warrants such status.

An actual entity realizes a quantum of the spatiotemporal continuum, but this *quantum is only individual and divisible in terms of its perspective rela-*

tionship with all the others. The complete interrelatedness of all regions as standpoints for realization is that aspect of the universe in virtue of which there can be transmission of feeling. Extensive relations "do not make determinate *what* is transmitted; but they do determine conditions to which all transmission must conform. They represent the systematic scheme involved in the real potentiality from which every actual occasion *arises*. This scheme is also involved in the attained fact that every actual occasion *is*. The 'extensive' scheme is nothing else than the generic morphology of the internal relations that bind the actual occasions into a nexus, and that bind the prehensions of any one actual occasion into a unity, coordinately divisible" (PR 288).

The scheme of extensive relationships expresses the basic geometry of the universe that exists in virtue of its constituents and to which all its constituents must conform. It is not modeled on any principle of quantitative individuality or discreteness; the extensiveness of an actuality does not refer to its "*numerical* self-identity" in any sense analogous to the counting of "ones." This latter notion is that pernicious, arithmetically derived concept of individuality that founds substance ontologies, and, according to Whitehead, "The admission of this fundamental metaphysical concept has wrecked the various systems of pluralistic realism" (PR 78). The Theory of Extension is designed to overcome the principle of numerical self-identity undergirding our conception of the quantitative reality of things. At the same time, it legitimates the move to quantification by showing that the primary notions from which we derive our sense of quantity (points, lines, etc.) in perception are grounded in a metaphysical scheme with quantitative features. Good science is a science whose measurements involving extended quantities approximates the relations established in the intensive quantitativeness of things, which intensity involves universal extensional relativity.

The conclusion of this discussion, as established in previous chapters on purely ontological grounds, is that the imputation of discrete numerical individuality, either to the prehensions revealed in a coordinate division, or to the actualities thus divisible, or to the future objectifications of an actuality, is a mistake of gravest metaphysical import, in fact the very mistake that the Theory of Extension was constructed so as to eliminate. The point of presenting the analysis of presentational immediacy in the context of the theory of extension is to show that, although perception is grounded in the metaphysical situation, the individuals selected out for emphasis or analysis in a coordinate manner have a certain derivative status, as the emergent characters of observable individuation (selected via determinate abstraction from full actuality) undermined ontologically by their intensive ecstasis. That extensive relations may suggest numerical differentiation between individuals divided coordinately does not license the ascription of images derived from the extensive quanta thus divided to the mode of self-individuation of entities that is an intensive quantity of feeling, of vibratory character.[22]

EXTENSIVE CONNECTION AND INTENSIVE INDIVIDUALITY

The conclusion to be drawn from the foregoing is that individuality is solely referent to the intensive aesthetic realization on the part of actualities. For even the relationships of extensive connection, though not dependent on any particular actuality for their nature, do depend on just that universe of actualities in process that exists. This raises two interesting questions for our consideration. First, if the relations of extensive connection are typical of the actualities that do exist, can they be metaphysically general and grounded nonarbitrarily? Whitehead comments that the scheme of extensive relations is "*sui generis*, and cannot be defined or explained" though he conjectures that some "general character of coordinate divisibility is probably an ultimate metaphysical character, persistent in every cosmic epoch of physical occasions" (PR 288).[23] By way of explanation, the concept of "God" as the principle in virtue of which there is "order" in the universe is introduced (PR 283). The "grounding" thus performed is no more arbitrary than the admittedly arbitrary appeal to our bodily experience of connection to a transcendent world cited earlier (SMW 92–93). I will return to the question of grounding this scheme in what follows and in the next chapter.

Second, if it is the case that all causality, and therefore all feeling, ultimately depends on extensive relation, could it not be argued that intensity is not metaphysically the most primitive notion in Whitehead's scheme as the present thesis has been suggesting? Indeed, the general characteristics of extensiveness are a function of the "objective species" of eternal objects, which are to be contrasted with the "subjective species" from which intensity of feeling is derived (PR 291). In virtue of the objective species of eternal objects one actuality can be objectified in another. The objective species of eternal objects are the purely relational, public characters, the "mathematical Platonic forms" that "concern the world as a medium" (ibid.). Thus, the "intensity of physical energy belongs to the subjective species of eternal objects, but the peculiar form of the flux of energy belongs to the objective species" (PR 292). The question becomes, which is more fundamental, in the sense of most metaphysically general—intensive relation or extensive relation?

But the question is misleading, for we must ask, more fundamental to what? If our concern is about the existence of actualities, the answer to the initial question is irrelevant. We are discussing the scheme of extensive relations that obtain in the *universe as actualized by entities seeking intensity* of feeling. In this light, extensity is a first fact about intensity and compromises nothing in regard to the arguments about individual existence that we have been entertaining. Without the achievement of a determinate intensity of feeling, a satisfied actual occasion does not, or will not, participate in the scheme of extensive relations; it will not *be*. On the other hand, however, what is to be made of the strong distinction between the eternal objects provident of intensity and those provident of connexity? Is this not in fact a distinction between public and private facts about the world?

Whitehead emphatically denies that any such distinction really obtains outside the realm of abstract analysis that discovers coordinate divisions. "The theory of prehensions is founded upon the doctrine that there are no concrete facts that are merely public, or merely private" (*PR* 290). The vast majority of references to intensity involve no ultimate existential distinction between the quantitative and qualitative dimensions of feelings; such a distinction is explicitly denied. There seems to be a contradiction between the general categoreal fundamentality of intensity and the distinction between species of eternal objects whereby only one of these species concerns intensity of feeling. But the contradiction is only apparent, for on Whitehead's own terms, the only fundamental (metaphysically general) concept of quantitative relation, and therefore pattern, is intensive.

To cite one of Whitehead's last insights on this topic, we note the observation that "geometry, as studied through the ages, is one chapter of the doctrine of Pattern; and . . . Pattern, as known to finite discrimination, is a partial disclosure with an essential relevance to the background of the Universe" (*MG* 671). It is the background *of* the universe, not *for* or *to* the universe: what is discovered via extensive or coordinate analysis are the emergent conditions of relation imposed by the intensive existential relationships of what exists. In calling extension the "scheme of possible relationships among actualities" Whitehead is not thereby creating a mode of possibility somehow systematically different from the modes of potentiality resident in things as intensive orders of becoming. Therefore, the objective species of eternal objects can be construed as not irrelevant to intensity, but expressive of conditions of intensive generality pertaining throughout the extensive continuum, in virtue, again, of the relations of actualities constitutive of that continuum.

Because the objective species of eternal objects can enjoy no status apart from the realm of actuality to which they are relevant, I choose to deny Whitehead's assertion that they are about a function that is not ultimately referable to intensity. The distinction between the quality of feeling and what appears to be the quantitative sense of the "form of the flux" carried by the objective ("mathematical") species is a nondistinction, or a distinction only of analysis. Perhaps if Whitehead had concluded his investigation of the full commensurability of genetic and coordinate analysis—how one can do both without imposing abstractions necessary to the latter on the concretenesses investigated in the former—the specious distinction between "species" (pardon the pun!) of eternal objects might not have been necessary. The unfortunate distinction is confined, at any rate, to the groping speculations of the last four pages of the chapter on coordinate division. It is introduced in a section that announces that it is addressed to "The antithesis between publicity and privacy" (*PR* 290) that we have seen to be indefensible on Whitehead's own terms and especially in the revised reading being offered here. There is an additional related discussion of what appears to be the "objective species of eternal objects" in *Adventures of Ideas*, where Whitehead claims, "Only the qualitative components of an actuality in the datum can pass into the subjective form" of a subject (*AI* 254). This claim would seriously undermine the ecstatic conception of individuality I am advancing here, where elements of the subjectivity of an occasion (its contrasts) are found in the subjectivities of other occasions, for here half of the existential pattern of the prior entity is excluded from the new entity.

Nobo cites this passage, and its surrounding discussion, as evidence that extensive relations form the ultimate basis for the transmission of feeling among entities, in the guise of a background of objective modes of relationship that need to be stipulated in the doctrine of the objective species of eternal objects, or the geometrical "Platonic forms" as Whitehead calls them.[24] But the *Adventures of Ideas* discussion, as was the case for the *Process and Reality* distinction between the qualitative and quantitative patterns, revolves around distinctions made *in analysis*. In fact, the distinction between the quantitative and qualitative, on which Nobo ultimately rests his strong distinction between causal (efficient) objectification and subjective (final) conformation, occurs, according to Whitehead, "when abstraction has reached its extreme limit. The extremity of abstraction from all qualitative elements reduces pattern to bare mathematical form—for example, triplicity or the abstract relationship of sets of numbers, such as the squareness of the number four. Such forms by their very natures cannot qualify subjective form. . . . Thus except in an indirect fashion—such as the qualitative feelings of smoothness of a sphere, of spikeyness of a square, of amplitude of a volume—, the doctrine of conformation does not apply to mathematical pattern. Here pure mathematics in its strictest modern sense is in question" (*AI* 254). In other words, the mathematical forms are discovered in a *mode of abstraction* from the actual intensive unities manifest in the actuated extensive continuum.

To my mind what Whitehead is doing here, and in the theory of extension generally, is showing that a mode of abstraction that may be adopted in regard to actualities discovers aspects of actualities that in a metaphysical sense may be taken to ground or legitimate the abstractions made, here those concerning "pure" mathematics. Science, too, needs to be shown to be more than a "daydream." Saying that the "doctrine of conformation does not apply to mathematical patterns" means that mathematical patterns *analytically (not existentially)* abstract from an intense subject's full range of feelings. Discovering "aspects" of an actuality does not mean that what is thereby discovered—in this case "mathematical" relations—are themselves a mode of potential definiteness that must be existentially different from forms of definiteness of "subjectivity."

In fact, the *Adventures of Ideas* discussion sets out an interesting clue as to how to resolve the present difficulties. The analysis of the abstract entertainment of an actuality continues: "Again the notion of an actual occasion—that is, of individual actuality—can be entertained in abstraction from any qualitative or mathematical components that in any sense are realized in its essence. . . . A particular actuality can also be abstracted from the mode of its first indication, so that in a later phase of experience it is entertained* as a bare 'It'. . . . In the sense in which an actuality can be indicated as a bare *It* for objective prehension—in that sense it does not enter into the subjective form of the prehension" (*AI* 254). The asterisk indicates Whitehead's own footnote to certain other texts, presumably for their clarificatory potential. One of the texts is *Process and Reality,* part III, chapter IV, which is a discussion of how the philosophy of organism revises the conception of individuality that is infected by the tendency to mean by "individual" something that is independent and viciously monistic in its inner nature.

Locke is once again lauded as the unwitting champion of a mutually synthesizing conception of individuals. Just as his "ideas" always find themselves "determine[d] to this or that particular existence," a Whiteheadian entity "repeats itself in another actual existent, so that in the analysis of the latter existent a component 'determined to' the former existent is discoverable" (*PR* 138-39). But the mode of analysis that discovers "components" needs to mind itself that it does not turn the component into a subordinate type of individual, which I think the doctrine of the objective species of eternal objects, as conveying *purely* quantitative relations undergirding actualities, *does*. The only individuation is intensive—particularity of existence and form, in any sense that can be designated qualitatively or quantitatively, belongs existentially to actualities and only *by abstraction* to the extensive relations discovered when something is *entertained* as a "bare 'It'."

At this point it would be helpful to set out the conclusion to be drawn from the latter sections of the present chapter and from the suggestions in earlier chapters about the metaphysical relevance of Whitehead's developing suspicions about the modes of linkage between genetic and coordinate analysis. Individuation in any ontologically relevant sense is intensive. Extended "individuation" of geometric or temporal "quanta" of any kind is derivative. In studying such extensive quanta via the discovery of the residence of prior actualities in later actualities—the division according to satisfactions—we acknowledge a scheme of relatedness among actualities, but cannot transfer the extend*ed* forms of the relations into the extens*ive* scheme of relations.

Discovery of mathematical pattern, and scientific "laws" subject to measurement, is a derivative abstractive process involving occasions of mental experience themselves abstracting subjective contents so as to make some (statistical) claims about the course of actual events. Such discovery stipulates quantitative relationships of a form that has emerged *from* process, primarily in the entertainment of existences in presentational immediacy. This I think is part of the point of the rejection of "infinitesimal quantities" (discussed earlier). The problem is that thought takes a form of quantitative determination that is indicated coordinately, "transmutes" this indication of coordinated quantity, and reads it back as an extend*ed* sense of unity into the actualities it purports to be describing genetically. Coordinate divisions are indeed referent to actualities—they are divisions of emergent satisfactions—but the abstract entertainment of certain of their features violates the real quantitative individuality of the entities, which is only intensive. Actualities possess quantity in the form of degree of presence of certain valuations in their ecstatic existence. The kind of quantities designated by any distinct geometrical forms of relatedness can only be a projection backward from abstraction, and not forward from actuality, unless the geometrical forms are themselves taken to be *intensive* elements of all actualities, which would collapse the distinction between the two species, leaving the interpretation developed here intact.

In general, thought must always ask itself: In what sense is something discriminated in any given method of abstraction (or, more importantly, simple verbal designation) being conceived as possessing a mode of conceivable individuality or particularity that it has *only because of its selection in thought* as a numerically single item of consideration? This is the question that Whitehead's satisfactory completion of the conception of the commensurability of the two modes of analysis would have helped address. As it is, his own discussion is replete with references to things in the realm of the actual as individuated or individually conceivable in a manner that undermines his more careful recognition of the merely derivative status of numerical unity from forms of intensive unification. Thought not only tends to "spatialize," to use Bergson's terms, it more fundamentally tends to treat its subject matters as numerically distinct in a manner that cannot help but distort the intensive character of unity as it is ontologically. Numerical unity is an abstract (i.e., it eliminates aspects of actuality) form of quantity that tends to infect any statement, because every sentence requires a subject that thereby purports to have an individual status that it may or may not. Whitehead's exceedingly strong distinctions between subjective and objective dimensions of the transmission of feelings, and the final and efficient causality therein involved, fall into the category of this infection of thought by modes of discrimination between individually conceivable things or elements of things. Individuated conception and individual existence suffer a relationship that is rooted in fact (the real interpenetration of satisfactions), but requisite of perpetual and deep critique.

The resolution of the question of the relation of extensity and intensity—via the assertion that extensive relations, being a function of the continuum of actualities as a whole, are subordinate to the general demand for intensity characterizing the continuum as processive rather than being a mere morphology—raises a further and more fundamental question of the grounding of Whitehead's scheme. For if extensity is a property of the community of fundamentally intensive atoms of becoming, it does not achieve that complete abstraction from particularity sought after in the Theory of Extension. Extensive connection may be free of any given empirical content, but it is not free of its grounding in an empirical intuition of the universe *as such*. On this score, Whitehead is in no worse straits than anyone concerned with the fundamental grounding of mathematical conceptions, and ultimately of metaphysical conceptions. But it must be noted that there is no transcending the general conditions of finitude in Whitehead's scheme, even for the purposes of grounding the scheme itself.

Indeed, Whitehead willingly acknowledges the ultimately probabilistic character of our metaphysical assertions, and entertains the further question as to whether anything in the experience of judgment as to probability ever serves to ground the propositions thus entertained (PR 194–207). There are many reasons for us to remain skeptical, though certain aspects of our situation afford some promise of a ground. These aspects concern our embeddedness, as occasions of mental experience, in an environment from which we abstract elements for consideration, though always under the conditioning force of the type of environment in question (PR 206–7). This promise does not escape probability, however. The one factor in my knowledge experience that transcends the metaphysics of probability involved in my judgments about my environment is the intuition of the reality of the "intensive relevance" of eternal objects to the discrete actual occasions about which I am trying to judge (PR 207). In other words, the intuition of intensive significance is the fundamental experience guiding any act of knowing, be it a judgment about my perception of an object, or a proposition regarding the grounding of the system itself. Knowledge is merely one instance of this "principle of intensive relevance" that is at work at all levels of experience for all subjects (PR 148–49). It is a nonstatistical intuition about that which lies at the base of things, the divine ordering of eternal objects such that there is evaluation and purpose (not mere mathematical form) at the base of any fact. Whitehead asserts that this is not a religious appeal, though it is urgent to explore a "secularization of the concept of God's functions in the world" (PR 207).

On what might such a secularization consist? A brief response to this question will serve as summary for the investigations of this chapter. It is my contention that the ultimate appeal in grounding this scheme, the insight that informs the relevance of intensity in all aspects of mental experience, including our decisions as to how to conceptualize individual existents in this scheme, is the appeal to the experience of value in human life. The interpretive leap of imagination is to the Platonic insight into the moral character of the universe as humanly experienced, rather than to the equally Platonic insight that mathematical relations seem pervasive. All entertainment of possibility in conceptual experience, all perceptual acts, all instincts for activity, all mathematical construction, all metaphysical speculation, to be mutually consistent and unified of purpose, must ultimately make this appeal, if our concern is the final rationalization of our experienced world.

Readying ourselves for the consideration of morality in the next chapter, we may end with the following passage from "Mathematics and the Good," an essay that is at once an encomium to Plato (and the forms of mathematical conception that he engendered), and Whitehead's own Platonic manifesto. The passage hints that Whitehead may finally have collapsed in his mind the distinction between abstract mathematical pattern and value-pattern, the distinction which, as argued previously, disrupts his own theory of atomic actuality. The centrality of 'pattern' to any and all philosophical considerations is emphasized:

> We cannot understand the flux which constitutes our human experience unless we realize that it is raised above the futility of infinitude by various successive types of *modes of emphasis which generate the active energy of a finite assemblage*. The superstitious awe of infinitude has been the bane of philosophy. The infinite has no properties. All value has the gift of finitude which is the necessary condition for activity. Also activity means the origination of patterns of assemblage, and mathematics is the study of pattern. Here we find the essential clue which relates mathematics to the study of the good, and the study of the bad. (*MG* 674, emphasis added)

The value that is the gift of finitude is the graded significance of the universe of actualities from the perspective of the occasion generated by the continuum-pervading actual and potential forms of emphatic evaluation. In Yeats's language the many "parts" of a single thought depend for their unity on the "glance" that runs "in the world's despite / To where the damned have howled away their hearts, / And where the blessed dance"—the finite experience is an evaluation of the totality of actual and possible modes of unity. As we hinted at the outset, the realm of alternative possibility realizable in thought, however intense, is not its own determination of moral "good" or "bad." There are serious deficiencies for subject and object—person and community—awaiting the intensive visionary who experiences him or herself as "needing nothing" in the sense of being "wound" like a "mummy" that is somehow sealed away from the processes comprehended in the thought. No thought is really the kind of closure that can seal itself in a sarcophagus of individual self-completeness. I think Yeats felt more positively about mummies than I imply here, for his interest in rituals of immortality was profound. But the actual course of realized immortality for ritualistically buried souls is one thing, and the potentially destructive contours of intense and finitely unifying intellection is another.

CHAPTER FIVE

An Essay on the Morality of Attention

> *Love, I shall perfect for you the child*
> *Who diligently potters in my brain*
> *Digging with heavy spade till sods were piled*
> *Or puddling through muck in a deep drain....*
> *Love, you shall perfect for me this child*
> *Whose small imperfect limits would keep breaking:*
> *Within new limits now, arrange the world*
> *Within our walls, within our golden ring.*
> —Seamus Heaney, "Poem" for Marie

Whitehead's contribution to moral discourse has as much to do with the problem of 'the one and the many' as does his metaphysics. One could argue that the main problem for moral thinking and action is the discernment of the relevant unities and diversities of value in the spheres of actuality and potentiality as they occur in human life. It takes much "digging with heavy spade" and "puddling through muck" to really come to terms with the acutely intensive realities pervading our moral environment. There is also to be considered our capacity to create "muck" via our profound capacity for what Whitehead calls "aesthetic destruction," the elimination of some intensities to the end of certain others. Heaney's poem, however, is a testimony of love, a promise of a kind of activity that is "perfecting" of the acts we bring forth from the "brain," our agentive intellect and imaginative power. The irony of moral life is the need to effect finite decisions that have inevitable transcendent repercussions, the choices, the "children" "whose small imperfect limits would keep breaking" despite their decisive singularity. The persistent quest for meaningful unity, particularly in human relationships—the "walls" of the "golden ring"—is undertaken in the midst of its perpetual breaking free of the "new limits" that "arrange the world." Moral experience is the rearrangement of the world in the quest for human subjective intensity of experience, and this rearrangement is swept into the rush of an ever-self-transcending temporal world. Problems of self-interest, responsibility, and care are born here. We hear in the poet's commitment to the ring of love the ever-present awareness of difficulty, of inconstancy, of fragility.

The purpose of this chapter will be to pose the question of how 'intensity' finds its moral application, with moral affairs taken as a special case of the problem of the one and the many conceived under the aspect of value-discernment. Problems regarding intellectual experience and its curious capacity to effect unities that may undermine the subjective unities of that which intellect perceives will be paramount, as will the issue of the moral agent's self-perception as transcendent creator. It is not my aim to construct, in so small a place, a complete ethic based on 'intensity' and drawing on concepts derived from all quarters of Whitehead's system, though this would be an interesting project. I will examine *some* of the implications of the ontology of intensity for the discussion of certain critical issues in moral thought, and on this level the discussion will have something in common with the attempts of other scholars, such as Lynn Belaief, to apply Whitehead's metaphysics to a study of ethics.[1] But my particular task here will be narrower, and will take the discussion of Whitehead's contribution to ethics in a new direction that, I think, adheres to the spirit of Whitehead's thought on questions as to the application of metaphysics. Specifically, this chapter will bring Whitehead's process philosophy into dialogue with the moral philosophy of philosopher-novelist Iris Murdoch.

Such a dialogue bears the burden of any comparison involving Whitehead's system: to marshal fertile concepts without being undermined by obfuscatory terminology. My general intent is to show how Whitehead's thought may be seen to contribute to the search for a new mode of conceiving the moral situation, the search for a "vocabulary of attention" as undertaken by Murdoch.[2] The notion of "attention" to which I think Whitehead's metaphysics has much to offer involves the self's ability to discern the realities with which it has to or can deal in its moral being, as created in particular moral acts. Thus my focus is not on the development of a moral *theory* based on Whitehead's system, but on the elaboration of a concept of moral *comportment*, allied to a fundamental commitment to a type of moral realism, that might be part of a number of theories, or a part of moral life in the absence of a theory about it.

Metaphysical Background

We saw in the articulation of the Category of Subjective Intensity the immediate relationship between the conditions of subjective becoming and the central concept of moral responsibility. To repeat, the category states that there is subjective aim at intensity of feeling not only in the present but in the relevant future. There is anticipatory feeling *in the present* respecting provision for intensity in the future, so that the double aim does not represent any strong division in experience. Whitehead explains that "[t]he greater part of morality hinges on the determination of relevance in the future. The relevant future consists of those elements in the anticipated future which are felt with effective intensity by the present subject by reason of the real potentiality for them to be derived from itself" (*PR* 27).

Almost every reference in Whitehead's writings to the concept of 'responsibility' refers us to this metaphysics of the intensive derivation of the future from the present, whereby present constitution is modified by the anticipation of future effect. In elaborating the notion that the feelings being integrated in concrescence "aim at the feeler" as the subject-superject of creative process, Whitehead writes: "In our own relatively high grade human existence, this doctrine of feelings and their subject is *best illustrated* by our notion of moral responsibility. The subject is responsible for being what it is in virtue of its feelings. It is also derivatively responsible for the consequences of its existence because they flow from its feelings" (*PR* 222, emphasis mine).[3] As I have argued in previous chapters, the "consequences" form *part of the being or existence* of the subject, as being some degree of anticipatable repetition of the intensive pattern and emotional tonality embodied in the actuality; this, coupled with the empirical fact (when it occurs) of our own quite determinate *feeling* of responsibility once those transcendent effects occur, shows that responsibility is internal to the act of self-constitution. Responsibility is not optional, though its conscious acknowledgment may be absent.

It is important to be absolutely clear on this point. It is integral to the doctrine of self-creation that the creature of this agency is internally connected to the process whereby it is created: "Its being is constituted by its becoming" (*PR* 23). Thus responsibility must be referred to the internal self-constitution of an actuality; in other words, it is primarily forward-looking. The morally important manner of experiencing responsibility is as anticipatory, and only derivatively as reflecting on the consequences of our acts as they come to pass. It is necessary to understand how this internality of responsibility is effected. The aim at intensity as immediate and anticipatory structures our responsibility in virtue of the "modification of subjective aim" in concrescent process. Subjective aim begins as a conceptual feeling regarding potentiality for complex achievement, and, over the course of the integrations occurring in each phase of feeling, undergoes modification according to the feelings as actually integrated. The modifications effect changes in the consideration of the relevant future as presently felt with some effective intensity.

Thus, in a discussion of the arbitrariness of the flux of metaphysical history, that there is no metaphysically general reason why the flux should have been precisely *this* flux (discussed in its metaphysical significance in Chapter Three, above), Whitehead refers the decision as to the form of the world-process to the individual free decisions of actualities, and remarks: "Further, in the case of those actualities whose immediate experience is most completely open to us, namely, human beings, the final decision of the immediate subject-superject, constituting the ultimate modification of subjective aim, is the foundation of our experience of responsibility, of approbation or of disapprobation, of self-approval or of self-reproach, of freedom, of emphasis. This element in experience is too large to be put aside merely as misconstruction. It governs the whole tone of human life" (PR 47). The "doctrine of responsibility," Whitehead remarks in the discussion of the emergent subject of feelings, "is entirely concerned with this modification" of subjective aim (PR 224). Responsibility is the intensively continuous perpetration of high-grade contrasts repetitively from one occasion of our experience to another. Its intensive, obtrusive presence in our lives (who has not felt the pangs of guilt, the pride of accomplishment?) is still further evidence of the realistic metaphysical hypothesis that asserts the possibility of a grasp of the not-present by present consciousness, alluded to in my introduction.

It is interesting to note this inclusion of references to the moral texture of experience at critical moments in Whitehead's metaphysics. Two implications arise: first, moral experience is frequently appealed to for its peculiar evidentiary status in describing the elements of experience in general, and in particular our experience of existential derivation from moment to moment. Second, this kind of evidence is one of the few Whitehead ever offers as to the intuitive plausibility of the metaphysics he erects, and is, moreover, central to his grounding of induction. I am tempted to forward the notion that the moral dimension of human experience (as a special case of the general aesthetics of experience) is a guiding thread in the construction of Whitehead's metaphysics. The introduction of moral considerations in the categoreal explanation of one of (if not *the*) central concepts of the system—subjective aim—is certainly suggestive in this regard, as is the comment that "this element in experience . . . . governs the whole tone of human life," thus standing as an element in any evidentiary experience. The human impress of intensive, self-transcending agency suggests itself as the most convincing evidentiary appeal to be made on behalf of the particular metaphysics Whitehead chooses to offer. This kind of moral appeal is not unusual in philosophy, but it does suggest that in Whitehead's case we had better be careful to attend to just how "intensity" might function as the intersection of metaphysics and ethics.

The perspective of metaphysical history in the passage cited previously calls our attention back to arguments forwarded earlier (chapter one)—that the consideration of any one actuality is never an affair of looking at it alone, but involves a look forward and backward such that its place in wider orders procurative of certain determinate intensive elements may be understood. These arguments are extremely significant for an understanding of present feeling of past, present, and future responsibility. The force of the following statement is thus most evident in moral affairs, though I have tried to argue to the ontological centrality of a particular slant on such notions: "[Y]ou cannot abstract the universe from any entity, actual or non-actual, so as to consider that entity in complete isolation. Whenever we think of some entity, we are asking, What is it fit for here? In a sense, every entity pervades the whole world; for this question has a definite answer for each entity in respect to any actual entity or any nexus of actual entities" (PR 28). Thus, too, the earlier arguments as to the dependence of genetic analysis on coordinate analysis (and the difficulties this raises for metaphysical conceptions of individuality) assume significance. What is noticeable about an actuality—that which prompts the analytical question about its fitness—depends largely on its solidarity with other occasions such that there is significant identity of form; the entity assumes a 'fitness' in the orders procurative of form or intensity of feeling. Moral responsibility is a poignant example of the importance of fitness of realization for a wider order that obliges some realization and that will suffer the consequences of this or any other such "child."

Transcendent Decision and Control of Process

Intensive incorporation of feelings regarding the relevant future is the doctrine underpinning the notion of "transcendent decision." Subjective aim, particularly as constituted by those intellectual operations whereby potentialities are introduced in high-grade experience, concerns the entity's experience of itself as transcendent creator, conditioner of creative action (cf. PR 273). Indeed, propositional feelings in general are devoted to the increase of intensity in the present *and* future. The key here, as in the general notion of subjective aim, is that a "lure" operates so as to maximize the experience of the importance of certain elements of the environment. The conditions of intensity—triviality, vagueness, narrowness and width—concern the valuative grading of importance of the elements in the actual world prehended in any occasion of becoming. Intellectual experience, which is the most morally obvious experience of "lures," is distinctive precisely in virtue of its capacity to enhance the importance or depth of what is felt in an occasion (ibid.). A lure is a temptation to a particular intensive depth.

In the description of experience, (particularly intellectual experience) in *Modes of Thought*, 'importance' is the fundamental notion developed to explicate the structural dynamics of process. The notion assumes critical significance in regard to morals: "Morality consists in the control of process so as to maximize importance. It is the aim at greatness of experience *in the various dimensions belonging to it*. . . . Morality is always the aim at that union of harmony, intensity, and vividness which involves the perfection of importance for that occasion" (MT 13-14). Systematically speaking, of course, harmony and vividness are aspects of intensity, and not separate considerations. Importance, or intensive valuation, is a multidimensional experience of the different "ecstases" proper to an individual as we have defined it here. Although all occasions seek to some extent to control process to the end of importance in the present and in transcendent effect, the inevitability of this control, and its intentional direction in human life, cannot be understated.

The moral significance of the aim at intensity of experience as the purposive enhancement of importance ultimately hinges on our interpretation of just how we are to construe 'control.' Control of process through high-grade intellectual experience of relevant novel alternatives for realization introduces the notion of "agency" or "will" central to any ethical scheme. To some extent, 'control' refers simply to the inevitable transcendent effects of whatever decisions are arrived at in the aim at intensity. At this level, being 'fit' for some purpose in a given order marks some exercise of control although the maintenance of that form of order depends on that actual entity rising to the occasion of its fitness, or to speak more systematically, its importance or intensity. But in those experients wherein importance is open to significant modification, control is more deliberate in the sense of being contingent directly upon the autonomous imaginative play of intellectual feeling, and not simply upon the weight of physical purposes.

We have here come upon the question of just what it is that constitutes moral agency in Whitehead's scheme. Traditionally this has been the search for a kind of will or intentionality that answers to our sense of the controllability of processes by purposeful action. Certainly, there is no room in this metaphysics for a substantive will, or faculty of mind corresponding functionally to such a will.[4] We have seen that "mind" in Whitehead's system assumes an apparently precarious status, "wandering in 'empty' space amid the interstices of the brain" (PR 339), existing in events not necessarily possessed of any strong degree of serial or personal order such as we are used to finding in accounts of moral personality or identity. This is a markedly criticized aspect of Whitehead's thought, easily remarkable as evidence for the moral unavailability or inadequacy of the system.[5]

Robert Neville, who also seeks to erect a cosmology premised on processive value-events, finds Whitehead's view to be seriously flawed in regard to its ability to account for and turn our attention toward the kind of consistent identity required of a theory of agency. Such a theory should be able to ground responsibility as well as our sense of self, although acknowledging the event-aspect of experience. On Neville's reading, Whitehead does not provide sufficient conditions of this kind of agentive unity.[6] Neville is absolutely correct. But this reading is a discovery of a flaw only if one is committed to a supposition that only a certain kind of agency can be legitimately said to experience responsibility and all of the other purposive elements of moral living. With the repudiation of modernism's belief in a substantive self, the search has continued in other guises for those conditions of unity that might overcome the partiality, shortsightedness, misdirectedness, inauthenticities, and genuine cruelties of our moral behavior. Or, conversely, the concern for morally illuminating theories is simply abandoned, as might be said of some post-modern gestures towards the inevitable fragmentation of experience.[7] The former tactic results in concepts of will or agency that do not meet the requirements of an event-based theory of reality, including human experience; the latter embodies none of the spirit of hope and adventure that Whitehead holds to be the non-negotiable fabric of rational as well as subrational experience.

Does a moral philosophy need to be a remedy to the momentariness and partiality of human behavior and thought, positing agencies and principles that transcend particularity to achieve satisfactory generality or even universality? Just what kind of moral individuality is really required to sustain the concepts of responsibility and intentionality that are, on Whitehead's own recognition, the strongest evidence of our place in a world beyond our own motives? In what follows I will argue that a picture of moral agency undertaken in light of the ecstatically intensive conception of the agency of all metaphysical subjects can find correctives to evil within the given framework of human nature, which seems to be so unregenerately partial, particular, unstable, non-universalizing, as to be so decisively *productive* of evil.

Neville's critique can be seen to operate within the interpretive thesis of Leclerc, disputed in chapter 3, that the macroscopic entities deemed to be moral agents (persons with bodies) have only derivative status qua 'actual' in Whitehead's scheme, and that this kind of derivative actuality is inadequate to the macroscopic concerns of responsibility. On my reading, the individual events constituting the life history of any such object are sufficiently connected in an existential, agentive sense with the other individual events constituting that macroscopic organism, such that the agency of the individual events considered severally carry the weight of agency for the society as a whole. It is simply not empirically evident that when acting as a moral agent, one acts as a totalized enduring object to which agency must be ascribed in some overarching form. This conception of agency begs the question of the nature of existence, deciding beforehand what type of entity we are looking for. Neville does himself develop an alternative theory of individuality so as to neither beg this question nor fall into any of the pitfalls of atomism. It is my claim, however, that atomism rightly understood does not possess such pitfalls, and more adequately comprehends the irremediable partiality and episodic character of our moral experience. As Murdoch puts it, half metaphorically, half literally, "The self is a divided thing and the whole of it cannot be redeemed any more than it can be known" (*SG* 99).

We can elucidate the elements of a working notion of moral comportment that functions within the historically evident limitations of human nature, without surrendering the capacity and respect for value and goodness presumably celebrated in any normative consideration of moral life, philosophical or otherwise. The notion of agency that I adopt is akin to that suggested by Lucas, "the occurrence of certain activities or events [rather] than the possession of fixed and determinate mental states or characteristics."[8] Agency is thus a kind of limiting concept, a way of describing the offices of human experience in regard to certain types of activity, namely the creation of some pattern of value in virtue of the realities present out of which that pattern shall be effected. It is at this point that Whitehead's potential contribution to moral discourse, offered within the confines of an event-theory of reality and human experience, interfaces with the perspective of Iris Murdoch.

The Metaphysics of Muddle

Though cool to constructive metaphysics in her earlier writings, Murdoch has recently, in *Metaphysics as a Guide to Morals*, undertaken generous discussions of speculative descriptions of reality in the context of her own attempt to articulate a form of moral realism. Her perspective is decidedly Platonic, attempting to elucidate the structures of reality constituting or evident in our moral intuition of the universe and of our existence in it. The elusive concept of goodness that has always haunted Murdoch's essays and novels is in this most recent project illuminated from multiple philosophic perspectives. In an era in which we are told that the traditional philosophical horizons of rational search for truths and persuasive argumentation on their behalf is being (Murdoch acknowledges using Nietzche's phrase) "sponged away," she sees herself as taking a hard look at the "entirely new mode of thinking" that is coming to be.[9]

The new mode of thinking of interest to Murdoch draws heavily on aesthetic experience as a model for moral intuition, and the various metaphysics imaginatively considered are explored for their bearing on how best to conceive of the aesthetics of moral life. There is, perhaps, no better arena in which to introduce Whitehead as a contributor to moral discourse. Although Murdoch is skeptical of any theory's ability (qua theory) to influence the ethical arena, the dense texture of ordinary life, she is yet hopeful in this work that theoretical exploration might awaken recesses of conception and imagination that contribute to our capacity to see and think about the reality that so often eludes us. Whitehead's metaphysics of aesthetic harmony, captured in the systematic notion of intensity, may provide a theoretical architechtonic through which to engage Murdoch's hope. Since in Whitehead's scheme experience is not (in the scheme's better moments) subjugated to intellectualistic categories, there may be a chance that it can deliver a contact with reality less open to our capacity to "deform by fantasy" the relevant aspects of the world that concern us morally.[10] Whitehead's metaphysics supplements Murdoch's intuition of a new way of seeing, and Murdoch's expressiveness in the sphere of moral discourse supplements and helps overcome Whitehead's idiosyncratic formulation of a new mode of conceptualizing reality.

Like Whitehead, Murdoch repudiates the notion of an existential distinction between fact and value, a distinction that can lead only, in her view, to a marginalization of value and morals in a world increasingly captured in discourse about facts (*MGM* 25–57). Her attitude toward twentieth-century science's attachment to positivistic and materialistic conceptions of "fact" is one of deep suspicion. Our encounter with reality is shot through with values, and "[i]nnumerable forms of evaluation haunt our simplest decisions" (*MGM* 26). All experience hence is tinged with the moral, with the question of how such evaluation can or should proceed in any instance. The title of this section, "The Metaphysics of Muddle," draws on Murdoch's pervasive sense of the particularity of action within which we must attempt evaluation. In a life of finite, particular acts and thoughts, we create 'muddle', or moral confusion, based on our experience of various spheres of evaluation often eluding any comprehensive sense of organization and moral clarity.[11] Most of the "muck," to recur to our poem, is of human origin.

Muddledness is the experience of competing forms of value in a situation in which it appears to be impossible to realize all competitors; it is an experiential rendering of what may theoretically be conceived as moral conflict. The sense of 'muddle' so often present in Murdoch's fictional characters' lives indicates the relevance of various spheres of evaluation competing for realization through the thought and action of a persona unable to effect the necessary balancing of values. In Whiteheadian terms, what fails is the aesthetic synthesis of intensities offering themselves as qualifications of the creative process. There is discord among values, mutual inhibitions of intensities, based on a failure to find an intensive evaluation (contrast) wherein all proffered values may be included (*AI* 254–57). A perfect harmonization of all relevant values is not achieved, indeed, may be nonachievable. A sensitivity to the inevitable tragedy of value-conflict is an important part of the work of its avoidance.

Perfection is an ideal that eludes the finite, while remaining relevant to it. The imperfection of value-balancing such that muddle or merely partial achievement results is a fact about our lives. The "small imperfect limits" of our designs "keep *breaking*." Breakage is a sign not only of limitation but genuine disruption; it sounds a note of discord, and it is experienced with a note of anxiety. For Whitehead, 'discord' provides an aesthetic background against which there is adventure and freshness of form. The discord of intensities breathes life into a processive universe, forcing a constant adjustment of aesthetic achievement. "Thus the contribution to Beauty which may be supplied by Discord—in itself destructive and evil—is the positive feeling of a quick shift of aim from the tameness of outworn perfection to some other ideal with freshness still upon it. Thus the value of Discord is a tribute to the merits of Imperfection" (*AI* 257). Murdoch likewise tenaciously affirms the isomorphic nature of evil and good in the recognition that "[d]iscord is essential to goodness," to our ability to recognize ourselves as obligated to produce better states of value-experience than those already at hand (*MGM* 488–89). Thus, we can assert that in a Whiteheadian-influenced ethics, discord and adventure are admitted as coordinated aspects of moral life with what we might call a categoreal status. Discord and adventure, attenuation of intensity and the commitment to overcome it, lie at the base of all moral experience, and constitute the first facts that must be recognized in the attempt to elaborate normative conditions for experience.

The admission of a principle of discord, of the experiential reality of 'muddle', is only a beginning. Whether discord be valuable or purely destructive and evil depends largely on its conditions of generation, which now require elaboration. The 'genetic' aspect of metaphysical description in Whitehead's system is highly suited to the habituation of our intellect to this search for the originating conditions of discordant experience. A conflict of intensities due to excess valuation of some elements of the world over others without due attempt at contrast effecting compatibility is "evil." The "clutch at vivid immediacy" that is "life" on Whitehead's terms requires care. A "living society" requires "food"—capture of environmental resources in the interest of some aim. An environment—be it in regard to actual nutrition or ideas, work, loyalty, or any other morally relevant capture of value—can sustain only a finite number of forms with sufficient dominance to procure significance. Thus, "whether or no it be for the general good, life is robbery. It is at this point that with life morals become acute. The robber requires justification" (PR 105). Life controls process to certain sought-after outcomes. Process as such seeks only intensities. "Living" processes procure intensities in culpable fashion. It is worth noting that the passage immediately following this acknowledgment of the need for "justification" is the section already cited wherein God as procurer of intensities has regard for each occasion *qua* individual intensity. The creative thrust is toward intense realization—it is up to the emerging subjects of such realization to find justifications, if they can, for such realization in the textures of actuality.

Two concerns emerge from this discussion. First, an understanding of the nature of individual intensity, particularly in regard to morals, is needed so as to clarify the sense in which intensity of individual achievement requires reference to other individuals. Second, the requirements for thoughtful reflection in the sphere of moral life must be explored such that the aesthetics of experience may be morally justifiable. How is it that moral experience may introduce an increase of beauty, instead of a destruction of value through irremediable partiality and vicious muddle?

The standard problem of subjectivism is held to be particularly acute in a scheme such as Whitehead's, since the scheme founds reality on subjects whose immediate aims suggest the extreme possibility of the most vicious and aestheticist moral solipsism. I hope that the concept of ecstatic individuality, founded on a thorough understanding of intensity, has already begun in the reader's mind to circumvent such a subjectivism, solipsism, or egoism. Since the subject is wherever its effects are, and in a nonderivative ontological sense, subjectivism in the solipsistic or egoistic sense is not an option, or at least not the primary form of moral experience derivable from the atomism. This argument against the allegedly subjectivist and aestheticist cast of Whitehead's description of experience will be expanded in what follows.

'Individuality' in Moral Experience

It is appropriate to pause at this point to emphasize what I think is one of Whitehead's major contributions to moral philosophy, a contribution that I snatch from what might be seen as its greatest weakness. Quite apart from the applicability of any given systematic notion to the demands of moral discourse and theory, there is a fundamental moral insight forming the background of Whitehead's analysis of human (and other) experience at all levels—from trivial events to the highest achievements of civilized life. This insight is that all experience, regardless of consequence and significance, is an individual, atomic, particular event. The facts of extensive and intensive connection compromise the absoluteness of particularity, as argued previously, but experience does remain atomic, the real temporal creation of events. The moral significance of this insight is its illuminative power as regards the texture of experience in regard to value and choice. If experience is atomic, we cannot count on the mere weight of past experience to bring to pass desired outcomes; we cannot depend on the mere entertainment of an idea to effect a change in behavior or thinking. Each moral event bears in itself the responsibility to effect the achievement of value appropriate and possible for it. The parallel with existentialism (raised earlier) here is strong. Each moral event, in its quest for intensity of feeling, stands forth as the locus of our moral being. The moral significance of our existence cannot be relegated to some dim "other" time, for we pervade all times by virtue of our very immediacy. Any given individual experience bears not only on the cumulative history of our past, but also on the real potentialities of our future. Identification of the self with some alternative time frame (past or future) that is not fundamentally a reference to the present is a form of inauthenticity and denial of the true contours of being an agent.

Thus Whitehead's contribution comes at the level of our conceptualization of 'individuality' in experience—the individuality of any given experience as it is undergone, and the individualities encountered (prehended or perceived) in the aesthetic synthesis of the present experience. Our moral assumptions about the 'units of being' involved in value-experience are conditioned by the fact of connected atomicity. There is no assumption of enduring *substance* as an account of one's own character, or the character of any other agent encountered. There is no enduring substantive mode of conceiving the relevance or importance of values—each moment is the realization of whatever value can mean to us. What will endure is the character of the present achievement, not a self that can disown it or "make up" for it. Two things follow. First, our understanding of moral individuality is conditioned so as to incorporate the significance of temporal creativity. Second, our attention is drawn to the individuality of each moment of choice and evaluation, that this event may be understood as the locus of agency that it is, as well as being understood to be partial and imperfect.

Returning to the two questions about agency raised prior to this digression, then, we may note that Whitehead's insistent atomism focuses our discussion on the question of the nature of individuality as it is to be conceived in the moral sphere, and couples this conception of individuality with considerations as to the conditions of aesthetic enhancement (increases of Beauty, over and against aesthetically destructive evil). The issue then, to reframe the question, is: What aspect or conception of moral comportment best exemplifies and works with this irremediably individual and aesthetic character of moral activity?

The answer to this question, as suggested at the outset of this chapter, is contained in the notion of 'attention to reality'. For Iris Murdoch, taking a cue from Simone Weil, "Moral change comes from an *attention* to the world whose natural result is a decrease in egoism through an increased sense of the reality of, primarily of course other people, but also other things" (*MGM* 52). Murdoch would have us recast the entire notion of "will" as "obedience to reality" (*SG* 41) in our particular attempts to realize value in our thoughts and actions in the moral sphere. Because of, among other things, the interests of the "fat relentless ego," the self's awareness of its environment, including other selves, is compromised and partial, perhaps even falsified.[12] "Human beings are obscure to each other, in certain respects which are particularly relevant to morality, unless they are mutual objects of attention or have common objects of attention" (*SG* 33). What the will requires is a principle of moral realism based on attention to the value present in the relevant entities in the self's world. In Whitehead's scheme existents are in essence common objects of agentive attention to one another, particularly the existents forming the high-grade societies at the basis of human physical and mental existence (though the "mind," we must remember, is not itself such a society, being merely sustained by them).

I have already noted that Whitehead's philosophy leaves no room for a substantive will, and noted that I may even be inclined, in the context of Whiteheadian thought, to reject the notion that moral agency requires the kind of unitary entitative status that may overcome our partialism and the fragmentariness of experience. If experience is irremediably individual, albeit connected via prehension (as real inclusion through reiteration conditioned by the "principle of intensive relevance"), and if the mind lacks unification precisely in order to entertain and realize the relevant novelties that we require in intellectual experience, ought we to posit any supervening form of agency designed to overcome certain fearsome results of these aspects of experience? It is my contention that in Whitehead's scheme agency must be conceived precisely along the lines articulated by Murdoch, as the organ of attention to reality. After a brief exploration of this idea, we may turn to a consideration of the normative considerations involved in attention as morally employed by Whitehead and Murdoch.

The freedom of human mentality in Whitehead's scheme is tied to a concept of 'attention' by Sherburne in his construction of the model of tangential inheritance involved in intellectual occasions. The freedom of mental occasions is likened, for phenomenological elaboration, to the notion of attention employed by James in his *Principles of Psychology*.[13] According to James, volition or will is precisely the effort of attention, and it is hypothesized that such attention is compulsive proportionate to interest.[14] James maintains quite boldly that attention is the *only* volitional act involved in human conscious experience.[15] This idea is quite congenial to Whitehead's scheme, especially on the somewhat antivolitional account of contrastive agency proffered by my reading. In mental occasions, there is significant "freedom" in that bonds of inheritance from the physical environment do not of themselves determine the arrangement of valuations possible in such occasions. Novel valuations and potentialities may be entertained in the interest of maximal intensive experience. The aspect of this imaginative entertainment of intensive possibilities that corresponds to the function of "will" as the organ of purpose and intention is precisely the attention accorded the various details being valued in the experience directive of process. In virtue of what is held in greatest importance, or "interest" in James' terms, there will be transcendent decision and thereby moral responsibility for the aesthetic synthesis achieved. The conferring of importance is the content of attention. The analysis echoes the claim of Alexander, that the "intensity" discoverable in thinking is that which is manifest in the effort of attention.[16]

Sherburne's helpful introduction of James in this context can be defended systematically. Whitehead himself not only praises James as formative for his own thinking (PR xii), but appeals, in the elaboration of the epochal theory of temporal atoms, to James's concept of the incremental nature of perception, citing the following passage: "Either your experience is of no content, of no change, or it is of a perceptible amount of content or change. Your acquaintance with reality grows literally by buds or drops of perception. Intellectually and on reflection you can divide these into components, but as immediately given, they come totally or not at all" (PR 68).[17] One hears in this passage overtones of the comments on *degree of presence* as constitutive of intensity in *Universal Algebra,* and of Whitehead's reformulation of the concept of metaphysical quantity argued above.

The application of this citation of James to the discussion of "will" as "attention" is direct: volition is determined by which totalities we admit and valorize through conferring importance in our aesthetic synthesis. Rather than seeing the will as some kind of magical property of origination, we can describe it as what happens qua valuation when attention is turned a certain way and paid with some kind of subjective quality. "Will" concerns precisely our "acquaintance with reality" in so far as such acquaintance is directed by mental experience of relevant possibilities coming to bear on the physical inheritances that to some degree occasion these mental events. This is exactly the office of metaphysics as a "guide to morals" in Murdoch's analysis. The function of the analysis of the structures of reality is to enhance our capacity to intuit the relevant "unities"or "wholes" represented in the entities (including humans) we encounter in moral experience (*MGM* 1–25). "Love," the fundamental value in Murdoch's view, "is knowledge of the individual," and the "endless task" confronting moral experience in the discernment of just what or who an individual reality *is* (*SG* 28). The endlessness of the task witnesses to our imperfection in realizing each other, our finitude in value-attainment, our "fallenness" (ibid.). Murdoch champions a moral "naturalism" or realism whereby through moral discipline we may comport ourselves with "a refined and honest perception of what is really the case, a patient and just discernment and exploration of what confronts one" (*SG* 38). The interests and motivations (for Whitehead, imaginative valuations and physical purposes) that form the texture of our experience and behavior partake of "Good" in so far as the individual realities taken account of in those interests and motives are *truly* seen or envisaged. Good remains undefinable or elusive in proportion to the partiality of our vision (*SG* 42).

In articulating the purposes of philosophy, Whitehead begins from the premise that our conscious experience is selective, emphasizing those things relevant to its own momentary purpose. The "task of philosophy" becomes the moral one, of "restoring the totality obscured by the selection" (*PR* 15). The morality of our experience is a function of what we have been calling "attention" to the realities constitutive of the actual world from which we emerge and about which we make transcendently effective decisions. Philosophy delivers a rational vision of reality such that the intensive significance of all that exists may be entertained.

> The selectiveness of individual experience is moral so far as it conforms to the balance of importance disclosed in the rational vision; and conversely the conversion of the intellectual insight into an emotional force corrects the sensitive experience in the direction of morality. . . .
>
> Morality of outlook is inseparably conjoined with generality of outlook. The antithesis between the general good and the individual interest can be abolished only when the individual is such that its interest is the general good, thus exemplifying the loss of the minor intensities in order to find them again with finer composition in a wider sweep of interest. (*PR* 15)

Given Whitehead's analysis, the notion of "attention" being developed here loses the tinge of passivity that, it could be contended, infects the contemplative characterization of moral life.[18] When it is recognized that attention to other realities is internal to the being of the agent, and thus integral and ultimate in any action, passivity is eliminated along with the exaggerated sense of ourselves as some kind of special freedom-nature in the cosmos. The merging of intensities in a broader, deeper contrast is the texture of a moral realism whose primary virtue is attentiveness and whose primary value is "love." The role of rational reflection in such a context is the disciplining of our capacity to see or attend to the individual realities present in the experience.

Whitehead accents the essentiality of attention in his own discussion of the intensive conditions of experience. Aware of the "superficial variability in our clear consciousness of qualitative detail," we introduce variation in the definiteness discerned in experience through "large scale transference of attention" (MT 108). But the purpose of attention is not mere rendering of detail, which is trivial experience; its purpose is the broad experience of totalities, the "worth" invested in the "vast issues vaguely haunting the fullness of existence" (MT 108-9). "Existence, in its own nature, is the upholding of value-intensity" (MT 110), and the purpose of attentive discrimination of individual existences is to enhance the experience of importance for the triad of self, others, and whole (MT 117). Thus, attention to individual aspects of the real world available in moral experience contributes not only an increased awareness *of* the individuals (human or otherwise), but also the increased possibility of interesting contrast of individuals in a broader, more holistic experience. The 'many' and the 'one' in moral experience are equally enhanced by the commitment to attentiveness about our world. Broad experience is, via attention, understood immediately to be sustained by the particulars whose massive, or perhaps gentle, intensive characters "haunt" existence. The particulars constituting minority, or perhaps unique, intensities in the environment are not levelled by the demand for holistic relevance. In fact such relevance is not "deep" unless it take seriously the realities pervading the entire actual world, each on its own terms. Breadth does not mean gross uniformity, given the focal arrangements of the "structural conditions" of intensity. A foreground may be occupied by any actuality, even the most unique, in the quest to effect deep and exquisite contrasts.

The Aesthetic Discernment of Individual Beings

Thus far our comparison of the moral thought of Whitehead and Murdoch has centered on the unity of general intent (realism in regard to moral experience), and analogy of general thesis (the reconceptualization of "will" as "attention"). But the comparison can and must be moved to a more fundamental level, systematically central for both thinkers and salient to the thesis being developed here, namely the aesthetic constitution of experience. The notion of the "discernment of definiteness" alluded to earlier, whereby our experience of value-intensity is deepened and broadened to coincide with the experiences of realities that transcend the self, is critical to the developed ethics of Murdoch and the implied ethics of Whitehead.

What does it mean to attend to individuals? As suggested previously, it generally means the ability to discern relevant unities, wholes, in our experience, of which those individuals as moral agents partake or which they as centers of value constitute. The discernment of an individual involves the recognition of that individual's value-achievement, its own purposive unification of aspects of its world, and this recognition takes place from the standpoint of one's own attempt at value-achievement—the standpoint of one's own interests, to speak in traditional ethical terms. This is the moral application of the systematic notion of anticipatory feeling regarding intensity in the future. Each aesthetic synthesis deliberately imposes itself on future individuals for entertainment and incorporation of the values realized in the original synthesis (what we have described as the concrescence resulting from a threshold of provocation by other imposing individuals). As one attempts this for oneself, one can and must recognize that other things and humans in our worlds have done likewise. Just as any novel subject incorporates its world in regard to the possibilities of intensive pattern, a moral agent evaluates its moral environment to effect an aesthetic pattern of incorporation or at least consideration. As I will impose value on my future, I must recognize that things in the past (other people, other things) have sought to impose value on me. In the patterning of importances, the contrasting of relevant aspects of experience so as to bring about a satisfactory unification of all relevant values may be attempted.

Skillfulness in moral comportment thus requires aptitude in apprehending patterned values and in turn effecting such patterns for oneself. In our particular, inevitably unifying experience, *some* pattern of value will be achieved. "The idea of a self-contained unity or limited whole is a fundamental instinctive concept," Murdoch's latest work begins (*MGM* 1). "The urge to prove that where we intuit unity there really is unity is a deep emotional motive to philosophy, to art, to thinking itself. Intellect is naturally one-making" (ibid.). Whitehead's philosophy is predicated, we have seen, on the intuition of relevant unity between one moment of experience and the next, and his metaphysics is a desciption of just how things are limited wholes. Morally, the question arises as to *what* pattern or limited, unifying whole should emerge or at least be attempted in our thought and action. Murdoch's use of metaphysics is in regard to its capacity to discipline our conception of individual unities in experience, either as attended to or achieved in activity. Her Platonism derives in large measure from her conviction that our capacity to attend to the relevant wholes (individuals or wide contexts) in experience is our mode of contact with the Good. The progression of Eros in the *Symposium* from lesser to greater objects of Beauty is appealed to as an example of that moral discipline of attention that we require. "The moral life in the Platonic understanding of it is a slow shift of attachments wherein *looking* (concentrating, attending, attentive discipline) is a source of divine (purified) energy. This is a progressive redemption of desire. . . . The movement is not, by an occasional leap, into an external (empty) space of freedom, but patiently and continuously a change of one's whole being in all its contingent detail, through a world of appearance toward a world of reality" (*MGM* 24-25).

In *Adventures of Ideas*, Whitehead uses this language of appearance and reality to exposit the relationship between any individual aesthetic event or experience (appearance) and the wider sphere of process out of which that individual emerges and to which it will return (reality) (*AI* parts three and four, 175-96).[19] One also recalls Whitehead's claim that for the achievement of morality, the individual interest must merge with the general interest, within the confines of the irremediably individual character of experience. The capacity to intuit the relevant unities of the general sphere transcendent of self is the first requisite in the determination of how individuals are to comport themselves amid others and in the environment as a whole. Loss of intensity is tolerated in the interest of the greater intensity of experience possible through a shift, or broadening, of individual perspective. The shift of perspective is literally a change in one's whole being. Shift of attention is the shifting or reconstruction of our activity, and the transformation will be morally characterized by the quality of the attention in its subjective form, its intensive structure.

To return this discussion to the notion of "pattern-recognition" originally asserted as the content of the discerning of individual realities, we note how Murdoch's Platonism is echoed in Whitehead's "Mathematics and the Good," wherein the human capacity to discern patterns of varying form, generality, and values is explored via the analogy between mathematical knowledge and knowledge of the Good. We require modes of conception that foster the capacity to discern patterns of definite achievement, or ideals yet to be realized. The moral effect of such discernment is the expansion, or at least conditioning, of individual value-interest in light of broader conceptions of what is going on in the way of value in the rest of the world. Patterns, experienced at the physical or mental level, invoke intensity of feeling in regard to the particular arrangements of qualities and quantities represented in the pattern (*MG* 679). Every aspect of our civilization (art, behavior, society) is affected by the creation, maintenance, modification, and discard of pattern, thus making our experience of pattern a "necessary condition for the realization of Good" (*MG* 678). In every case of the experience of pattern, of unification of detail according to some intensely felt form or style of synthesis, the issue is the relation of the individual and that which transcends the individual. "The crux of philosophy is to retain the balance between the individuality of existence and the relativity of existence. Also each individual entity in one pattern may be capable of analysis, so as to display itself as the unity of achieved pattern. The point that I am emphasizing," Whitehead writes, "is the function of pattern in the production of Good or Evil in the finite unit of feeling which embraces the enjoyment of that pattern" (MG 680).

The concept of ecstatic existence is helpful in appreciating the fusion of privacy and publicity in the comments just cited, and, I must confess, the development of "ecstatic existence" as a systematic interpretation was undertaken in part so as to underwrite an appreciation of the ethical relevance of Whitehead's thought. Unity and value are the achievement of pattern in an interlocking, pulsing mesh of existence, and the discipline of philosophy is to attend to pattern in the transcendent environment that provides the context of existential relativity for any individual pattern of value one might achieve. Thus, any mode of "division" of the concrete (coordinate analysis) will proceed along the lines of some recognized pattern that has emerged as the formed activity of individual intensive subjects. An intellectual or coordinate division will always to some extent abstract from the full actuality of the existents standing in the pattern so "divided" out. Patterns are abstracted from the extended natural orders testifying to the "relativity of existence" that sustains such orders. But the individualities so related are thereby problematized. Moral experience is the excruciating process of unpacking what patterns we have opted to see, and testing them against the welter of detail we may have left out in order to see just that. What have I ignored so as to see the processes of putting a life together on the part of a friend as "lovable"? What are the losses to the competing patterns of valuation involved in that ignorance?

Moral experience is the awareness that the patterns we readily perceive (in presentational immediacy) have existential footing in reality, combined with the awareness that we ignore a great deal of that footing in order to "present" some details to ourselves. Our "small imperfect limits . . . keep breaking." The recognition that the objective patterns we have discovered as emergent from process cannot be isomorphically assumed to be precisely the modes of individuation causing such emergence constitutes our commitment to moral improvement. In other words, moral responsibility is the commitment to not mistake extended quanta for the intensive quantities that make them possible to entertain in experience.

A Defense of Whitehead's Concept of Value

Here we come to a point that enables us to respond to a criticism leveled at Whitehead's notion of value, as articulated in "Mathematics and the Good" as well as in his systematic work, by John Goheen. The doctrine of feeling as the achievement of value through patterned intensive unification—the achievement of definiteness—is not enough, according to

Goheen, to supply the moral Good in experience. "Pattern or form, in the ordinary sense of defining or limiting an event, may well be a condition of existence, but, as such, throws no light on the nature of value or the Good. This is clear from Whitehead's analysis of value in terms of feeling, for it is satisfaction which distinguishes the Good from all other experiences."[20] On this reading, Whitehead's subjectivistic position emerges as a kind of aestheticism, or at best, as noted by Beliaef, a theory similar to Hume's, wherein moral values are determined "by the likes and dislikes of men."[21] Belaief repudiates Goheen on the basis of the claim that the analysis of experience undertaken by Whitehead does not prejudge whether an ethic to be derived from it would be subjectivist or objectivist. She goes on to cite, against the analogy with Hume, Whitehead's claims as to the intuition of eternal ideals and of purposes at work in creativity as a whole (*MT* 141; *AI* 292).

I will return to the notion of ideals later. But Goheen's objection must be met at a different level, one that does not from the start concede the accuracy of his analysis of Whitehead's theory of feeling. First, on Goheen's view, every entity, including those involved in the human apprehension of value, is self-enclosed and self-determining in the highly particularized manner that I have been disputing throughout this book. Although it is true that the experience of good will be an individual satisfaction, it is not true that there is no broad perspective of pattern and value that directly influences (without compromising the ontological principle) the intense feeling of any single agent. On Goheen's view, entities are wrenched from their place in social orders, or in histories of enduring objects, and conceived as if free-floating value-determiners. We have seen that this is not the case. The existential character of value experience is inherently self-transcendent on Whitehead's view, and most deeply so on the "ecstatic" interpretation.

Second, Goheen does not take into account the discipline of philosophy that Whitehead elaborates throughout his systematic writings, and again in "Mathematics and the Good," such that the interpretation of value as achieved in any single patterner or subject is measured against precisely the wider perspective of process within which it occurs. If Goheen is concerned with the ambiguity of value if left to the determination of subjective human experients, then his position must take into account the analysis of the requirements of rational thought as offered by Whitehead for those subjects. Although it is true that "[i]n itself a pattern is neither good nor bad" (*MG* 679), it is not true that in experience, particularly rational experience, a pattern is left to "itself." The moral interpretation of any achieved unity of patterned intensity is undertaken from the perspective of thought disciplined in the discernment of pattern across time. Intellectual experience is particularly well-equipped to "compare" patterns, given its freedom from determination by the physical societies on which it depends for its generation.

It is here that the notion of "fortunate evolution," used by Whitehead as a mode of justification for symbolic reference, is important. An act of symbolic reference is in essence an act of perception of an environment, an act in which attention to the relevant unities or individuals is crucial. The test of such a symbolic reference is "pragmatic," in the sense that the effect of the symbolism on future states of the percipient "person" or the environment is analyzed. What is desirable is that the effect manifest an evolution that is "fortunate," meaning that the mutual enhancement of what is experienced at the levels of causal efficacy and presentational immediacy occurs not only in the present event, but is capacitated in relevant future events (PR 181). A moral determination about an achieved value hinges on that value's place in the wider orders in which that intensity *qua that intensity* will impose itself. Importance is conditioned by reflection when the question of justification is relevant. "It is in the nature of the present that it should . . . transcend itself by reason of the immanence in it of the 'other'. But there is no necessity as to the scale of emphasis that this fact of nature should receive. It belongs to the civilization of consciousness, to magnify the large sweep of Harmony" (AI 291). Consideration is given to the role of any individual value, realized or conceptually entertained, in transcendent process, and to the role of that value in bringing about a state of sensitivity whereby the agent is more able to effect the contrasts procurative of a cooperative relationship with the environment, particularly the environment of other agents.

Whitehead's conception of "Beauty" as the achievement of intensity of feeling arising from patterned experience is not, then, an aestheticism unmeasured by a perspective transcendent of individuality. The celebration of finite intensity, in the recognition that "value is the gift of finitude," does not condemn that finite beauty to a status of absolute moral vagueness. There will be some vagueness as to the good fortune or ill fortune represented in any finite achievement—this is the essence of Tragedy, that finite realization may and in fact must be imperfect, somehow inhibitory. But Tragedy, like discord, serves to goad the creative process towards finer achievement. The intuition of "Peace," Whitehead's recommended apex for civilized thought, is the recognition that in the midst of the inevitable destruction of some intensities by other intensities, given the atomicity of experience, there is the impetus to transcend destruction in an aim at a wider, broader intensity or Harmony. Peace witnesses to the tragedy in experience "as a living agent persuading the world to aim at fineness beyond the faded level of surrounding fact. Each tragedy is the disclosure of an ideal:—what might have been, and was not: What can be" (AI 286).

What this rather romantic statement means is that the transcendent efficacy of individual subjects is dependent upon the maintainance of the original subject's satisfaction to some significant degree. The extent to which an occasion devalues the intensities of a provoker occasion, the provoker occasion will diminish in degree of presence at least for the present occasion in question. The moral challenge is to be an agent of diminishment only in those broader harmonic circumstances that demand it in the existential long-run. Since many of the dismissals of relevance possible for intellectual experience would be undertaken precisely in ignorance of this long run, the moral agent does so at her own eventual expense (as well as at the expense of "loss to the social environment" that sustains her). Moments of crass subjectivism are deliberately solipsistic in their consideration of finalities—that is what gives them their special appeal, their acute raising to significance only of the forefront of presently (subjectively) entertained ends. My argument for the elimination of the strong distinction between final and efficient causality allows what in subjectivistic experience is relegated to the status of merely efficient cause of one's own ends to be considered as possessing the same kind of agentive finality as one's "own" private ideal. In other words, the subjectivist is seen as inauthentically denying the ecstatic presence of other subjects in him or her, and his or her ecstatic presence in the agency (not merely the exploitable efficiency) of other beings. This explains how subjectivism does characterize our moral experience, as well as explaining the metaphysically normative conditions that demand its avoidance.

"On God and Good": Ideals, Religion, and the Discipline of Attention[22]

With the introduction of 'Peace' as the simultaneous intuition of the possibilities of Beauty and Tragedy, the compatibility of Whitehead and Murdoch re-emerges. The concept of moral comportment suggested by both is primarily concerned with the question of moral improvement, not with the static measure of value by non-temporal standards or principles, either internal (Kant) or external (utilitarianism) to the will. Both adopt a faith that value-experience, disciplined by the refinement of the skills of attention to patterns of achieved value, may be adequate to the ongoing task of purifying the subject of its excess of emphasis on this or that aspect of its own desires or feelings. "Freedom is not the sudden jumping of the isolated will in and out of an impersonal logical complex, it is a function of the progressive attempt to see a particular object clearly" (*SG* 23). What remains to be seen, in this exploration of common themes in Whitehead and Murdoch, is the normative ideal conditioning the apprehension of pattern, whereby there is moral improvement or education, whereby there is "magnification of the wide sweep of Harmony," whereby attentive will might be said to genuinely seek the good.

For Murdoch, the "Form of the Good" to which we are drawn in "the morass of existence" by a kind of spiritual energy (the Platonic Eros)

> may be seen as enlightening particular scenes and setting the specialized moral virtues and insights into their required particular patterns. This is how the phenomena are saved and the particulars redeemed, in this *light*. . . . The sovereign Good is not an empty receptacle into which the arbitrary will places

> objects of its choice. It is something which we all experience as a creative force. This is metaphysics, which sets up a picture which it then offers as an appeal to us all to see if we cannot find just this in our deepest experience. (MGM 507)

The Good is that in virtue of which our particular experience of particular entities occurs as an ever-enlarging vision of and respect for reality.

In Whitehead's philosophy, the metaphysical account of the redemption of individual entities' intensities of value-achievement is offered in the concept of God, that "final interpretation" of the metaphysical situation undertaken by way of melding systematic content with the civilized needs and achievements of humanity in art and religion. The role of God is the ultimate mutual adjustment of intensity of feeling, such that the unavoidable partiality, discord, and tragedy of finite, particular realization might be regarded as redeemed in an infinite harmony of diverse intensities. The fulfillment of God's subjective aim is conceived as the infinite adjustment of the finality—the value intensity—of all individuals (PR 345). The ideal is perfection of subjective aim in the widest possible sense.

> The wisdom of subjective aim prehends every actuality for what it can be in such a perfected system—its sufferings, its sorrows, its failures, its triumphs, its immediacies of joy—woven by rightness of feeling into the harmony of the universal feeling, which is always immediate, always many, always one, always with novel advance, moving onward and never perishing. The results of destructive evil, purely self-regarding, are dismissed into their triviality of merely individual facts; and yet the good they did achieve in individual joy, in individual sorrow, in the introduction of needed contrast, is yet saved by its relation to the completed whole. The image—and it is but an image—the image under which this operative growth of God's nature is best conceived, is that of a tender care that nothing be lost. (PR 346)

This aspect of the nature of God is the fulfillment of the promise made possible through the initial provision by God for the maximal intensity achievable in any creative actuality. The realization of individual intensity via contrast is brought to ultimate fruition in the universal contrast, a perfected aesthetic realization that transcends the evils of partiality. "God" is the ideal, to be specific, of the contrastive unity of all agents; not as one supervening agency, but a universal ecstasis of perspective harmonization.

The issue is now 'Picturing' the Ideal. In the midst of muddle, the sufferings and sorrows as well as joys and triumphs of experience, "the morass of existence in which [the human spirit] always at every moment finds itself immersed" (*MGM* 507), the Good is a lure in the moral purification of our desires and of our ability to see (*MGM* 400), the "progressive destruction of [false] images" in the name of an unrealized but intuitively apprehended "perfection" (*MGM* 329). The function of the concept of God in Whitehead and Good in Murdoch is to stand as an image—a "picture" of that perfection of pattern that conditions all finite engagement. This image of perfection remains indefinable to any finite agent, but is at the same time experienced as operating in the activities of that agent: "Good is indefinable . . . because of the infinite difficulty of the task of apprehending a magnetic but inexhaustible reality" (*SG* 42). The image of the perfect apprehension and adjustment of reality is that picture whereby our individual agency is conditioned in the direction of goodness: "The ideal situation . . . is . . . to be *represented as* a kind of 'necessity.' This is something of which the saints speak and which any artist will readily understand. The *idea of* a patient, loving regard, directed upon a person, a thing, a situation, presents the will not as unimpeded movement but as something very much more like 'obedience'" (*SG* 40, emphasis mine). This portrait of the virtue of obedience to reality on the part of a moral agent is echoed in Whitehead's description of the divinity as operating with "tender patience" (*PR* 347) in regard to the world, instituting a universal virtue of "love" as the "tender care" taken in regard to each individual. The divine "dwells upon the tender elements in the world, which slowly and in quietness operate by love; and it finds purpose in the present immediacy of a kingdom not of this world" (*PR* 343). Such moral "pictures" are regulative ideals (in Kant's sense) and more—for a picture is an intrusive imagination that concretely reconstructs the picturer to some extent.

It is important to keep in mind that Whitehead's 'God' is an *interpretive* concept, at least in the grand function of mutual adjustment of intensity. Such a concept introduces metaphysical difficulties if taken as a statement of categoreal necessity. I wish simply to take the concept of God in terms of its interpretive capacity in regard to human experience, particularly as regards our capacity to make moral discernments of value, and our motivation to understand and improve the contours of moral experience in light of the irremediably particular character of every agentive act. This is the kind of functionalist (but not reductive) use of a God-concept undertaken by Murdoch in "One God and Good," and throughout *Metaphysics as a Guide to Morals*. Moral life requires, and obtains in Murdoch and Whitehead, a "metaphysical background" (*SG* 42) of ideality *pictured* or *imaged*, or *represented* in the concepts of God and good.

The function of ultimate conceptions of the metaphysical background against which the moral drama unfolds is in both Whitehead and Murdoch the image of a perfect condition of mutual adjustment of reality, the condition in which attention to the reality and value of the world transcendent of self has been successful. In a sense, this is a moral application of the general metaphysics of intensity that we have been developing. In light of the ideal of the "Harmony of Harmonies," "the World receives its persuasion towards such perfections as are possible for its diverse individual occasions" (*AI* 296). An individual is apprehended, and apprehends its world, in virtue of transcendent orders of reality conditioning its possibility of aesthetic achievement, and within which its aesthetic achievement will find itself and be responsible. The function of an ideal is to be a lure to the perfection of individual experience, to be a standard of perfect mutual adjustment of intensity of feeling.

Thus, the critical role of metaphysics in ethics is to provide a "picture" of the ideal, that individual agents may attempt that ideality in the muddled individuality of experience. Since no intellectual apprehension—no "division"—can render the full intensive determinacy of what it divides, though it is itself intensively captured by the intrinsic interest of its division, an aesthetic and regulative picture may be used alongside or within any selective mode of emphases. The "control of process" is guided by the ideal of care, expressed in the virtue of Love.[23] Moral responsibility emerges as the loving obedience to the values proffered but perhaps ungrasped in the reality in the midst of which we act. "Love" is the idealization of the "attachment" that characterizes any attentive volition. It is, thereby, grounded in and normative for the kind of will we have.

The crucial skill in this kind of moral engagement is the ability to discern those patterns, or intensities, of value that impose themselves on us for consideration, and to project or anticipate the intensive impact of those patterns of value that we may set out to realize. The moral problem in Whiteheadian terms concerns our ability to conform to those intensive patterns dictated by the environment, but more importantly to be able to hold out as lures for ourselves, in our intellectual experience of as yet unrealized possibilities, those kinds of ideals that will be least partial, least destructive of intensity in other quarters, most likely to engage and foster the wider "sweep of harmony." The imposing and obliging aspect of entertained value does not mean dumb reiteration. The fact remains that each individual will create a pattern of values that is its own, somehow a modification of its world. The undertaking of obligations is not blind conservatism, for that would result in what Whitehead calls "tedium" or "fatigue"—a condition directly opposite to the very texture of rational life (*FR* 23). Obligation and creativity together characterize the moral scene.

The implications of the concept and functioning of *ideals* for the understanding of the demands of moral *agency* may be elaborated by returning to the notion that the primary virtue, indeed the primary experience of volition, on the part of a moral agent is its capacity to attend, to see, to envision. The metaphysical situation, according to Whitehead, is such that the achievement of individual realization of value attains its "aesthetic importance" in virtue of its "claim to attention" (*AI* 264). Realities demand attention in virtue of the intensity achieved in their aesthetic synthesis. What is required morally is an education of the capacity to appreciate the need to attend, the duty to attend imposed by the very fabric of intense becoming, and the skill of attention in its formal aspects. Murdoch suggests an education of our aesthetic capacities of attention to limited wholes through the experience of art (especially literature) as well as metaphysics. Likewise, Whitehead recommends art not only for its capacity to offer fundamental principles of aesthetic arrangement that might be metaphysically employed (*PR* 162-63, 317) and thereby stand as images for thought in general, but for its educative role in the reconstruction of our capacity to see and comprehend the real. Art and aesthetic education, perhaps most importantly literature, are the means to the apprehension of the concrete in our actions. "There is no substitute for the direct perception of the concrete achievement of a thing in its actuality. We want concrete fact with a light thrown on what is relevant to its preciousness" (*SMW* 199), and "It is in literature that the concrete outlook of humanity receives its expression" (*SMW* 75). We hear echoes of Murdoch's commitment to the redemptive force of "light" as a metaphor for our vision of the real.

Aesthetic education increases the "depth of individuality" of percipient as well as the perceived. It is quite literally, as "deepening of individuality," the moral education or formation of the will. The primary virtue, we might call it, accorded to our capacity to perceive individual existents by Whitehead is "sensitiveness" (*SMW* 200). Sensitiveness is the "apprehension of what lies beyond oneself," and finds its paradigmatic exemplification in "art" conceived in the general sense of "any selection by which the concrete facts are so arranged as to elicit attention to particular values that are realizable by them." The "habit of art is the habit of enjoying vivid values" (ibid.). The "aestheticism" issue seems to construe the moral problem of life in decidedly Nietzschean terms, and perhaps this is unavoidable in this century. But a good part of evil is a function of the nonvivid structures of what Arendt called the "banality" of human self-imposition on the world. In so far as our experience tends towards banality, it will be habituated in the avoidance of the delicate and fragile value-realities that die under our feet and shuffle off to the gas chambers. Art and the interpretive metaphysical ideal of the divinity serve the same purpose—the appreciation, incorporation, and experiential retention of intensities of achieved value. Both offer refinements of our *capacity to see or picture the real and the good*. There is moral improvement to be gained, according to Murdoch, through the "ability to sustain and *experience* imagined syntheses," through "looking carefully at something and *holding* it before the mind" (*MGM* 3). This is more than the experience of a proposition—it has the existentially transforming effect of a physical purpose in all of its intensive consideration of the worldly place of the subject.

A similar ethic of attention is developed in a process vein by Robert Neville in *A Puritan Smile*. The primary "corrective" source for the partiality or even vicious ideology of our values and theories in the sphere of action is "cultivated intuitive perception," issuing in the ability to grasp "things on their own terms," a sort of "increased empathy" with other realities.[24] This notion is broadened by Neville into the concept of moral discernment, the perfection of intuition for the purposes of grasping the "immediate unities" of reality that are "harmonies as contrasts."[25] Neville adopts Whitehead's analysis of experience as an aesthetics of contrasts issuing into intensities of feeling, and offers a development, via the notion of discernment, of the kind of intuition required to grasp such aesthetic realities. The ideal of intuition is the ability to truly attend to what is there, or to project responsibly those forms of unity of potential achievement productive of harmony. "The norms for imagination are not so much moral ones comparing patterns of integration as aesthetic ones of cohesion and intensity of contrast with the patterns."[26] We should note, of course, that the aesthetics of contrast in the interest of intensity *is* comparative, and so Neville's distinction between moral and aesthetic norms should not be taken too strongly. For Neville as well as Murdoch and Whitehead, the responsibility of every agent, in its very being as an agent, to discern the values present in reality passes over into the religious experience of the reality of the ideal harmonization of all values.[27]

If the ideal for responsible moral discernment is attention to the real, guided by an ideal harmony of all realities of value, the question remains as to what practice might effect the realization or efficacy of this ideal in any given agent. The practice most likely to refine and idealize our capacity to attend is, according to Murdoch, "prayer" (*SG* 55). The human attitude toward reality is to be reverential. This is the sense of "religion" advocated by Murdoch—the discipline of our sensibilities in light of an ideal of perfected reverence for all individuals (*MGM* 80–85, 183, 391–430). Reverence is perfected in proportion to an agent's capacity to perceive the relevant objects of our experience. On Murdoch's reading, the Allegory of the Cave is a "religious myth" disclosing the reality of different grades of awareness and experience of existence (*MGM* 183). The significance of the Cave parable is its provision, with metaphysical background, of an image for *thought in general*, a spiritual image that attests to the idea that moral thinking and perception are obligated by what there is to perceive (*MGM* 400). Likewise for Whitehead, the "religious" character of education has the function of inculcating "duty and reverence." Whitehead continues on this notion of obligation with a statement that strongly supports the concept of ecstatic subjectivity: "Duty arises from our potential control over the course of events. Where attainable knowledge could have changed the issue, ignorance has the guilt of vice. And the foundation of this reverence is this perception, that the present holds within itself the *complete sum of the existence, backwards and forwards*, that whole amplitude of time, which is eternity" (*AE* 26, emphasis mine).[28]

Conclusion: Sketch of an Ethics of Intensity

The "virtue" of sensitiveness, guided by the ideal of "love," issues in the requirement that our "control of process" be engaged under the image of a divine adjustment of all individual processive events. Moral education, or moral improvement, consists in the refinement of our skills of apprehension of pattern. The images offered in metaphysics and religion, and the formal experiences of aesthetic unities in art, conspire to effect this education of sensibilities. In the absence of a substantive will, in the absence of a fixed structure of reality, moral principles can emerge only as expressions of how events may be internally conditioned so as to achieve those values of mutual adjustment productive of a civilized, enduringly satisfying life.[29]

By way of summary of the foregoing, and speculation as to the development of an ethic conceived in a Whiteheadian context, we may pause here to articulate the contributions of the metaphysics of intensity to moral discourse. This contribution may be roughly distinguished into two spheres: those aspects of the scheme that may be taken to undergird morally categoreal aspects of experience, and those aspects of the scheme that are suggestive of techniques for the normative improvement of our directed experience given the categoreal conditions of that experience. Neither of these spheres should be confused with a Kantian search for a "categorical imperative," for the logic that might underwrite such a search is repudiated in Whitehead's thought.

MORAL CATEGORIES

The moral categories articulated here, and any others that may emerge on further inquiry, are to be conceived on the analogy of the Categoreal Obligations, as conditions that are exemplified in processes of subjective becoming. The difference between moral and metaphysical categories is that the former are undertaken in the context of entities exemplifying a good deal more "freedom" or entertainment of conceptual alternatives than the "average" metaphysical entity, and so the obligatory character of the categories requires special interpretation. The moral categories offered here are directive of a more satisfying texture of human life, productive of what will be more likely than mere egoistic self-concern to bring about "fortunate evolution" in value-production. Thus the adoption of the term "categoreal" rather than "categorical," distinguishing these moral categories from the type of ethics derivable from Kant. There is no universal categorical demand in atomic creativity, beyond the demand for intense creation. Norms can emerge only as practical guidelines for the creation of an enriched experience.

There are at least four general moral categories derivable from the metaphysics of intensity, conditioned by our comparison with Murdoch's ethics of "attention." They form the basis of the moral realism derivable from both thinkers.

The Category of Objective Attention

A moral agent must attend to the 'individuals' constitutive of the morally relevant world. This category has two dimensions. First, it forces a recognition that each moment of moral life is an act of construction emerging as a unification of world-elements, and that those world-elements are themselves analogous constructions of patterned value. Thus, prior to intense incorporation of my environment in my experience, what is required is the attempt at understanding what the achieved values of the individual realities of my environment truly are. The question in regard to any individual in my world is, What value was attempted or achieved in this constructive experience—how did it emerge, and where does it stand relative to the wider orders of the moral environment (social processes, family lives, institutional affiliations, vocation, etc.) in which it or I do or might participate? My individual intensity of experience is greatly bound up in the intensities represented in the other individuals in the existential network(s) in which I find myself. My ecstatic existence requires my acknowledgment of the ecstatic presence of other existences.

Second, this category forces a recognition that the discrimination of relevant individuality is not always obvious, and requires effort. The contribution of discrete realities to my intense experience hinges on just *how* those realities are "individuals" or "limited wholes." Care is to be taken to critique the intellect's tendency to project extensive conceptions of individual unities on existences that are in themselves intensive unities. For example, does a species in an ecosystem stand out with a determinate individuality, or does its individuation include aspects of the ecosystem so as to be essentially unextractable? The theory of ecstatic existence deepens the already acknowledged relevance of Whiteheadian connectionism to environmental ethics. The case of abortion is another poignant example of the vagueness characterizing the selection of relevant individuality in moral decision making. There may be times, moreover, when human beings or other entities are more relevant as single agents, and times when a collectivity of agents is the relevant "individual," or limited whole, in a certain moral sphere—the relevant form of individuation may be "*our* golden ring," to recur to Heaney's poem. This vagueness attends not only considered individualities, but the operations of agency as well. Is my agency always discrete, or are there not times when I am a factor in a wider agency of creativity? Sometimes it is my participation in a species or society or team that is my functional role in process, for good or ill. Failure to recognize this vagueness in the discrimination of individuality, either in regard to what I must *consider* in my agentive acts, or in regard to the agentive *status* I have in my activities, vitiates much utilitarian philosophy, particularly in the arena of 'preference calculation'.

The Category of Value-Diversity

A moral agent is to recognize the genuine contrastive diversity of elements (a) taken into consideration in explicit choice-making, and (b) operating at the levels of unexplicit awareness that might, with alteration of attentive focus, be rendered more susceptible to conscious discrimination. The values represented by the genuinely diverse individuals of which I take account are the metaphysically formative values out of which my intense experience will emerge, both in conscious deliberation and subconscious motivation. Since definiteness of existence depends on contrast, diversity of value is an irremediable fact about the moral situation. Any given value achieves definiteness as a contrast with other values, and more comprehensive values may emerge on the basis of such contrasts. In other words, in order to be individually definite, value must be relative (contrastive) to other values. Note that this is not a condition of *mere* diversity, but of diversity as a necessary functional component in the experience of the *connection* and *individual identity* of discrete values, including those to which I might be tempted to give exclusive attention. This kind of category would be particularly relevant in the context of certain contemporary debates as to cultural pluralism. There is *no* cultural value without diversity of value at some level; likewise, there is no diversity without some structural conditions of comparison effecting unification to some degree. The principle of 'contrast' celebrates diversity and unity without either the risk of mere trivial multiplicity or leveling uniformity. In virtue of this category, no position on moral values exists in isolation from the consideration of other values.

The Category of Transcendent Creativity

Given the insurmountable individuality of each moral occasion, and its necessary finitude in regard to value perfection, the task of any moral agent is the genuine creation of values that address or perhaps to some extent overcome the particular limitations of previous occasions. There is no ultimate overcoming of destructive partiality except in the ideal, and so attention may be focused on the consideration of concrete realities of value conflict and the creativity whereby this situation may be transcended. Attenuated intensive experience in the moral sphere forces the question, What are the conditions of attenuation, and how may they be passed beyond via a broader intensive aim?

This category has the effect not only of forcing a recognition of our partiality, and hence the encouragement of such virtues as humility and forgiveness, but also of fixing our sights on the possibility and necessity of real improvement of concrete situations, thus recommending courage, cooperation, and respect for the attempt at value creation.[30] There is also the recognition that unflinching conservatism and unbounded liberality are alike aesthetically destructive, the former due to an absence of intensifying novelty, the latter due to an absence of a background of achievement against which novelty may be relevant. Adventure is the categoreal obligation to effect a satisfactory balance between change and endurance: "Permanence can be snatched only out of flux; and the passing moment can find its adequate intensity only by its submission to permanence" (PR 338).

The Category of Emotional and Intellectual Complementarity

Agency is at once emotional and intellectual. There is no absolute separation between the emotional and intellectual conditions of agentive action. The doctrine of subjective form expresses the very texture of reality as intensity of feeling. We have thus the obligation to consider not only our consciously entertained ideas but also our emotional states in our attempt to understand and responsibly employ our purposive capacities. Also, there can be no expunging of emotional content from the ideals guiding our directed activities. Intellectual abstraction is always abstraction from ever-present emotional (aesthetic) content. This category thus has the effect of forcing a realistic recognition of the irremediable presence of emotion in our purposive actions, both within and below the level of consciousness. Intensity is sought in the emotional texture of experience at all levels of the human organism (from physical purposes to the entertainment of propositions), thus the drivenness of our experience is neither to be underestimated nor deplored. The question is whether we will experience emotions as a form of bondage (*pace* Spinoza) or as a source of adventure, the creation of value in the interest of finer attainments of human experience. A determination as to this question is to be made in light of the other categories and the following techniques as elaborations of the normative possibilities of attentive experience.

ETHICAL PRACTICES

There are at least three ethical practices that may enable an agent to successfully engage the moral categories elaborated previously. These techniques are mutually illuminating and pragmatically overlapping. They are functionally analogous to the deliberations undertaken in finding the "mean" in Aristotelean ethics, as they simultaneously address the concerns of any single moral experience, and the issues of moral formation Aristotle collected under the notion of "habit."

Patterning

An agent achieves intense value experience and the attention to relevant individuals in virtue of the possibilities of *pattern*. Thus, skill in apprehending and creating pattern is to be encouraged through the education of aesthetic sensibilities. The appreciation of *any* experience for its embodiment of pattern is a constant source of such refinement. Keeping in mind that what I find in my world are patterns and not substances is a first step in this education—thus the morally instructive value of metaphysics. This practice stipulates that aesthetic experience is not an epiphenomenon of culture but the very essence of human civilization, and therefore is *not optional*. The agent who effectively shuts him or herself off from opportunities for aesthetic experience, or is so shut off by another, is operating in a diminished, and in the former case culpable, state of agency.

Interaction of Rationality and Intuition

The discrimination of individuals proceeds by aesthetic intuition, but the discernment of patterns of value in those individuals may require the enlargement of perspective possible only through rational reflection. Two things follow from this technique. First, our attention is turned to the fact that any individual about which I have some intuition of form emerges out of a temporalized ordered process—there is a history to be considered. Without the appreciation of the temporal patterns in which any atomic pattern emerges, an intuition will be defective.[31] Second, both our rational and intuitive capacities are refined by those activities that refine our sensitivity to pattern. Thus, rationality and intuition are influenced by aesthetic and religious education as outlined previously; they are not atemporal faculties, but aspects of process constitutive of human events and typified by certain structural conditions. The practice of detailed analysis interacting with broadly synthetic patterns of unification is a staple of meaningful education.

Envisagement

The Practice of 'Envisagement' is closely allied to both pattern and the interactive complex of rationality and intuition. It is the undertaking of imaginative foresight in the interest of controlling process. I adopt the term 'envisagement' rather than simply 'imagination' because of the former term's close connection to the normative condition of attention to—'redemptive vision' of—realities. Murdoch's recommendations as to 'prayer' may be taken as a subsidiary function of envisagement. The entertainment of novel possibilities of intense patterned arrangement, coupled with the Platonic insight that human apprehension of reality demands the enlargement of our sphere of connection—emotional and rational—to reality, constitutes the normative employment of the technique of envisagement. The practice is the moral analog of the systematic notion of subjective aim as derived from the divine envisagement of the relation of the realm of potentiality to each individual occasion of experience. Our production of 'lures' for more satisfactory experience can be normed by the demand for the fusion of individual and general outlook, minimally represented in the ecstatic existence of intensive events. The technique of envisagement reinforces, moreover, the general attitude of attention to realities. It is the futural dimension of the 'vision' undertaken in present contemplation.

TOWARD A CONTEMPORARY MORAL PLATONISM

The foregoing is meant only as a suggestive sketch of what might be developed in more elaborate form in a larger project that would advance Whiteheadian ethics in light of the concepts of intensity and attention as the cornerstones of a moral realism. The categories and practices, functional equivalents of a theory of virtues, emerge from and condition our consideration of the reality of both muddledness and high ideals in the fabric of moral existence. Any ethic must take its start from the simultaneous recognition of these two seemingly contrary facts of our experience.

The Platonic insight that mathematics is an image of the Good is borne out in the moral philosophy of Murdoch and Whitehead through the conviction that experience is measured by its capacity to perceive and effect arrangement of form, the intensity of pattern involved in value experience. The connection of the idea of formal arrangement with the idea of Goodness comes in our characterization of the offices of human thought in general. Murdoch and Whitehead seek those images or metaphors that best express the obligations and capacities of thought at its moments of deepest penetration into human experience. Metaphysics emerges as that picture of reality possible given the forms of thought available to humankind, and the first requirement of metaphysics is that it understand its historical conditions of emergence. The forms of thinking in which we presently engage have emerged from a history that has witnessed the production and passing away of forms of thought answering to the deepest purposes of civilization, as expressible in the various historical epochs.[32]

And yet alongside its embeddedness in history, metaphysics may explore as well the image of God as an infinite, enduring harmonization of all irreducibly individual intensities of value, and the image of the Good as the inscrutable and yet immediately, magnetically felt ideal of a reality that transcends the fragmenting limitations of individual experience. The historical and ideal elements of a metaphysics cooperate to picture for us that factor in the universe that conditions all present striving and attainment (cf. *AI* 293). Although there is no value that is imagined to supervene over all individual values, no principle or determinate good to be obeyed in our willing, there is the corrective and inspirational force of an ideal that speaks to the intrinsic comparability and coexistence of all individual values in the creative process. Both Whitehead and Murdoch name this ultimate comparative and creative force in experience, after Plato, "Eros." The Adventure (cf. *AI* 252–95) undertaken in its name, and under its inspiration, is not subject to scrutiny in the form of proof or the elaboration of stable normative principles. Philosophy can attempt an experiential description, in the form of "imaginative generalization," or "divination," of its "generic traits" (*PR* 4-5, 10). But in the end, "The sole appeal is to intuition" (*PR* 22). The contemporary Platonism forwarded in this guise by Whitehead and Murdoch offers a welcome addition to the scene of contemporary moral theory, balancing the Aristotelean traditionalism of Alasdair MacIntyre.[33]

It is of the essence of individual creative synthesis, and is thereby a categoreally ultimate fact about the universe, that subjects emerge as contrastive unifications of the values present in their worlds. It is the office of moral philosophy to emphasize the importance of the comparative nature of value, and of its potential conditioning by images of an ideal of comparison wherein there is no loss, no evil of destruction, of reality. We harbor an anxious hope, incanted in Heaney's verse: "Love, you shall perfect for me the child." Moral philosophy, and moral education, is the refinement of our recognition of the fact of value-comparison in our lives, and of the Erotic zeal to effect creative advance rather than aesthetic destruction. The conscious recognition of responsibility for the reality and effects of our moral acts hinges on an understanding of the dynamic texture of value experience, and of the ideal possibilities by which we might be guided. "Within new limits now, arrange the world." The final appeal is to the intuitive plausibility of the concept of Love, the general concept of attachment of the self to others and others to the self (*SG* 103). If we are to be attached to, or moved by, a moral ideal, that ideal should itself be founded in the fabric of attachment and mutual emotive effect that constitutes the nature of existence itself. Walt Whitman, the great denier of the modes of abstractness that tear humans out of the rich web of life, captures the insight of an atomistic ethics conceived in light of the ecstatic concept of existence:

> I celebrate myself, and sing myself,
> And what I assume you shall assume,
> For every atom belonging to me as good belongs to you.
> —"Song of Myself"

This essay has been a first sketch of how light may be cast, through a metaphysical elaboration of structures and ideals implicit in our experience, on the existential conditions of an ethics of Love whose primary virtue is reverent attention to what is real.

Epilogue
Notes
Bibliography
Index

Epilogue on Atomistic Metaphysics

The moon in the bureau mirror
looks out a million miles
(and perhaps with pride, at herself,
but she never never smiles)
far and away beyond sleep, or
perhaps she's a daytime sleeper.

By the universe deserted,
she'd tell it to go to hell,
and she'd find a body of water,
or a mirror, on which to dwell.
So wrap up care in a cobweb
and drop it down the well

into that world inverted
where left is always right,
where the shadows are really the body,
where we stay awake all night,
where the heavens are shallow as the sea
is now deep, and you love me.
 —Elizabeth Bishop, *"Insomnia"*

The narrator of this poem deals with the isolation of sleeplessness by a consideration of self that reveals the possibility of connection and unity with nonself that overcomes the merely apparent alienation of solitude. I think this poem, which is printed in its entirety, offers several images through which to conceive key points of the interpretation of Whitehead's metaphysics that I have been developing here. A subject, in virtue of being reflected in beings beyond itself ("the moon in the bureau mirror") achieves a depth of actuality that is real and internal to its own subjective existence (it "looks out a million miles"). Deep actuality is a revelation of the "greatness" (as Whitehead calls it) of each thing as it achieves an intensive unity of felt connections with the universe beyond itself. An entity looks *out* with "pride, at itself," *not inward*; feelings are directed "at the superject, and not from the subject," and an entity is not so much a private enjoyment of a final satisfaction but a projected, ecstatic self-manifestation in its emergence from and transcendence into a creative universe of other such subjects.

Ecstatic individuality is "far beyond sleep" in the sense that actuality is a remorseless repetition "to the crack of doom," as Whitehead puts it, of achieved intensive contrasts inherited and modified and linking actualities in a solidarity of creative emphasis. On the other hand, there is a sort of "daytime sleep" that might be said to attend actuality, in so far as the concrescent center of full intensive achievement of an individual may be said to "perish," relative to its partial presence (via anticipated or prehended contrasts) in other actualities. Something about an actuality perishes, or sleeps, but something else does not. Whitehead's strong doctrine of subjective perishing needlessly introduces an ontological distinction between temporal states of an actuality, when the difference between "subjectivity" and "objectification" could just as easily have been cashed out in terms of the degree of presence of a certain unity of intensive contrasts. Had Whitehead not adopted ontological categories such as the distinction between "formal and objective reality" to discuss the difference between subjects and superjects, he might have realized that his own concept of intensity of feeling and the transmission of contrasts could by itself account for enough diversity between an entity's concrescence and its presence in other actualities to account for real temporal advance. This would have avoided the doctrine of temporal advance commonly associated with his atomism whereby individual actualities seem to be "By the Universe deserted," which to my mind could never have been the intended meaning of a connectionistic atomism.

Whitehead seems to have thought that his atomism was of a sort to sustain the kinds of relations among events that would prevent serious problems arising in regard to the ontological status of the past and in regard to the relations between a subject and its superject. Atomistic metaphysics is such a dubious metaphysical hypothesis that it seems unlikely that Whitehead would have adopted it unless he thought he had arrived at a version that successfully avoided the typical issues raised by this kind of theory (mainly regarding the existential connections among things that any atomism could legitimately be said to problematize). "Intensity" is of prime importance, I have argued, in coming to terms with what in the nature of Whitehead's atomism may be called upon to meet the ontological needs of what must be a nonisolated sense of atomicity, one that connects individuals in terms of the agency that makes them individuals, rather than by an objectified satisfaction that has been denuded of actuality by the perishing of concrescence. The system as it stands, replete with distinctions between final and efficient causality, subjective and objective dimensions of the actual, and so on, leaves the atomism in a genuine danger of looking indeed as if the Universe deserts, or merely uses, each actuality as it comes to pass.

I have tried to "wrap" this care, this possible implosion of the atomism into a solipsism of the present moment or a dual-level ontology, in the "cobweb" of intensity. It seems to me that "cobwebs" in this poem represent the ever-present matters that a mind has wisping about which are both the subconscious sources of wakeful insomnia and the equally subconscious recesses of personal capacities for overcoming the isolatedness of the insomniac form of waking experience. Intensity is both what makes an entity unique, a form of individual value-achievement, and what makes it a genuine contribution to the becoming of other subjects. The challenge is to conceive the existential unity of the intensive subject in its own experience and its role as itself in the experience of other such subjects, in a manner that does not endanger the atomistic conception of actuality by splitting it into two distinct types of operation.

We have no language in which to express a concept of individuation that is not a way of specifying a discrete being (or becoming, for that matter) incapable of location in other such individuals. But Bishop's poem points us in the right direction: In its final stanza the poem goes through a rhythmic change, to a form almost reminiscent of Gerard Manley Hopkins's inscaping; the poem comes to reflect in its rhythms the actual processes of overcoming the ordinary distinctions between things that are alleged to be opposite: left-right, shadows-body, wakefulness-night, shallow-deep. We are faced with a similar overcoming of distinctions in regard to subject-object, final-efficient cause, subject-superject—all the dualities of description that permeate the philosophy of organism's description of atomic individuality. The repetition of "where . . ." the opposites come to be one eventually resolves itself into the conviction of being loved, of the individual having made existential contact with another and with the entire world of harmonized opposites: ". . . and you love me." The incantatory and unifying rhythm, and its movement of the reader's awareness of the poem's subject, suggests the kind of "inversion" involved in thinking of individual actualities as ecstatically dispersed throughout the spatiotemporal continuum in a vibratory array of contrastive agency. We must be moved through our conceptual inertia, our philosophical insomniac isolation, to an awareness of the unity of that which seems distinct.

Unless the unity-in-diversity of an aesthetic occasion is really an existential unification of actualities via intensive incorporation of one another, the description of subjective experience offered in this philosophy is at risk for seeming to be a tale of pure privacy. It also makes the objective adventures of an entity a different kind of ontological event from the original contrastive agency of becoming. But if we interrogate an occasion, we need to ask whether it can be anything besides its achieved intensive structure of qualitative and quantitative detail, and the answer seems to be "No." If intensity of feeling describes both what and how an entity achieves a harmony of contrastive incorporation, then we may ask, further, if it can be said to "perish" in anything like the sense Whitehead often describes, and if it can be said to be in some different kind of ontological state in the various temporal dimensions belonging to it. I see no way of calling this system an atomism of connected individuals without a negative answer to this question as well. This does involve a selective emphasis on certain strains of the system at the expense of others, and may indeed amount to a serious revision of process as Whitehead seems to have described it. But the revision is premised on what seems to be the undercurrent of Whitehead's own thinking, by relying on the metaphysical vocabulary of intensive becoming that he developed to express his systematic insights, rather than relying on his use of terminology borrowed from forms of metaphysical thinking at odds with the novel project of the philosophy of organism.

Several times throughout this discourse I have contended that the distinction of final and efficient causality is unnecessary in Whitehead's system. This claim is premised on my sense of the seriousness of the ontological problems that seem to follow on the distinction, and on certain extra-systematic considerations that I will now briefly indicate. Aristotle's doctrine of four causes has been an indispensable tool of metaphysical analysis throughout the history of philosophy, and in particular the distinction of final and efficient causality that allows us to consider "finality" or "purpose" or "endhood" as not limited to the influence of one existent on another has been critical in ontological and moral spheres. But what is a useful distinction for selective emphasis on this or that dimension of process ought not to be ontologized into distinct modes of existence. It is my contention that nothing in nature advertizes itself as quadratically organized in a causal sense, such that the four causes and especially the two that become focal for Whitehead's discussion are not descriptive but analytical. A distinction of causes inexorably leads to interpretive decisions as to which cause to privilege in the metaphysics of process. Traditionally, Whitehead scholarship has privileged final cause, or purpose. Some commentators such as Jorge Nobo now seek to cut a wide swath in process for the operations of efficient causality alongside the concrescent final causality. My suggestion is that the interpretive option of denying the causal distinction yields a view that can distinguish events from one another while preserving their internal connection, by a serious consideration of the difference between the total presence of an intensity and its subordinate contrasts (concrescence) and their partial repetition elsewhere in the cosmos ("objectification," or ecstatic location). The immediate objection that collapsing this distinction leads to the dissolution of freedom and purpose in the acid-bath of remorseless natural processes is neutralized by the counter-claim that if the distinction is denied, we cannot privilege any of the previously entertained poles of the distinction (in the case of this objection, efficient causality). Thus the description of what look to be the merely efficient causes in nature requires as much revision as the description of that which is purely purposive or agentive.

The ecstatic interpretation of contrastive or intensive individuality faces at least one really serious objection, and that is the possible tendency towards a monistic scheme of internally related actualities.[1] But I think there are several solid points against this possibility. First, there is the genuine differentiation among events in terms of the difference between full and partial realization of the contrasts or intensities that belong to individual actualities. In many of the more stable social organizations in nature, inheritance of intensities is relatively complete and compulsory, the agency of one event differing from another only, or primarily, in terms of minor differences in detail. In other words, in many of the orders characterizing nature, we simply do not need in our metaphysics to guarantee a great deal of intensive differentiation between events. Once we move into the kinds of orders typical of living and human societies and minds, the merely partial incorporation of intensities of past actualities in present agents, in virtue of the consideration of alternative possibilities for becoming typical of such agents, renders unlikely the possibility that actuality might be said to collapse into a single nondifferentiating unity.

Second, if we recall the important distinction between (a) merely numerical or geometrical forms of discrete "oneness" and (b) the complex, multiply located sense of "one" developed here, we are reminded that a conglomerate or numerical monism of a universal oneness of all things is no more possible than the numerical monism of individual actualities. The kind of unity denied of constituent occasions in a processive cosmos must also, and more vehemently, be denied of the creative universe in toto. This renders the ontological perspective from which a monistic cosmos might be conjectured unavailable. This leads to a third, and related consideration. For the monistic argument to hold sway, it must reasonably be said that the actuality of any given entity somehow reduces to the actualities of any and all other actualities. The mutuality of agency on my interpretation suggests this kind of reduction. But in addition to the fact that this agentive mutuality is always and everywhere merely partial, we must keep in mind that the intensive presence of one thing in another can no more be said to reduce any one subject than it reduces *all* of them collectively, which I have just argued cannot be the case. Because there is nothing but everything else considered *severally* and *intensively* (not numerically) for entities to reduce to, there can be no proper "reduction" in the sense feared by the monistic critique. The reductionistic dimension of the monism argument is denied by the rejection of the conception of individuality that might underwrite it. The "thing" to which another "thing" might be agentively reduced is not the kind of individual that can own or hijack in a totalistic sense the agency of the individuals it includes in its intensive depth of actuality.

An actuality is a perspective within a universe of actualities whose genuine differentiation is a condition of the intensive feeling whereby they might be argued to collapse into one another monistically. A creative cosmos of vibratory intensities is a perpetual manifold of felt connectivity in an ever-changing array of worlds, and of potential contrasts whereby such worlds may be made one and rendered part of the perpetual many. The increase of the many by one must locate the one inside any possible many the universe may contain. This entails the intensive incorporation of actualities by one another, and the genuine preservation of an ontological status in the course of this incorporation.

The ethical consequences of this view, explored earlier, may likewise be subject to the criticism that significant individuality of agentive status is not sufficiently preserved, with the result that our construal of moral agents and the experience of moral responsibility may be said to be undermined. Although I think the arguments just advanced might apply to the nonreducibility of moral agents to one another just as much as the nonreducibility of actual entities to one another, we must remember that a moral agent is a vastly complex integration of the events associated with the "mind," the body, personal history, and so on. The dependency of moral behavior on the types of events characteristic of "consciousness" and their attendant capacity for, nay requirement of, novel intensities prevents their collapse into one another. Moreover, the *array* of social organizations involved in the complete definition of the "human being" possessed of moral agency establishes a noncoincidence of many dimensions of the causal continuities of what it means to be such an agent. The practical possibility of such massive overlap of human beings that their agencies could meaningfully be said to be nondistinguishable is negligible at least, if not nonexistent. In a very general sense, the ways in which our mentalities insinuate themselves in one another guarantees that our agencies intersect—meaningfully enough to be a genuine threat or delight to one another—and demands that our view of responsible action diminish our attachment to the concept of radical individuation in moral agency. Thus a balance is struck in this interpretation between our need for mutuality and agentive responsiveness and our need for moral distances from which to reflect on those interests and responsibilities we own relatively uniquely.

No interpretation of Whitehead's metaphysics can be conclusive, given the tensions and complexities that pervade the corpus of the philosopher's work. Yet Whitehead's indecision on this or that conception engenders in his commentators and critics a commitment to novel inquiry and hypothetical reasoning that might further free our ontological conceptions from the bonds of presupposition that tend to infect all human reasoning about such matters. It is nearly impossible to clear thought of those kinds of determinate fixing of boundaries between this and that which Whitehead describes as the fruits of derivative forms of quantitative construal (the infection of thought by the belief in extensive quantity's absoluteness). Thought cannot proceed without distinctions, and yet for every dialectical or discursive step in understanding made possible by the discrimination of actualities from one another, we are forced back to the beginning of understanding, to undermine the false discreteness imposed by the necessities of cognition as we know it.

Perhaps in poetry and art we near that mode of imagination that transcends the limitations of intellectual distinctions in virtue of being *productions* with similar creative proportions and operations to those realities they convey or remind us of. The writer Donald Hall has observed:

> Philosophy in its more logical incarnations strives to eliminate powers of association because they are subjective and uncontrollable. Poetry, on the other hand, wants to address *the whole matter of the human*—including fact and logic, but also the body with its senses, and above all the harsh complexities of emotion. Our senses, excited by sound and picture, assimilate records of feeling that are also passages to feeling. Poems tell stories; poems recount ideas; but poems *embody* feeling. Because emotion is illogical—in logic opposites cannot both be true; in the life of feeling, we love and hate together—the poem exists to say the unsayable.[2]

Because it is Whitehead's contention that an understanding of an actuality is knowledge of "a complete fact," analogous to "the whole matter of the human" referred to by Hall, it is important to render our philosophy somehow inclusive of a mode of describing, referring to, or from time to time manifesting, that embodiedness that attends all actualities and their relations, the embodiedness that defies logical discrimination and undermines the applicability of logic's very substance.

I have included poetry as the contextualizing realities, embodied complete facts, at each step of this analysis so as to suggest and begin to ameliorate the likely inadequacies of the conceptual representation of what is ultimately not subject to such representation. "Intensity" is in particular a notion that defies adequate "saying" in philosophical speech, for it is the existential denial of the radical distinctness of that which is genuinely concrete and individuated. The rhythmic vortex of Elizabeth Bishop's last stanza of "Insomnia" comes close to the representation of what cannot be "thought" true but what must be real in fact—that every individual finds its reality in its looking out through a universe whose deep seas and shallow heavens are genuine reflections of one another. To be alone is to be everywhere, an inversion of logical expectations in favor of limited, but satisfying, ontological union.

Notes

CHAPTER ONE

1. This is not to deny that Aristotle's categories have a logical or epistemological status, for surely they do, but this status is in virtue of or simultaneous with their ontological significance. Kant's categories of understanding, being transcendental conditions for the possibility of objects of experience, are part of a propaedeutic to metaphysics, and are not metaphysical or ontological in their explicit construction.

2. Immanuel Kant, *Critique of Pure Reason*, trans. Norman Kemp Smith (New York: St. Martin's Press, 1965), 114 (A81/B107).

3. In this Whitehead is quite similar to John Dewey, who treated the human experience of nature as an occasion in nature which we could expect to reveal certain, though perhaps not all, of the "generic traits" of nature as such. See Dewey's *Experience and Nature*, The Later Works, vol. 1, ed. Jo Ann Boydston (Carbondale: Southern Illinois University Press, 1988).

4. Parts two and three of *Process and Reality* are wonderful philosophical exercises in the explorations of common notions to be discovered among philosophers who quite deliberately set out to differ from one another, and to say something that fundamentally contradicts what Whitehead claims to find in them.

5. The reader will no doubt notice an idiosyncracy about the spelling of 'categoreal', supplanting at times the more usual 'categorical' in standard English. Whitehead uses the 'categoreal' spelling in cases involving fundamental metaphysical arrangements, much the way Kant used 'categorical' to indicate judgments that could not be otherwise. 'Categorical' is reserved for discussions where it is the status of something qua analytic category, and not metaphysical function, which is at stake.

6. Whitehead's doctrine of "feeling" is largely derived from that of F. H. Bradley. For both, the concept of feeling denotes real connection or continuity amongst realities, while maintaining the diversity of aspects of reality felt in a complex feeling of the universe as a whole. However, Bradley's idealism rejects the individuality of existence of the realities feeling and felt, while Whitehead's atomism is premised on the real plurality of existents. This difference results in a wide gap between the two theories on the topic of the metaphysical status and function of relations, as we shall see. For an excellent discussion of the important connection between Whitehead and Bradley, see Leemon McHenry, *Whitehead and Bradley: A Comparative Analysis* (Albany: State University of New York Press, 1992). On the topic of "feeling" see especially pp. 28–45 of McHenry's analysis.

7. The most extensive use of the concept of intensity in post-Whiteheadian scholarship has been made by Robert Neville, who borrows it in relatively unmodified form as part of the structural analysis of existents as "harmonies" in his own metaphysics. See, for example, *Reconstruction of Thinking* (New York: State University of New York Press, 1981). Because Neville constructs his own metaphysics in this and other works, his primary objective is not the systematic elucidation of Whitehead's particular employment of the term. Interestingly, however, I think such

an elucidation yields a possible alternative ontology to Neville's, which was conceived in part to overcome certain problems he notes in Whiteheadian atomism.

8. Dorothy Emmett, *Whitehead's Philosophy of Organism* (New York: St. Martin's Press, 1966), 199.

9. Ibid.

10. For an interesting exchange on the problems posed for key Whiteheadian concepts by the idea of modification of subjective aim through the phases of concrescence see John Cobb,
"Freedom on Whitehead's Philosophy: A Response to Edward Pols," *Southern Journal of Philosophy* 7 (1969–1970), 409–13; Lewis Ford, "Can Whitehead Provide For Real Subjective Agency? A Reply to Edward Pols's Critique," *Modern Schoolman* 47 (1970), 209–25; Edward Pols, "Freedom and Agency: A Reply," *Southern Journal of Philosophy* 7 (1969), 415–19.

11. "The Harvard Lectures, for 1924–25," ed. Jennifer Hamlin von der Luft, printed as Appendix 1 to Lewis Ford, *The Emergence of Whitehead's Metaphysics* (Albany: State University of New York Press, 1984).

12. William A. Christian, *An Interpretation of Whitehead's Metaphysics* (New Haven: Yale University Press, 1959), 23.

13. Ibid.

14. Ibid.

15. Ibid., 29.

16. Ibid.

17. Ibid., 30.

18. I will resist digressing here into a discussion of how curious it is for Whitehead to attach the all-important "formal reality" of an epochal occasion to the concrescent process wherein it is *not yet in time*. One might build some interesting ontologies from this curiosity, including the notion that things that are in time do not in the truest sense of the word "exist." This would put Whitehead's ontology very much in line with either certain eastern conceptions of the illusoriness of temporal existence, or the Sartrean conception of existence as characterless activity, the "pure spontaneous upsurge" of consciousness in *Being and Nothingness*. Given Whitehead's interest in concreteness, however, these developments, tempting as they may be, would mark a serious departure from some of his major intentions in constructing a metaphysics. They would not, however, be in much tension with some of Whitehead's comments about the function of "solitariness" in religious experience, as the manner in which the self throws off the encrustations of social determination of character and assumes the capacity for penetrating sincerity. *Revising* Whitehead's total system in these directions would itself constitute an interesting project. See *Religion in the Making* for the discussion of religious solitariness.

19. Lewis S. Ford, "A Sampling of Other Interpretations," Afterword to *Explorations in Whitehead's Metaphysics*, ed. Lewis S. Ford and George L. Kline (New York: Fordham University Press, 1983), 321. See also A.H. Johnson's discussion with Whitehead on this and other issues in "Some Conversations with Whitehead Concerning God and Creativity," in Ford and Kline, *Exploratons*, and in another version with more attention to "satisfaction" in *Philosophy and Phenomenological Research* 29(1968–1969):351–76.

20. See his "Whitehead's Principle of Relativity," *Process Studies* 8(1978):1–20.

Related issues regarding individuation on Nobo's reading will be discussed in later chapters.

21. Christian, *Interpretation*, 39.

22. Ibid., 43.

23. Jorge L. Nobo, *Whitehead's Metaphysics of Extension and Solidarity* (Albany: State University of New York Press, 1986), 259–67.

24. Christian, *Interpretation*, 46, emphasis mine.

25. Elizabeth M. Kraus, *The Metaphysics of Experience* (New York: Fordham University Press, 1979), 61–62.

26. Ibid., 63.

27. Robert C. Neville, *The Cosmology of Freedom* (New Haven: Yale University Press, 1974), 156.

28. Neville does in fact develop his own conception of individuality, the notion of "discursive individuals," which is designed to rise above just the kinds of ontological problems I am exploring in Whitehead's system. What I suggest is that there may be a way within Whiteheadian atomism to rise above such problems, a way that emphasizes a certain kind of ontology of individuals which might then be evaluated alongside Neville's ingenious constructions. It is crucial to the historical development of Process Philosophy that numerous contending images of individual reality be developed, to create a body of work conceptually rich enough to challenge the long-standing attachment to substance-ontological notions of individual existence, as well as their existentialist alternatives.

29. For another take on the status of eternal objects as what I am calling "potential contrasts," one should look to Jorge Nobo's very important treatment of the metaphysics of "envisagement" in *Whitehead's Metaphysics of Extension and Solidarity*. Nobo delineates the different metaphysical contexts wherein "envisagement" of forms of definiteness is crucial to processual creativity, most importantly in regard to how such envisaging provides a formative matrix of mutual relevance from whence felt contrasts in actual things may take their start. Forthcoming studies by Nobo explore the concept of "envisagement" still further.

CHAPTER TWO

1. Interestingly, Donald Sherburne adds a fourth phase, beyond the three to be elaborated here, to accommodate the forms of feeling involved in the "higher phases of experience" (alluded to in chapter one) typical of intellectual occasions. These special forms of feeling involve complex comparisons (contrasts) of the simpler feelings of the earlier phases, warranting a separate phase, according to Sherburne. See his *Key to Whitehead's "Process and Reality"* (Chicago: University of Chicago Press, 1966), 39.

2. This idea will be explored at length in chapter three, in which the real existential solidarity of Whitehead's atomic actualities is argued.

3. Paul Weiss, *Beyond All Appearances* (Carbondale: Southern Illinois University Press, 1974), 20–25.

4. Readers should note that the position being taken in the present study precludes any important conceptual distinction in metaphysics between individuality and particularity, because I take it to be the thrust of Whitehead's atomism that

things exist in some state of singularity that would undermine the force of such a distinction. I realize the controversiality of rejecting this distinction, but I hope the analyses in this essay might be taken together as an argument that sets us on the path of rejecting an abstract philosophical distinction in favor of a description of the existential conditions of concreteness.

5. Sherburne, *Key*.

6. Ford, *Emergence*, p. 239, 260.

7. This theme is amplified at *PR* 215n, where Whitehead asserts his agreement with Kemp Smith's analysis of Kant on the question of an "object." Whitehead claims to be using the same sense of "object" as Kemp Smith in the following: "When we examine the objective, we find that the primary characteristic distinguishing it from the subjective is that it lays a compulsion upon our minds, constraining us to think about it a certain way. By an object is meant something which will not allow us to think at haphazard." Whitehead then adds: "There is of course the vital difference, among others, that where Kemp Smith, expounding Kant, writes 'thinking', the philosophy of organism substitutes 'experiencing'." The interesting point in terms of our current analyses is that the substantial aspect of objectivity over and against subjectivity is simply its compulsoriness in the experience of other things (rather than any special ontological status which gives it that compulsoriness). And it may also be noted that despite Whitehead's substitution of 'experience' for 'thought', as metaphysical thought is a form of experience, it too must answer to the compulsions of its objects as well. If something cannot become an object of thought except as it is insinuated in other things, then this insinuation becomes an element in our concept of the thing, in this case an individual entity. Here we see the grounding of some of Whitehead's affinity with Hegel.

8. cf. Sherburne, *Key*, 42–45; Nobo, *Whitehead's Metaphysics*, 341, 400; Ivor Leclerc, *Whitehead's Metaphysics: An Introductory Exposition* (Lanham, MD: University Press of America, 1986), 167–70.

9. This experiential realism seems to echo the sense of "objectivity" Whitehead applauded in Kemp Smith, the tendency of something to impose itself in the experience (or knowledge) belonging to other things. See note 7.

10. Edward Pols famously argued that Whitehead's portrait of subjective becoming is undermined by the doctrine of eternal objects as forms of definiteness. The fact that the character of actualities stems from the character of eternal objects robs the actualities of their ultimate status as free self-creators. See his *Whitehead's Metaphysics: A Critical Examination of Whitehead's "Process and Reality"* (Carbondale: Southern Illinois University Press, 1967), 171–95. Any defense of Whiteheadian ontology must face Pols' challenge. I do not see, however, how the argument that eternal objects do the work in this metaphysics addresses the *agency of contrast* that is the crucial character of actuality qua creativity. As also acknowledged by George Lucas, Lewis Ford advances an interpretation of the scheme whereby Pols' position amounts to the error of confusing the forms of definiteness recognizable in an occasion once completed, with the agency of composition required during concrescence. See Ford's "Can Whitehead Provide for Real Subjective Agency?" *Modern Schoolman* 47(January 1970):209–25. Also see George Lucas, *The Rehabilitation of Whitehead* (Albany: State University of New York Press, 1989), 151–54, for a discussion of Pols' extended argument against Whitehead's account of subjective free-

dom. My own interpretation will modify Ford's somewhat by claiming that completed forms of definiteness do not lost subjective agency, thereby eluding Pols' criticism and avoiding the ontological difference between subjects and objects implicit in Ford's position.

11. Editors' notes to *Process and Reality*, PR 408.

12. I am indebted for certain refinements in the following discussion to the helpful comments of Professor Nobo, though of course I am wholly responsible for any interpretive indiscretions contained herein.

13. Nobo, *Whitehead's Metaphysics*, 29–32, and passim; and "Whitehead's Principle of Process," *Process Studies* 4 (Winter 1974), 278–84.

14. Nobo, *Whitehead's Metaphysics*, 154.

15. Ibid., 155.

16. This would be a good place to remind the reader that my intentions in challenging Nobo's two-process view is not to suggest that it is incorrect, because I think it is one of the more powerful readings of Whitehead's metaphysical project, a project that Whitehead himself failed to adequately characterize. My intent is to offer an *alternative* that adheres *somewhat* more closely to the atomistic claim at the basis of Whitehead's axiological ontology, because, as I will argue later, I think there is something valuable to defend in the *kind* of atomism Whitehead may have intended to develop in his obscure system.

17. Nobo, *Whitehead's Metaphysics*, 31.

18. See Nobo's *Whitehead's Metaphysics*, chapters five through seven, for his developed argument of this important point.

19. See *Whitehead's Metaphysics*, chapters one through three, and eight.

20. Jean-Paul Sarte, *L'Etre et le Neant* (Paris: Editions Gallimard, 1943), 210. The translation that follows is from *Being and Nothingness*, trans. Hazel E. Barnes (New York: Philosophical Library), 170.

21. In future studies I will be interested in drawing out the obvious parallels between the concept of "ecstatic existence" being developed here and that found in Heidegger's thought.

22. An important contribution to the understanding of Whitehead's system would be made if one were to undertake the unpacking of the scheme from the perspective of what it says *about* the experience from which it derives its conceptual vocabulary. A systematic understanding of the convergence between the existential conditions of knowing, and the knowledge of the conditions of existence would then be possible, and with it a greater appreciation of Whitehead's philosophical relevance to much philosophy since Hume and Kant.

CHAPTER THREE

1. Charles Hartshorne, *Whitehead's Philosophy: Selected Essays, 1935–1970* (Lincoln: University of Nebraska Press, 1972), 161–62.

2. George Kline, "Form, Concrescence, Concretum," in Ford and Kline, *Explorations*, 104.

3. Kline, "Form, Concrescence, Concretum," 105, 117, and passim.

4. Ibid., 132–33.

5. Ibid., 119.
6. Ibid., 104.
7. Ibid., 106.
8. Ibid.
9. Ibid., 107.
10. Ibid., 118–22.

11. There may be any number of metaphysically plausible time-theories consistent with Whiteheadian atomism, including perhaps the possibility that time is reversible, a wild and provocative notion now receiving some attention from speculative cosmologists. On the more mundane level, however, in a recent study Robert Neville has advanced a manner of conceiving the unity of the three temporal modes of past, present, and future under a proper conception of "eternity." See *Eternity and Time's Flow* (Albany: State University of New York Press, 1993). Neville's view captures a dimension of eternality that I am trying to advance in a more atomistic sense, and in light of which I have privileged the imaginative notion of the "eternal" by placing the Blake quote at the head of this chapter.

12. Kline, "Form, Concrescence, Concretum," Ibid., 124.

13. Ibid., 125.

14. Nobo's project explores in great detail this provocative notion of the "modal" presence of one thing in another. See *Whitehead's Metaphysics of Extension and Solidarity*, passim, but especially 222ff.

15. Kline, "Form, Concrescence, Concretum," 134. For a later formulation of Kline's position, see his essay, "The Systematic Ambiguity of Some Key Whiteheadian Terms," in *Metaphysics as Foundation: Essays in Honor of Ivor Leclerc*, ed. Paul A. Bogaard and Gordon Treash (Albany: State University of New York Press, 1993), 150–63.

16. Ivor Leclerc, *The Nature of Physical Existence* (Lanham: University Press of America, 1986), 284.

17. Ibid., 288.

18. Ibid., 291.

19. Ibid., 290.

20. Kline objects to Whitehead's use of the language of "feeling another feeling" in "Form, Concrescence, Concretum," 119; Leclerc notes that there is a subjective and objective use of the concept of feeling, denoting the cumulative character of time provided for the objective presence of past feelings in present actualities. See *Whitehead's Metaphysics*, 156–62. I do not think this reading resolves the ontological questions at hand, for the existential status of subjectivity versus objectivity is precisely at stake. However, Leclerc's view is not inconsistent with mine. Christian offers an analysis of what he takes to be Whitehead's careless suggestion in many passages that there is "feeling of feeling" or a "flow of feeling" between actualities in *Interpretation*, 67–73. Hartshorne, however, is comfortable with the language of "feeling another feeling"; see his *Whitehead's Philosophy*, passim.

21. It must be noted that the "deadness" in this citation does not unambiguously establish a static characterization of completed actualities. The expression is poetically appealing, doubtless, for anyone seeking to effect such a characterization, but the actual passage, read in toto, seems to establish the incurably dynamic character of being in this scheme. In the process of transition from entity to entity, "the creativity, universal throughout actuality, is characterized by the datum from the past;

and it meets this dead datum—universalized into a character of creativity—*by the vivifying novelty of subjective form* selected from the multiplicity of pure potentiality. In the process, the old meets the new, and this meeting *constitutes the satisfaction* of an immediate particular individual" (PR 164, emphasis mine).

22. Leclerc, "Being and Becoming in Whitehead's Metaphysics" in Ford and Kline, *Explorations*, 62–64.

23. In note 11 of this chapter I remarked that a theory of time as reversible might be consistent with Whitehead's atomism. The current passage would certainly undermine that claim. A determination on this issue would depend on a rather substantive analysis of whether or not the "cumulative" character of time requires its strict "irreversibility," which analysis must unfortunately be postponed for another occasion. I will make some brief speculations on this issue later. Certainly irreversibility is suggested by common sense, but it may not have to be in the nature of things.

24. To indulge one more comment on cumulation versus irreversibility: Whitehead is at pains to guarantee the cumulative character of time in order to avoid the "stage play" conception, which would appear to be another dig at Bradleyan idealism, or perhaps at Leibniz. Idealism and Leibnizian monadology are problematic, however, because of their stipulation of a unitary sense to the "whole" of things, which is not a reference to its component parts. If what happens "in" time is merely a factor in the experience of some very grand scale "individual" (the absolute, or Leibniz's divine arrangement of things) then it is a stage play, and the directional sequence is irrelevant. Remove the totalizing effect of the perspective of the "whole," and we can ask whether cummulative time requires nonreversibility in the sense of a time-system in which one can never move backward or forward. If the relevant form of cumulation is the happening of events, intensities, with ecstatic location throughout the continuum, then the abstract question of "direction" might be reformulated as movement amidst actualities and not the attempt to "count" backward or forward (there is nothing to "count" intrinsically except the intense satisfactions of entities). These are mere speculations, of course.

25. William Garland, "The Ultimacy of Creativity," in Ford and Kline, *Explorations*, 212–38.

26. William A. Christian, "The Concept of God as a Derivative Notion," in *Process and Divinity: Philosophical Essays Presented to Charles Hartshorne*, eds. William L. Reese and Eugene Freeman (LaSalle: Open Court Publishing, 1964), 183–84.

27. Garland, "Ultimacy," 228.

28. Ibid.

29. Garland, "Ultimacy," 288. I am intrigued by Garland's suggestion, in a private conversation, that perhaps Whitehead should have introduced a Category of *Objective* Intensity, to resolve the being and becoming issue. I fear, however, that this would simply relocate the same ontological problem to another unexplained distinction between intensities of two varieties.

30. Kant, *Critique of Pure Reason*, A162-63/B203. Note that Whitehead is using Max Müller's translation of Kant.

31. Whitehead mistakenly attributes this passage to the Axioms of Intuition, where the other passage in question is to be found.

32. Kant, *Critique of Pure Reason*, A 169/B211.

33. Ibid., A 169/B 211.

Notes to Chapter Three

34. George Lucas, *Rehabilitation*, 77.

35. Ibid., 76–92.

36. This point of origin in part accounts for that aspect of Whitehead's thought that Norman has labeled "aesthetic mathematicism." See Ralph V. Norman, Jr., "Whitehead and 'Mathematicism'," in *Alfred North Whitehead: Essays on His Philosophy*, ed. George L. Kline, 34.

37. Granville Henry, "Whitehead's Philosophical Response to the New Mathematics," in Ford and Kline, *Explorations*, 17.

38. Henry, "Mathematics," 16–17.

39. If Whitehead is using "intensity" here in a manner not really parallel to its later employment in a much more elaborate philosophy, I am unable to discover it. I am told by experts more knowledgeable than I in mathematical theory that the presence of "intensity" is idiosyncratic to Whitehead's own *Universal Algebra*, and does not appear in those constructed by other thinkers in mathematics. At any rate, I am not asserting an absolute symmetry of conceptual functioning between the "intensity" of *Universal Algebra* and the "intensity" of *Process and Reality* and *Adventures of Ideas,* but it does seem duly plausible that the conception of quantitative degree so fundamental to Whitehead's mature ontology was born in *Universal Algebra*.

40. See Elizabeth M. Kraus, *The Metaphysics of Experience*, 127–57, for a clear exposition of Whitehead's Theory of Extension, especially 141.

41. Morris Kline, "Projective Geometry," in James R. Newman, *The World of Mathematics*, vol. 1, 622–41. It is to be noted that Cayley performed similar services for algebra in the theory of quantics: see Eric Temple Bell, "Invariant Twins, Cayley and Sylvester," in Newman, *World*, 355.

42. Kraus, *Metaphysics*, 15–16, and note.

43. Bishop Berkeley, "The Analyst," excerpted in Newman, *World*, 292. Interestingly, Whitehead's mathematical inquiries led him to the same conclusions as those reached by Berkeley, though there is no evidence as to his having read Berkeley's works on this point (Newman, *World*, 291n).

44. Samuel Alexander, *Space Time and Deity*, vol. 1, 307.

45. Ibid., 310.

46. Ibid.

47. Jorge Nobo, "Whitehead's Principle of Relativity," *Process Studies* 8 (1978), 1.

48. Lucas, *Rehabilitation*, 170.

49. Ibid., 172.

50. Ibid., 174.

51. For a cogent summary of the critical disputes centering on Whitehead's theism, see Lucas, *Rehabilitation*, 161–66. Some scholars attempt to defend Whitehead's concept of God and its function in the system from charges of incoherence and superfluity (see, for example, Christian, *Interpretation*, and Ford, "An Appraisal of Whiteheadian Non-Theism," *Southern Journal of Philosophy* 15(1)(Spring 1977):27–35). Others either advance the charge of incoherence or attempt to offer naturalistic alternatives to God's cosmological role from within Whitehead's scheme (see Donald Sherburne, "Whitehead Without God," *The Christian Scholar* 40(3)(Fall 1967):251–72; Victor Lowe, *Understanding Whitehead* (Baltimore: Johns Hopkins University Press, 1962), 87ff.

52. The language of "massiveness" of inherited feeling, allied constantly to a strong sense of "perishing," is used by Whitehead throughout *Adventures of Ideas* in

an attempt to explain experience with particular emphasis on intensification. This coupling lends credibility to the position I am forwarding as to the nature of Whiteheadian atomism. Real penetration of one reality by another does not vitiate the atomic cosmology, if experience is at once "massive" and transitory.

53. I can hardly avoid a comment here since this issue is so prevailingly raised by readers and (especially) nonreaders of Whitehead alike (it was in fact the subject of philosophically stimulating papers delivered by Leemon McHenry and Lewis Ford at a recent meeting of the Society for Study of Process Philosophy, New York, 1996). There is no escaping the subjectivist cast of Whitehead's mature philosophy, but this does not amount to the kind of ridiculous panpsychism often attributed to him, whereby every event is possessed of at least a little of what we know as conscious thought. To assert the metaphysical continuity of the conditions of process in all events is not to assert the absolute identity of character (which, in Whitehead, is a type of functioning, as my notion of intensive contrast is designed to highlight) among all factual existents. All that is asserted is the universal generality of the conditions of character, not the emergent forms designated as "the" character or natures of things. The entertainment of possibility, which is the essence of mentality, has to be described as a kind of agency, and some find it very difficult to attribute any such powers to nonintellectual types of existents (rocks, lamps, trees, etc.).

First of all, I think some of the difficulty we have in sharing a metaphysically general conception of "agency" is due to an overevaluation of just what such agency means in us (I will discuss this in chapters four and five). How genuinely "productive" is an agent? That nonintellectual agents cannot be productive in the sense we take ourselves to be productive seems clear. But we may not be taking our own productivity for what it is in this denial of its presence in subhuman or subanimal species.

Second, the kind of subjectivity Whitehead attributes universally is just so much as to avoid the vacuous actuality of mechanistic materialism, but not so much as to imply that rocks think. The accusation that Whitehead is a panpsychist of any "ridiculous" (not to imply that radical panpsychism *is* ridiculous, which is a separate issue, but only to answer those who think that *Whitehead's* is) kind stems from the refusal to entertain his philosophy on its own terms. Now, Whitehead is himself responsible for this refusal to an extent because he frames the crucial notions of his philosophy in the crucible of decidedly idealist philosophies. We should keep in mind, however, that what Whitehead discovers in these philosophies is a manner of thinking and conceiving of things in a systematic sense, and not so much a doctrine of what those things are.

It may be that even contemporary discussion in the philosophy of mind is coming around to a view that has to entertain the viability of a revised and prototypically mental concept of the "physical" world in which minds are said to reside and from which, more importantly, minds are said to have emerged (both in the evolutionary sense and in the minute by minute sense in which minds may be emergent phenomena produced by the physical brain). The problem of consciousness in nature, including the "hard" problem of phenomenal qualia, has led David Chalmers to just this sort of reconstruction of the "physical" in *The Conscious Mind: In Search of a Fundamental Theory* (New York: Oxford University Press, 1996).

54. Whitehead goes so far as to claim that God's existence, which imposes limitation or relatedness on the realm of potentiality and its relevance to the course of

actual events, is "the ultimate irrationality" (*SMW* 178). It might be worth pointing out that God's existence is *no more* irrational than the alternative materialistic (non-valuative) hypothesis Whitehead is trying to undermine. That the world should be composed of matter in elaborate dynamic arrangements but without purpose effecting its arrangement is no less a faith than the hypothesis that self-value is the reason for any arrangement. That the latter constitutes simply a better *explanation*, and not just a better *faith*, is Whitehead's rational project in doing metaphysics.

CHAPTER FOUR

1. Yeats was painfully aware of the pitfalls of excessive awareness and imaginative thinking, and his poetic corpus is testimony to his life-long struggle with the enriching and disabling functions of intellectual fancy. It is worth noting here that Yeats read Whitehead's *Science and the Modern World* and was extremely taken by it, especially by how it shed light on the philosophical vision Yeats himself was developing. I had the opportunity to study Yeat's copy of *Science and the Modern World* in his daughter's library in Dalkey, Ireland, and will bring the results of these researches to publication in the near future. "All Soul's Night," the poem quoted here, was written in 1920, before Yeats read Whitehead in 1926.

2. Alexander, *Space*, vol. 1, xiv: "There are no two separate mental acts, one of enjoyment and one of contemplation. The mind, in enjoying itself, has before it, and therefore contemplates, the object. Contemplation is the same act as enjoyment, only in reference to the object. The enjoyment is at once a state of being of the mind itself, and that to which the object is revealed, and so is an act of knowing. Reciprocallly, in knowing the object I know myself, not in the sense that I contemplate myself, for I do not do so, but in the sense that I live through this experience of myself." For Alexander, as for Whitehead, the ordinary subject-object antithesis in occasions of knowledge is compromised. For Whitehead this is an extension of his general reconstruction of the distinction.

3. The language of experience as 'enjoyment' in Whitehead, particularly in regard to its application in the human realm, has its echoes in Dewey's philosophy. Both thinkers share the conviction that the attribution of qualities of enjoyment or suffering to any given experience is metaphysically a function of both the natural environment and the experient subject. See Dewey's *Experience and Nature* (Carbondale: Southern Illinois University Press, 1988), passim, but especially 89–96.

4. Ernst Wolf-Gazo, "Negation and Contrast: The Origins of Self-Consciousness in Hegel and Whitehead," in *Hegel and Whitehead, Contemporary Perspectives on Systematic Philosophy*, ed. George R. Lucas (Albany: State University of New York Press, 1986), 213.

5. References to the developments in the psychology of his day are scattered throughout Whitehead's *Process and Reality* (18, 32, 103, 326).

6. Donald Sherburne, "Whitehead's Psychological Physiology," *Southern Journal of Philosophy* 7 (1969), 403–6.

7. Ibid., 406.

8. William J. Gallagher, "Whitehead's Psychological Physiology: A Third View," *Process Studies* 4 (1974), 273.

9. It is important to note that in the second species of physical purposes, there

is origination of additional conceptual feeling, via the Category of Reversion, such that intensity is increased due to the enlargement of the sphere of relevant potentialities entertained under contrasts. This second species is characteristic of high-grade experience with ample capability for anticipatory feelings regarding the future.

10. See, for example, Dewey, *Experience and Nature*, 198–207.

11. Alexander, *Space*, vol. 2, 161–64.

12. Ibid., 162.

13. Henri Bergson, *Creative Evolution*, trans. Arthur Mitchell (New York: Henry Holt and Company, 1911), 211–12.

14. Ibid., 150–65.

15. Alexander, *Space*, vol. 2, 137.

16. Ford, *Emergence*, 238–40.

17. Ibid.

18. Henri Bergson, *Matter and Memory*, trans. Nancy Margaret Paul and W. Scott Palmer (London: George Allen & Unwin, 1911), 234–36.

19. Ibid., 239–43.

20. Ibid., 244.

21. Ibid., 259.

22. Whitehead's attempt to resolve the tensions between realities *in concreto* and realities qua analyzed might here be interestingly compared to or supplemented by Justus Buchler's concept of the "discrimination" of "natural complexes" effected by various forms of human apprehension. Both try to maintain a realistic, naturalistic scheme while asserting some limitation of our statement of nature's forms by the forms imposed by intellect. See Justus Buchler, *The Metaphysics of Natural Complexes*, 2d expanded edition, ed. Kathleen Wallace and Armen Marsoobian, with Robert S. Corrington (Albany: State University of New York Press, 1989).

23. Whitehead offers one argument, about the fundamental relationship of whole and part, to suggest a substantiation of the thesis that there is some general character of extensivity that is metaphysically general. It is true of all entities that the relationship of whole and part is so intimate and fundamental that "[i]f you abolish the whole, you abolish its parts; and if you abolish any part, then *that* whole is abolished" (*PR* 288).

24. Nobo, *Whitehead's Metaphysics of Extension and Solidarity*, 199.

CHAPTER FIVE

1. See Lynn Belaief, *Toward a Whiteheadian Ethics* (Lanham: University Press of America, 1984); Richard Davis, "Whitehead's Moral Philosophy," *Process Studies* 3 (Summer 1973), 75–90; Arthur Henry Jentz, *Ethics in the Making* (Doctoral Thesis, Columbia University, 1965); Daniel Metzgler, *Essay in Whiteheadian Ethics* (Doctoral Thesis, Emory University, 1987); John B. Spencer, *The Ethics of A. N. Whitehead* (Doctoral Thesis, University of Chicago, 1967).

2. Iris Murdoch, "Against Dryness: A Polemical Sketch," in *Revisions: Changing Perspectives in Moral Philosophy*, eds. Stanley Hauerwas and Alasdair MacIntyre (Notre Dame: University of Notre Dame Press, 1983), 43–50.

3. Belaief and others commonly acknowledge the self-creative responsibilities involved in becoming as central to the moral significance in Whitehead. My analysis

seeks to extend this acknowledgment via the sustained intensive analysis of what it means to exist at all in this system.

4. Whitehead repudiates not only the metaphysics of substantive agents, but the abandoned "faculty-psychology" on which it is based (*PR* 18).

5. See Neville, *Cosmology*, 40–51; Paul Weiss, *Man's Freedom* (New Haven: Yale University Press, 1950); D. Browning, "Whitehead's Theory of Human Agency," *Dialogue* 2 (1963–1964), 424–41.

6. Neville's critique in *Cosmology* involves the development of his own theory of "discursive individuals," hypothesized to remove the inadequacies of Whitehead's insufficiently unified agents.

7. For Murdoch's analysis of these moves, see *The Sovereignty of Good* (New York: Schocken Books, 1971), 47, 76 and passim. Hereinafter cited in text as (*SG* page number).

8. George Lucas, "Moral Order and the Constraints of Agency," in *New Essays in Metaphysics*, ed. Robert Neville (Albany: State University of New York Press, 1987), 123.

9. Iris Murdoch, *Metaphysics as a Guide to Morals* (New York: Viking Penguin, 1992), 2. Hereinafter cited in text as (*MGM* page number).

10. Murdoch, "Against Dryness," 49.

11. The frequent allusions to 'muddledness' in Murdoch's novels and essays are indicative of the genuine complexity of the moral situation as faced by even well-intentioned agents—see for example *A Fairly Honourable Defeat* (New York: Penguin Books, 1970), wherein even the most seemingly 'virtuous' protagonists frequently find themselves bemoaning the "muddle" in which they find themselves, usually due to a failure of their own to justly evaluate the competing claims on their attention, claims that put those very characters in a position of responsibility that they resist claiming. It is also interesting to note Whitehead's affinity with the very notion of 'muddledness', highlighting as it does the finite, sometimes tragic complexity of human experience as well as the modes of thought through which humans try to conceive of reality. The rhythmic fluctuation between periods of conceptual clarity and intellectual muddledness are described by Whitehead in these and other terms in his frequent discussions of the progress of human knowledge and civilization (see *SMW*, *AI*, *FR*, passim). Paul Kuntz associates Whitehead with the tolerance of nonvicious muddledness in thought [see his "Whitehead the Anglican and Russell the Puritan: The Traditional Origins of Muddleheadedness and Simplemindedness," *Process Studies* 17 (Spring 1988), 40–44], even while appreciating the centrality of the concept of "order" in the system [see his *Alfred North Whitehead* (Boston: Twayne Publishers, 1984)].

12. Murdoch, "Against Dryness," 49.

13. Sherburne, "Psychological Physiology," 409.

14. William James, *The Principles of Psychology* (Cambridge: Harvard University Press, 1981), 1164.

15. Ibid., 424, 1166–67.

16. Alexander, *Space, Time, and Deity*, vol. 2, 137.

17. Whitehead is quoting from *Some Problems of Philosophy*, chapter 10.

18. Murdoch defends the contemplative characterization of the task of moral life in *Sovereignty of God*, by way of aligning herself with Moore against his critics. She defends Moore's use of "quasi-aesthetic imagery of vision in conceiving the

good," and the "contemplative attitude" thus pictured as the core of agency, over and against an overly moving image of will as advanced by Hampshire as well as Sartre (*SG* 3).

19. Interestingly, Murdoch ends *Metaphysics as a Guide to Morals* with a consideration of Bradley's metaphysics, suggesting that the parallel established here with Whitehead is methodologically legitimate. Bradley stands as a determinate link between the two, given the profound and formative influence of Bradley's system on Whitehead's own.

20. John Goheen, "Whitehead's Theory of Value," in *The Philosophy of Alfred North Whitehead*, ed. Paul A. Schilpp (LaSalle: Open Court Publishing, 1941), 437–59.

21. Belaief, *Whiteheadian Ethics*, 121.

22. I borrow the title of this section from Murdoch's essay, "On God and Good," in *The Sovereignty of Good*.

23. On this point Whitehead's contributions to moral philosophy can lend insight into Gilligan's dispute with Kohlberg as to the relative status of principles and intuitive caring in morally mature decision making. See Carol Gilligan, *In a Different Voice: Psychological Theory and Women's Development* (Cambridge: Harvard University Press, 1982); John Michael Murphy and Carol Gilligan, "Moral Development in Late Adolescence and Adulthood: A Critique and Reconstruction of Kohlberg's Theory," *Human Development* 23 (1980), 77–104. Whitehead's ecstatic conception of existence is also provocatively similar to Abraham Maslow's notion of "peak experiences," whereby the individual's identity "is more able to fuse with the world, with what was formerly not-self. . . . That is, the greatest attainment of identity, autonomy, or selfhood is itself simultaneously a transcending of itself, a going beyond and above selfhood." *Toward a Psychology of Being*, Second Edition (Princeton: D. Van Nostrand Company, 1968), 105.

24. Robert Neville, *The Puritan Smile: A Look Toward Moral Reflection* (Albany: State University of New York Press, 1987), 89.

25. Ibid., 103.

26. Ibid., 112. This concept of aesthetic imagination in the realm of moral experience has deep resonances with Dewey's notion of "dramatic imaginative rehearsal" in *Human Nature and Conduct* (New York: Modern Library, 1922), especially 178–86.

27. Neville, *Puritan Smile*, 197–200.

28. Neville's *Eternity and Time's Flow* (Albany: State University of New York Press, 1993) is of interest here. In this work Neville argues for the necessity of the perspective of eternity for a complete appreciation of the metaphysical and moral implications of finitude.

29. David Hall, *The Civilization of Experience: A Whiteheadian Theory of Culture*, (New York: Fordham University Press, 1973), passim.

30. Neville's ethics in *The Puritan Smile* acknowledges similar virtues.

31. The temporal character of moral experience receives interesting attention from Charles Sherover in "Toward Experiential Metaphysics: Radical Temporalism," in Neville, ed., *New Essays*, 77–100.

32. There is a decidedly historical cast to Whitehead's conception of the doing of philosophy, such that not only are the insights of the history of philosophy culled for explanatory force, but the historical dimensions of philosophic thought in itself

are also acknowledged in a quasi-Hegelian manner (without the eschatology of the absolute). See the historical sections of *Process and Reality,* part 2, chapters 1, 5, 6, 7.

33. In his review of *Metaphysics and a Guide to Morals,* MacIntyre faults Murdoch for her failure to provide normative values (akin to his own adaption of Aristotelean ethics) that would meaningfully support functioning moral communities. This is not surprising given MacIntyre's generally dim view of the Enlightenment. But Murdoch's position, as well as Whitehead's, focuses on the absolute *necessity* for *individuals* to undergo the purification or education of their capacity to envision the good in situations that resist satisfactory interpretation by the tradition of experience or communities or theories. (*New York Times Book Review,* January 3, 1993, 7, 9.) See Davis, "Whitehead's Moral Philosophy," for a discussion of the "social" dimension of ethics in a Whiteheadian vein.

EPILOGUE

1. The necessity for the following reflections was made clear to me thanks to the helpful critique offered by members of the Society for the Study of Process Philosophies, to whom I gave a digest of my researches at the 1994 APA Eastern Division Meeting, in Boston. These reflections are forwarded here in the Epilogue because I think the problems regarding the possible monism of my interpretation are matters which pertain to the general and extra-systematic consideration of what it means to do metaphysics in an atomistic process perspective, which is the specific point of offering this epilogue as a conclusion to the current project.

2. Donald Hall, "The Unsayable Said," in *Principle Products of Portugal* (Boston: Beacon Press, 1995), 85.

Selected Bibliography

I. BY WHITEHEAD

Adventures of Ideas. New York: Free Press, 1967.
Aims of Education and Other Essays. New York: Free Press, 1967.
The Concept of Nature. Cambridge: Cambridge University Press, 1971.
An Enquiry Concerning the Principles of Natural Knowledge. New York: Dover, 1982.
Essays in Science and Philosophy. New York: Philosophical Library, 1947.
The Function of Reason. Boston: Beacon Press, 1958.
The Philosophy of Alfred North Whitehead, edited by Paul A. Schilpp. LaSalle: Open Court, 1951.
An Introduction to Mathematics. New York: Henry Holt, 1911.
The Philosophy of Alfred North Whitehead, edited by Paul A. Schilpp. LaSalle: Open Court, 1951.
Modes of Thought. New York: Free Press, 1968.
Principia Mathematica. With Bertrand Russell. Cambridge: Cambridge University Press, 1950.
The Principles of Relativity with Applications to Physical Science. Cambridge: Cambridge University Press, 1922.
Process and Reality. Corrected Edition, edited by Donald W. Sherburne and David Ray Griffin. New York: Free Press, 1978.
Religion in the Making. New York: Fordham University Press, 1996.
Science and the Modern World. New York: Free Press, 1967.
Symbolism. New York: Fordham University Press, 1985.
A Treatise on Universal Algebra, with Applications. New York: Hafner, 1960.

II. OTHER SOURCES

Alexander, Samuel. *Space, Time and Deity*. 2 vols. London: Macmillan, 1927.
Allan, George. *The Importances of the Past: A Meditation on the Authority of Tradition*. Albany: State University of New York Press, 1986.
Auxter, Thomas. "The Process of Morality." In *Hegel and Whitehead: Contemporary Perspectives on Systematic Philosophy*, edited by George R. Lucas, 219–38. Albany: State University of New York Press, 1986.
Belaief, Lynne. *Toward a Whiteheadian Ethics*. Lanham: University Press of America, 1984.
Bergson, Henri. *Creative Evolution*, translation by Arthur Mitchell. New York: Henry Holt and Company, 1911.
———. *Matter and Memory*, translation by Nancy Margaret Paul and W. Scott Palmer. London: George Allen & Unwin, 1911.
Bracken, Joseph A. "Energy-Events and Fields." *Process Studies* 18 (Fall 1989): 153–65.
Bradley, F. H. *Collected Essays*. 2 vols. Oxford: Clarendon Press, 1935.
Brumbaugh, Robert S. *Whitehead, Process Philosophy, and Education*. Albany: State University of New York Press, 1982.

Buchler, Justus. "On a Strain of Arbitrariness in Whitehead's System." *Journal of Philosophy* 66 (1969): 589–601.

Chappell, V. C. "Whitehead's Theory of Becoming." In *Alfred North Whitehead: Essays on His Philosophy*, edited by George L. Kline, 70–80. Englewood Cliffs, NJ: Prentice Hall, 1963.

Chiaraviglio, Lucio. "Whitehead's Theory of Prehensions." In *Alfred North Whitehead: Essays on His Philosophy*, edited by George L. Kline, 81–92. Englewood Cliffs, NJ: Prentice Hall.

Christensen, Darrell. "On Rendering Whitehead's 'Complete Fact' Complete." *Idealistic Studies* 12 (May 1982): 135–55.

―――. "Whitehead's 'Prehension' and Hegel's 'Mediation'." *Review of Metaphysics* 38 (December 1984): 341–74.

Christian, William A. *An Interpretation of Whitehead's Metaphysics*. New Haven: Yale University Press, 1959.

Christian, William A. "Whitehead's Explanation of the Past." In *Alfred North Whitehead: Essays on His Philosophy*, edited by George L. Kline, 93–101. Englewood Cliffs, NJ: Prentice Hall, 1963.

Cobb, John, and Donald W. Sherburne. "Regional Inclusion and Psychological Physiology." *Process Studies* 4 (1974): 263–74.

Code, Murray. *Order and Organism: Steps to a Whiteheadian Philosophy of Mathematics and the Natural Sciences*. Albany: State University of New York Press, 1984.

Crosby, Donald A. "Religion and Solitariness." In *Explorations in Whitehead's Philosophy*, edited by Lewis S. Ford and George L. Kline, 149–70. New York: Fordham University Press, 1983.

Dewey, John. *Experience and Nature*, The Later Works, vol. 1, edited by Jo Ann Boydston. Carbondale: Southern Illinois University Press, 1988.

―――. *Human Nature and Conduct*. New York: Modern Library, 1957.

―――. "The Philosophy of Whitehead." In *The Philosophy of Alfred North Whitehead*, edited by Paul A. Schilpp, 641–62. LaSalle: Open Court, 1951.

Early, Joseph E. "On Applying Whitehead's First Category of Existence." *Process Studies* 11 (Spring 1981): 35–39.

Emmett, Dorothy C. "Creativity and the Passage of Nature." In *Whitehead's Metaphysik der Kreativität*, edited by Freidrich Rapp and Reiner Weihl, 71–80. Munich: Alber, 1986.

―――. *Whitehead's Philosophy of Organism*. London: Macmillan, 1966.

―――. "Whitehead's View of Causal Efficacy." In *Whitehead and the Idea of Process*, edited by Harald Holz and Ernest Wolf-Gazo, 161–78. Munich: Alber, 1984.

Fetz, Reto Luzius. "Aristotelean and Whiteheadian Conceptions of Actuality: I." *Process Studies* 19 (Spring 1990): 15–27.

―――. "Aristotelean and Whiteheadian Conceptions of Actuality: II." *Process Studies* 19 (Fall 1990): 145–55.

Findlay, J. N. "Hegel and Whitehead on Nature." In *Hegel and Whitehead: Contemporary Perspectives on Systematic Philosophy*, edited by George R. Lucas, 155–66. Albany: State University of New York Press, 1986.

Ford, Lewis S. "The Concept of 'Process': From 'Transition' to 'Concrescence'." In *Whitehead and the Idea of Process*, edited by Harald Holz and Ernest Wolf-Gazo, 73–101. Munich: Alber, 1984.

———. *The Emergence of Whitehead's Metaphysics, 1925–1929.* Albany: State University of New York Press, 1984.

———. "Neville's Interpretation of Creativity." In *Explorations in Whitehead's Philosophy*, edited by Lewis S. Ford and George L. Kline, 272–79. New York: Fordham University Press, 1983.

———. "Whitehead and the Ontological Difference." *Philosophy Today* 29 (Summer 1985): 148–55.

Ford, Lewis S., and George Kline, editors. *Explorations in Whitehead's Philosophy.* New York: Fordham University Press, 1983.

Frankenberry, Nancy. "The Emergent Paradigm and Divine Causation." *Process Studies* 13 (1983): 202–217.

Garland, William. "The Ultimacy of Creativity." In *Explorations in Whitehead's Philosophy*, edited by Lewis S. Ford and George L. Kline, 212–38. New York: Fordham University Press, 1983.

Goheen, John. "Whitehead's Theory of Value." In *The Philosophy of Alfred North Whitehead*, edited by Paul A. Schilpp, 435–60. LaSalle: Open Court, 1951.

Hall, David L. *The Civilization of Experience: A Whiteheadian Theory of Culture.* New York: Fordham University Press, 1973.

Hartshorne, Charles. "The Compound Individual." In *Whitehead's Philosophy: Selected Essays, 1935–1970*, 41–62. Lincoln: University of Nebraska Press, 1972.

———. "The Immortality of the Past: Critique of a Prevalent Misinterpretation." *Review of Metaphysics* 7 (1953): 98–112.

———. "Is Whitehead's God the God of Religion?" *Ethics* 53 (1942–43): 219–27.

———. "On Some Criticisms of Whitehead's Philosophy." *Philosophical Review* 44 (1935): 323–44.

———. "Ontological Primacy: A Reply to Buchler." *Journal of Philosophy* 67 (1970): 979–86.

———. "Whitehead and Contemporary Philosophy." *The Relevance of Whitehead*, edited by Ivor Leclerc, 21–43. New York: Humanities Press, 1961.

———. "Whitehead's Novel Intuition." In *Whitehead's Philosophy: Selected Essays, 1935–1970*, 161–70. Lincoln: University of Nebraska Press, 1972.

———. "Whitehead's Theory of Prehension." In *Whitehead's Philosophy: Selected Essays, 1935–1970*, 125–28. Lincoln: University of Nebraska Press, 1972.

———. *Whitehead's View of Reality.* New York: Pilgrim Press, 1981.

Henry, Granville C. "Whitehead's Philosophical Response to the New Mathematics." In *Explorations in Whitehead's Philosophy*, edited by Lewis S. Ford and George L. Kline, 14–30. New York: Fordham University Press, 1983.

Hocking, William Ernest. "Whitehead on Mind and Nature." In *The Philosophy of Alfred North Whitehead*, edited by Paul A. Schilpp, 381–403. LaSalle: Open Court, 1951.

James, William. *The Principles of Psychology.* Cambridge: Harvard University Press, 1981.

Johnson, A. H. "Some Conversations With Whitehead Concerning God and Creativity." In *Explorations in Whitehead's Philosophy*, edited by Lewis S. Ford and George L. Kline, 3–13. New York: Fordham University Press, 1983.

———. "The Status of Whitehead's 'Process and Reality' Categories." *Philosophy and Phenomenological Research* 40 (March 1980): 313–23.

———. *Whitehead's Theory of Reality*. Boston: Beacon Press, 1962.

Kline, George L. "Concept and Concrescence: An Essay on Hegelian-Whiteheadian Ontology." In *Hegel and Whitehead: Contemporary Perspectives on Systematic Philosophy*, edited by George R. Lucas, 133–54. Albany: State University of New York Press, 1986.

———. "Form, Concrescence, Concretum." In *Explorations in Whitehead's Philosophy*, edited by Lewis S. Ford and George L. Kline, 104–48. New York: Fordham University Press, 1983.

Kraus, Elizabeth M. "Existence as Transaction: A Whiteheadian Study of Causality." *International Philosophical Quarterly* 25, no. 4 (December 1985): 349–366.

———. *The Metaphysics of Experience: A Companion To Whitehead's Process and Reality*. New York: Fordham University Press, 1979.

Kuntz, Paul Grimley. *Alfred North Whitehead*. Boston: Twayne, 1984.

———. "Whitehead the Anglican and Russell the Puritan: The Traditional Origins of Muddleheadedness and Simplemindedness." *Process Studies* 17 (Spring 1988): 40–44.

———. "Whitehead on Order." *Nous* 8 (1961): 1–12.

Lango, John W. "Whitehead's Actual Occasions and the New Infinitesimals." *Transactions of the Charles S. Peirce Society*, 25 (Winter 1985): 29–39.

Lawrence, Nathaniel. *Whitehead's Philosophical Development: A Critical History of the Background of Process and Reality*. Berkeley: University of California Press, 1956.

Leclerc, Ivor. "Being and Becoming in Whitehead's Philosophy." In *Explorations in Whitehead's Philosophy*, eds. Lewis S. Ford and George L. Kline, 53–67. New York: Fordham University Press, 1983.

———. "Form and Actuality." In *The Relevance of Whitehead*, edited by Ivor Leclerc, 169–89. New York: Humanities Press.

———. *The Nature of Physical Existence*. Lanham: University Press of America, 1986.

———. "Process and Order in Nature." In *Whitehead and the Idea of Process*, edited by Harald Holz and Ernest Wolf-Gazo, 119–36. Munich: Alber, 1984.

———. "A Rejoinder to Justus Buchler." *Process Studies* 1 (1971): 55–59.

———. *Whitehead's Metaphysics: An Introductory Exposition*. Lanham: University Press of America, 1986.

Lowe, Victor. "The Concept of Experience in Whitehead's Metaphysics." In *Alfred North Whitehead: Essays on His Philosophy*, edited by George L. Kline, 24–33. Englewood Cliffs, NJ: Prentice Hall, 1963.

Lucas, George R. "Moral Order and the Constraints of Agency: Toward a New Metaphysics of Morals." In *New Essays in Metaphysics*, 117–40, edited by Robert C. Neville. Albany: State University of New York Press, 1987.

———. "Outside the Camp: Recent Work on Whitehead's Philosophy, Part One." *Transactions of the Charles Sanders Peirce Society* 21 (Winter 1985): 49–76.

———. "Outside the Camp: Recent Work on Whitehead's Philosophy, Part Two." *Transactions of the Charles Sanders Peirce Society* 21 (Summer 1985): 327–82.

———. *The Rehabilitation of Whitehead*. Albany: State University of New York Press, 1989.

———. *Two Views of Freedom in Process Thought*. Missoula: Scholar's Press, 1979.

Lucas, Hans Christian. "Spinoza, Hegel, Whitehead: Substance, Subject, and Superject." In *Hegel and Whitehead: Contemporary Perspectives on Systematic Philosophy* , edited by George R. Lucas, 39–60. Albany: State University of New York Press, 1986.

Martin, R. M. *Whitehead's Categoreal Scheme and Other Papers*. The Hague: Martinus Nijhoff, 1974.

McGilvary, Evander Bradley. "Space-Time, Simple Location and Prehension." In *The Philosophy of Alfred North Whitehead* , edited by Paul A. Schilpp, 209–39. LaSalle: Open Court, 1951.

McHenry, Leemon B. *Whitehead and Bradley: A Comparative Analysis*. Albany: State University of New York Press, 1992.

Murdoch, Iris. "Against Dryness: A Polemical Sketch." In *Revisions: Changing Perspectives in Moral Philosophy*, edited by Stanley Hauerwas and Alasdair MacIntyre, 43–50. Notre Dame: University of Notre Dame Press, 1983.

———. *Metaphysics as a Guide to Morals*. New York: Viking Penguin, 1991.

———. *The Sovereignty of Good*. New York: Schocken Books, 1971.

Neville, Robert C. *The Cosmology of Freedom*. New Haven: Yale University Press, 1974.

———. *Eternity and Time's Flow*. Albany: State University of New York Press, 1995.

———. *The Puritan Smile*. Albany: State University of New York Press, 1987.

———. *Reconstruction of Thinking*. Albany: State University of New York Press, 1981.

———. *Recovery of the Measure*. Albany: State University of New York Press, 1989.

———. "Sketch of a System." In *New Essays in Metaphysics,* edited by Robert C. Neville, 253–74. Albany: State University of New York Press, 1987.

———. "A Thesis Concerning Truth." *Process Studies* 15 (Summer 1986): 127–36.

———. "Whitehead on the One and the Many." In *Explorations in Whitehead's Philosophy*, edited by Lewis S. Ford and George L. Kline, 257–71. New York: Fordham University Press, 1983.

Nobo, Jorge Luis. *Whitehead's Metaphysics of Extension and Solidarity*. Albany: State University of New York Press, 1986.

———."Whitehead's Principle of Process." *Process Studies* 4 (1974): 275–84.

———. "Whitehead's Principle of Relativity." *Process Studies* 8 (1978): 1–20.

Norman, Ralph W. Jr. "Whitehead and 'Mathematicism'." In *Alfred North Whitehead: Essays on His Philosophy*, edited by George L. Kline, 33–40. Englewood Cliffs, NJ: Prentice Hall, 1963.

Pailin, David A. "Narrative, Story, and the Interpretation of Metaphysics." In *Hegel and Whitehead: Contemporary Perspectives on Systematic Philosophy,* edited by George R. Lucas, 268–84. Albany: State University of New York Press, 1986.

Palter, Robert M. "The Place of Mathematics in Whitehead's Thought." In *Alfred North Whitehead: Essays on His Philosophy,* edited by George L. Kline, 41–52. Englewood Cliffs, NJ: Prentice Hall, 1963.

Pols, Edward. "The Non-Speculative Basis of Metaphysics." *Process Studies* 15 (Summer 1986): 95–105.

———. *Whitehead's Metaphysics: A Critical Examination of Process and Reality*. Carbondale: Southern Illinois University Press, 1967.

Reeves, Gene. "God and Creativity." In *Explorations in Whitehead's Philosophy*, edited by Lewis S. Ford and George L. Kline, 239–59. New York: Fordham University Press.

Ritchie, A. D. "Whitehead's Defense of Speculative Reason." In *The Philosophy of Alfred North Whitehead*, edited by Paul A. Schilpp, 329–49. LaSalle: Open Court, 1951.

Rorty, Richard. "Matter and Event." In *Explorations in Whitehead's Philosophy*, edited by Lewis S. Ford and George L. Kline, 68–103. New York: Fordham University Press, 1983.

Ross, Stephen David. *Perspective in Whitehead's Metaphysics*. Albany: State University of New York Press, 1983.

Schilpp, Paul A. "Whitehead's Moral Philosophy." In *The Philosophy of Alfred North Whitehead*, edited by Paul A. Schilpp, 561–618. LaSalle: Open Court, 1951.

Schindler, David L. "Whitehead's Inability to Affirm a Universe of Value." *Process Studies* 13 (1983): 117–131.

Sherburne, Donald W. "Decentering Whitehead." *Process Studies* 15 (1986): 83–94.

———. "Whitehead's Psychological Physiology." *Southern Journal of Philosophy* 7 (1969): 401–7.

Sherover, Charles M. "Toward Experiential Metaphysics: Radical Temporalism." In *New Essays in Metaphysics*, edited by Robert C. Neville, 77–100. Albany: State University of New York Press, 1987.

Vlastos, Gregory. "Organic Categories in Whitehead." In *Alfred North Whitehead: Essays on His Philosophy*, edited by George L. Kline, 158–67. Englewood Cliffs, NJ: Prentice Hall, 1963.

Wallack, F. Bradford. *The Epochal Nature of Process in Whitehead's Metaphysics*. Albany: State University of New York Press, 1980.

Weiss, Paul. *Beyond All Appearances*. Carbondale: Southern Illinois University Press, 1974.

———. *Man's Freedom*. New Haven: Yale University Press, 1950.

Wolf, George. "Psychological Physiology From the Standpoint of a Physiological Psychologist." *Process Studies* 11 (1981): 274–91.

Wolf-Gazo, Ernest. "Negation and Contrast: The Origins of Consciousness in Hegel and Whitehead." In *Hegel and Whitehead: Contemporary Perspectives on Systematic Philosophy*, edited by George R. Lucas, 207–18. Albany: State University of New York Press, 1986.

Index

abortion, 198
abstraction: from actual intensive unity, 166–7; from complete being of entity, 89
actual world, 11, 108
actualities (*see also* actuality): past, as post-concrescent, 90; pragmatic effectiveness of, 129; as transcendent creators, 64, 129
actuality, 55; agentive subjectivity of, 129; atomic, 14; as concrescence, 41; as "datable," 57; as deep, 207; derivative, 104ff.; grades its universe, 125; as haunted by potentiality, 16; individual, 28; intensive, x; as intensive satisfaction, 86; past, 54; subjective and objective dimensions of, 54; temporal states of, 208; vacuous, 223n.53; vibratory character of, 131
actualization, process of, 27
adventure, 177
adversion, 60ff.
aesthetic achievement, 145; as "self-retentive," 97; subjective conditions of, 128
aesthetic destruction, 171
aesthetic discernment, 185ff.
aesthetic education, 195
aesthetic experience, 68 (*see also* experience); as model for moral intuition, 178
aesthetic occasion, 209
aesthetic order, 8, 14
aesthetic relationship, law of, 119
aesthetic splendor, 44
aesthetic unity, superject as internal conditions of, 98
aestheticism, 69, 195
affirmation–negation contrast, 137
agency, 10, 223n.53; as belonging exclusively to actual occasions, 88; as comparison, 88; of contrast, 130;
discrete or wide, 198; ecstatically intensive conception of, 177; as emotional and intellectual, 200; intensive, 91; as merely private, 95; as occurrence of certain activities, 177; and process of concrescence, 95; subjective, 62; vs. will, 176ff.
agent, not a totalized enduring object, 177
agentive attention, 182
agentive intellection, 171
agentive unity, 176
aim, 51 (*see also* subjective aim)
Alexander, Samuel, 120ff., 157ff.; and effort of attention, 183; on knowledge, 224n.2; on knowledge as enjoyment, 133–4
analysis (*see also* division): coordinate, 49; coordinate and genetic, 76; genetic, dependent on coordinate analysis, 175; relation of genetic and coordinate, 52ff.; unity of coordinate and genetic, 79
appearance and reality, 187
appetition, 31, 147; constitutes subject, 65; and objective functioning of superject, 31
Arendt, Hannah, 195
Aristotle, 4; categories of, 215n.1; ethics of 200; logic of, 34, 120; metaphysical categories of, 4, 6; naturalism of, 5; universals of, 6
art, 213; and divinity, 195
atom: of experience, 82; not a most small portion of space-time, 122; temporal, 98
atomic actualities (*see also* atomic actuality): internally related, 117; multiplicity of, 162
atomic actuality, 14, 32 (*see also* atomic actualities); as belonging more to superject than to subject, 32; individual, 72

235

INDEX

atomic becoming, 126
atomic reality, vibratory conception of, 73
atomicity: connected, 181; non-isolated, 208
atomism, x, 23, 60, 63, 65, 68, 87ff., 217n.28; connectionistic, 208; creative, 85; and crypto-substantialism, 95; and final causality, 15; Leclerc on, 104; organic, 96
atomization, of creative universe, 125
attention, 145, 158, 185; to reality, Murdoch on, 182; subjective form and, 187; vocabulary of, 172
Auden, W. H., 44
aversion, 60ff.
axiological metaphysics, 39
axiology, 81

Buchler, Justus, 225n.22
balanced complexity, 14, 51, 83 (*see also* contrasts; eternal objects); and subjective form, 14
Beauty, 148, 179, 190–1
being, 47, 155–6; and categorical description, 4; constituted by becoming, 160, 173; as ecstatic, 97, 103; as emergent, 41; of entity as objective, 94; knowledge and, 155; as value, 145
Belaief, Lynn, 172, 189, 225
belief, 134, 139ff.; as form of enjoyed origination, 140
Bergson, Henri, 72, 157ff., 168
Berkeley, George, 94, 120
Bishop, Elizabeth, 207–8
Blake, William, 84
body, 142, 150
Bradley, relations in, 56, 63
breadth of thought, 155

care, 171
Categoreal Explanations, 53
Categoreal Obligations, 4, 7, 8, 42, 110, 130, 197; arbitrariness of, 7; as overlapping, 82–83. Individual Categoreal Obligations: Category of Conceptual Reversion, 67ff.; Category of Conceptual Valuation, 58ff.; Category of Freedom and Determination, 80; Category of Objective Diversity, 54ff.; Category of Objective Identity, 49ff.; Category of Subjective Harmony, 77ff.; Category of Subjective Intensity, 8, 64, 80, 149, 172; Category of Subjective Unity, 46ff., 63; Category of Transmutation, 74ff., 108
categories, 4, 7; and classification, 6; of explanation, 7, 8; unity of, 4
Categories of Existence, 7, 8, 40ff., 90–91, 110; fourth, 14; "pastness" as absent from, 90
Categories of Explanation, 110
Category of Emotional and Intellectual Complementarity, 200 (*see also* Moral Categories)
Category of Transcendent Creativity, 199–200 (*see also* Moral Categories)
Category of the Ultimate, 7, 8, 58, 84–85; Creativity as, 103
Category of Value Diversity, 199 (*see also* Moral Categories)
causa sui, really real things as, 80
causal efficacy, 150
causal power of one thing in another thing, 67
causality, xi, 55
causation, final and efficient, 60ff. (*see also* final and efficient causality)
Cayley, Arthur, 118
Chalmers, David, and "hard problem" of phenomenal qualia, 223n.53
change, 108
character, 13; causal transmission of, 60 (*see also* transmission); emergence of, 100; as everlasting, 126; individual ontological, 64; intensity and, 139; ontological, 126; and ontological status, 126; qualitative, and quantitative extension, 161; and symbolic reference, 152; vibratory, 163
Christian, William A., 26ff., 85, 105
Cobb, John, and phases of concrescence, 216n.10

community of environment, 75
comparison, as basis for theory of nature and knowledge, 116 (*see also* contrast; value)
compatibility, 50 (*see also* contrast); for contrast, 107; of elements in complex of feeling, 13
"complete fact," 213
conception, modes of, 133
conceptual inertia, 209
conceptual representation, inadequacies of, 213
concrescence, xi, 7; distinction between concretum and, 85ff.; emerging subject of, 130; as epochal whole, 51; heart of, 8; implied subjects of, 78; phases of, 22, 45, 51; as "process," 26; termination of, 100; theory of, and theory of extension, 159; theory of, linked to theory of extension, 115; Whitehead on, 12
concrescent, vs. post-concrescent, 90
concreta (*see also* concrete): Kline on, 90–92; provocation by, 92
concrete (*see also* concreta): Kline on, 90; as subjective, 87
conditions (*see also* contrasts, conditions of): for occurrences of natural events, 5; of order, 125, 151; of satisfaction, 12; subjective, of becoming, 159
conformation, 20
connection, extensive and intensive, 181
consciousness, 137ff.; importance and, 138; intentional, 137; negation in, 138; as subjective form, 134
consequences, form part of being of subject, 173
constitution of entities, 87, 88, 89
contrast, 8, 18; affirmation–negation, 137; agency of, 130; agentive, transfer of, 156; as basis of unity of feeling, 12; compatibility for, 18, 107; and compatible elements for feeling, 12; and complex eternal objects, 13; conditions of, 67; and enhancement or diminishment of intensity, 13; as maximally intense, 18; private–public, 29ff.; proposition and, 136; and repetition, 125; and solidarity, 55; and synthetic character of process, 13; valuation of, 64
contrasting: activity of, 63; and diversity, 54
contrastive agency, 183
contrastive complexity, 46
contrasts, 82; full and partial realization of, 211; hierarchy of, 37; subordinate, 42
creative existence, 44
creative process: aspects of, 8; "passing" character of, 84; as pulse or throb, 129; transcendent, 51; value as end of, 147
creative unification, 99
creative universe, as demand for intensive unification, 148
creative urge, 20
creativity, 18, 96; character of, 64; not a predicate, 98; and ontology, 109ff.; temporal, 181; as ultimate principle, 110
Creativity, 81; as Category of the Ultimate, 103
critical philosophy, post-Kantian, 49
crypto-substantialism, 86, 95, 103ff.

data, as "welter," 93, 111
datum: pattern of objective, 102; objective, 55
defining characteristic of society, 108
degree, 116, 121; of presence, 183, 208
depth: of actuality, 76, 147; of experience, 69ff.; of intensity, 153; as presence of one thing in another, 71; of value, and intensive structure, 81
Descartes, René, 23–24, 32, 34, 129
determinacy, 42, 68; and subjectivity, 47
Dewey, John: on "dramatic rehearsal," 227n.26; and experience, 215n.3, 224n.3
discord, 179

disorder, 20ff. (*see also* order)
diversity (*see also* Category of Objective Diversity; Category of Value Diversity): contrastive, 199; objective, 83; and particularity, 55; relevant, 67; relevant, and repetition, 124
divine decision, 74 (*see also* God)
divinity (*see also* God): and art, 195; as tender patience, 193
divisibility, 161ff. (*see also* analysis); arises from relatedness, 161; coordinate, 164; of entity, 52; as revelation of internal complexity, 52
division (*see also* analysis): of concrete, 188; connection of genetic and coordinate, 115, 159
dualism, 24, 155
Duty, 196

ecstatic actuality, 128
ecstatic existence, 71ff., 84ff. (*see also* existence); as fusion of privacy and publicity, 188; as underwriting ethical relevance of Whitehead's thought, 188
ecstatic individuality, xii, 84ff. (*see also* individuality); and remorseless repetition, 208
ecstatic unity, of vibrations referable to intensity, 112
education: of aesthetic capacities, 195; moral, 197
efficient cause, x, 45 (*see also* final and efficient causality)
elegance, 36, 38
emergent evolution, 40
Emmet, Dorothy, 19
empiricism, 155; solipsistic, 155
ends (*see also* purpose; subjective aim): pervade nature, 149
enfeeblement: as aesthetic destruction, 14; and evil, 14; of intensity, 14
entities (*see also* actualities; actuality; entity): actual, as res verae, 108; as nothing but intensity of feeling, 103
entity (*see also* actualities; actuality; entities): atomic, 3; cannot be conscious of its satisfaction, 110; fitness of, 175; as in its essence social, 26; integrity of as objectified, 51; objective existence of, 45; pervades whole world, 175; as pragmatic and processive, 93; pragmatic consequence of, 98; pragmatic usefulness of, 100,110; self-constitution of, 45; as self-creative, 59; self-identity of, 95; self-transcendence of, 97; superjective nature of, 98; transcendent creativity of, 21, 27, 52;
environment: contemporary, 150ff.; extended, 151
environmental ethics, 198
envisagement: as analog of subjective aim, 201; Nobo on, 217n.29
Envisagement, as practice, 201–2
epistemology (*see also* knowledge): two-stage, 150
Eros, 202; as spiritual energy, 191
essences, 156 (*see also* eternal objects)
eternal objects, 11, 156; and balance, 16; and balanced complexity, 16; as comparable to one another, 16; and contrasts, 13; as forms of definiteness, 11; and God, 16–17; implied with "actual world," 11; individual essences of, 16; ingression of, 13; maximum number of, 16; objective species of, 164–8; as pattern, 11; pattern of, 57, 139; as pure potentials, 11, 12; relational essences of, 16
ethical practices, 200–2
event (*see also* actualities; actuality; entities; entity; existents): comparative, 119; location of, 123; as locus of moral being, 181; Whitehead on, 96
event-based theory of reality, and ethics, 176
events (*see also* event): come to "be" comparatively, 121
everlastingness, and God, 126
evil, 180 (*see also* enfeeblement); as aesthetic destructiveness, 79, 182; banality of, 195

existence, x, 55 (*see also* being; ecstatic existence); ascribable only on basis of aesthetic complexity, 110; creative, 44; of one thing in another, 58; physical, 73; public, as a function of contrastive activity, 77; ultimate claim of, xi; vibratory, 112

existences, 6; subjective and objective, 43

existent (*see also* existents): as comparable to others, 126; manifest in another, 3

existential ecstasis, 128 (*see also* ecstatic existence)

existents (*see also* actualities; actuality; ecstatic existence; event; existent): individuality of, 94; ontological separateness of, denied, 39–40; separateness of, 156

experience: as atomic, 82, 85; atoms of, 82; character of, as derivative from intensive pattern, 114; conscious, 133; conscious, as selective, 184; of contemporary objects, 149ff.; depth of, 69ff.; as embedded, 169; of embeddedness, 157; emergence of as individual, 98; and empirical underpinning of Whitehead's thought, xi; episodic character of, 177; as foundation for systematic description, 157; higher forms of, 18; higher phases of, 16; individual act of intense, 119; and induction, 5; intense internal, 80; intensity of, 42; intensive, 199; linguistic practices as, 6; logical predication as, 6; moral, 174ff.; in phenomenology, 137; quantitative and qualitative aspects of, xi; refined intensity of, 152; religion and private intensity of, 10; sensitive, x–xi; subjective, in actual entity, ix; subrational, 177; and unity of intensity, 68; value, 147; of value, as ground of scheme, 169; value-ladenness of, xi

explanation, 49; and embodied percipient, 154

extended quanta (*see also* extensive quantity; oneness): mistaken for intensive quantities, 188

extension: theory of, 122, 133, 159, 160ff.; theory of, and sense perception, 160; theory of, linked to theory of concrescence, 115

extensity, as first fact about intensity, 164

extensive connection, 124; and intensive individuality, 164ff.

extensive continuum, 49; individual entities in, 97

extensive quantity, 112ff., 158ff.; as assumed in conception of individual event, 117

extensive relations, 114, 117, 123–24, 164

extensive solidarity, 65, 123

extensiveness, not numerical self-identity, 163

externality, sense of, in feeling, 91

Ezekiel, 78, 93

fact–value distinction, 34, 178

faculty-psychology, 226n.4

Fallacy of Misplaced Concreteness, 7, 154

fatigue, 194

feeling, 8, 105 (*see also* feelings); as achieved intensity of contrast, 106; aesthetically supplemental, 66; agentive, 3; anticipatory, 74, 172, 225n.9; and Bradley, 215n.6; comparative, 45–46; complex of, 9; as conducting its own process, 48; conformal, 45, 105; as directed at superject, 61; of externality, 66; intensity of, 8; intensive, as marking interpretation of individuals, 84; massiveness of, 108; modification of, 15; perceptual, 139; physical vs. supplemental, 36; reproduction of, 45; sense of externality in, 91; subjective, 3; transmission of, 45; uniqueness of, 15

feelings (*see also* feeling): conceptual, 129; intellectual, 134–42; propositional, 134ff.; propositional, subjective forms of, 135

239

"feels another feeling," 105
final and efficient causality, 21, 156, 191, 208–9
final cause, x, 9 (see also final and efficient causality); and atomism interconnected, 15
finitude, and Whitehead's scheme, 169
fitness of entity, 175
Ford, Lewis: on agency, 218n.10; on coherence of God concept, 222n.51; on connection of coordinate and genetic analysis, 159; *The Emergence of Whitehead's Metaphysics*, 53; panpsychism, 223n.53; on William Christian, 28
form, 4 (see also eternal objects); magnitude of, xi; transfer of, 156
"formal" reality: and agentive concrescence, 25; and objective reality, 208; and objective reality, and existential status of occasions, 26; and time, 216n.18
fortunate evolution, 189, 197; as pragmatic test, 152, 153
freedom, 20, 142, 189; and inheritance, 147; of mentality, 183
functioning (see also entity, pragmatic usefulness of): objective, 3, 159; of objectified entity, 51
future, xi, 46; immediacy in, 95; relevant, 9, 62, 64

Gallagher, William J., 145
Garland, William, 110ff.
geometry: intuitive content of, 122; projective, 117ff.
Gilligan, Carol, 227n.23
God: absolute end of, as intensity, 146; character of, vs. will, 20; and everlastingness, 126; existence of, 223–4n.54; as ground of intensity, 148; as ground of relevance, 130; and harmonization, 126; as harmonization, 202; as harmony of intensities, 192; as ideal of contrastive unity, 192; and incoherence of scheme, 222n.51; as interpretation, 127, 192–3; Murdoch on, 193; and ontological principle, 146; as original actuality, 16; primordial envisagement of potentiality by, 47; primordial nature of, 19, 73, 130; as principle of concretion, Emmet on, 19; as principle of order, 164; as procurer of intensities, 180; and realm of potentiality, 16; and relevance of eternal objects to one another and to actuality, 17; role in temporal realization, 146–7; in *Science in the Modern World*, 16; secularization of functions of, 169; and subjective aim, 126; subjective aim of, 192; and valuation, 16
Goheen, John, 188ff.
Good, 184ff.
goodness, Murdoch on, 178
ground and consequent, 68–69, 71, 119
grounds of order, 12, 18, 20ff., 79

Hadas, Rachel, ix
harmonization, God and, 126
harmony, 4, 175; subjective, 82
Harmony, 190–1
Hartshorne, Charles, 84–85
Heaney, Seamus, 171
Henry, Granville, 115
Hegel, G. W. F., 138, 218n.7
historical narratives, 6
history: arbitrariness of, 173; as incapable of rationalization, 81–82; realism about, 56
hope, 177
Hopkins, Gerard Manley, 209
human, 212
Hume, David, 5; on custom, 139–40; *Dialogues on Natural Religion*, 19; and subjectivism, 137; on vivacity, 141

ideal, 33 (see also subjective aim); as lure for perfection, 194; picturing of, 192ff.
ideal forms, 24 (see also eternal objects)
idealism, 17, 56, 155, 161
imagination, 138, 201, 213
immediacy, 9, 84, 129; of experience, 143; of feeling, 10; in present and

future, 95; presentational, 150ff.
importance, 37, 50, 175, 190 (*see also* value); and consciousness, 138; as James's "interest," 183; patterning of, 186; referent to unity, 154; for self, others, whole, 185
individual, 52 (*see also* actuality; entity; individuality); act of intense experience, 119; agency of, 131; attending to, 186; and community, 148; decision, 81; as ecstatic, 102; emergence of entity as, 98; requires reference to others, 180
individuality, 25 (*see also* actuality; entity; existent; individual); absolute, repudiation of, 117; atomic, 99; and atomism, 39; character of, 69; of character, as present in other entities, 100; concept of, ix; depth of, 195; does not mean substantial independence, 94; of events, and massive unity of enduring objects, 97; of existence, as rejection of Cartesian notions, 26; of existents, 94; identified with superject, 99; insurmountable, 199; moral, 177ff.; in moral experience, 181ff.; and objectification, 54; and particularity, 217n.4; of prehensions, 14; relevant, 198; and sameness, 127–8; as satisfaction, 32; and subjective form, 15; and Subjective Units, 48; thought and, 168
individuals, in existential network, 198
individuation (*see also* individuality): "extended," as derivative, 167; of moral agency, 212; observable, 163
infinitesimals, repudiation of, 119–20
ingression, 13
inheritance: and freedom, 147; tangential, 146
instinct, 158
integral: infinitesimal, of distance, 114; and integrate, 98
integration, 11, 51, 68; as central to concrescence, 47; and feeling, 16; and integral intensity, 48 (*see also* integral)

intellect: as "one-making," Murdoch on, 186ff.; "spatializes," 158, 168
intelligence, and latent geometry, 157
intensification, by valuation, 59
intensities (*see also* intensity): patterned, 76; re-enaction of, 108
intensity: aesthetic, 103; as aesthetic experience of existential comparison, 122; as application of freedom and agency, 33; as augmented by mutual compatibility of eternal objects, 18; and character, 139; as crossroads of subjectivity and objectivity, 85; deepening of, 67–68; defies adequate "saying," 213; as degree of manifestation, 116; enfeeblement of, 14; enhancement of, 136; as expressive of felt unity of data, 10; and extension, unitary source of theories, 122; as heightened, 13; as imposing itself, 190; integral, 107; as intersection of metaphysics and ethics, 174; involves extensional relativity, 163; is an occasion of experience, 103; moral applicability of, xii; moral application of, 171; not a predicate, 98; as privacy, 34; provision for future, 131; qualitative, 157ff.; quantitative, as presence or absence of an element in a manifold, 116; quantitative and qualitative dimensions of, 165; of satisfaction, xii; of satisfaction, power of effecting, 129; as secondary property, 116; of sensitive experience, 155; "structural conditions" of, 46, 119, 185; structural considerations in, 34ff.; subject to geometrical expansion, 18; of subjective form, 110; in symbolic reference, 151ff.; in thinking, 158; in *Treatise on Universal Algebra*, 115, 229n.39; as useful to understanding system, 4; as what entity is objectively, 34
intensive achievement, 101
intensive contrasts, 158 (*see also* contrasts; intensity)

241

intensive features of metaphysical situation, 133
intensive magnitudes, 112–3 (*see also* quantity)
intensive re-enaction, in societies, 105–7
intensive regularity, among mental acts, 140–1
intensive significance, intuition of, 169
intensive structure, 209
intensive subject, 209
Interaction of Rationality and Intuition, as practice, 201
interestingness, 141
intuition, 162, 196, 201, 203

James, William, 183–4
Johnson, A. H., 216n.19
joy, 84, 131
joyful naturalism, 44
judgment, 134, 139, 140ff.; invariance of style of intensity in, 140
justification of perception, 152

Kant, Immanuel, 4, 112–24, 120ff.; categorical imperative of, 197; categories of, 5–6, 215n.1; and certainty, 5; and degree, 121; on quantities, 112ff.; on quantity, 162; and subjectivism, 137; and unorganized flux of sensations, 111; on will, 191
Kemp Smith, Norman, 218n.7
Kline, George, 22, 85, 105; on concreta, 90–92; on concrete, 90; on systematically confusing terms, 86
knowledge, 5 (*see also* epistemology); and being, 155; as enjoyment, 133–4; and immediacy, 150; as instance of principle of intensive relevance, 169
Kohlberg, Lawrence, 227n.23
Kraus, Elizabeth, 38, 73, 120
Kuntz, Paul, 226n.11

Leclerc, Ivor, 104ff.
Leibniz, 19, 104, 123
life, 143ff.; as captive of intensity, 143; and originality, 143; as "robbery," 180
location (*see also* ecstatic existence): of events, 123; in future entities, 97; simple, 96; singular, of a reality, 96
Locke, John: on perpetual perishing, 23; on power, 128, 129; and repetition, 167; and subjectivism, 137
love, 185, 194
Lucas, George, 113
lure (*see also* subjective aim): as temptation to intensive depth, 175

McHenry, Leemon, 215n.6
MacIntyre, Alasdair, 203, 228n.33
"many become one, and are increased by one," 11, 85, 128, 148
Maslow, Abraham, 227n.23
massiveness of feeling, and perishing, 222n.52
materialism, 161
mathematics, as image of Good, 202
measurement, 114
memory, 142
mental and physical life, interplay of, 142
mental pole, 59
mentality, human, 132ff.
metaphysical assertions, as probabilistic, 169
metaphysical impulse, 49
metaphysics: description, x; and generality, 8; as "guide to morals," 184; hypothetical, 4, 6; "intensity" does work in, 18; as picture of reality, 202; speculation, xi
mind, 134, 182, 212; non-social nexus as, 144; and substance, 142; as wandering, 144, 148–49, 176
misplaced concreteness (*see also* Fallacy of Misplaced Concreteness): abstraction of, 7
monism: of current interpretation, 211; and repetition, 124
Moore, G. E., Murdoch and, 226n.18
moral agency (*see also* agency): individuation of, 212
moral being, 172

Moral Categories, 197–200
moral comportment, 172
moral engagement, 194
moral experience: and atomism, 180; and beauty, 180; unities in, 184
moral realism, Murdoch on, 178
morality, 171–206passim; and relevance in future, 9
"muddledness," 179; in Murdoch, 226n.11; in Whitehead, 226n.11
Murdoch, Iris, 172ff., 202

narrowness, 34, 36ff., 46, 50, 69, 75, 82, 107, 119, 151, 175
negation, in consciousness, 138
negative prehensions, 14, 15, 18; and balanced complexity, 17; and enfeeblement of intensity, 17; subjective forms of, 17, 125; and triviality, 35
Neville, Robert: on agency, 176; on discursive individuals, 217n.28; on "elegance" and "contrast," 38–39; on intensity, 215n.7; on moral discernment, 196
Newton, Isaac, 121
nexus, 21; non-social, as mind, 144
Nobo, Jorge, 22, 28, 76, 111, 123ff.; on objective species of eternal objects, 166; on physical purposes, 61ff.; on transition and concrescence, 61ff.; *Whitehead's Metaphysics of Extension and Solidarity*, 57, 61, 123ff.
novelty, 20, 59, 132

obedience, to reality, 193
object, 218n.7; macrocosmic, 108
objectification (*see also* objective immortality): as ecstatic location, 210; vs. immediacy, 28
objective, presence of, in subjective, 93
objective immortality, 29, 57 (*see also* objectification)
objectivity, x
objects: enduring, 97; as provocative of characters of occasions, 92
occasions: intellectual, 132ff.; mental, 134; purposiveness of, 151

one and the many, the, relevance to ethics, 171ff.
oneness, 127ff.; not extensive, 131; intensive nature of, 121; and multiple realization, 127–8; numerical form of, 211
ontological principle, 20; God and, 146; and propositions, 135
ontological status (*see also* actuality): and character, 126; derivative, xii
order, 20ff., 37, 107; concept as coextensive with "causality," 20; environmental, 100; inside an entity, 75; in world, 111
order of nature, 19, 48
originality, and soul or mind, 142
origination, Whitehead on, 14

panpsychism, 59–60, 129, 147, 223n.53
particularity, 50 (*see also* individuality)
passing vs. perishing, 84
past, x, xi, 46; as more than inert, 124; non-passivity of, 93; ontological status of, 29, 90; ontology of the, 69; reiteration from, 143–4
"pastness": as absent from categories of existence, 90; and agency, 92
Pater, Walter, 3, 42
pattern, 11, 45, 50, 101ff. (*see also* contrasts; intensity); abstract intensive, 101; centrality of, to philosophy, 170; of contrast, 68; of eternal objects, 139; fused, 102; intensive, 73; intensive, as modified, 85; of intensive quantity, 101; and intensive relationship, 165; mathematical, 167; as more than arrangement of eternal objects, 130; objectification of, 64; of objective datum, 102; predicative, 135; qualitative and quantitative, 101ff.; recognition, 187; rhythm and self-identity of, 73; of value, 178
Patterning, as moral practice, 200–1
patterns, competing, 188 (*see also* contrasts)
Peace, 190–91

243

perception, 94 (*see also* epistemology)
perishing, xii; "perpetual," 98
persistence, 58
personal identity, 145
personality, Whitehead's inadequacy on, 176
perspective: foreground and background in, 36; individual, 38; on past, 55; and projection, 118; and valuation, xii
phenomenology, 137
physical purposes, 59ff., 76; and ethics, 195
Plato, 23, 98, 170
Platonic forms, objective species of eternal objects as, 164
Platonic insight into moral character of universe, 169
poetry, 213; and explanation, xiii
Pols, Edward, on eternal objects, 218n.10
position, 123
positional manifold, 115
positive prehensions, 17
possibility (*see also* eternal objects; subjective aim): entertainmnet of, in higher experience, 134
postmodern fragmentation, 176
potentiality, 19, 47; as graded in relevance, 73; real, 88; vectoral directedness of, 48
power, 128–30; Locke on, 128, 129; substance as, 128
prayer, 196
prehension (*see also* negative prehension; positive prehension): mutual, 57; as positive and negative, 27; vector character of, 31
presence of one actuality in another, 124
present, x, 46; immediacy in, 95
principle of intensive relevance, 125–26, 129–30, 182; knowledge as instance of, 169
privacy, 10, 15 (*see also* subjectivity); intensive, 70; vs. publicity, 77
private: intense enjoyment of, 69; and public, distinction of, 164
private act of becoming, 143

private enjoyment, as emergent feature, 100
private matters of fact, 14
probabilistic knowing, 5
process: control of, 176ff.; control of, divine image of, 197; control of, and Love, 194; nature of, 18; principle of, 53; seeks only intensities, 180; teleological concerns of, 9
projection (*see also* geometry, projective): as perspective, 118; and presentational immediacy, 150; as scheme of morphology, 151
proposition: as Category of Existence, 134–5; and contrast, 136; entitative status of, 135; as lure for feeling, 135, 141; as pattern, 135; society and, 136; as species of contrast, 43; truth and falsehood of, 139
provocation: by concreta, 92; by past, 129; threshold, 129
provoking, efficient causality as, 81
psychological physiology, 142ff.
public: and private, distinction of, 164; presence of in private, 70
public matters of fact, 91
purpose, 210
purposes, metaphysical import of, 149

quantity, 161ff.; emotional, 98; intensive, 112ff.
quantum emotional intensity, as determining character of individuality, 100
quantum of existential character, 127

rationalism, 155
real potentiality, 9, 10, 130
realism: atomistic, as communitarian, 109; experiential, 218n.9; in philosophy, ix, x, xiii; pluralistic, 163; self-justifying thoughts in, xi
realization: as creative achievement of intensity, 97; texture of, 97
reduction: of agents, 212; of entities to one another, 211
region, extensive, 161
reiteration, 25, 68; and adjustment, 97

relatedness, extensive, 161ff. (*see also* extensive relations)
relations, 4; and atomism, 3; spatial and temporal, 118–9
relevance (*see also* principle of intensive relevance): as deep, 185; in future, 172
religion, 196; as experience, 6; and metaphysics, x; and private intensity of experience, 10
Renaissance art, 118
repetition, 58, 103, 124ff.; monism and, 124; and relevant diversity, 124
responsibility, 171; feeling of, 173; and high-grade contrast, 174; and metaphysics of intensive derivation, 173ff.; in past, present, and future, 174
reversion, 74, 83, 133, 149 (*see also* Categoreal Obligations: Category of Conceptual Reversion)
rhythm, 73
Romantic poets, 154

sameness, individuality and, 127–8
Santayana, George, 156
Sartre, Jean-Paul, 72; on existence, 216n.18
satisfaction, 22, 24, 26–27, 55, 85; and becoming, 30; and classification, 34, 40–41; as completion of entity, 103; entity cannot be conscious of its, 110; and forms of definiteness, 42; as "immediately felt," 27; individuality as, 32; intense, 78; ontological status of, 27ff., 39; as "product," 26; quantitative, 98ff.; as quantitative achievement of emotional intensity, 99; quantitative intensity of, 100; and substance, 24; and temporality, 28; as transcendent creator, 9
satisfactions, 82 (*see also* satisfaction); and agency of subjects, 67; as emergent, 84; intensive, as making up the universe, 83
science: as experience, 6; and induction, 5; and metaphysics, x

scientific observation, and presentational immediacy, 160
self, as divided, 177
self-constitution, 3, 45 (*see also* agency; self-creation)
self-creation, 12, 15, 20, 65 (*see also* agency; self-constitution); conscious control of, 153
self-interest, 171
self-value, and relevance, 81
sensation, 76; and intensity, 157
sense-data, 150–1
sensitiveness, 195–7
Sherburne, Donald, 51, 144ff., 183; and phases of concrescence, 217n.1; on psychic depths, 145
social order, 79, 108, 142
societies (*see also* society): living, 142ff.; as procurative of intensity, 107
society (*see also* societies): as aggregate, 105; defining characteristic of, 108; massiveness of emphasis in, 107; as procurative of intensity, 136; and propositions, 136
solidarity: of creative emphasis, 208; as necessary to achievement of subjective experience, 123
solipsism, 96, 209; moral, 180
spatiotemporal continuum, 100
Spinoza, Baruch, 19; Emmet on, 19; on emotion as bondage, 200; and modes, 94
spiritual energy, Eros as, 191
Stadt, Karl von (*see* von Stadt, Karl)
subject (*see also* actuality; agency; existent): emergent, 47; emerges as contrastive unification, 203; as locus of agency, 16; and relation to objectifications, 10; self-production of, 48; as superject, 45
subjective aim, 9; and complexity, 133; and decision, 141; and ethics, 174; as general nature of the universe, 127; and God, 127; as ideal, 12; at intensity, 78; as in entity, 10; as "lure," 9, 175; modification of, 22, 173–4; as provided by divine nature, 130

245

subjective existence, 29
subjective form, 8, 59, 102, 200; attention and, 187; and concrescent individuality, 15; as emotional tonality, 14; enrichment of, 68; and ideal intensity, 14; and importance, 45; intensity of, 110; and negative prehension, 17; Whitehead on, 14
subjectivism, 180ff., 191; repudiation of, 158
subjectivity, x, 4, 223n.53 (*see also* agency; immediacy; privacy); agentive, of actuality, 129; Cartesian version of, denied by idea of emergent intensity, 34; and determinacy, 47; intensive, of agents, 123; intensive considerations of, 66; and objectification, 208; and ontological status, xii; private, error of seeing as sole locus of individuality, 84; vs. objectivity, 84
subject–object relations, in *Adventure of Ideas*, 92
subject–predicate language, Whitehead's rejection of, 101
subject–superject, 21, 103ff. (*see also* actuality; ecstatic existence; entity; existent); ethics of, 173; as one ontological reality, 89; perplexity of notion, 85; and sameness, 128
substance, 23, 33; composite, derivative status of, 104; composite, Leclerc on, 104; enduring, 181; isolates individual, 95; and mind, 142; as power, 128; rejection of, 127
superject, 21; causal objectification of, 45; objective functioning of, 29; status of in future, 79
supplementation, conceptual, 151
symbolic reference, 150ff. (*see also* epistemology)

tedium, 194
temporal description, xii
temporal passage, 44
temporalization, 91
theory of feeling, 68, 189
thought: and distinctions, 212; and individuality, 168; transmutes intensities into extended unity, 168
time: cumulative character of, 107; epochal theory of, 112; as incurably atomic, 90; in philosophy of organism, 91
Tragedy, 190–1
transcendence, and transition, 110–1
transcendent creative action, and proposition, 141
transcendent decision, 175
transcendent efficacy, of individual subjects, 149, 190 (*see also* entity, transcendent creativity of)
transition, 96; and transcendence, 110–1
transmission: of character, 21, 25; of feeling, 45
transmutation, 83, 133, 149 (*see also* Categoreal Obligations: Category of Transmutation); as abstraction, 75
triviality, 34ff., 46, 50, 69, 75, 107, 119, 151, 175
truth, and falsehood, of propositions, 139

ultimacy, of intensity, xi
ultimate conceptions, in Whitehead and Murdoch, 193
unification, 120; creative, 99
unity (*see also* Categoreal Obligations: Category of Subjective Unity): agentive, 176; and diversity, 154; intensive character of, 168; intensive nature of, 121
Unity of Adventure, 148
universals, 57
utilitarianism, 191, 199

vagueness, 34ff., 46, 50, 69, 75, 82, 107, 119, 151, 175
valuation, 59, 133, 149 (*see also* Categoreal Obligations: Category of Conceptual Valuation); degrees of, xii; emergent significance of, 34
value, 188ff. (*see also* importance); ambiguity of, 189; competing forms of, 179; as end of creative

process, 147; and feeling, 189; as fundamentally comparative, 117; as "gift of finitude," 190; and ideal, 13; marginalization of, 178; patterning of, 37; and perspective, 145; as referable to individual existents, 83; and structural pattern, 34; ultimacy of, for inquiry, 154; unities and diversities of, 171
vector character of prehension, 31
vectoral flow, 48
vibration, 84
vibratory character, 163; of actuality, 131; as intensive imposition, 131
vibratory cosmos, 148
vibratory creative process, 83
vibratory intensities, 211
virtual unity, and vibratory actuality, 74
volition, determined by totalities admitted in aesthetic synthesis, 183
von Stadt, Karl, 118

Weil, Simone, 182
Weiss, Paul, 49
Whitehead, Alfred North: expositional weakness of, 7; obscurity of, xii; as realist, 120. Works: *Adventure of Ideas*, 92, 148; *An Enquiry Concerning the Principles of Natural Knowledge*, 73; *The Function of Reason*, 142; "Immortality," 145; "Mathematics and the Good," 170; *Modes of Thought*, 51, 142, 175; *Process and Reality*, 3, 18, 25; *Religion in the Making*, 24–25, 68, 126; *Science and the Modern World*, 16, 24, 96, 126; *A Treatise on Universal Algebra*, 115, 118
Whitman, Walt, 203
wholes and parts, 14; entity taken as, 15
width, 34, 36ff., 46, 50, 69, 75, 107, 119, 151, 175
will, 147; as effort of attention, 183; as obedience to reality, 182
Wolf-Gazo, Ernst, 138
world (*see also* actual world): perspectives of, 57; physical, 223n.53; as self-transcending, 171
worth (*see also* importance; value): Whitehead on, 185

Yeats, William Butler, 132–3; reading of Whitehead, 224n.1

Zeno, 113

Judith A. Jones, assistant professor of philosophy at Fordham University, has focused in her writings on Whitehead, Dewey, and process philosophy. She wrote the introduction for the recently published reprint of Alfred North Whitehead's *Religion in the Making*.

INTENSITY

was composed electronically using Berkeley Book types,
with displays in Berkeley, Berkeley Black, and GillSans Ultra Bold.
The book was printed on 60# Booktext Natural acid-free paper
and was Smyth sewn and cased in Roxite B cloth by BookCrafters.
The dust jacket was printed in three colors by Vanderbilt University Printing Services.
Book and dust jacket designs are the work of Deborah Hightower.
Published by Vanderbilt University Press
Nashville, Tennessee 37235